Shock and the Senseless in Dada and Fluxus

Interfaces: Studies in Visual Culture

Editors Mark J. Williams and Adrian W. B. Randolph, Dartmouth College

This series, sponsored by Dartmouth College Press, develops and promotes the study of visual culture from a variety of critical and methodological perspectives. Its impetus derives from the increasing importance of visual signs in everyday life, and from the rapid expansion of what are termed "new media." The broad cultural and social dynamics attendant to these developments present new challenges and opportunities across and within the disciplines. These have resulted in a trans-disciplinary fascination with all things visual, from "high" to "low," and from esoteric to popular. This series brings together approaches to visual culture—broadly conceived—that assess these dynamics critically and that break new ground in understanding their effects and implications.

For a complete list of books that are available in the series, visit www.upne.com

Dorothée Brill, *Shock and the Senseless in Dada and Fluxus*
Janine Mileaf, *Please Touch: Dada and Surrealist Objects after the Readymade*
J. Hoberman, *Bridge of Light: Yiddish Film between Two Worlds*, updated and expanded edition
Erina Duganne, *The Self in Black and White: Race and Subjectivity in Postwar American Photography*
Eric Gordon, *The Urban Spectator: American Concept Cities from Kodak to Google*
Barbara Larson and Fae Brauer, eds., *The Art of Evolution: Darwin, Darwinisms, and Visual Culture*
Jeffrey Middents, *Writing National Cinema: Film Journals and Film Culture in Peru*
Michael Golec, *The Brillo Box Archive: Aesthetics, Design, and Art*
Rob Kroes, *Photographic Memories: Private Pictures, Public Images, and American History*
Jonathan Beller, *The Cinematic Mode of Production: Attention Economy and the Society of the Spectacle*
Ann B. Shteir and Bernard Lightman, eds., *Figuring It Out: Science, Gender, and Visual Culture*
Anna Munster, *Materializing New Media: Body, Image, and Interface in Information Aesthetics*
Luc Pauwels, ed., *Visual Cultures of Science: Rethinking Representational Practices in Knowledge Building and Science Communication*
Lisa Saltzman and Eric Rosenberg, eds., *Trauma and Visuality in Modernity*

Shock and the Senseless in Dada and Fluxus

Dorothée Brill

Dartmouth College Press
Hanover, New Hampshire

Published by
University Press of New England
Hanover and London

Dartmouth College Press
Published by University Press of New England
www.upne.com

Manufactured in the United States of America
Designed by Katherine B. Kimball
Typeset in Sabon by Alice W. Bennett

University Press of New England is a member of the Green Press Initiative. The paper used in this book meets their minimum requirement for recycled paper.

Library of Congress Cataloging-in-Publication Data

Brill, Dorothée.
Shock and the senseless in Dada and Fluxus / Dorothée Brill. — 1st ed.
p. cm. — (Interfaces : studies in visual culture)
Includes bibliographical references and index.
ISBN 978-1-58465-902-0 (cloth : alk. paper) — ISBN 978-1-58465-917-4 (pbk. : alk. paper)
1. Dadaism. 2. Fluxus (Group of artists) 3. Art, European—20th century—Psychological aspects. I. Title.
N6494.D3B75 2010
709.04'062—dc22 2010023307

5 4 3 2 1

Contents

Note on Translations

For my research on this book I used the original version of the primary texts wherever possible, notably with regard to the writings of the Dadaists, Walter Benjamin, Sigmund Freud, and Georg Simmel. However, for the sake of readability, all quotations are in English. Wherever possible, these are taken from published translations with the respective bibliographical details given in the notes. In the case of hitherto untranslated texts the renderings are my own and the respective bibliographical details refer to the original-language version I consulted.

As to the use of titles of texts, the original is first cited, followed by the title of the published English translation where one exists. All subsequent references use the English title alone. Untranslated texts are referred to by their original title only.

Shock and the Senseless in Dada and Fluxus

1 Introduction: Shock of the Senseless

The provocation of a sense of shock is a recurrent feature of works of art dating from the mid-nineteenth century to the present, from Gustave Courbet or Édouard Manet to the Young British Artists. The Dada and Fluxus movements of the twentieth century can be considered to have played a crucial part in this tradition, at times even being reduced to their supposedly exclusive interest in inducing scandal. Regardless of whether this was truly their sole interest, we are certainly dealing with two movements that deliberately generate shock and allocate a specific function to such experience. Both embed shock within a larger conceptual framework, making it part of their artistic endeavor at large, and provide sufficient evidence to elucidate their concepts of shock and the reasons for their interest in this experience.

In pairing Dada and Fluxus my aim is to conduct a comparative analysis of both movements' concepts and uses of shock, which in turn will be shown to be linked to an artistic engagement with the senseless, a relationship that can be examined as one of cause and effect. Yet I am not only interested in attesting differences and similarities on the basis of such comparative analysis, but also in exploring the implications of and reasons behind either continuation or change, and in deducing from these the interconnection between a particular artistic approach (toward shock) and its sociocultural context. In fostering and contributing to a theoretical understanding of shock within artistic expression while focusing on an approach I describe as the "shock of the senseless," I seek to address a deficiency within art-theoretical studies.

With its focus on Dada and Fluxus—the latter initially describing itself as neo-Dada—this book pairs "the most radical movement within the European avant-garde"[1] with "the most radical and experimental art movement of the sixties,"[2] which has been considered "the last risk" and "one of the last Avant-gardes" within twentieth-century art.[3] Both movements base their understanding of art on its necessary reconnection with life, upon the desire for art to have an effect upon external reality, and upon some notion of the "end of art." Indeed, as contemporary press accounts of both movements agreed, "these presentations have evidently nothing to do with art,"[4] and are performed by a "clique of bunglers."[5] Dada's and Fluxus's mutual interest in the generation of shock, which is not only a distinctive but also an intentional feature of both groups, can be considered a manifestation and consequence of these objectives. Shock functions as part of the movements' attempt to change society or—to formulate it less strongly—to have an impact upon the artists' sociocultural context and the recipient's engagement therewith. This endeavor will be shown as being linked to the artists' rejection of the idea that artistic production must make sense and be meaningful. Both movements, to name but one example, claim to have found their names by flipping open a dictionary and sticking a finger randomly on the open page—a doubtful enough assertion for Dada and even more difficult to believe in the case of Fluxus.[6] As the Dadaist Georges Ribemont-Dessaignes stated, Dada "means nothing, aims to mean nothing, and was adopted precisely because of its absence of meaning."[7] In a similar vein, Fluxus artist Robert Watts observed, "The best thing about Fluxus is that nobody knows what it is."[8] *Bashing the Head through the Wall . . . and Find Something New*,[9] as a Fluxus retrospective was entitled, the postwar movement repeated Dada's desire for "something new at all costs."[10] Both Dada and Fluxus launched an intentional attack on the audience's presumptions about artistic production in particular and their understanding and perception of the world in general. As a consequence, "the public's horror . . . [became] a pride to behold,"[11] as it testified to a successful provocation of the audience.

For both Dada and Fluxus, shock, one might argue, is used "as a stimulus to change one's conduct of life,"[12] and—as Peter Bürger maintains—as a "means to break through aesthetic immanence and to usher in . . . a change in the recipient's life praxis."[13] As Raoul Hausmann emphasizes, Dada was not concerned with "aesthetic revolutions, but with stirring the general insight that the state of the world has become unbearable."[14] This intention, as Tristan Tzara recalls, was "at the time of which I am speaking the mark of so subversive a spirit that we were bound to scandalize society, to scandalize it so drastically that it could only regard us as criminals or imbeciles."[15] Dada's interest in shock cannot be understood without taking into consideration the distinct sociocultural context characterizing the beginning of the twentieth century—and the artists' discontent with this context.

Correspondingly, the comparative analysis of Fluxus's approach to shock will need to take not only the changed artistic and art-historical framework into consideration but also the changes to have occurred in the broader sociocultural context. Hence, rather than confining myself in the present analysis of the concept of shock within Dada and Fluxus to a straightforward registration of similarities and differences between the two, I seek to examine why certain aspects were either continued or modified and to determine the extent to which the modifications developed in response to the changing sociocultural climate. In this endeavor, I share Klaus von Beyme's conviction that "an approach which takes into consideration aspects of social and political history assesses the artists" theories as more than mere background music to their works of art. Their own comments are taken seriously as the continuation of artistic expression with the means of language."[16]

Indeed, in my attempt to clarify the movements' understanding of shock and its functioning, an important part will be played by artists' statements and manifestos alongside theoretical and artistic inquiries. This approach necessitates a caveat insofar as it occupies the frequently hazy borderline separating artistic manifestation from its accompanying explanation. There is no unambiguous separation between literary or performative texts and explanatory comments. The artists' statements I refer to—most notably in the case of Dada—often require a twofold interpretation, since they both manifest and explain an artistic approach, thereby creating a blurred zone in between. The diverging readings of Tzara's "Manifeste Dada 1918" that can be witnessed in the studies of Peter Bürger, Hubert van Berg, Alfons Backes-Haase, and Hanno Ehrlicher attest to this dilemma,[17] the dissension being fueled by differences in approaching the manifesto as a work of art on the one hand and an explanatory document on the other.

The sociocultural anchoring of the two movements' interest in shock is, however, not only a response to their specific conceptual layout. As the discussion of the writings of Georg Simmel, Sigmund Freud, and Walter Benjamin will show, the emerging preoccupation with shock is not only a paradigm of twentieth-century art but of a theoretical engagement developing simultaneously in a variety of disciplines, most notably in sociology and psychoanalysis. Emerging at the turn of the century, this burgeoning interest allows for the postulation of shock, more generally, as an issue of the twentieth century. It was first used within medical and psychological research—predominantly in a German speaking context—and was subsequently adopted in both literary and colloquial language, being spelled variously as "choc," "chok," "chock," "shock," and "schock."[18] It is a development that can be shown to be linked to the notion and, more important, the experience of the senseless. Recognizing the encounter with the senseless as a trigger of shock, this relationship will come to be specified as one of cause and effect, giving shape to what I call the "shock of the senseless." While the term *senseless* is used here to denote meaninglessness as opposed to insensibility, the word's dual connotation, referring to both a cognitive and a perceptive level, will nevertheless prove a useful asset in the course of the present examination.

Copious scholarly work has been produced on Dada, crowned by the substantial catalog published a few years ago to accompany the Dada retrospective organized by the National Gallery of Art in Washington.[19] It is only in comparison to this relative abundance that the literature on Fluxus appears modest. When it comes to the pivotal question of shock, however, only a few accounts of the two movements do more than mention its relevance, each stopping short of full analysis. The two texts that advance the furthest in this direction both focus on Dada. In her interesting and profound essay "'See: We Are All Neurasthenics!' or, The Trauma of Dada Montage" (1997), Brigid Doherty analyzes representations of traumatic shock within individual works from Berlin Dada. She considers the artists' use of montage as a materialization of traumatic shock, seeking to "demonstrate the meaningfulness and vitality of trauma as a category of historical and interpretative interest in Berlin dada."[20] The second text worth mentioning is Elizabeth Allen Chabert's doctoral thesis from 1995, entitled *Transforming Impact: The Shock Experience in Dada and Surrealist Poetry*.[21] Focusing on the use of language, Chabert's argument parallels my own approach inasmuch as she considers related ideas in Walter Benjamin's sociocultural embedding of the movement's use of shock. We considerably differ, however, in that I consider it necessary to explore Dada's use and understanding of shock in connection to the movement's interest in the senseless and to locate both within the larger framework of intellectual and social developments in the early twentieth century. A quite solitary position is held by Greil Marcus's book *Lipstick Traces: A Secret History of the Twentieth Century* (1989),[22] in which the author examines three countercultural tendencies of the twentieth century: Dada, the Situationist International, and punk. Without focusing on the experience of shock in particular, Marcus revisits in unconventional manner their shared nihilist approach toward established society and their verve and impetuosity in challenging its purportedly indisputable values.

In comparison with Dada, the academic investigations into the use of shock within Fluxus are truly marginal—an absence that is not surprising, given the lesser exposure of the manifestation of shock within Fluxus coupled, as we will see, with the movement's interest in triggering a reaction of quite a different kind.

Aside from scholarly discourse with an explicit focus on either Dada or Fluxus, a number of publications over the past decade or so have turned their attention to the survey of scandalous art with a view to arriving at some kind of classification for transgressive artistic activity. Key examples can be found in Anthony Julius's *Transgressions: The Offences of Art* (2002),[23] Paul Ardenne's *Extrême: Esthétiques de la limite dépassée* (2006),[24] and most notably Kieran Cashell's recent study *Aftershock: The Ethics of Contemporary Transgressive Art*,[25] which was published in 2009 and to which I shall return later in more detail. Less recent but impossible to overlook are the two seminal books *The Shock of the New* (1970) by Ian Dunlop,[26] and Robert Hughes's 1980 publication of the same title, the latter having been based on Hughes's BBC television series on the history of modern art, which was produced in the late 1970s and inspired by Dunlop's book.[27] While both explore the transgression of the limits of established artistic practice, and thus pursue a line of inquiry close to my own, they do not venture in any depth into the concept and theory of shock underlying this transgressive act.

Two prominent essays investigating the relationship between shock and the insensible or the unknown, both focusing on the first part of the twentieth century, deserve mention: in "Aesthetics and Anaesthetics" (1992), Susan Buck-Morss delivers a conscientious account of the notion of shock as developed in Walter Benjamin's "Artwork Essay,"[28] and Albrecht Riethmüller's "Hermetik, Schock, Fasslichkeit" (1980) delivers a very good exploration of the notion of shock within music theory of that time, with a focus on Theodor W. Adorno and Ernst Krenek as well as Walter Benjamin.[29]

Perusing publications of the last decade, one can discern an increasing attention to the artistic use of the human body, bodily material, or organic matter in a shocking or disgusting manner: Francesca Alfano Miglietti's *Extreme Bodies* (2003) delivers an art-historical survey of twentieth-century body art;[30] Linda S. Kauffman's book *Bad Girls and Sick Boys* (1998) explores artists' use of "the body as material in every sense of the word";[31] and Monika Wagner provides a material history of twentieth-century art in her compendium *Das Material der Kunst* (2001).[32] These discussions of the artistic appropriation of unusual materials, often considered unsuitable and highly contentious, have been accompanied by a range of scholarly publications providing a comprehensive examination of the cultural and intellectual history of disgust, such as William Ian Miller's *Anatomy of Disgust* (1997), Winfried Menninghaus's *Ekel: Theorie und Geschichte einer starken Empfindung* (*Disgust: The Theory and History of a Strong Sensation*, 1999), Robert Rawdon Wilson's *The Hydra's Tale: Imagining Disgust* (2002), and a Ph.D. dissertation by Chris Turner on the disgusting and unrepresentable from Kant to Kristeva (2000).[33]

When it comes to shock and its intellectual history, there is no counterpart to the distinct theoretical engagements with the concept and experience of disgust—and with the notion of the abject as its philosophical-psychoanalytical companion. One of the thinkers having ventured into this direction is Karl Heinz Bohrer,[34] who has pursued a lasting academic engagement with shock, but also with related notions such as the evil, the gruesome, and the sudden. Like Friedrich Nietzsche or Georges Bataille before him, Bohrer is a disputatious and acclaimed advocate for the evaluation of evil as an independent aesthetic and ontological category.[35] Closest to my own approach is his study on *Plötzlichkeit* (*Suddenness*, 1981), which, focusing on structural rather than representational issues, explores whether "the boundary between the aesthetic and the nonaesthetic phenomenon [can] be represented by means of the temporal modality of 'suddenness.'"[36] Another more cursory approach toward an aesthetic theory of shock has been undertaken by Paul Crowther in his *Critical Aesthetics and Postmodernism* (1993), and, in his wake, by Laura Wixley Brooks in 1995,[37] both proposing an integration of the experience of shock into the aesthetic tradition of the sublime.

Returning to the trajectory of my own investigation in the present volume, namely the experience of shock triggered by an encounter with the senseless in artistic production, I implicitly formulate a number of assumptions. The first of these pertains to the suggestion that there are a variety of distinguishable ways to trigger shock within artistic produc-

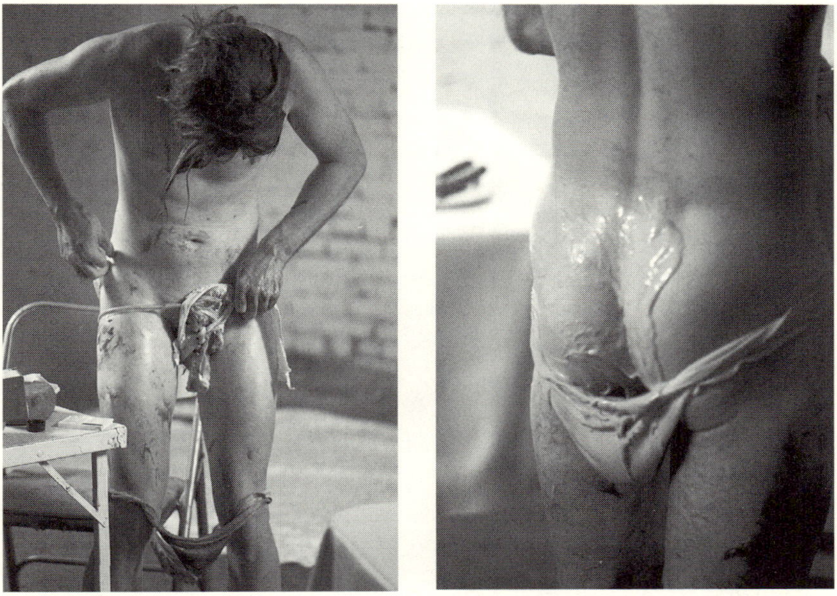

Figures 1 and 2. Paul McCarthy, *Hot Dog*, 1974. Performance, video, black-and-white and color photographs. Videography by Mike Cram; photos by Spandau Parks/Karen McCarthy.

tion. The second refers to the lack of sense as constituting one of these approaches. And third we have the insinuation that either this strategy in particular or others of its kind can be defined as artistic, thus suggesting a distinction between artistic and nonartistic strategies of shock.

The first assumption (the existence and distinction of various ways to trigger a reaction of shock within art) is easily verified by considering late nineteenth- and twentieth-century works of art that have been deemed shocking. Such a selection could include, among others, Édouard Manet's *Déjeuner sur l'Herbe* and *Olympia* (both 1863),[38] Gustave Courbet's *L'Origine du Monde* (1866), Pablo Picasso's *Demoiselles d'Avignon* (1907), Marcel Duchamp's *Fountain* (1917) or *L.H.O.O.Q.* (1919). Similarly, it could encompass Paul McCarthy's exuberant and transgressive performances from the mid-1970s, deploying excessive amounts of ketchup, mayonnaise or chocolate sauce in a Freudian state of regression (figs. 1, 2, and 8), Robert Mapplethorpe's nude photographs from the 1980s, which were considered not only obscene but an intolerable reference to homosexual attraction (fig. 3), or Dread Scott's answer to the question of *What Is the Proper Way to Display a U.S. Flag?* (1988): by using it as a carpet on the floor. Martin Kippenberger's *Fred the Frog*

Rings the Bell (1990, fig. 4), a wood-carved sculpture of a crucified frog, which, when exhibited at Galerie Gisela Capitain in the year of its creation, carried the alternative title *What's the Difference between Casanova and Jesus: Their Facial Expression During Nailing*,[39] has been excluded from exhibitions due to its shock value. Marc Quinn's series

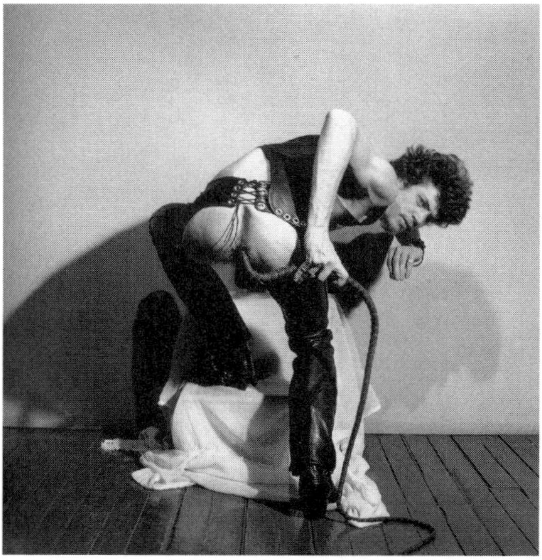

Figure 3. Robert Mapplethorpe, *Self-Portrait with Whip*, 1978. Gelatin silver print.

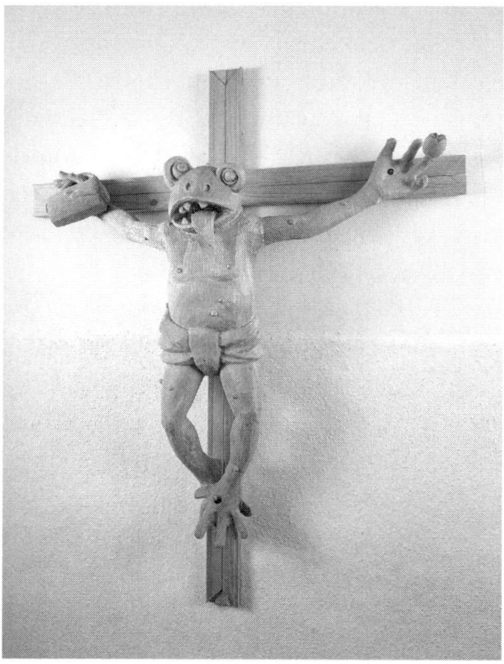

Figure 4. Martin Kippenberger, *Fred the Frog Rings the Bell*, 1990. Wood, nails. Carved by Johann Widauer; photo by Egbert Haneke. Sammlung Falckenberg, Hamburg.

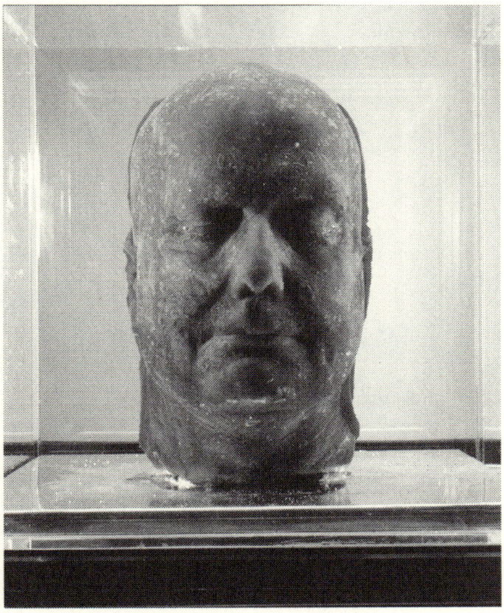

Figure 5. Marc Quinn, *Self*, 2001. Artist's blood, stainless steel, perspex, refrigeration equipment. Photo by Stephen White.

of self-portraits made about every five years, each consisting of 4.5 liters of the artist's frozen blood (fig. 5), Stelarc's project of growing an *Extra Ear—¼ Scale* (1997) on his arm or cheek and Orlan's heavy cosmetic surgery carried out on herself as part of *The Reincarnation of St. Orlan* in the pursuit of an ideal incarnation of female beauty based on the canon of art, have been considered as shocking and unacceptable due to their potential or actual harm to the artists' bodies. Xiao Yu's *Ruan* (1999, figs. 6 and 7) consists of an array of glass jars filled with formaldehyde and containing a jackalope-like creature in various stages of growth. The creature combines a variety of dead animal body parts stitched together with a foetal human head (a Chinese specimen dating from the 1960s). Upon being exhibited at the Kunstmuseum Bern it was accompanied by the warning: "This work might be found shocking." Thus, the visitor was encumbered with full responsibility for looking at this "omnivorous mammal with wings."[40] Jake and Dinos Chapman's *Hell* (2000), which comprises a series of exuberant three-dimensional model-scale depictions of Nazi atrocities, offers a truly apocalyptic version of what at first glance might seem to be a harmless scene of model railroads. Both works were received as repulsive and heavily criticized for what was seen as an inappropriately justified—and thus unjustified—use of a particular subject matter or material.

The range and diversity of these works reveal that shock is a possible reaction to a great variety of heterogeneous artistic expressions and

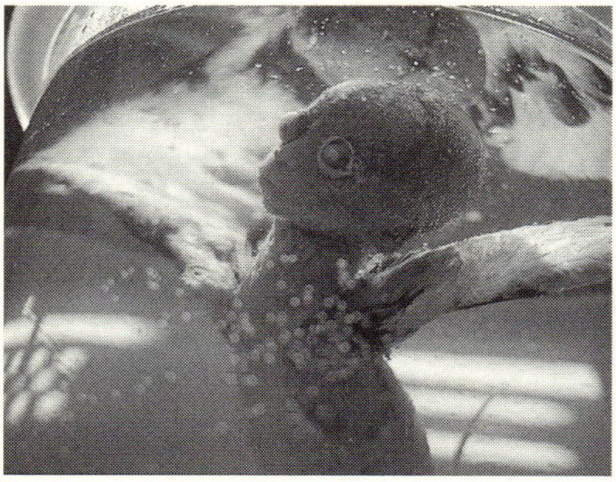
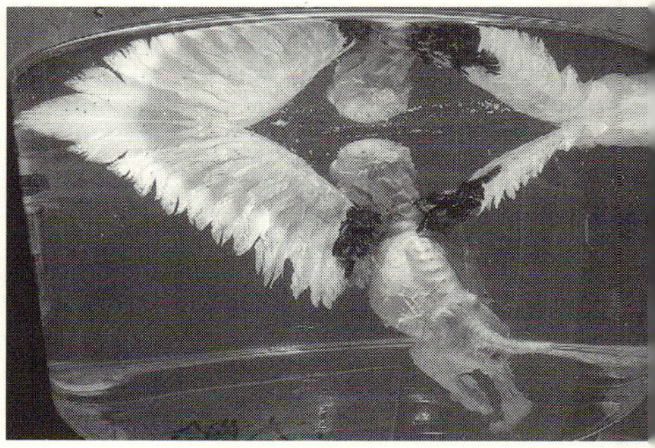

Figures 6 and 7. Xiao Yu, *Ruan*, 1999. Installation in six parts. Glass containers, formaldehyde, animal body parts, fetal human head.

that experiences of shock can be triggered for quite different reasons. It is consequently possible to classify these works of art according to the source from which their shock potential derives or, to put it differently, according to the type of transgression they perform. Here, we touch upon their common denominator: they all share an act of transgression of some kind, a transgression—as I would argue—of either moral or artistic values. Yet whereas Manet, Courbet, and Mapplethorpe seem to transgress the limits of decency, bordering on pornography, Scott is alleged to disrespect feelings of patriotism, loyalty, and national pride. In contrast, Quinn, Stelarc, Xiao Yu, Orlan, and the Chapman brothers were reproached for a morally dubious and unjustified exploitation of either subject matter or material—unlike Kippenberger, who was accused of blasphemy, "the very model of transgression," as Anthony Julius states.[41] All of these offenses—blasphemy, pornography, a lack of national ethos, or an unethical use of subject matter and material—can be characterized as offenses against moral values in one way or another. In the case of Paul McCarthy's materially excessive and self-absorbed performances, for example, the reasons why we are unsettled, irritated or even shocked when watching McCarthy's infantile play with lubricious substances or when seeing him crouching on all fours while shitting and subsequently playing around with his excrement, have little to do with the fact that McCarthy claims these activities to be artistic. We would have similar reactions irrespective of whether we came face to face with these activities at a museum or in any other public, or even private, context. Here, the experience of shock can indeed be explained in psychoanalytical terms as an infantile regression and a return to primordial and suppressed drives. Equally, the activity's senselessness and inexplicability does not result from the fact that McCarthy deems the activities and their documentation to be art. Although he makes this claim—and we might have our difficulties in accepting it—it is not our foremost "problem" in engaging with the work.

So these examples of potential sources of shock are not limited to the field of artistic expression, nor has their appearance within the context of art had a primary effect—mitigating or otherwise—on their "shock value." The effervescent discussion sparked by an MTV advertisement in Germany announcing *Pope Town*, a satirical British cartoon series about daily life at the Vatican, offers just one example. Accompanied by the slogan "laugh, don't hang around," it featured a jovial Jesus laughing and lolling about in front of a television set, remote control in hand, with an empty cross in the distance. Another well-known example of shock in the interest of product promotion is Oliviero Toscani's much-contested Benetton campaign. Then there is the so-called "Cannibal of Rotenburg," who killed and ate parts of another man with the latter's consent—and filmed these activities. He made no claim to be creating art, but his acts probably shocked people even more than the supposed eating of a stillborn foetus by Chinese artist Zhu Yu. The experience of shock is inherent

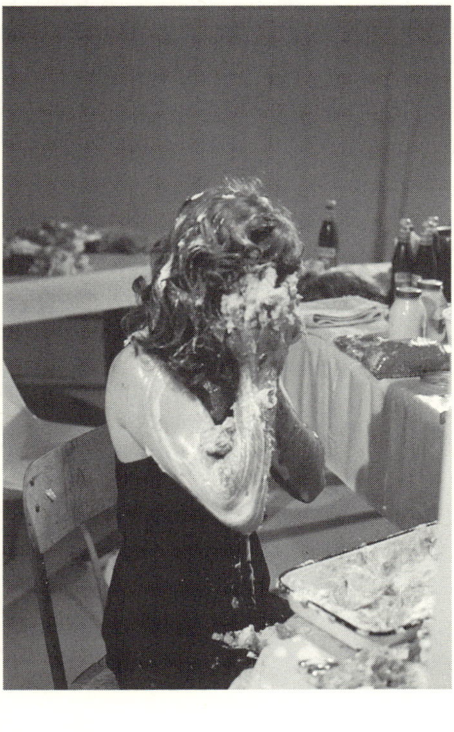

Figure 8. Paul McCarthy, *Meat Cake #5*, 1974. Performance, video, black-and-white and color photographs. Videography by Mike Cram. Photo by Spandau Parks.

to the witnessing of such acts, largely regardless of whether or not they are claimed to be art.

In respect thereof, the examined works are different from the aforementioned examples by Picasso and Duchamp. Works such as *Demoiselles d'Avignon*, *Fountain*, or *L.H.O.O.Q.* caused a reaction of shock due to their utter disrespect for the principal guidelines and values of artistic creation. They violated the established principles of how a work of art was meant to look and undermined the given "understanding of the nature and purpose of art."[42] It is this cause of shock to which Ian Dunlop alludes in the above-mentioned book *The Shock of the New*, which analyzes seven "outrageous" modernist exhibitions from around the turn of the century, each of which provoked a full-blown scandal. Dunlop sets out to investigate why the exhibitions in question, which were widely received as "quite incomprehensible,"[43] triggered a reaction of shock. Rather rhetorically, he begins by asking whether it is "subject matter, technique, colour, or something less specific like newness"[44] that caused the audience's reaction of shock. His answer is self-evident: Dunlop considers the reason for the shock he examines to lie in the artworks' "newness."[45] Phrased differently, the works were hardly capable of being understood as art—let alone good art—as they did not adhere to established notions of a work of art accepted at the time and thus did not correspond to the concept of art to which the viewer was accustomed. They were received, as was written in a review of *Entartete Kunst*, the notorious exhibition of so-called "degenerate art" (and thus of a dense accumulation of avant-garde art) mounted in 1937 in Munich, as "tendencies which are pure nonsense."[46]

As I shall go on to argue, I do not conceive of the shock of the senseless as an approach altogether different from the shock of the new, but rather as a more appropriate description of the same artistic procedure. By this I mean that it might not be so much the fact of something's being new that causes the reaction of shock, but the fact that what is new is perceived as senseless. In other words, the new does not shock because it is new, but because it does not disclose its potential meaning, thus depriving the recipient of the capacity to explain and thereby justify a work's creation. As Karl-Heinz Bohrer puts it:

> The artist is no friend of art but its true opponent, that is, the opponent of the kind of art that predominates up to his or her arrival. This provocation, which is inherent in every creative act, lies not only in the work's provocative

message. Rather, it is contained already in the work's pure presentness, which can elicit a "confusion of feelings" if no known structure can immediately be recognized.[47]

Bohrer adds that this presentness of a new artistic production that ignores its antecedents is what gives rise to the scandalous, the "scandal [that] is presented to us as criminal but is in reality part of every imaginative, creative act."[48]

A senseless artistic production can thus function as a source of shock for artistic, as opposed to moral, reasons. Transgressive acts can be identified as being of artistic character not, I would argue, by the realm in which they appear (i.e., art), but by the type of values that are dismissed in the process. All the same, I would willingly concur with Kieran Cashell's statement that "aesthetic transgression can be defined as any act of violation presented under the alibi of art."[49] As Cashell argues, it is impossible to receive works of art in a disinterested mode of perception *and* to experience them as transgressive in nature. If we were to follow Immanuel Kant, "one kind of ugliness alone is incapable of being represented conformably to nature without destroying all aesthetic delight and consequently artistic beauty, namely, that which excites disgust."[50] Cashell widens this irreconcilability to include any transgressive act performed within art. Whatever type of values an artistic production transgresses, it is—according to Cashell—inevitably also always an aesthetic transgression: "All transgressive art . . . is driven by a similar intent to menace the emotionally distanced perspective associated with the aesthetic attitude, by deliberately provoking emotional responses or visceral reactions that refuse to be assimilated to the disinterested mode of perception."[51]

The difference between the arguments evinced by Cashell and those informing my own analysis is the difference between artistic and aesthetic transgression. As Cashell sees it, aesthetic transgression occurs in utter independence from the specific nature of the transgressive act but is a consequence of any act of transgression happening in a work of art: "Because ethical judgement is institutionally considered to be anathema to aesthetic appreciation, such art can be identified as paradigmatically transgressive precisely because the reaction it provokes is a *moral* reaction."[52]

Whereas I differentiate between ethical and artistic transgression—with a transgressive act being located in either one or the other realm—Cashell distinguishes between ethical and aesthetic transgression—with the ethical being the primary and the aesthetic the secondary act of transgression. By pushing the recipient into an engagement with ethical issues, the work unhinges a disinterested approach, thus transgressing—as a second step—the precondition for the appropriate reception of art. This second step is, I would argue, unlikely to be a source of shock and by no means entails a challenge of established artistic criteria. The discussion it is likely to instigate has more to do with the ethical value and legitimacy of a given work than its artistic quality. In contrast, my own focus on the shock of the senseless clearly coincides with a challenge of this artistic quality. This does not imply that a state of disinterest is secured or that we are dealing with an endeavor that can only aim at a revolution within the realm of artistic production. Surveying Dada and Fluxus, Théophile Thoré's dictum that "art changes only through strong convictions, convictions strong enough to change society at the same time"[53] can even be modified a little: The urge to influence and change society requests changes in artistic production in order to keep it worthwhile and relevant. Both Dada and Fluxus can be regarded—and will be examined—as primary manifestations of such an endeavor that respond to sociocultural aspects as much as they seek to influence them.

A possible critique of my enterprise to trace the genealogy of a specific strategy of shock and to interpret it as an intended interaction with the sociocultural field could be founded upon a school of thought initiated by Peter Bürger. In his *Theory of the Avant-Garde* (1974), Bürger urges us to consider that "nothing loses its effectiveness more quickly than shock; by its very nature, it is a unique experience."[54] As much as Bürger is right in affirming "the impossibility to make permanent this kind of effect,"[55] it is not the experience of shock that loses its jolting and thus potentially initiating capacity, nor, as I will argue, does a particular strategy of shock fade in this way; instead, it is the specific act of transgression that is of limited effectiveness. Not long after a work's creation and shocking impact, it will "require a great deal of imagination to understand why one of these pictures ever caused a scandal."[56] Thus, in applying Bürger's hypothetical criticism to the shock of the senseless, I would argue that it is not the strategy itself that stops functioning, although it might be shown to lose its relevance. Instead, what changes is that which is actually perceived as a transgression of the concept of art.

But Bürger's criticism of the neo-avant-garde is not only directed at the continuation of an avant-garde strategy of shock that he considers outdated. More specifically, it is based on the conviction that the first use of this approach was unsuccessful. According to Bürger, the avant-garde's shock of the senseless failed to support and bring about the changes that motivated its use. These changes can be summarized as the desired "reintegration of art and life,"[57] and the consequent disappearance of art within life. The failure to achieve this aim is proved by the fact that a movement that set out to abolish art is itself retrospectively assessed as an art movement. Looked at from this angle, the neo-Dada tendencies of the late 1950s and early 1960s—of which Fluxus forms a vital part—appear to unwittingly discredit their predecessor's credibility by referring to a movement that had set out to achieve "the annihilation of aestheticism, of the autonomous, the institutionalized status of art, or even . . . the overcoming of art itself."[58] By making reference to Dada, Fluxus can be said to have compelled its precursor "to reveal itself as what it has always been: Anti-art art."[59] Within Bürger's argument, this discrediting of Dada also weakens Fluxus's own standing, as it perpetuates a demand, namely the integration of art into the "praxis of life," that has already been proved unachievable.[60] By attesting to this failure in referring to the avant-garde as an artistic manifestation, "the gesture of protest" of the neo-avant-garde proves itself apocryphal from the start.[61] Following this line of thought, the neo-avant-garde and thus neo-Dada could consequently be reproached for turning "the antiaesthetic into the artistic, the transgressive into the institutional,"[62] thus declaring their own intentions as noncredible. Contrasting Bürger's negative evaluation of the avant-garde's repetition as being inauthentic and invalid from the outset, Hal Foster suggests a Freudian rereading of the functioning of such repetition:

> The avant-garde work is never historically effective or fully significant in its initial moments. It cannot be because it is traumatic: a hole in the symbolic order of its time that is not prepared for it, that cannot receive it, at least not immediately, at least not without structural change.[63]

The supposed inauthenticity of a continuation of the avant-garde's revolutionary intentions is of interest to us insofar as it affects not only the pursuit of these intentions but equally the continuing use of shock as a tool to put them into practice.[64] As a newspaper article from 1965 argues, Dada "shocked to reveal the demonical and intellectual vacuum in the heart of a civilization being dragged by its own dead weight into self-destruction." In contrast to this, neo-Dada only "exploits the ideologies where Dada at its purest, stood up and fought them."[65] Neo-Dada—

and thus Fluxus—is here considered an "empty" repetition, having lost both a real cause and the authentic means to pursue it. My reasons for dissenting from such a verdict can be expressed in terms of Karl Heinz Bohrer's conviction:

> From the beginning of this century, the radicalism with which artists have staged the new, the incomprehensible, and—let us not hesitate to name it—the unknown has gone far beyond mere formal techniques. . . . The new, the incomprehensible, the unknown does not simply equal the most advanced style; instead, it is what fits the moment [*das dem "Augenblick" Adäquate*]. . . . The historical misunderstanding that keeps repeating itself is to imagine postmodern art as a merely technical repetition of the avant-garde and thus to dismiss it as something outworn. . . . The proof that formal techniques exhaust themselves over time does not prove anything.[66]

Taking Bohrer's statement as my point of departure, I will consider the shock of the senseless as not necessarily based on formal innovations, but rather on the question of if and why it formulates that which "fits the moment." Put differently, the problematic aspect of Peter Bürger's approach consists in his omission of a nuanced distinction and comparison between the intentions and means of the predecessor and its heir.[67] Although Fluxus does indeed continue Dada's claim to challenge and change the "praxis of life"—and might even have a similar vision of these changes—Fluxus pursues its aims along a different course. Examining both the continuities and changes marking some of the most distinctive avant-garde paradigms, I will show that while shock and the senseless did indeed continue to play a dominant, if slightly weakened, role in the 1960s, they adopted both a different function and a different relationship to one other. Hence, if this book were to be read as a response to Hal Foster's question about whether "the postwar moments [are] passive repetitions of the prewar moments"[68] and thus "cancel the project of the historical avant-garde,"[69] or whether the neo-avant-garde does "act on the historical avant-garde in ways that we can only now appreciate,"[70] it would clearly align itself with the latter claim.

2 The Notion of Shock in Early Twentieth-Century Europe

"Art has often generated disgust, but only with the rise of the avant-garde two centuries ago did shock become a major artistic device."[1] As Chris Turner here suggests, art's engagement with shock is a distinct phenomenon of modernity and, more specifically, of the avant-garde. I would like to both widen and limit his postulation: *Shock* is a term of the twentieth century, that is, it is not only a paradigm of twentieth-century art but of critical engagement in general. Having indeed seen its preparation in the nineteenth century, the intellectual and artistic engagement with this term seems distinctly specific to the early twentieth-century. Saying this, however, I ignore neither the fact that the term's etymology dates back to the late sixteenth century nor that terms related to the idea of shock possess a long aesthetic tradition. Scanning philosophical inquiries into the sublime and the experience of catharsis, exemplarily those by Edmund Burke and Immanuel Kant, adjacent terms do indeed make repeated appearances, notably the words *shudder*, *fear*, or *fright*. When Jeffrey Schnapp thus argues that shock "as a secular experience was already fully underway" during the two preceding centuries,[2] the seeming opposition between his approach and my characterization of this term as inherently belonging to the twentieth century is based on mixing up a reflection on the use of the term itself with investigations into what this term might refer to. When Patricia De Montfort thus analyzes the nineteenth-century sensation novel and sensation painting, concluding that this genre intended "to shock the sensibilities of its original viewers" or readers,[3] she is describing an experience by using a terminology belonging to her own time and context, the early twenty-first century. In contrast, Henry Mansel in 1863 describes the same genre as "producing a somatic effect on readers"[4] and as "preaching to the nerves."[5] Quite significantly, Mansel does not use the word *shock*, although his physical and neurological approach toward sensation anticipates the understanding and use of the term as it will emerge at the turn of the century when it becomes the subject of scientific and theoretical considerations.

With the ground having been prepared in the nineteenth century—as is shown, for example, by the way Walter Benjamin anchored his investigation into shock in Baudelaire, or the way Karl Heinz Bohrer examines Jünger's early writings within the context of romanticism[6]—"theories of shock" simultaneously emerged in the fields of psychoanalysis, sociology, and aesthetics. The contemporaneous appropriation of the term within a number of disciplines might be understood as a consequence of the sociocultural and historical circumstances of the time. But which sociocultural and historical circumstances are we talking about?

As I will show in some depth, there are two dominant realms providing the breeding ground for the eventually unavoidable necessity for a theoretic engagement with the experience of shock. On the one hand, we have increasing urbanization and a swiftly growing population, together with the rapid technological development of means of transportation and communication, which changed the conditions of daily life considerably and created utterly new demands on the individual's sensorial and cognitive capacities. On the other hand, there is World War I, the "primal catastrophe of the twentieth century,"[7] which presented itself as an unprecedented and extraordinary event and confronted the individual with a technologized warfare machinery, resulting in a "battle of equipment,"[8] and over 9 million deaths. "The world war between 1914 and 1918 is one of the significant experiences of this century, if not the most significant one,"[9] and widely considered to be "a turning point of both secular and global significance, at which momentous historic developments of the present century took their beginning."[10] Leading to the total mobilization of all human and material resources, World War I consumed this material in an unprecedented quantity and an unparalleled speed. Having been described the "father of all things," World War I has not only significantly shaped the history of the twentieth century, but it has also proved to be of lasting influence on its sociocultural and its critical development.

The focused concern with the experience of shock was certainly one of the war's consequences, and inevitable at that: "The conflict manifested on the battlefield between technological development and human mindset brought home the shock of modernity: rather than arriving quietly, it crashed in uncomfortably (and often fatally)."[11] To name one example among many, the war made psychoanalytical research into shell shock indispensable and thus furthered the rise of psychoanalysis and the development of a psychoanalytical concept of shock. One of the first usages of the term *shell shock* for a traumatic psychic disturbance caused during combat is to be found in a text from 1916, in F. W. Mott's "Special discussion on shell shock without visible signs of injury."[12]

The unparalleled event of the war combined with an utterly new shape of what were becoming the ordinary parameters of daily life called for psychological and sociological research into the individual's capacity to cope with a new quantity and type of unprecedented, unavoidable, and unexpected experiences. "A modern man registers an hundred times more sensory impressions than an eighteenth-century artist," as Fernand Léger observes.[13] Sociological and psychological research analyzed the individual's psychic and perceptional constitution as affected by the mentioned changes. In this attempt, it might be said that the notion of shock came to describe the interface between the conditions of modern life and the individual's experience of these conditions. Shock, as Walter Benjamin famously concluded, became the paradigm for the modern individual's experience.

Walter Benjamin is, of course, the key figure linking the emerging sociological and psychoanalytical investigation of shock to the realm of art, notably in his approach toward Dada. His view of the movement, formulated about ten to fifteen years after its emergence, not only clarifies their mutual approach to shock, it also emphasizes that their joint interest in shock is a consequence of their respective responses to similar sociocultural features. These features' impact on emerging concepts of shock cannot be ignored and can be shown to determine the rising relevance of shock in the first place.

Although not the first to use the term within the field of sociocultural thinking, Benjamin is the first to provide what can be considered the corner points for an aesthetic—or, as will be argued, an anaesthetic—theory of shock. That said, we should make clear that such a theory of shock finds no explicit formulation within Benjamin's writings, but is to be deduced from the variety of his texts. Besides his two late works "Das Kunstwerk im Zeitalter seiner technischen Reproduzierbarkeit" ("The Work of Art in the Age of Its Technological Reproducibility," 1935–36)[14] and "Über einige Motive bei Baudelaire" ("On Some Motifs in Baudelaire," 1939), where the author's ideas on shock find their most overt formulation, the term appears occasionally in Benjamin's earlier writings. Benjamin's thoughts on shock can be furthermore read as the conclusion of a number of ideas vital to his philosophy, developing and uniting preceding strands in his works as well as responding to positions of contemporaries. Again, they are mutually grounded within the relevant social and historical backdrop of the early twentieth century.

Two figures are here of specific importance to Benjamin. First, there is his response to Georg Simmel that is accommodated within an exploration of the changing parameters of urbanity and urban lifestyle. Second, there is his engagement with the ideas of Sigmund Freud, which sheds light on the implications of World War I for the development of a scientific occupation with shock. In the way that modern urbanism had a crucial influence on sociology, World War I had an extraordinary impact upon psychoanalysis. Both of these interrelations are of interest because they outline the basis on which Benjamin came to ground his concept of shock a couple of decades later, adopting and adapting the definitions the term had received within recent sociological and psychoanalytical research. As this book argues, urbanism as a sociological concept on the one hand and the war as an issue of psychoanalysis on the other generated the principal features of the notion of shock developed by Benjamin, elucidating his concept of shock as the distinct outcome of its time and context.

Shock and Urbanity: Walter Benjamin and Georg Simmel

Throughout the nineteenth century, Europe's population rose significantly, from 180 million prior to 1800 to 460 million in 1914, as Ortega y Gasset reports.[15] As he describes in *La Rebelión de las Masas* (*The Revolt of the Masses*, 1929), society had produced "a gigantic mass of humanity which, launched like a torrent over the historic area, has inundated it."[16] This gigantic mass of humanity was not spread evenly, but represented a swiftly rising tendency toward urbanization notably during the second half of the nineteenth century. This trend continued throughout the early twentieth century, so that by 1935 almost 70 percent of the population lived in an urban environment.[17] To name a relevant example, the urban population of Germany rose from 36 percent in 1871 to 60 percent in 1910, with the number of cities with a population exceeding 100,000 growing from eight to forty-eight, and incorporating a population of 14 million in total.[18] Staying with Germany, this process of urbanization coincided with a rapid growth in population of over half a million per year, rising from 40 million in 1872 to 67 million in 1913. France had a total population of 45 million at the time and Great Britain around 40 million.[19]

However, numbers alone do not tell the story of the sociocultural relevance of urbanism. As Louis Wirth writes, "The city is not only in ever larger degrees the dwelling-place and the workshop of modern man, but it is the initiating and controlling centre of economic, political, and cultural life that has drawn the most remote parts of the world into its orbit."[20] With this statement, Wirth points up the fact that urbanity is inseparably interwoven with the concept of modernity and that it is within urbanism and urban life that the characteristics of modern life find their most accentuated expression. The representative manifestation of modern man is the urban dweller, having "come under the spell of the influences which the city exerts by virtue of the power of its institutions and personalities operating through the means of communication and transportation."[21]

In the following, the sociological and psychological impacts of urbanism, the growth of population, and the related phenomenon of the masses will be analyzed as the framework within which the first concepts of shock emerge. The notion of shock seems to have been adopted to describe a particular and paradigmatic experience of the individual resulting from being positioned within an urban context, a social and technological framework representing a new range of sensorial challenges and impacting the individual's self-perception. The "cumulative accentuation" of the distinctive characteristics of modern life in the metropolis became widely considered to have reached an etiological quantity. "Especially big cities provide the predisposition to fall ill, as it is here where the entire range of technical innovations find their application,"[22] as Wilhelm Graff was not alone in pointing out. The metropolis was the breeding ground for what George Miller Beard, the New York–based specialist for neuropathology and electrotherapy, described in the title of an 1869 essay as "neurasthenia, or nervous exhaustion."[23] With his publication, which was followed by the two books *Practical Treatise on Nervous Exhaustion (Neurasthenia)* in 1880 and *American Nervousness: Its Causes and Consequences* in 1881, Beard established neurasthenia as a phenomenon of the time, thus preparing the assumption that "our times can rightly be named as the nervous ones."[24] In 1916 Carl Ludwig Schleich, a popular German neurologist and anaesthetist, elaborated as follows: "Possibly, neurasthenia is not an illness as such, but rather a process of adjusting to a cultural development happening too fast. The nerves are required to become excursive in order to remain able to cope with the delusional agitation of our time and with the consequent nervous stimulations."[25]

A large number of scientific, popular, and literary texts explored the changed nervous disposition of the modern urban individual at the turn of the century, and they reveal Georg Simmel's and Walter Benjamin's investigations of these changes as part of a much wider preoccupation at the time. *Über die wachsende Nervosität unserer Zeit* (1893) by Wilhelm Heinrich Erb, *Die Pathologie und Therapie der Neurasthenie* (1896) by Ludwig Binswanger, *Nervosität und Kultur* (1902) by Willy Hellpach, and "Die 'kulturelle' Sexmoral und die moderne Nervosität" ("'Civilized' Sexual Morality and Modern Illness," 1908) by Sigmund Freud are some of the numerous scientific engagements with the subject matter. Martin Beradt's *Der Neurastheniker* (1913) and Alice Berend's *Spreemann & Co.* (1916), to name two examples, engaged with the theme in the field of literature.[26]

Within Germany, the center of the sociocultural and technological upheaval was Berlin, the home of both Simmel and Benjamin. The following investigation into this city's influence on both authors' ideas on sense perception in general and the experience of shock in particular can thus be understood as a testing of John Bornemann's nomination of Berlin as "the twentieth century's paradigmatic space,"[27] mirroring Walter Benjamin's conception of Paris as the "capital" of the nineteenth century.

Toward the end of the nineteenth century, Berlin underwent a decisive transformation, its population doubling between 1871 and 1892. Having passed the 1 million mark in 1885, its population reached 2 million only twenty years later, notwithstanding the fact that most of today's major districts, such as Charlottenburg, Rixdorf/Neukölln, and Schöneberg, were not yet incorporated and were thus counted as separate cities, having up to 300,000 inhabitants each.[28] After their incorporation in 1920, the city's population rose to almost 4 million, a mark that was exceeded a few years later. However, within Europe, Berlin was by no means the largest city, with London having a population of 6.5 million at the turn of the century, and standing at just over 8.5 million in the late 1930s. (Paris's population was 2.7 million at the turn of the century, reaching its maximum in the 1920s with just under 3 million.) Berlin's specificity was not the size of its population but its density: it had become the most densely populated city in Europe and possibly in the world.[29]

Thus, the experience that can be considered as particular to Berlin was that of the mass of its populace. At the end of the nineteenth century, an average of 77 people lived within the same building, having increased from 55 in 1873.[30] Many of the typical five-story blocks, fitted with two or three backyards, often incredibly narrow, had between 100 and 300 inhabitants.[31] Some big housing complexes, such as the infamous tenement "Meyers Hof" in Berlin-Wedding that was demolished in 1972, housed more than 2,000 individuals. The rapid increase of the population and its density within the city limits made overpopulation and a lack of individual space the city's predominant characteristic. Berlin was labeled the "largest tenement city in the world,"[32] and the birthplace of tenement housing. The lack of sufficient housing and income supported the extreme crowding of the available space and fostered the resulting social problems. Already in the 1840s, as Heinrich Grunholzer noted in his travel diary, an average of seven to eight people shared a flat of about 250 square feet (approx. 23 square metres).[33] In a newspaper of 1928, Kurt Tucholsky—using the pseudonym Ignaz Wrobel—delivered a touching description of the living conditions of the working class in Berlin, entitling his article "Die Kinderhölle in Berlin, a children's hell."[34]

In accord with the growing population, Berlin became one of the major centers of industrialization and technological progress. Within a few decades, the new-born capital was the leading and largest industrial center in continental Europe and took up its role as "electropolis," with Siemens and the A.E.G. securing Berlin's leading position within the electrical industry and its world market.[35] Both the growing population and the technological advances furthered a swiftly developing system of transportation. The world's first electric locomotive, developed by Werner von Siemens and presented to the public on the occasion of the industrial exhibition in Berlin in 1879, was inaugurated in 1881 and had replaced horsepower by 1902.[36] In the same year, an underground and overhead railway system was added, and buses began circulating in 1905.[37] By 1914, Berlin had more than 130 trams,[38] 7,400 registered automobiles, and an extensive underground and overhead railway network.[39] In 1912, the Vienna-born Egon Friedell described Berlin as "a wonderful modern machine shop, a colossal electric motor, which performs an amplitude of complex mechanical operations with an unbelievable precision, speed and energy."[40] The electric trams moved at about fifteen to twenty kilometres per hour, speeds that appear slow today but were exhilarating at the time.

However, as perfectly as the system of public transportation performed, the enormous demands made on it not only led to traffic jams, but resulted in a number of disastrous accidents.[41] In September 1883, the overcrowding of a platform at one of Berlin's stations led to the worst train accident in the Berlin area since the emergence of this means of transportation, killing forty-three people.[42] In 1908, two trains on the newly expanded subway network crashed into each other at an overhead crossing, pushing one of the trains off the elevation.[43] Both the rising quantity and new quality of accidents, emerging as a consequence of the modern means of transportation, drew attention to a previously unrecognized disease that became known as "railway spine." It was a term coined and developed in 1866 by John Eric Erichsen, who considered internal hemorrhages along the spine resulting from a violent shockwave to be the cause of a consequent neurological defect.[44] It was equally believed that the slight, constant vibrations during a train ride were a source of nervousness and ultimately neurasthenia.[45] Other terms used in the 1860s and 1870s were "spinal concussion" and "brain concussion,"[46] before the phenomenon was later renamed "shell shock" or "traumatic neurosis." Defined as "triggered by an event outside the normal range of human experience,"[47] it is now known as post-traumatic stress disorder. As Inka Mülder-Bach points out, the preoccupation with shell shock developed in two batches between 1860 and 1920: before World War I fostered the second wave of focused research into this disease, investigations had been triggered by the unparalleled number and severity of these train accidents.[48]

Such was the Berlin of Walter Benjamin's childhood and adolescence, growing up in the midst of this atmosphere of transition, growth, and acceleration. He was born into a bourgeois family that was thus well able to profit from the technological innovations. During the first years of his life, Benjamin's family moved a couple of times within the very center of Berlin before moving from the "old to the new West,"[49] that is, from Berlin's center to the prestigious area of Charlottenburg, still a separate administrative district at that time. Among the many urban areas neighboring Berlin, Charlottenburg was not only the largest (numbering 200,000 inhabitants at the turn of the century and 325,000 in 1919), but also the richest, having the highest per capita income of all cities within Prussia.[50] Benjamin's year of birth, 1892, also saw the death of Werner von Siemens, whose groundbreaking inventions in the field of telegraphic communication and heavy-current electrical engineering had been indispensable to the changes in communication and transportation shaping the city. With his company, Siemens & Halske, comprising 10,000 employees in 1906, he initiated the emergence of an industrial and residential area bordering Charlottenburg, called Siemensstadt. In 1881, Siemens & Halske provided the telegraphs for Berlin's first telephone network. It also outfitted the city center with the first electric lighting system, putting an end to the flickering, dim light of gas lamps and creating a contrast that was "brutally shocking [*brutalen Chock*] with the spectacle of entire cities suddenly being illuminated by electric light,"[51] as Benjamin described it.

Benjamin's autobiographical notes from spring 1932, entitled *Berliner Chronik* (*A Berlin Chronicle*), only posthumously published, although extracts were included in a published work of that year entitled *Kindheit um neunzehnhundert* (*Berlin Childhood around 1900*), reflect upon his childhood in Berlin. Here, the memories of a powerful city and an experience of menace and peril prevail. Being out on the streets, Benjamin describes his feelings of exposure, abandonment, and danger, culminating in the sensation of senselessness and unconsciousness.[52] This early experience of Berlin as a labyrinth triggering a lack of orientation and the consequent feeling of being lost within the massive and incomprehensible corpus of the surrounding city appears to be more than just a general feature of large cities. If one believes Karl Scheffler's severe condemnation of Berlin, written in 1910, the utter incapacity to perceive this city as a sensible organism and the absence of cornerstones for an orientation within it were specific consequences of Berlin's urban planning or, rather, the lack of such planning.[53] Equally significant is the opening sentence of Mark Twain's travelogue of Berlin, "The German Chicago," which encapsulates the author's experience: "I feel lost in Berlin." Later in the same piece, Twain described Berlin as "the newest [city] I have ever seen."[54]

For Benjamin, his early experience of an inability to cope with his urban surroundings seems to affect his mode of perception, requiring and generating "a gaze that appears to see not a third of what it takes in [*auffasst*]."[55] In this, Benjamin was not alone. Whereas Franz Kafka, for example, described a similar experience in view of film turning looking into overlooking,[56] other reports, such as that of Richard Hamann from 1907, focus on the urban environment in a similar manner:

> The crossing of the Potsdamer Platz or simply a walk through Friedrichstrasse during busy times of the day, [requires] a presence of mind, which contents

itself with impressions of inarticulate kind and with visual impressions seen allusively and which directs its volition accordingly. Those who feel the need to look around more carefully in order to complete the hints received will be doomed in these turbulences.[57]

In a famous quotation, Benjamin describes the very same situation going yet a step further: "Moving through this traffic involves the individual in a series of shocks and collisions. At dangerous intersections, nervous impulses flow through him in a rapid succession, like the energy from a battery."[58]

As a consequence of the social milieu and prosperous neighborhood into which he was born, Benjamin came into direct contact with the new means of transportation and communication. In his childhood memories, he mentions the horse-drawn trams and the steam-powered city trains among his earliest experiences,[59] and he describes the frightening sound of the family's first telephone emerging from a dark corridor of the apartment. He also describes his experience of feeling exposed to the voice coming through the new apparatus and exceeding the young boy's control.[60]

As another consequence of his bourgeois circumstances, Benjamin's childhood developed well removed from the overcrowded and poorly heated tenant housing complexes so typical of Berlin's extensive blue-collar areas, which were a recurrent issue of contemporary social disputes and conflicts. In retrospect, Benjamin comes to describe the socio-geographical framework of his childhood as an imprisonment, as "confined to this affluent neighbourhood without knowing of any other."[61] At the same time, and despite his distance from those areas and milieus where the density of Berlin's population manifested itself most explicitly, Benjamin speaks of his early abhorrence of being part of a crowd and states that "solitude appeared to me as the only fit state of man"[62]—but also, we might add, the most anachronistic. In seeming aberrance from this, we find a sort of plea for Berlin's infamous tenement blocks in Benjamin's review of Werner Hegemann's publication *Das steinerne Berlin: Geschichte der grössten Mietskasernenstadt der Welt* from 1930, which was reprinted as the foreword in later editions of Hegemann's book. "Even the desultory crudeness of this settlement," as Benjamin states here, "has its own beauty, not only for the strolling snob from the West but also for the Berliner, the Zille-Berliner himself." It is a love-hate relationship, indeed, based on Benjamin's conviction that "what we seek to annihilate may not be standing in front of us as an abstract 'negativum,' a counter-example. . . . It is not sufficient to know what one wishes to extinguish, one has to have . . . felt it."[63]

Benjamin is highly aware of the inevitable influence of his sociocultural milieu on his production, locating his "small writing factory" in Berlin's Westend. "Where is my productive base?" he asks in a letter to Gershom Scholem.

> It is—and I have not the slightest illusion about this—in Berlin W. WW, if you will. . . . That is, it is not within my power to relocate my productive base to Berlin east or north. (I would be able to emigrate to Berlin E. or N., but only to do something different from what I do here. . . . I am determined to do my thing regardless of the circumstances, but this thing is not always the same thing under every set of circumstances. It is instead something that corresponds to the circumstances.[64]

In addition to the explicit examination of his childhood city contained in his autobiographical writings, Benjamin's socialization at a distinct point in Berlin's history and development is also implicit within his consistent interest in modern metropolitan life or, more precisely, its consequences for the conditions of the individual's perception. "Just as the entire mode of existence of human collectives changes over long historical periods, so too does their mode of perception," as Benjamin famously states in the "Artwork-Essay." "The way in which human perception is organized—the medium in which it occurs—is conditioned not only by nature but by history."[65] With this statement, Benjamin points toward a distinct focus within his analysis of contemporary society. It is not simply directed at the phenomenon of the metropolis, but asks specifically for its impact upon the individual living in it, examining the sociohistorical determination of sensory perception. In this, too, Benjamin was not alone. Georg Simmel is well known to be "the first sociologist, who . . . broached the issue of an excess of information in the streets, the incessant bombardment with shocking contacts and who deduced the metropolitan habitus from this situation."[66] In 1902–3 the sociologist, economist, and philosopher had published his essay "Die Grossstädte und das Geistesleben" ("The Metropolis and Mental Life"), examining the impact of metropolitan life upon the individual's perceptual and psychological condition.

> The psychological basis of the metropolitan type of individuality consists in the intensification of nervous stimulation which results from the swift and

> uninterrupted change of outer and inner stimuli. Lasting impressions, impressions which differ only slightly from one another, impressions which take a regular and habitual course and show regular and habitual contrasts—all these use up, so to speak, less consciousness than does the rapid crowding of changing images, the sharp discontinuity in the grasp of a single glance, and the unexpectedness of onrushing impressions. These are the psychological conditions which the metropolis creates. With each crossing of the street, with the tempo and multiplicity of economic, occupational and social life, the city sets up a deep contrast with small town and rural life with reference to the sensory foundations of psychic life.[67]

Simmel specifies the effect of this change of the individual's psychic condition as bound to "the permanent knowledge of a certain danger" affected by increasing traffic, speed, overcrowding, and so on, which "has to necessarily generate a modification within the psychological disposition of men."[68] According to Simmel, the increased challenge imposed on the nervous system cannot (or cannot solely) be met by an increased awareness but by its opposite. As a consequence of the constant strain and excessive demand, "an incapacity thus emerges to react to new sensations with the appropriate energy."[69] Benjamin not only agrees with this observation in his theoretical writings, but confirms it by his own experience. The feeling of unconsciousness, by which he found himself overwhelmed on the streets of Berlin, and the impossibility of a fully conscious visual reception, correspond closely with the phenomenon Simmel describes. Benjamin, who attended some of Simmel's lectures during his first semester at the Berlin university in 1913 (briefly before the elder left the city), names Simmel among those professors he considers of particular interest and influence.[70] Although there is no explicit and focused engagement with Simmel's work—and only little secondary literature exploring the affinities between Simmel's and Benjamin's thinking[71]—quotations from and references to the sociologist are frequent and diverse in Benjamin's writings. Having previously shared a preoccupation with Johann Wolfgang Goethe, it is in *Das Paris des Second Empire bei Baudelaire* (*The Paris of the Second Empire in Baudelaire*), finished in 1938, that Benjamin turns to Simmel's sociohistorical enquiries. For both his research on Baudelaire and for his fragmentary and unfinished *Passagen-Werk* (*The Arcades Project*) Benjamin read Simmel's seminal book *Philosophie des Geldes* (*Philosophy of Money*, 1900), as he reports in a letter to Adorno.[72] Much earlier even, in 1917, he had already consulted *Das Problem der historischen Zeit* (*The Problem of Historical Time*, 1916), which he described, however, as an "utterly miserable botch."[73]

What becomes of explicit interest to Benjamin in the mid-1930s is Simmel's account of the sociohistorical determination of sense perception, notably referring to the elder's essay "Soziologie der Sinne" ("Sociology of the Senses," 1907). This text was included in the French edition *Mélange de philosophie rélativiste*, which Benjamin consulted while conducting research at the Bibliothèque Nationale in Paris.[74] As his written correspondence with Adorno tells us, a debate arose precisely around a quote from this text, which Adorno wanted removed before publishing Benjamin's essay in the *Zeitschrift für Sozialforschung*, but Benjamin refused.[75] Implicit references herald this quote, giving expression to the authors' shared conviction of a causal relation between a certain sociocultural context and the disposition of the individual living in this context. Both consider it to affect, as Simmel phrased it, "the sensory foundations" of the individual's "psychic life"[76]—but more than this, they also correspond with regard to the kind of effects the increase of stimuli has upon the individual's sensory and psychological condition. In this, both differ from other contemporary approaches, such as Willy Hellpach's, who equally observed the stated increase of stimuli but considered it to result in an amplified state of alert and awareness,[77] detecting a vigilance of the senses (*Sinneswachheit*) in utter opposition to Benjamin's state of insensibility (*Ohnmacht*) or Simmel's paralysis of the perceptional capacity (*Paralyse des Wahrnehmungsvermögens*).

In view of these intellectual correspondences, the similarities in their social circumstances are perhaps unsurprising. Both not only were born and grew up in the very center of Berlin, but each continually reflected upon their specific urban socialization and the distinct characteristics of Berlin. Born in 1858 as the youngest of seven children to a prosperous entrepreneur (who belonged to a Jewish family of merchants of Silesian origin), Simmel also grew up accustomed to the bourgeois lifestyle.[78] After some economic difficulties, the family's financial well-being was secured through the support of a close friend, Julius Friedländer, who later included Georg Simmel in his will and thus secured Simmel's own family's prosperity. Although both his parents had converted to Christianity (one to Catholicism, and one to Protestantism), Simmel considered himself Jewish, and the memories of his son give clear expression to the culturally Jewish but unorthodox orientation of Georg Simmel's own household.[79] With Benjamin's and Simmel's birthplaces only several hundred meters apart as the crow flies, Simmel's social, cultural, and architectural impressions of Berlin were also those of a prosperous, flourishing, and mercantile city center. For the major part of his life he stayed in this city—living at its heart—and his own house was to become a hub for the city's intellectual life. However, in view of these socio-geographical correspondences in both biographies, one distinct difference has to be taken into consideration: namely that, thirty-four years Benjamin's senior, Simmel was born into a quite different Berlin. In 1858, the German Empire was yet to be established and Berlin was yet to become its capital. Though it was already a large city, Berlin was not yet a metropolis.

In his comparison of E. T. A. Hoffmann's "Des Vetters Eckfenster" ("My Cousin's Window Corner") from 1822 and Edgar Allan Poe's "The Man of the Crowd" from 1840, Benjamin explains the protagonists' differing attitudes by referring to their dissimilar socio-geographical contexts:

> In the difference between the two observation posts lies the difference between Berlin and London. On the one hand, there is the man of leisure. He sits in his alcove as in a box at the theater; when he wants to take a closer look at the marketplace, he has opera glasses at hand. On the other hand, there is the anonymous consumer who enters a café and will shortly leave it again, attracted by the magnet of the mass which constantly has him in its range.[80]

The stated difference is rooted in the different locations insofar as London in 1840 was already a metropolis of about 2.5 million, whereas the population of Berlin in the 1820s was only about 220,000 and the groundbreaking transitions of what came to be known as the *Gründerjahre*—the period of industrial expansion in Germany from 1871 onward—were yet to come.

When these transitions started to take effect, notably in the last two decades of the nineteenth century, Simmel found himself at the very heart of these changes, living at the northwest corner of the intersection of Friedrich- and Leipzigerstrasse, where he was born. The fact that Ralph Hoppe's book *Die Friedrichstrasse—Pflaster der Extreme* is dedicated exclusively to the social and architectural history of a single street is indicative of the exemplary status of Friedrichstrasse for Berlin, the development of one mirroring that of the other.[81] "Just over twenty years after the birth of the empire," as Hoppe confirms, "the old Western city center with its streets Unter den Linden, Leipziger- and Friedrichstrasse had become the heart of the metropolis."[82] The very junction of Friedrich- and Leipzigerstrasse became a center for national and international corporations, such as insurance companies and banking. In 1888, to name an example, the *Equitable Life Assurance Society* of the United States built their impressive and famous headquarters at the northeast corner of the junction. A few meters down the street, the area's first shopping mall was inaugurated in 1873 on the emperor's birthday.[83] Baroness Hildegard von Spitzemberg's graphic description of the Berlin of 1898 could not have been written forty years earlier:

> The hustle and bustle of the main roads, such as Leipziger- and Friedrichstrasse, is downright deafening; the electric cars and trams form an incessant line; cars of all kind, droshkies, three- and four-wheeled vehicles drive beside, before, and behind each other and frequently on top of each other. The ringing of all these vehicles and the rattling of the wheels is ear-splitting; crossing the street is a daring feat for the city slicker and an ordeal for the provincial. Mrs von Beulwitz even affirms that people used to embrace each other emotionally once they had found refuge on the other side having safely negotiated the Potsdamer Platz![84]

As mentioned earlier, it was not Berlin's size that marked it apart from other European capitals such as London and Paris, nor its wealth or the city's transformation effected by new technology and emerging means of transportation; it was the remarkable density of its population and the consequent omnipresence of the masses. The second aspect that gave Berlin its exceptional position in the decades around the turn of the century was the speed and scale of these transitions, having started at quite a different point than other major European cities.[85] When Lessing in 1913–14 looked back on Simmel's neighborhood of the year 1858, he described it wrongly as the noisy and crowded hubbub it was yet to become.[86] The industrialist, politician, and writer Walter Rathenau, born in Berlin in 1867, described his home city in 1899 as "not grown but transformed. . . . The royal Prussia has no place within the imperial Berlin; Spree-Athens is dead, but Spree-Chicago is growing up."[87] Berlin's development was normal in that it experienced the changes of all other European metropolises. It was abnormal in as far as the changes occurred in an unprecedented speed, thus providing the platform to experience the effects of these changes in an exemplary and drastic manner.

Based on these observations, Dietmar Jazbinsek asserts convincingly "that Simmel was called to be the theoretician of the urban setting precisely because he had not become accustomed to the 'tumult of the metropolis' from early life on but rather had been confronted again and again with what was new and what needed getting used to. He had been confronted with the strangeness of a city in which nothing today is like it had been yesterday."[88] Jazbinsek's argument finds further support in Hans Simmel's *Auszüge aus den Lebenserinnerungen*, where the author describes his father's birthplace: "Having once been removed from the old city center, these streets became later two of the most typical and most important shopping streets; hardly anyone could have been more responsible within Berlin, than the person being born at the crossing of the Leipziger and Friedrichstrasse."[89]

Reviewing Simmel's seminal book *Philosophie des Geldes* (*Philosophy of Money*, 1900), Karl Joël is convinced that "this book could only have been written in Berlin and at this time."[90] The relevance of both the place and time of his birth is confirmed by Simmel himself, who states, "Berlin's development from a city into a world metropolis in the years around and after the turn of the century coincides with my own broadest and most intense development."[91] Simmel continues elsewhere: "Would I have lived in a different city, I might have possibly achieved something equally valuable; but the distinct achievement, which it seems I accomplished during the last decades, is undoubtedly bound to the Berlin milieu."[92] He thus corresponds strikingly with Benjamin's own rootedness in the Berlin context, and is equally attached to this city, which he only leaves reluctantly in 1914, at the age of fifty-six, having finally been appointed to a full professorship in Strasbourg. The three decades separating Simmel and Benjamin in age might explain the divergence in their evaluations of the situation they analyze. Having witnessed the city's considerable transformation as an adolescent and young adult, Simmel deplores the effects of these changes upon the individual's perceptional and psychic capacities as phenomena of decadence and decline. Having been born into the newly risen metropolis, Benjamin takes instead an ultimately neutral and impartial view, scrutinizing rather than evaluating the given situation.

Simmel's awareness of a close link between the experience of the emerging urban lifestyle and changes within sociological theory is far from unique. Rather, as Ilja Srubar argues, it was the metropolitan experience that generated and shaped modern sociology in the first place.[93] The fact "that sociology received its theoretical tools largely in its observation of the big city, can be recognized by help of the observation that . . . its [i.e., the big city's] analyses were always a constitutive component within each of its [i.e., sociology's] developed theories."[94] Both Simmel and Benjamin confirm this assumption on an implicit and explicit level. Considering the human capacity and structure of sense perception as shaped by historical determinants, Simmel presents sense perception not as the neutral basis for social interaction, but rather as determining this interaction as a consequence of its own transformation. As Simmel elaborates in "Sociology of the Senses," social interaction changes depending on whether or not such interaction is based, for example, on the predominance of visual or acoustic stimuli. "The prevalence of one or the other sense in the contact of individuals often provides this contact with a sociological nuance that could otherwise not be produced."[95] With regard to the parameters of the modern, urban lifestyle, Simmel observes a predominance of the visual over acoustic sense perception. As he comes to conclude, it is as a consequence of the increasingly dense population and new forms of transportation that intersubjective interaction and evaluation had become predominantly based on visual rather than acoustic information. This turned the individual into an anonymous member of a mass, since it was "infinitely easier to form a general conception of human beings whom we only see than if we could speak with each of them,"[96] thus leading to the anonymity of cities so frequently deplored.

However, Simmel not only precedes Benjamin in his awareness of the sociocultural determination of sense perception and an investigation into the impacts of the modern urban environment on the sensory system. More specific to our context, Simmel precedes Benjamin in adopting the term *shock*, using it to describe the reaction to a particular type of sensory impression. "The modern person is shocked by innumerable things, and innumerable things appear intolerable to their senses."[97] A couple of pages later in his essay "Sociology of the Senses," Simmel specifies this by speaking of "shocks to the sense of smell [*Chockierung des Geruchssinnes*],"[98] thus using the notion of shock to describe a type of sense perception unbearable to the sensory system. Shock becomes defined as an experience resulting from a transgression of the subject's sensorial capacity and tolerability. Such a use of the term in relation to the act of smelling significantly illustrates the transgressive character of a shocking experience by combining it with a lack of distance: "Now, from the outset, the olfactory sense is already adapted to short distances by comparison to sight and hearing," writes Simmel.[99] Perceiving another person via his or her smell confirms a lack of distance, an insufficiency of space between two people. Simmel fosters such link between shock, smell, and a lack of distance by referring to the phenomenon of the mass: "Indeed, in general, shocks to the sense of smell will be directly quantitatively proportional to the mass of people in the midst of which they strike us."[100] Here, Simmel describes shock explicitly as an experience produced by a paradigm of urban life, that is, the density of urban population. In accordance with his earlier assumption of the reciprocal relationship between sense perception and the social context, the potentially shocking effect of sense perception fostered by the conditions of urban living in turn has an impact on living conditions: "The social question is not only an ethical one, but also a question of smell [*eine Nasenfrage*],"[101] Simmel concludes poignantly: "Personal contact between educated people and workers often so vigorously advocated for the social development of the present and the rapprochement of the two worlds 'of which the one does not know how the other lives,' advocated by the educated classes as an ethical ideal, fails simply because of the insuperability of impressions of smell."[102] Evidently, this insight is rooted in Simmel's own experience of Berlin and his knowledge of the contemporary social discussion: The lack of decent living space for the working class is a recurrent issue within the social and political debate of the time, and the issue of smell—or rather of revolting stench—features recurrently within it.[103]

This survey of Simmel's writings allows three conclusions. First, the sociologist defines shock as the reaction to a certain type of sense perception. Second, this type of sense perception can be described as one that transgresses the subject's personal sphere, incorporating something alien and external. In the case of another person's or an object's smell, something external literally penetrates the subject. Third, Simmel considers the shocking capacity of sense perception as a phenomenon of the modern urban society and time. Shock appears as the peak of the intensified nervous stimulation, which Simmel recognizes as paradigmatic of modernity. When Susan Buck-Morss affirms that "Benjamin's understanding of modern experience is neurological,"[104] thus pointing toward the primordial importance that Benjamin allocates to sense perception and the nervous impulses thus triggered, she indirectly points us toward Benjamin's affinity with Simmel. Antedating an element that will become significant for Benjamin's preoccupation with shock, Simmel not only states an increase in the density and strength of potentially shocking sensorial experiences, he also outlines the indispensable necessity of developing mechanisms to protect the individual from such experiences. For Simmel this protection is accommodated by an automatically generated change within the disposition of the big-city dweller, whom he considers to develop an increasing "incapacity . . . to react to new sensations with the appropriate energy."[105]

Simmel considers such a "blasé attitude" (*Blasiertheit*) as the necessary consequence of "the rapidly changing and closely compressed contrasting stimulations of the nerves. From this, the enhancement of metropolitan intellectuality, also seems originally to stem."[106] Using a terminology that will become apparent as strikingly close to that of Sigmund Freud, Simmel states that the intellect "has its locus in the transparent, conscious, higher layers of the psyche, . . . [being] the most adaptable of our inner forces."[107]

> In order to accommodate to change and to the contrast of phenomena, the intellect does not require any shocks [*Erschütterung*] and inner upheavals; it is only through such upheavals that the more conservative mind could accommodate to the metropolitan rhythm of events. Thus the metropolitan type of man . . . develops an organ protecting him against the threatening currents and discrepancies of his external environment which would uproot him. He reacts with his head instead of his heart. In this an increased awareness assumes the psychic prerogative. Metropolitan life, thus, underlies a heightened awareness and a predominance of intelligence in metropolitan man. The reaction to metropolitan phenomena is shifted to that organ which is least sensitive and quite remote from the depth of the personality.[108]

Simmel considers intellectuality as a mechanism "to preserve subjective life against the overwhelming power [*Vergewaltigung*] of metropolitan life."[109] Thus he considers an increasing intellectualism as the individual's escape route from its permanent exposure to incidents of shock by responding to any incoming impulses intellectually and not with an emotional or psychological reaction: "The essence of the blasé attitude consists in the blunting of discrimination. This does not mean that the objects are not perceived, as is the case with the half-wit, but rather that the meaning and differing values of things, and thereby the things themselves, are experienced as insubstantial."[110]

The blasé attitude is the individual's necessary reaction to the increasing "concentration of men and things," that "stimulate the nervous system of the individual to its highest achievement so that it attains its peak." However, by such "quantitative intensification of the same conditioning factors this achievement is transformed into its opposite" resulting in the nerves' "refusal to react to their stimulation," thus withdrawing to "the last possibility of accommodating to the contents and forms of metropolitan life."[111]

Simmel's understanding of the mechanisms of shock prevention is thus based on the combination of a decreasing capacity of the individual's emotional, psychic, and sensorial ability to respond to impulses, on the one hand, and an intensification of intellectual activity on the other. As we shall see, Benjamin's definition of shock corresponds with Simmel's as a transgression of the capacities of sensual perception. We shall also see that he shares Simmel's conviction of the necessary proliferation of mechanisms to protect the individual from shock, although he adopts this conviction from Freud rather than from Simmel. However, as will become apparent in what follows, Benjamin does not share the sociologist's belief in the intellect's capacity to provide such protection. Recognizing the mode of distraction as both the paradigmatic receptive attitude for the modern society and the gateway of shock, he acknowledges the necessity to provide a protection from shock on the very same level on which experiences of shock occur.[112] Consequently, as will be shown later, his protection from shock is identical neither with Simmel's blasé attitude nor with his metropolitan intellectualism.

Shock and World War I: Walter Benjamin and Sigmund Freud

As the preceding focus on Berlin illustrates, the sociocultural changes brought about by urbanization and technological development at the turn of the century generated a specific focus within sociological research, culminating in the work of Georg Simmel. Urbanism, as both experience and concept, generated an interest in the sociological determination of sensory perception and in the latter's reciprocal effect on social dynamics. In this context, we encounter the term *shock* as it was used to define a transgressive experience within sense perception. A sociohistorical development had here effected a change within a scientific and theoretical approach and had consequently created the need for a new terminology. A parallel interrelation can be observed between the unprecedented experience of World War I and the emergence (or, more precisely, the widespread acknowledgment) of psychoanalysis in the wake of what became the era of the Great War.

Born in 1856, Sigismund Schlomo Freud—better known to us as Sigmund Freud—was only two years older than Simmel. Like both Simmel and Benjamin, Freud belonged to an assimilated Jewish family. Apart from the first four years of his life and until his emigration to London in 1938, one year before his death, Freud lived and worked in Vienna, and thus in the very center of the Austro-Hungarian empire. It became the capital of the republic of Austria after the monarchy's downfall in the aftermath of World War I.

At the turn of the century, Vienna was widely seen as the antipode of Berlin. Whereas the Prussian center was considered a modern hubbub, shaped by a shallow Americanism, superficiality, and speed, the capital of the Austro-Hungarian monarchy was seen as firmly grounded on solid traditions, having a rich cultural and architectural history and possessing emotional warmth and substance.[113] However, Vienna's population had also risen rapidly and approached the 2 million mark in the 1910s: by 1916 its population had reached a new high of just over 2.2 million.[114] As was illustrated by six social studies edited by Hans Ostwald, which formed part of his ambitious fifty-one-volume project of the *Grossstadt-Dokumente* (1904–1908), the social problems arising from such growth were not solved in Vienna, but were merely better ignored. With the monarchy's declaration of war on Serbia, triggered by the killing of the Habsburg's heir apparent, Franz Ferdinand, in Sarajevo, Austro-Hungary set off what were to become "great and terrible times,"[115] as Freud put it, of disastrous and endless fighting and killing.

Freud remained in Vienna throughout the war, finding himself physically exposed to its effects, notably experiencing the lack of food and heating, which hit Austria particularly hard.[116] All three of his sons were involved in front-line combat and were thus in permanent danger of life. (They survived, but Freud lost his nephew.) This created a situation of constant fear, which forced their father to conclude that "getting killed is only a function of time, anyway."[117] Freud's participation in the ongoing events of war is thorough and emotional. In the attempt to gain accurate and objective information, he adopted the habit of reading four newspapers daily.[118] His attitude toward war meandered between euphoria and patriotism, on the one hand, and an ultimately dominating abhorrence and condemnation of the war on the other. Instead of the expected "chivalrous passage of arms"[119] Freud had hoped for, the war turned out to be a horrendous and mechanized slaughtering of masses and proved to have fully abandoned the idea of chivalry and a fight man against man.

For Freud, it was thus less the event of war itself than the way in which it was fought that he thoroughly despised. In his numerous letters of the time, Freud repeatedly described his incapacity to continue with his own research, finding it "completely impossible to do anything sensible," as he put it in 1914; in 1916 he wrote, "My thoughts are mostly not with analytic work,"[120] and the following year he told Abraham, "I am at daggers drawn with writing,"[121] also giving expression to the despair effected by the emblazing war. "I am well aware that human sciences suffer only apparent death, but it seems that humanity is actually dead."[122] With the war only a few months old, Freud confided to Ernest Jones, his friend and colleague in London: "I have no illusion that the blossoming of our science has now been abruptly cut short, that we are approaching a bad period, and that it can only be a matter of maintaining a glimmer of the fire in individual hearths until a more favourable wind allows it to blaze again."[123]

Freud's verdict on the stagnation of psychoanalytical research and its acknowledgment by the scientific community at large appears only partly accurate. Obviously, the war generated difficulties for daily psychoanalytical practice and Freud had to close down his own surgery during large parts of the war due to a shortage of clients.[124] Research and academic exchange between the Freudian psychoanalysts living and working all over Europe was difficult, especially where they belonged to opposing and warring countries. With Jones in London, for example, Freud was only able to communicate via an intermediate address in the Netherlands. Furthermore, the widespread suspicion toward the new science, emanating from the ranks of medicine, neurology, and psychiatry, was fostered by a general dislike by the allied countries of anything considered to be of German origin or closely related.[125] However, despite these impediments and his stated reluctance to write, Freud was in fact remarkably productive during the years of war, probably due to his reduced workload as a practicing psychoanalyst. During the first few months of 1915, he wrote a series of essays with outstanding speed, some of which, notably those that he published under the title "Zeitgemässes über Krieg und Tod" ("Thoughts for the Times of War and Death"), showed an immediate connection to the experience of the war, containing the chapters "Unser Verhältnis zum Tode" ("Our Attitude Toward Death") and "Die Enttäuschung des Krieges" ("The Disillusionment of the War"). Other essays written that year include "Triebe und Triebschicksale" ("Instincts and Their Vicissitudes"), "Die Verdrängung" ("Repression"), "Das Unbewusste" ("The Unconscious"), and "Metapsychologische Ergänzung zur Traumlehre" ("A Metapsychological Supplement to the Theory of Dreams").

However, more important to us than Freud's individual productivity is the fact that World War I generated the basis for the first widespread acknowledgment and support of psychoanalysis. Having been looked at as inferior, psychoanalysis now became an essential means of war medicine.[126] This recognition emerged from a distinct area of psychoanalytic research: an investigation into the heteronymous phenomena summarized as traumatic neurosis, war shock, or—most commonly—shell shock, which Jones considered an "unfortunate catch-word," as it referred to one specific etiological factor, rather than to the illness itself.[127] In her translation of Jones's contribution to the Fifth International Psycho-Analytical Congress in Budapest in 1918, Anna Freud uses the terms "*Granatshock*" and "*Kriegshock*," whereas the German term *Kriegszitten* was mostly used with a pejorative connotation.[128] On the occasion of the mentioned congress, which took place in Budapest in September 1918, Sándor Ferenczi exclaimed, "We cannot spare neurologists the reproach of having so long disregarded the pioneer researches of Breuer and Freud concerning the psychical determination of many nervous disturbances, and of having required the terrible experiences of the war to set them right in this respect."[129]

As psychoanalysts repeatedly stated, World War I did not generate new diseases, but delivered new data on existing diseases.[130] Shell shock was a primary but by no means an exclusive example. Another disease of this kind, developing in the aftermath of the war, was encephalitis lethargica or "sleeping sickness," an often fatal disease affecting several million people.[131] In opposition to the view held by neurology and traditional psychology, psychoanalysis revealed the source of the malfunctions of the nervous system summarized as shell shock as based on a psychological instead of a physical defect. It thus abandoned the prevailing assumption that shock resulted from a violent *mechanical* impact on the human organism. In 1920 Freud summarized as follows:

> Although the war neuroses manifested themselves for the most part as motor disturbances—tremors and paralyses—and although it was possible to suppose that such gross impact as that produced by the concussion due to the explosion of a shell near by or to being buried by a fall of earth would lead to gross mechanical effects, observations were nevertheless made which left no doubt as to the psychical nature of the causation of these so-called war neuroses.[132]

A growing number of soldiers were disqualified from duty due to the effects of shell shock; "the stuttering, shaking and writhing neurotics, supported by canes and crutches," populated the streets, presenting a "sad and heart-wrenching image."[133] This observation by Ewald Stier is misleading insofar as it wrongly suggests the author's sympathy for the diseased. In fact, he rather considered shell shock patients as mostly faking their disease, whether consciously or not. According to their own official figures, the German army had 313,000 shell shock patients treated in hospitals during World War I, with the estimated number of unregistered cases being considered significantly higher.[134] Pressured by the lack of efficient therapeutic means, the aforementioned Budapest congress was rather hastily summoned, receiving unprecedented interest and participation from government and military officials. "For the psychoanalytical movement, the Budapest Congress of September 1918 represented a pinnacle. It was an *event of war* [*Kriegsereignis*]; its subject: the war neuroses."[135] Indeed, the congress resulted in governmental plans to support psychoanalytical centers for the treatment of soldiers affected by shell shock. This sudden support contained an obvious conflict for the researchers themselves, emerging from the fact that the official interest in psychoanalysis was solely motivated by the need for a swift return of the shell shock patients to the front.

In the preceding years, shell shock patients had been subjected to a range of cruel methods of treatment, including electric shock, incessant exercising to the point of total exhaustion, and isolation. Since it had become apparent that there was no physical cause in the majority of cases, the brutal treatments were motivated by the attitude that the diseased were simply inferior malingerers lacking courage and patriotism who had developed their illness, consciously or not, in order to escape their duty.[136] An important aspect in this argument of whether or not shell shock patients largely fake their disease was bound to the issue of the war-veteran pension scheme, as over 50 percent of all pensioned veterans in the early 1920s received their pension due to some form of nervous ailment. The so-called "pension neurosis" even became established as an official diagnosis.[137]

Both the diagnosis and treatment of shell shock by and large differed depending on the military rank of the patient: whereas shell shocked officers were generally diagnosed as suffering from neurasthenia (i.e., nervous exhaustion), shell shocked infantrymen were instead diagnosed as hysterics and thus as of inferior character.[138] On the same grounds, officers were generally spared the electrical shocks and other tortures that were the usual form of treatment for sufferers of war neuroses.[139] It is hardly surprising that these treatments did not achieve lasting results and instead resulted in violent deaths and a rising rate of suicides among the diseased.[140] The official acknowledgment of psychoanalysis following the Budapest congress and the assurance of financial support of the new science was unprecedented. However, the plans remained unrealized due to the termination of the war and the consequent loss of interest on the part of governments. In a letter to Ferenczi, Freud states sarcastically, "Our analysis has actually also had trouble. No sooner does it begin to interest the world on account of the war neuroses, the war ends, and once we find a source that affords us monetary resources, it has to dry up immediately."[141]

In his keynote speech for the Budapest congress, Sándor Ferenczi asserted that the countless cases of shell shock generated by the war had proved that a mechanical impact on the body was not an essential cause of the symptoms summarized as shell shock. These symptoms were of both a physical and a psychic nature. Tics, tremors, paralysis, catatonia, rhythmical screaming, and crawling on all fours were some of them. Others concerned more specifically the overstimulation or understimulation of sensory organs, such as hyperesthesia of one or all senses in the former, or blindness, deafness, stuttering, and numbness in the latter. Psychological symptoms such as depression, anxiety, and terror would also occur.[142] The research enabled by the war had furthermore made apparent that a considerable percentage of shell shock patients were not even involved in front-line combat. Although a mechanical impact often coincided with the psychological experience triggering shell shock, it was revealed to be neither a mandatory nor an optional source for the traumatic neurosis, but only an accompanying aspect. Going yet a step further, Freud concluded that a simultaneous injury might even minimize the danger of falling ill with traumatic neuroses.[143]

Freud's famous description of shock as an "extensive *breach* [*Durchbruch*] of the protective barrier [*Reizschutz*] . . . around the psyche"[144] aligns the psychological wounding of the "apparatus of the soul [*Seelenapparat*]" with the physical wounding of the body. Similar to a projectile, breaking through the skin and entering the flesh, shock describes such penetration on a psychological level.[145] "We describe as 'traumatic' any excitations from outside that are powerful enough to break through the protective shield,"[146] Freud summarizes. Thus, the conclusion drawn by psychoanalysis did not consist in abandoning the link between shock and a moment of impact, but in discarding the assumption that this impact was necessarily of a *physical* nature, as medicine believed.

> The latter regards the essence of the shock as being the direct damage to the molecular structure or even to the histological structure of the elements of the nervous system; whereas what we seek to understand are the effects produced on the organ of the mind by the breach in the shield against stimuli and by the problems that follow in its train.[147]

Shock became recognized as a destructive blow to the psychological apparatus, and thus consolidated the isolated attempts of late nineteenth-century neurology to consider the traumatic effects of accidents as of functional rather than organic origin.[148]

An eloquent and early testimony of such nonorganic causes of shock is to be found in Charles Dickens's account of a severe train accident in Staplehurst in 1865, which the writer survived unharmed. In a letter written soon after the event, Dickens confides that "in writing these scanty words of recollection I feel the shake and am obliged to stop."[149] Weeks later, Dickens still suffered from the effects of the experience, both physical (fatigue, dizziness, tremors) and psychological (states of anxiety).[150] However, the reasons why he developed such a variety of symptoms had yet to be examined. It would not be until more than half a century after Dickens's observation and after the experience of World War I that Freud would conclude in 1920: "We may . . . tentatively venture to regard the common traumatic neurosis as a consequence of an extensive breach being made in the protective shield against stimuli."[151] Thus, the approach toward shock and trauma had completed its journey from traditional medicine into psychology, and from body to psyche.

However, the swiftly emerging preoccupation with shell shock phenomena (and the consequent recognition of psychoanalysis) is not sufficiently explained by the war's proliferation of copious research material. There is a further reason requiring consideration, which substantiates the assumption that shell shock is indeed a phenomenon of the early twentieth century. The many case studies provided by the war showed the diversity of possible etiological factors, which were seen to be optional instead of necessary sources of the disease. In other words, an identical shocking experience could well prompt a traumatic neurosis in one person but not in another, depending on the individual's disposition.[152] This observation substantiated Freud's assumption that the ultimate precondition to fall ill from traumatic neurosis was to be found in a certain psychological disposition of the individual. Consequently, the striking rise of cases of shell shock during the war was not exclusively explained by the war's generation of innumerable potentially etiological experiences. Rather, it was the underlying psychological disposition, supporting the development of a trauma, that was revealed as being furthered by the war. In other words—and contrary to what might seem likely—psychoanalysis considered the military's unprecedented epidemic of shell shock to be brought about not so much by the excessive deployment of artillery, nor by the strenuous exposure to physical suffering during a tedious static warfare. Psychoanalytical research of the time, rather, came to conclude that the emergence of shell shock mainly resulted from a change in the type and relevance of intersubjective relations within the army and from the ensuing affective disposition of the individual. "In contrast to the wars of the nineteenth century, the world war presented the preconditions for a widespread affective depletion," Wietfeld stated, consequently coming to define shell shock as a "psychic-social deficiency disease."[153] Freud concurred: "We know that the war neuroses which ravaged the German army have been recognized as being a protest of the individual against the part he was expected to play in the army; and according to the communication of [Ernst] Simmel (1918), the hard treatment of the men by their superiors may be considered as foremost among the motive forces of the disease."[154]

In the publication by Ernst Simmel that Freud cites, shell shock is described as "pathogenic reactions" to the "mental experience of the war."[155] The affective depletion generated by the felt annihilation of the individual through the bureaucratic and coldhearted structure of the warring machinery constituted the psychological breeding ground for an experience of shell shock to take effect. The depersonalized mechanical and bureaucratic structure behind the war machinery gave rise to an experience of a loss of individuality and individual value and the simultaneous loss of autonomy and self-determination, which manifested itself poignantly in one of the innumerable letters from the front, in which its author concludes that "nobody here feels human anymore."[156] This sense of dehumanization finds confirmation in statements by Dada artist Hugo Ball, who later founded the Cabaret Voltaire: "The war is based on a crass error. Men have been mistaken for machines."[157] And he concludes elsewhere: "Everything is functioning; only man himself is not any longer,"[158] being tossed into an "unutterable age."[159] As Wieland Herzfelde remembers in his account of George Grosz, who (like John Heartfield and possibly Richard Huelsenbeck) is believed to have fallen ill with shell shock,[160] "the dread of [the] Prussian barracks drill" was "almost worse than the idea of death or being crippled."[161] Heartfield, Herzfelde's brother, is said to have indeed experienced the military drill and authority as a traumatic shock. The artist suffered a severe nervous breakdown after a sergeant smirked when hearing his claim to be mentally ill.[162] As Wietfeld concludes, "it was the psychological isolation and affective depletion which functioned as the disposing and setting factor."[163]

Johannes Volmert comes to a similar conclusion in examining the very few moments of panic, irritation, and psychological vulnerability experienced by Ernst Jünger's otherwise coldhearted and combative stormtroop officer: "Loneliness and inaction ('no clear orders') as well as symptoms of dissolution within their own military collective are experienced by the soldier as the greatest danger to his ego."[164] The primary problem in terms of a psychological protection against shell shock was thus not that of being at the front but of being in the army. The loss of individuality and of affective and personalized intersubjective relations are recognized as endangering the individual psychologically, and as devastating as the immediate physical danger. As Freud points out, this challenge and threat finds its paradigmatic expression in the army, its failure to respect and protect the subject's individuality. Ultimately, it can be stated that Freud considered the increase of shell shock suffered by the warring forces during World War I to be not primarily a consequence of new technology and the consequent physical dangers, but as emerging from a new social structure that weakened the subject's psychological condition and resistance to psychological disease. As historian Jules Michelet claimed, every century can be recognized by its significant disease. If hysteria was the illness of the nineteenth century, traumatic neurosis—also called "male hysteria" (*männliche Hysterie*)—might be considered that of the twentieth century.[165]

Besides representing an actual physical danger to life, the new material and structural challenges of World War I exposed the subject to a certain psychological threat, where one's individual value was largely diminished if not erased, coinciding with a total loss of criteria for self-orientation. This disappearance of the individual is complemented and coincides with a disappearance of sense and meaning. In "The Disillusionment of the War" (1915), Freud gives expression to this loss of any parameter of reason, intelligibility, and orientation:

> In the confusion of wartime in which we are caught up, relying as we must on one-sided information, standing too close to the great changes that have already taken place or are at the beginning to, and without a glimmering of the future that is being shaped, we ourselves are at a loss as to the significance of the impressions which press in upon us and as to the value of the judgements which we form.[166]

The opening pages of Ernst Jünger's *In Stahlgewittern* (*Storm of Steel*) from 1920, based on fourteen diaries that the author kept during his service in the war, feature a similar description: "The impression of something arising entirely from beyond the pale of experience was so strange that it was difficult to see the connection of things. It was like a ghost at noon."[167] As variously stated in both theory and artistic expression, World War I was the paradigmatic breeding ground for new experiences that were in their nature unexpected, experiences that exceeded the individual's ability to imagine or anticipate and that consequently could not be made sense of. In view of "this event, so far beyond anything we had experienced," recalls Jünger's storm-troop officer, "it was difficult to understand."[168] Similarly, in *Goodbye to All That* (1929), an autobiographical account of the war, Robert Graves's alter-ego comes to "realize that the war's all wicked nonsense."[169] In his autobiographical notes, *Die Flucht aus der Zeit* (*Flight Out of Time*), Hugo Ball writes in autumn 1914, "You know, I would really like to understand, to comprehend,"[170] but he realizes that "we must break with the system of reason [*Vernunftsystem*], because a higher reason exists."[171] The system in place is no longer able to provide meaning or to structure the incomprehensible and overcome extreme disorientation:

> Once the possibility of generating meaning had been left behind, there was the experience of the absurdity of existence. . . . The absurd moment flags the fracture; the continuity of traded symbols is torn apart—without having a new symbol already in place, which would allow for the production of meaning. The absurd moment is an instant of both loss and search.[172]

As Ulrich Linse continues in his psycho-historic analysis of World War, it is in "its least disguised manner" that "the collapse of meaning presents itself as the collapse of mental sanity."[173]

Having analyzed the psychological and ultimately social preconditions that Sigmund Freud considered as paving the ground for experiences of shock to occur, we can now look at what he considered to constitute the experience of shock itself. Freud described shock as an "extensive breach being made in the protective shield against stimuli,"[174] and he specified this psychological "breach" as that of "excessive amounts" of stimuli (*übergrosse Reizmengen*) and "unsuitable kinds of stimulation" (*unangemessene Reizarten*),[175] disturbing the psyche's internal "store of energy" (*Energievorrat*). In Freud's opinion, such disturbance and imbalance between the internal and external energy level is to be prevented where possible:

> Protection against stimuli [*Reizschutz*] is an almost more important function for the living organism than reception of stimuli [*Reizaufnahme*]. The protective shield is supplied with its own store of energy and must above all endeavour to preserve the special modes of transformation of energy operating in it against the effects threatened by the enormous energies at work in the external world—effects which tend towards a leveling out of them and hence towards destruction.[176]

Interestingly, Freud defined the "apparatus of the soul," which he divides into "various organs,"[177] with spatial-bodily terminology, describing it as a structure of several layers, of which the outer layer presents itself as the least sensitive and therefore the least vulnerable. In this he formulated a structure and organization of the psyche very much akin to that of Georg Simmel. The use of the body's physical layout to describe the psychological layout of the soul allocates image and shape to something invisible and shapeless, thus making it easier to imagine. More specifically, psychoanalysis's early research into the phenomenon of shell shock presents this adaptation of a spatial-bodily model as a consequence of the transfer of shock from being understood as a physical injury to a psychological harm.

As explained by Freud, shock results from an attack of excessive external energy insofar as it is not met by a similarly high energy level within the human psyche. Preventing an experience of shock requires a preparatory rise of the internal store of energy. Such preparation occurs whenever something potentially shocking is both expected and its occurrence is imaginable. For this reason, Freud clearly separates the notion of fear or anxiety from the notion of *Schreck*, translated alternatively as "shock" or "fright."[178] In opposition to shock, the emotion of fear precisely consists in such a preparatory rise of the internal energy level, thus conditioning the psyche for the anticipated encounter. "Through fear," concludes Freud, "man protects himself from shock" (*Schreck*).[179] In distinction from this, shock is defined precisely by its being an utter surprise, thus wounding the individual's unprepared psychological disposition. Freud underlines "that the chief weight in their causation seems to rest upon the factor of surprise, of fright" (*Schreck*).[180] The lack of anticipation and thus preparation gives way to the penetration of the most external and least sensitive layer of the soul, which is understood to be the level of consciousness. Such penetration—or, in other terms, the leaving of an impact unregistered (and consequently uncontrollable) by consciousness—creates permanent memory traces (*Gedächtnisspuren*) that are considered to be inaccessible to voluntary and guarded retrieval.

> "Anxiety" describes a particular state of expecting the danger or preparing for it, even though it may be an unknown one. "Fear" requires a definite object of which to be afraid. "Fright," however, is the name we give to the state a person gets into when he has run into danger without being prepared for it: it emphasizes the factor of surprise. I do not believe that anxiety can produce a traumatic neurosis. There is something about anxiety that protects its subject against fright and so against fright-neuroses.[181]

Within early psychoanalytical research, shock is considered to result from excessive external energy, the devastating effect of which is seen in connection with an insufficiency of internal energy. This insufficiency is given where there is a lack of preparation, in other words where such attack of excessive energy is unexpected or, even stronger, where it is in its nature unexpectable.

At this point, the link between Freud's investigation into the army's effects upon the individual's psyche and his description of shock as arising from an inequality of the internal and external energy levels becomes apparent. The lack of preventive preparation on the one hand and the experience of a loss and a lack of orientation on the other both appear as related to an insufficiency of meaning or, more precisely, to the impossibility of allocating meaning to an experience. Lacking a system of parameters from which sense could be deduced, the individual experienced loss, isolation, and abandonment as well as the incapacity to predict and consequently prepare for further potential experiences of similar kind.

The parallel aspects of the sociological and psychoanalytical approaches toward shock at the beginning of the twentieth century thus become apparent. Both approaches can be said to anchor an experience of shock in the relationship between the individual and the mass, which can furthermore be specified as an experienced lack of distance and control and a consequent threat to the individual as an individual. "There is one fact which, whether for good or ill, is of utmost importance in the public life of Europe at the present moment," Ortega y Gasset states in the opening sentence to his analysis of the mass, written in 1929. "This fact is the accession of the masses to complete social power."[182] Inducing "the greatest crisis that can afflict peoples, nations, and civilisation," the experience of crowdedness turns the "social mass" into a "psychological fact."[183] For Ortega y Gasset, the psychological impact of the mass primarily results from the individual's changing self-perception, recognizing itself as a member of the mass and thus as identical with its other members. As the author points out, this changed self-perception might function as a source of pride and empowerment, but might equally result in the experience of danger and the loss of power if the individual lacks sufficient affective quality, as Freud and contemporary psychoanalysts outlined. The mass can provide the grounds for the individual's experience of shock. Whereas Simmel investigated the effects of the mass upon the individual's sense perception, Freud focuses on the psychological effects of a challenge to or diminution of the individual's sense of self. In both cases the experience of shock coincides with a discounting of the individual.

Shock and Tactility in Walter Benjamin

The writings of Georg Simmel and Sigmund Freund are examples of the sociological and psychoanalytical research that preceded Walter Benjamin's investigation into both the experience and the concept of shock, which he then transferred to the realm of aesthetic theory. Benjamin's borrowings from psychoanalysis are more obvious than his affinities with sociological approaches of the time. His references to Freud in particular are crucial and explicit, providing the basis for his concept of shock. Benjamin adopts the psychoanalyst's use of a spatial-bodily terminology and accepts the description of shock as the intrusion of excessive energy and the enabling of such intrusion by an insufficiency of the internal energy level.

The interplay between Freud's sufficiency and insufficiency of *energy* will recur in Benjamin's work as the sufficiency and insufficiency of *awareness*. Whereas Freud investigates shock with regard to its effects upon the "apparatus of the soul,"[184] Benjamin investigates its interplay with the "human apparatus of perception."[185] His turn toward the notion of awareness is indicative of the fact that Benjamin's interest in shock is not directed toward its psychological results, but focuses on shock as a sensorial experience. For Benjamin, shock is of interest as an immediate sensorial encounter enabled by an insufficiency of awareness of a received impulse and by the consequent failure of the intellect to process it. As mentioned earlier, Benjamin develops his concept of shock most explicitly within the two famous texts "The Work of Art in the Age of Its Technological Reproducibility" (1935–36) and "On Some Motifs in Baudelaire" (1939). Although thus developed within essays on the means and media of artistic expression, Benjamin's concept of shock is not derived from the history of art or aesthetics. Rather, his approach to shock is the symbiosis and continuation of preceding sociological and psychological approaches, which culminate in Benjamin's affinities with Georg Simmel and Sigmund Freud.

Although it emerges from his investigation into artistic expression, Benjamin's explicit preoccupation with the idea of shock does not necessarily imply that he developed it in response to a situation or need observed within the realm of the arts. Put differently, Benjamin's interest in Dada and film can be considered as not of artistic but of sociological origin, resulting not from their furtherance of artistic developments and art-historical genealogies, but from their reaction to an art-external (i.e., social) situation. Benjamin considers Dada and film as appropriately responding to a specific, socially generated need, and it is this facility of response that defines their relevance. Both the Dada movement and the medium of film possess the capacity to formulate an appropriate reaction or to give appropriate expression to the given sociocultural context, and this is the basis of Benjamin's interest in them. (The tachistoscope from the late 1880s, which can be seen as a predecessor of film with regard to the recipient's perceptional situation, was developed as a scientific, not an artistic, device to examine the workings of perception in a brief sensation, that is, in the perception of a single glance.)[186]

With this in mind, it becomes indispensable to turn first toward Benjamin's perception of his sociocultural context and to examine the tasks he considers to emerge from it. An analysis of Benjamin's notion of "tactility" serves as an entry into this issue, since it elucidates not only the connection between Benjamin's understanding of his sociocultural context and Dada or film, but also the resulting relevance of shock. Early in 1927, Walter Benjamin traveled to Moscow at the invitation of his longtime friend (and former lover) Asja Lacis. One of a number of texts resulting from this two-month stay was published in *Die Kreatur* later that year.[187] "More quickly than Moscow itself, one learns to see Berlin through Moscow."[188] With this insight, Benjamin opens his straightforward, factual account of the foreign city, in which he allocates barely any space for interpretation and theorization. In a letter to Siegfried Kracauer, he fittingly proclaims, "It has been my intention to return only enriched in impressions not in theory, and I consider this a benefit."[189] The kind of benefit he has in mind becomes clearer in a letter to Martin Buber, the magazine's editor, where Benjamin refers to the submitted text by stating that within it "everything factual is already theory."[190] (It was this closeness in Benjamin's argumentation between an empirical approach and its theorization that became now and then a point of discord with Adorno.)[191] Exaggerating a little, it is through the mere description of the city that the text of 1927 implicitly embodies a sociocultural theory, containing the vertices of Benjamin's "theory of shock," which will only find its more explicit formulation nine years later. Such close linkage is hardly surprising, considering that Benjamin recognizes the urban environment as constitutive of modern experience and that he will come to perceive shock at the very heart of this experience.[192]

In a letter to Hugo von Hofmannsthal, written at the beginning of June 1927, Benjamin reports of his visit to Moscow: "I concentrated even more on rhythmic experiences than I did on visual ones."[193] He thus appears to anticipate Robert Musil's description of "all big cities" as being "made up of irregularity, change, forward spurts, failures to keep step . . . ; made up of . . . one great rhythmic beat as well as the chronic discord and a mutual displacement of all its contending rhythms."[194] Like Musil's "man without qualities," a city dweller, Benjamin does not experience the city's rhythm as a constant, steady, and anticipatable beat, but rather as determined by frequent a-rhythmical and unexpected interferences. Thus, it is not so much the rhythm but its continual disturbance that define this specific experience of the urban environment. Going on to describe "travel by streetcar in Moscow [as] . . . more than anything else a tactile experience,"[195] Benjamin indicates the relationship between the rhythmical character of the city and the individual's body, the first directly affecting the latter. It is only in the much later "Artwork Essay" that Benjamin elaborates on the notion of a tactile experience and calls it exemplary of the type of experience generated by modern urban life: "For the tasks which face the human apparatus of perception at historical turning points cannot be performed solely by optical means—that is, by way of contemplation. They are mastered gradually—taking their cue from tactile reception—through habit."[196] Put differently, the increasing challenge to the individual's capacities for sense perception (a consequence of the growing number, frequency, strength, and discord of external sensorial impulses) requires a new type of perception in order for the individual to be able to deal at all with those impulses and react to them. The individual can only hope to master the changed external situation by undergoing a corresponding change in its internal response to this situation.

Besides this, Benjamin's words illustrate that neither the notion of the "optical" nor that of "tactility" refer to the perception of a specific sensory organ. He thus indicates that his focus on tactility does not deny the predominance of visual perception, which Georg Simmel described as paradigmatic for the modern, urban context, an idea Benjamin explicitly agreed with in his text on "The Flaneur."[197] Instead, the notion of tactility is used to specify the particular character of this new attitude of perception, defined by a state of distraction and processed in a mode of habituation. "Opticality" is thus not to be understood as an exclusive reference to the act of seeing, nor is "tactility" an exclusive reference to the act of feeling or touching. Rather, the optical and tactile modes of perception define a certain *attitude of reception*. Whereas the optical mode describes reception as taking place within an act of contemplation, tactility refers to reception within a mode of distraction: "On the tactile side, there is no counterpart to what contemplation is on the optical side. Tactile reception comes about not so much by way of attention as by way of habit."[198] Benjamin specifies this mode as "reception in distraction."[199] In recognizing distraction as paradigmatic for the modern subject, Benjamin was partaking of the spreading awareness of distraction as the counterpart to self-conscious contemplation.[200] Frederic Schwartz concludes:

> Distraction is a hypothetical mode of visual attention, one described as routine, active and not absorbed, one representing a mode of technical problem-solving and not aesthetic enjoyment, one addressing bits and pieces from the inside and not unified wholes from a distance.[201]

My investigation into the influence of Benjamin's childhood experiences of Berlin upon his later work finds a primary example in his "theory of distraction." Modern living conditions, culminating in the metropolitan environment, produce a specific mode of perception and reception, in which one (consciously) sees a fraction of what is (unconsciously) perceived. This mode develops in response to the impossibility of processing the increasing number of incoming impulses in their entirety. As Richard Shusterman observes with regard to Benjamin, "our immediate experience of things no longer forms a meaningful, coherent whole but is rather a welter of fragmentary, unintegrated sensations—something simply lived through [*erlebt*] rather than meaningfully experienced."[202] Importantly, a mode of *reception* in distraction requires a mode of *reaction* in distraction, that is, a mode of action and reaction not based on a fully conscious process of reception and decision making.[203]

With this in mind, it becomes clearer what Benjamin means when describing his experience of Moscow as a tactile rather than an optical experience. His way of looking, gained within the urban surroundings of Berlin, reused in Moscow, and performed without the full participation of consciousness, is considered as necessary in order to cope with the multitude and diversity of sensual impulses. Being definable as a tactile mode of visual perception, it is considerably different from Filippo Tommaso Marinetti's call for "Tactilism, or the Art of Touch."[204] In contrast to the Futurist, Benjamin—who also pleads for "tactile art"—does not focus on the sense of touch in order to dissolve the superiority of the visual. As was argued, his interest is not in a particular sense organ, but in a different level of sense perception applicable to all senses. Tactility, as has been shown, defines the paradigmatic and indispensable mode of perception for the new and incomprehensible living conditions of the modern world.

It is not surprising that Benjamin's fragmentary "Theorie der Zerstreuung" ("Theory of Distraction") is thought to have been drafted between 1935 and 1936, making it contemporaneous with his two principal texts on the concept of shock.[205] In the unfortunately sparse draft, Benjamin defines the receptional mode of distraction as an inevitable and indispensable consequence of the modern urban environment, necessary in order to be at all capable of coping with the changed quantity and quality of stimuli. Whereas attention is a normative form of reception, as Jonathan Crary elaborated, distraction is rather a mobile one, thus defining the two extremes of a receptive disposition.[206]

It is at this point that, for Benjamin, the inevitability of experiences of shock in modern times emerges. Having recognized the receptional mode of distraction as a necessity to cope with the new sensorial challenges, it is in this mode where he finds the gateway of shock, thus opening up the dilemma of the modern individual. In the mentioned fragment, Benjamin consequently comes to consider "distraction and destruction as the subjective and objective sides, respectively, of one and the same process":[207] the first (distraction) becomes the paradigmatic attitude of reception, the latter (destruction) emerges as the consequent experience. This relationship between distraction (as a mode of reception) and destruction (as a type of experience) finds further exemplification in Benjamin's text on Baudelaire, where the mode of distraction is recognized as lacking the means to prevent an experience of shock. This insufficient shock-protection derives first from distraction's consisting of a deficiency of attention and second from the fact that an involvement of attention would be able to parry and prevent potential experiences of shock. Indeed, Benjamin considers the occurrence of shock and attention as mutually exclusive.[208] Although abrupt breaks or harsh disjunctions within perception can of course have the effect of revivifying our cognitive awareness within perception, a lack of such awareness and attention can allow such breaks and disjunctions to have an effect of shock. Being defined by a lack of attention, the distractive mode of reception thus paves the ground for shock to become a paradigm of modern experience. Recapitulating Freud's conviction that an experience of shock is enabled by an insufficiency of the internal energy level, the proximity of Freud's psychoanalytical and Benjamin's perceptional approach becomes apparent. As was the case for Freud's insufficient internal store of energy, Benjamin's receptive mode of distraction coincides with a lack of awareness and thus with a lack of expectation and preparation.

When Susan Buck-Morss concludes that "Walter Benjamin's understanding of modern experience . . . centers on shock,"[209] we can simultaneously argue that Benjamin's understanding of modern experience is centred on shock *prevention*. Although two sides of the same coin, there is a decisive difference between the two with regard to the implications for the individual. Like Freud, Benjamin distinguishes between a conscious and an unconscious level of experience—or, to describe them differently, between a level that is sensitive and another that is insensitive to experiences of shock. These levels are furthermore distinct from each other with regard to both the permanence and accessibility of their contents. Benjamin adopts Freud's assumption "that the inexplicable phenomenon of consciousness arises in the perceptual system *instead of* the permanent traces [*Dauerspuren*]."[210] In other words, the content of each level is mutually exclusive. Impacts received consciously do not leave traces on the underlying level of unconsciousness. As Freud continues, the level of consciousness is "characterized by the peculiarity that in it (in contrast to what happens in the other psychical systems) excitatory processes do not leave behind any permanent change in its elements but expire, as it were, in the phenomenon of becoming conscious."[211] Consciousness does not allow for its uncontrolled modification. The capacity of consciousness to function as an instance of shock prevention results from the combination of the following two assumptions: First, an incoming impulse is *either* accommodated within the conscious *or* within the unconscious level of experience. Second, any consciously received impulse cannot set off an experience of shock. "By its death, the outer layer has saved all the deeper ones from a similar fate—unless, that is to say, stimuli reach it which are so strong that they break through the protective shield [*Reizschutz*]."[212] Successful shock defense thwarts the dispersal of "traces of memory" within the unconscious.

However, as much as these traces represent a potential danger for the individual's psychological well-being, they also represent an enrichment of the individual's experience. Consequently, successful shock defense thwarts such enrichment as much as it thwarts the damage this experience might impose. In one of the autobiographical episodes in *A Berlin Chronicle*, Benjamin compares the enriching aspect of an experience of shock to a magnesium flash imprinting an impression onto the photosensitive surface of memory: often "the half-light of habit denies the plate the necessary light for years, until one day from an alien source it flashes as if from burning magnesium powder, and now a snapshot transfixes the . . . image [of perception] on the plate,"[213] thus leaving behind a new trace. An amelioration of shock-defense consequently reduces the likeliness and frequency of such traces. "The greater the shock factor [*Chockmoment*] in particular impressions, the more vigilant consciousness has to be in screening stimuli; the more efficiently it does so, the less these impressions enter long experience [*Erfahrung*], and the more they correspond to the concept of isolated experience [*Erlebnis*]."[214] The prevention of shock thus reveals itself as "a peak achievement of the intellect,"[215] as Benjamin concludes. Benjamin and Freud agree not only that the mechanisms of the *Reizschutz* (protective barrier) and the *Schockabwehr* (shock defense) are of predominant importance, despite the resulting impoverishment of the scope of experience, but also that an amelioration of these protective mechanisms can be achieved via conditioning through repeated exposure to similar impulses of shock. Both authors would describe such an increase in the individual's protective capacities as a thickening and conditioning of the shielding "skin" surrounding the soul or psyche, thus rendering less likely its penetration and the consequent incorporation of shock within the individual's psychological disposition. Thus, one can also perceive Simmel's sociological observation of the city dweller's numbness as a consequence of his exposure to repetitious sensorial impulses mirrored in Freud's psychological description of the consequences of repetitious stimuli. In both approaches it becomes less likely for a potentially shocking impulse to have an impact on the subject. In Benjamin's account of shock, however, the new element is the involvement of distraction. For Freud, being fully focused on the individual's mental disposition, the receptive mode and perceptional situation is of minor relevance.

Due to Benjamin's shift of focus to the relationship between shock and modes of reception, he finds himself in an intricate situation, resulting from the combination of three assumptions: First, Benjamin understands prevention of shock as "a peak achievement of the intellect" and thus as being part of a conscious mode of reception. Second, the mode of reception predominantly required by the modern urban environment is precisely *not* a conscious mode of reception, but rather that of "reception in distraction." As Max Horkheimer correspondingly observed, "the ready response is what counts, affinity to every kind of machine, technical, athletic, political."[216] Third, an increase in the capacity to protect against experiences of shock is necessary and desirable. The ensuing dilemma is evident: the need for an increase of protection is augmented by the increasing likelihood of experiences of shock to occur, which is brought about by the growing quantity and new quality of potentially shocking impulses, surpassing the capacities of consciousness. This surpassing of the capacity of conscious reception requires its support and supplementation by a mode of reception based on distraction.

From these three observations, Benjamin draws a logical conclusion, which he elaborates implicitly rather than explicitly. He recognizes the need to develop an alternative mechanism of shock-prevention, no longer exclusively based on the intellect's capacities, as Georg Simmel assumed, because the intellect's capacities are exhausted. Consequently, the receptive mode of distraction, which allows external impulses to effect an experience of shock, has to be made more resilient against these impulses. Such increase of resilience must be achieved via processes of training and conditioning. It is at this point that Benjamin appropriates Freud's use of repetition—but changes its role, its manifestation, and the moment of its intervention. For psychoanalysis, a shock is repeatedly appropriated after its original encounter, for example during psychoanalytical therapy or in dreams, in order to "prepare for a trauma that ha[s] already come."[217] Benjamin's priority is prevention rather than cure. Having already played a role within the traditional treatment in the form of electric shocks, psychoanalysis transferred repetition from a physical to a psychological level. Given that it transgresses the borderline from involuntary reliving to voluntary replication (or, in Freud's terms, from repetition to remembrance), repetition is a method of healing. A person suffering from shock "is obliged to repeat the repressed material as a contemporary experience instead of . . . remembering it as something belonging to the past."[218] Intentional repetition thus strives to transfer a previous experience of shock from the level of unconscious onto that of conscious memory, thus making it available to voluntary, self-directed access.

In contrast, for Benjamin the aim of repetition is not to effect an appropriation of a prior experience but to anticipate a potential experience in order to enhance the individual's perceptional resilience. Such training of perceptional resilience is obviously not something achieved during the psychoanalytical dialogue or in a state of hypnosis. Instead, Benjamin locates repetition firmly within sense perception, as for example in the process of receiving works of art. It is thus at a fairly late point within Benjamin's concept of shock that art comes into the picture, being an a priori means for a conditioning repetition. In coherent continuation of his focus on the individual's perceptional capacity as the interface between the individual and the exterior world, Benjamin's training does not focus on the psyche but on the perceptional capacities. The desired resilience consists in increasing the capacity to trigger a reaction that is not based on a fully conscious perception. Consequently, it is not only within Benjamin's concept of shock but also within his (inseparable) concept of shock prevention that the artwork, as a deliberate generation and manipulation of sensory impulses, finds its function.

It is in this context that Benjamin's appreciation of Dada is to be understood, and he himself is explicit about the criteria for this appreciation. Dada works frequently attempt to deliver both the type and quantity of sensory impulses that necessarily require a tactile mode of visual reception, thus training the related capacities. As indicated earlier, the achievement of Dada in the eyes of Benjamin depends on the extent to which the movement succeeds in responding to the significant features of its sociocultural context (i.e., to the modern, urban environment) by *repeating* these features. Dada mirrors and responds to Benjamin's observation that "everything perceived . . . [is] something that befalls us,"[219] by triggering a similar type of experience through works of art. "From an alluring visual composition or an enchanting fabric of sound, the Dadaists turned the artwork into a missile. It jolted the viewer, taking on a tactile quality."[220] Benjamin's appreciation of film is based on the same grounds: "Reception in distraction—the sort of reception which is increasingly noticeable in all areas of art and is a symptom of profound changes in apperception—finds in film its true training ground. By virtue of its shock effects, film is predisposed to this form of reception."[221] Benjamin continues this line of thoughts in his fragments toward a "Theory of Distraction," establishing an analogy between the relationship of distraction and film on the one hand and that of catharsis and tragedy on the other.[222] With such comparison he underlines the specific function he allocates to film as a means to train and educate the recipient—this time not on the level of contemplation but of perception. Fostering distraction, both film and Dada replicate the experience of parrying the shock factor in daily life. Thus, a work of art appears to gain its relevance where it retraces the phenomenological features of contemporary society.

Benjamin considers art and, more specifically, the reception of art as training for the individual's perceptive capacities to prevent incidents of shock from taking place. In contrast to the common understanding of art as working toward a refinement of perception, Benjamin directs art toward the opposite aim. In being "marshalled to parry technological stimuli in order to protect both the body from the trauma of accident and the psyche from the trauma of perceptual shock," the reception of art, once expected to train and modify the individual's capacity for sensory perception, now seeks "to numb the organism, to deaden the senses, to repress memory: the cognitive system of synaesthetics has become, rather, one of anaesthetics."[223] As will be discussed later, Dada does indeed seek to put this conversion of the aesthetic experience into practice, an endeavor inseparable from the artists' central interest in shock and their equally ferocious rejection of meaning. In summary, the theoretical preoccupation with shock arising in the early twentieth century amid the decisive sociocultural changes taking place at the time coincides with a shifting evaluation of the intellect and of intellectual reception. This shifting evaluation is by no means the same in the works of Simmel, Freud, and Benjamin; however, they do share an understanding of shock as not evolving on an intellectual level. For them, shock is not a cognitive experience. Consequently, the intellect—or, to use a term nearer to Freud, consciousness—is able to prevent an experience of shock from taking place. This shared element of the three approaches differs in the details. All three positions agree in theory about the shock-preventive capacity of the intellect, but differ with regard to its capacity of performing this protective activity in practice. The "intellectualization" of metropolitan man, perceived by Simmel, which coincided with an emotional indifference and reduced affective engagement, might even be shared by Freud and Benjamin—but they do not consider it to be sufficient to defend against the increasing number of potentially shocking impressions. As a consequence of this insufficiency, Benjamin came to focus on an alternative mode of reception beyond a purely cognitive approach. It is not so much this aspect in itself that is significant for our purposes, but the fact that this mode of reception is relevant in the realm of art or, more precisely, in the perception of art. This puts into question the previously uncontested position of contemplation as the primary mode of art reception. At the center of this new engagement with the receptive process in art was a concerted attempt by artists themselves to generate an experience of shock; Dada is a primary example.

3 Shock and the Senseless in Dada

In lieu of the *Blue Flower* Dada focused on the effect of the surprising and the unusual.
—*Raoul Hausmann, "Massenpsychologie Dadas"*

Over the decades, the aspect of Dada that has been most often commented on in art-historical criticism is its link with the scandalous. "Scandal was Dada's main aesthetic strategy of appeal"[1]—thus reads Hanne Bergius's confirmation of a general assumption. As Peter Bürger correspondingly concludes, it is thereby representative of "the historical avant-garde movements [for which] shocking the recipient becomes the dominant principle of artistic intent."[2] Matei Calinescu even goes a step further when arguing that "the avant-gardist, far from being interested in novelty as such, or in novelty in general, actually tries to discover or invent new forms, aspects or possibilities of crisis. . . . Art is supposed to become an experience—deliberately conducted—of failure and crisis."[3] Focusing on Dada in particular and choosing Tristan Tzara's "Manifeste du Monsieur Antipyrine" ("Manifesto of Mr. Antipyrine," 1916) as his example (which Tzara himself described as a "boxing match with words"),[4] Bürger describes the Dada works as having been "geared to shock the reader or listener respectively—with the reader or listener assumed to have a bourgeois background.[5] Contemporaneous accounts on Dada give proof of the same focus. A review in the *Berliner Börsen-Courier* answers its own question "for what Dadaism is," with some perplexity: "I don't know. Dadaism is everything; most prominently, however, it is row. Row in all keys."[6] The same author states elsewhere: "Dadaism's soul is row, the most intense movement."[7] In most cases, however, criticism has stopped at the point of stating the scandalous, using it to label Dada rather than to understand the movement's intentions and to investigate the conceptual function of scandal in the fulfilment of these intentions.

The assumption that Dada's engagement with the scandalous and shock is indeed deliberate and might have been given some role in its understanding and concept of art, is confirmed by the manifold artists' statements on the subject matter. They bear eloquent witness to the fact that Dada's generation of scandal was indeed of an explicit and intentional nature and show their restless striving for shock and arousal and the importance of succeeding in triggering such a reaction. The Dadaists' intent, as Tzara described it, was to "scandalize society."[8] Of the Dada activities in Berlin, Raoul Hausmann states with approval that "the performances always took their course with the greatest scandal."[9] Walter Mehring describes a Dada matinee in Berlin on December 7, 1918, as "such a triumphant scandal that we repeated it,"[10] a repetition, which was, in fact, flooded by hordes of those "covetous for outrage."[11] In his biography, George Grosz remembers: "As Dadaists, we held meetings and charged a few marks admission but gave in return no more than truisms. By that I mean, we just insulted the people roundly."[12] During one of the first Dada events in Paris in January 1920, the audience, as Tzara put it, was like a "pot with boiling water," whose "dissatisfaction found expression in acrimonious vociferation."[13] In his account of a very early Dada soirée in Zurich on July 14, 1916, Huelsenbeck delivers an equally graphic description:

> A massive roar. "We want our money back." First tributes in form of apples, potatoes and rotten eggs. People rush towards the podium, crying, moaning and howling: the dadaist spirit, which will then spread like a pandemic, starts to infect the people.[14]

In his "Erinnerungen an Dada" (1927), Tzara recalls a Dada soirée in Paris in the early summer of 1920: "For the first time since the world's existence, not only eggs, heads of lettuce and loose cash were thrown onto the stage, but also beefsteaks. This was an ample success, the audience was very much dada."[15]

With Tzara's criteria in mind, the last Dada soirée to take place in Zurich on April 9, 1919, can indeed be rated an overwhelming triumph, being terminated by an angered audience dragging the protagonists off the stage.[16] Hausmann, remembering a Dada soirée in Berlin, writes that the performance's "effect on an audience gripped by an epileptic rage was extortionate and instantaneous."[17] It thus made a "formidable evening and a DADAistic success."[18] It is only much later, in the early 1960s, that Hausmann seemed to become anxious to widen this distinct focus on shock and scandal, stating that this "intention . . . is not the exclusive preserve of Dada."[19]

However, the statements by Dadaists give expression to their enormous interest in triggering a reaction that is variously described as "scandal," "outrage," "a massive roar," "acrimonious vociferation" and "epileptic rage." All these terms refer to a certain type of public debate arising in response to an activity regarded as unacceptable. They define a reaction that is indeed of primary interest to Dada, but is not—as I will argue—its proper purpose. Whereas scandal is always a collective phenomenon, Dada's primary interest lies in the necessarily individual experience of shock. The creation of a scandal is appreciated by Dada as proof of having successfully triggered experiences of shock in individual recipients. In other words, Dada was not primarily interested in the infamous "*épater le bourgeois*," but in prompting the immediate emotional and sensational reaction of shock in the individual. It is thus worth analyzing Dada's concept of shock and the motives behind its pursuit, as well as its connection to Dada's equally strong refusal to make sense. How must we understand the sociocultural context from which it arose, and which role did it play in the formation of Dada's concept of shock?

In retrospect, the dominant achievements of Dada appear to be confined to the realm of art and to culminate in a fundamental transformation of the concept of art. This transformation consists primarily in two interlinked aspects. The first can be described, with Kurt Schwitters, as "the principle of using any material" regardless of how, why, and by whom it was produced, and whether on purpose or accidentally.[20] The second point of transformation is less prominent and harder to define, but it could be described as a shift of attention from the object of art itself to the experience of perceiving it. This latter achievement will be of major importance to us inasmuch as senselessness and shock are only manifested within the process of reception, and it is this shift from the object of art to the experience of perceiving it that provides the grounds for Dada's interest in shock.

However, the movement's own objectives were far from focused on a transformation of art. Although Dada intended to alter the concept of art or, more precisely, to turn it into a concept of anti-art, this endeavor is only to be understood as an integral part of the movement's critique of society at large, and as an attempt to have an effect upon its sociocultural context. When Marcel Duchamp was asked whether he considered Dada only a critique of art or also a critique of society, he chose the latter.[21] One could yet go a step further, arguing that Dada was primarily and predominantly a critique of society, "some sort of cultural criticism,"[22] according to Raoul Hausmann. Hans Richter put it more strongly: "We wanted to bring forward a new kind of human being, one whose contemporaries we could wish to be, free from the tyranny of rationality, of banality, of generals, fatherlands, nations, art-dealers, microbes, residence permits and the past."[23]

Continuing Richter's vision, Huelsenbeck attests that the desired generation of a "new kind of human being" requires the demolition of "all the slogans of ethics, culture, and inwardness."[24] In other words, it entails the destruction of precisely those values generally perceived as the basis of civilization and a humane culture—a somewhat Nietzschean claim.[25] "Dada is the blastocyst of a new type of man" and negates "the meaning of life hitherto and . . . a culture, which was not tragic but shrivelled."[26]

> We want to radically demolish the sophistries of kindness, beauty, value, we want to destroy everything, we want to tear it to shreds—we want to hurl that new world from within ourselves, which is not security and repose, but upheaval and renewal. We don't want to hide behind philosophies and religions any more. We want to be what we are: self destroyers! . . . We are beyond the good, just society.[27]

All these statements share a common ground: the conviction that the age of humanism in its established understanding has come to an end and that the state of present society has become intolerable. This conviction is an unsurprising reaction to the artists' experience of the devastating war—but it is also a critique of modern times more generally, which are seen as a threat to a humane world and to each individual. Both war and the changes in modern society diminished the individual's ability to make sense of the encounters it experienced. As I will argue, it is this spreading experience of a lack of sense that not only provides the basis for Dada in general—finding its first and foremost expression in the movement's name—but also fuels Dada's specific interest in shock.

Dada's Notion of Art and Its Sociocultural Context

Unbar your head, at last! Make yourself available for the demands of today.
—Poster at the First International Dada Fair, 1920

"Art wants to and has to return to life,"[28] reads the heading of a 1919 text by the Dadaist Marcel Janco. "We are not only artists but human beings and as such we feel obliged to reassume a positively operating power within life."[29] This mission and conviction is crucial for the Dada artists, as Hugo Ball states in his diaries, later published as *Flucht aus der Zeit* (*Flight Out of Time*): "For us art is not an end in itself—more pure naïveté is necessary for that—but it is an opportunity for the true perception and criticism of the times we live in."[30] The seminal "Dadaistisches Manifest" ("Collective Dada Manifesto") of 1918,[31] which inaugurated the Dada movement in Berlin and was signed by Zurich and Berlin Dadaists alike,[32] stated unequivocally that "art in its execution and direction is dependent on the time in which it lives, and artists are creatures of their epoch."[33] Francis Picabia confirms that "art is, and can only be, the expression of contemporary life,"[34] and Raoul Hausmann is more specific when he writes that "within this loony climate, within this dull destruction, it is impossible to be a good type of conventional artist."[35]

As these quotations eloquently illustrate, the Dadaists' self-conception is based on the conviction that there is a link between art and its time—or art and life—that is inevitable and unavoidable and that also gives rise to the artist's consciousness of a duty that must be fulfilled. As Owen F. Smith concludes, the Dadaists "realized that the potential power of art existed in its potential for altering the practices of life."[36] In a retrospective account on Dada, Richard Huelsenbeck describes "the dadaist movement [as] an immediate child of its time," consisting of people, "who understood the essence of their time most intensely"[37] and who were, in Leah Dickerman's words, "seismically sensitive to historical shifts."[38] Huelsenbeck concludes that "the Dadaist positions himself in the midst of things and in the midst of the danger of things and does not shirk the 'duties of the day.' "[39] This corresponds with Hausmann's description of Dada as "a necessity" and consistent manifestation of its time, being both generated and required by the "spiritual climate of the world."[40] The Dada artists, as Hausmann observes, shared the conviction that "all genres and artistic techniques require a revolutionizing change, should they maintain any connection with the life of our time."[41] Stating that "all inventions are made when they become necessary,"[42] he anticipates the primary grounds for Walter Benjamin's later interest in Dada[43]—as well for Adolf Hitler's very rejection of this movement, contradicting his vision of art as eternal and constant.[44] As if wanting to suggest a proof of Hausmann's claim, John Heartfield considered the artistic technique of photomontage as generated by World War I or, more precisely, by the soldiers' need for means of communication that were able to seep through the military's censorship by formulating their messages in ways that did not easily disclose their meaning.[45] More generally, this interlocking of active innovation and passive reaction to the requests of time and context can be also considered the basis for the frequently simultaneous but independent discoveries of new artistic methods or techniques, of which the claimed concurrent discovery of the photogram by Raoul Hausmann and Man Ray in 1921 might be one example.[46]

Dada's conviction of a necessary connection between artistic expression and the sociocultural context to which it responds, ultimately forms the background for Man Ray's initially surprising statement that New York Dada did not exist. As he argues, it did not exist because the principles of Dada, notably the ideas of scandal and provocation, were "entirely foreign to the American spirit." Consequently, Americans were unable to "appreciate or enter into the spirit of Dada,"[47] due to the fact that this spirit lacked a direct connection to their own sociocultural context and experience of life. It was thus notably in Germany, as Huelsenbeck underlines, where Dada could be received appropriately "as the symbol of destructive art. In this lies its immortal service."[48]

Of course, Dada was not alone in stating the inextricability of art and its time. We can find similar statements and manifestos from the realms of Futurism or Cubism, for example. In his *Contemporary Achievements in Painting* from 1914, Fernand Léger states that "a work of art must be significant in its own time, like any other intellectual manifestation." Talking about painting, changes are necessary in order to remain "representative, in the modern sense of the word, of the new visual state imposed by the evolution of the new means of production."[49] Wassily Kandinsky wrote in 1912 that "every artist, as the child of his epoch, has to express what is particular to this epoch."[50] And in the first issue of *Blast* from 1914, the Vorticists attested "that an Art must be organic with its Time."[51] One could go on. However, what is important for an understanding of Dada is not just this conviction in itself, but the ways in which it manifested itself in the movement's artistic production. Merely stating the necessity that art react to the contemporary sociocultural context does not tell us what it is that art should react to or the forms that such a reaction should take. What does Dada conceive of as the appropriate and required reaction to life? "Despite the critics' almost universal lack of comprehension," writes Hausmann, "some have recognized that the Dada movement represented the spirit of the twentieth century, whereas even Futurism still hung on to semantic and formal problems of post-classical art."[52]

Hausmann's quoted critique of Futurism repeats itself much more strongly with regard to the Expressionists. Dada's condemnation of Expressionism exemplifies the movement's conviction that art must respond to life in an *appropriate* way. Appropriateness in this context will come to be defined as art's successful response to those features considered as paradigmatic for the given time and context. Expressionism, as Dada criticizes, not only failed to achieve this, but did not even aim at doing so. Thus, Dada's assessment of Expressionism can help to characterize its own aims *ex negativo*, despite the existing ties to that movement within Dada's own genealogy (notably visible in the artistic career of Hugo Ball),[53] and despite the fact that Expressionism's requests do at times appear highly akin to Dada's own statements. In his "Anleitung zum Malen von Grossstadtbildern" (Instructions for Painting Pictures of the Metropolis) from 1914, for example, Ludwig Meidner uses a language that is anything but foreign to Dada. Here, the Expressionist par excellence asks the artists of his time to paint "the metropolis that we love without reserve" and to depict with "feverish scrawling hands . . . everything that is strange and splendid, everything that is monstrous and striking, about our great avenues and railway stations, our towers and factories."[54] Nevertheless, Dada criticizes the Expressionists for lacking the "'infallible sense of what is presently required,"[55] for having failed to face the paradigms of the present reality and to direct their artistic production accordingly. "Has expressionism fulfilled our expectations of such an art, which should be the expression of our most vital concerns? No! No! No!"[56] The movement's most extensive condemnation of Expressionism is to be found in Huelsenbeck's "En Avant Dada" from 1920:

> Now came the expressionists, like those most famous medical quacks who promised to "fix everything up," . . . [and] pointed to "the rich treasures of our literature," pulled people gently by the sleeve and led them into the half-light of the Gothic cathedrals, where the street noises die down to a distant murmur and, in accordance with the old principle that all cats are grey at night, man without exception are fine fellows. Man, they have discovered is good. . . . On the basis of all these considerations and the psychological insight that a turning-away from objective reality implied the whole complex of wariness and cowardice that is so welcome to putrescent bourgeoisie, we immediately launched a sharp attack on expressionism in Germany, under the watchword of "action."[57]

Clinging on to a "hocus-pocus of inwardness" (*Innerlichkeitshokuspokus*),[58] as Dada argues, Expressionism refers to outdated qualities of life, having lost their value and justification for the present day. In a polemical passage of the "Collective Dada Manifesto," the Expressionist artist finds himself endowed with the following attributes: "Hatred of the press, hatred of advertising, hatred of sensations, archetypical of people who prefer their armchair to the noise of the street, and who even make it a point of pride to be swindled by every small-time profiteer."[59] For the Dadaists, the bourgeois approach to life as based on logical systems and rationalized cause-and-effect relationships had proven out of sync with reality. Quite the opposite, life was dominated by irrationality, contradictions, and arbitrariness.[60]

In view of this critique of Expressionism, we need to ask how Dada itself reacts to society. How does art's stipulated obligation manifest itself within Dada works? In what ways does Dada formulate a critique of its sociocultural context? Although heterogeneous with regard to their political inclinations and degree of engagement,[61] none of the Dadaists can be considered as politically indifferent. Notably Franz Jung, Wieland Herzfelde, George Grosz, John Heartfield, and Hans Richter (all members of the Club Dada Berlin) were of an explicit Marxist-Communist mind-set and pursued party activities. Jung, Herzfelde, Heartfield, and Grosz were original members of the Spartakusbund, a revolutionary left-wing association founded at the very beginning of 1919, which merged with the KPD (German Communist Party). Having been excluded from the party at one of its conventions in 1919, Franz Jung became one of the founders of the KAPD (Communist Workers Party of Germany).[62] By contrast, with the noteworthy exception of the works of George Grosz and John Heartfield, Dada's artistic production is comparatively apolitical, notably in its early days in wartime Zurich. Hardly any explicit statement of political or, more specifically, of antiwar subject matter is to be found in that period. And if Robert Motherwell in the introduction to his anthology describes Tzara's "Manifesto of Mr. Antipyrine" (1916) as being "clearly a protest against the war,"[63] I would argue that this clarity only emerges once Dada's strategies of opposition are made familiar. In fact, Hugo Ball's poem "Totentanz" ("Dance of Death") from 1916 was virtually unique in having an explicit antiwar subject matter, and was promptly printed on flyers by the allies in their attempt to demoralize the German troops.[64] Its first and last verses read as follows:

And so we die, so we die
And die every day,
Because we can die so comfortably.
In the morning still in sleep and dreams
At midday we're already gone
In the evening deep within our grave.

We thank you, we thank you,
Herr Kaiser, for the kindness,
Of choosing us to die.
Sleep, sleep gently and still.
Until our poor flesh, covered by grass,
Wakes you up.[65]

With regard to Berlin Dada, some examples of an artistic-political engagement can be found. In the manifesto "Was ist der Dadaismus und was will er in Deutschland?" ("What Is Dadaism and What Does It Want in Germany?") from 1919, the artists request "the international revolutionary union of all creative and intellectual men and women on the basis of radical Communism," and the "introduction of the simultaneist poem as a Communist state prayer," thus linking artistic production with a political positioning.[66] And the *Erste Internationale Dada-Messe* (First International Dada Fair) in Berlin in 1920 resulted in the organizers being convicted and fined for insulting the German military, as one of the exhibited sculptures consisted of an officer's uniform suspended from the ceiling and fitted with a plaster pig's head (fig. 9).[67] In 1919, so-called "Oberdada" Baader disrupted an assembly of the German Reichstag, distributing flyers that called for the dissolution of the national assembly.[68]

However, although Dada Berlin's artistic activities included more overtly political statements, the existing imbalance between the artists' political agenda and the relatively weak engagement with political subject matter in their works requires us to look beyond the level of content for Dada's reaction to (and rejection of) its sociocultural context. One possible reason for this imbalance is offered by Dadaist Walter Serner, who claimed that "in the middle of the world war, the Dada artists didn't mention it with a single word," because "to ignore the war was the most noble way to protest against it."[69] But this form of a silent protest can be equally understood as being the result of Dada's attempt to register its critique on the level of artistic expression—or, more specifically, on the level of form rather than that of subject matter.

> What is socially decisive in artworks is the content (*Inhalt*) that becomes eloquent through the work's formal structures. . . . It is one thing to show one's political colours . . . ; it is quite another to preface the work with the instruction "to be sung in an ugly manner," for it is an open question whether an artistic attitude of howling and crudeness denounces reality or identifies with it.[70]

These words are taken from Theodor W. Adorno's posthumously published *Ästhetische Theorie* (Aesthetic Theory), where the author denounces "the open or covert treatment of social matters" within artistic expression as "the most superficial and deceptive."[71] Without mentioning Dada, Adorno implicitly describes its strategy of transposing a political opinion and sociocultural critique from the level of content to the level of form and structure. "If no word which enters a literary work ever wholly frees itself from its meaning in ordinary speech, so no literary work . . . leaves these meanings unaltered,"[72] he writes, thus stating how sociocultural cri-

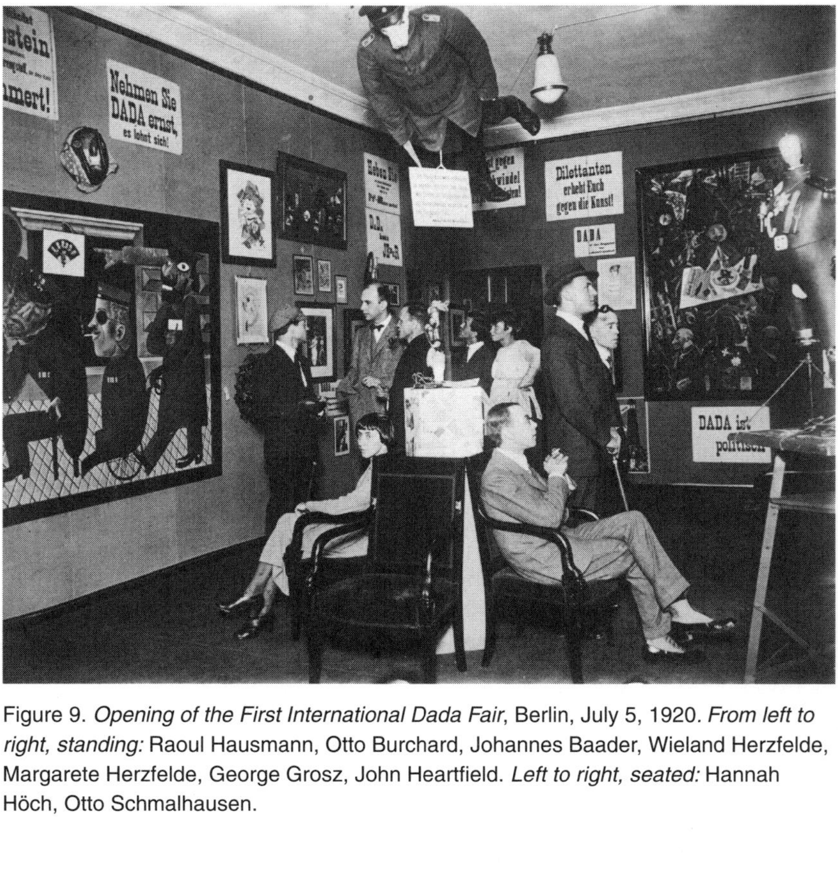

Figure 9. *Opening of the First International Dada Fair*, Berlin, July 5, 1920. *From left to right, standing:* Raoul Hausmann, Otto Burchard, Johannes Baader, Wieland Herzfelde, Margarete Herzfelde, George Grosz, John Heartfield. *Left to right, seated:* Hannah Höch, Otto Schmalhausen.

tique is, to his mind, inevitably inherent in any artistic expression. "What is social in art is its immanent movement against society, not its manifest opinions. . . . Insofar as a social function can be predicated for artworks, it is their functionlessness."[73] With Dada, however, an artwork's lack of function exceeds the common denominator of all art being free of any usefulness by definition. Dada's lack of function consists of an absence not only of practical use but also of any intellectual one by refusing to make sense and to contain meaning. Dada's "orgiastic devotion to the opposite of everything that is serviceable and useful" is precisely where the movement's social stance and political opposition is manifested.[74] An example of the subversive capacity of such renunciation of sense occurred already during Hugo Ball's pre-Dada activities in Berlin. A journal that published Ball's poem "Der Henker" ("The Hangman") was confiscated soon afterward, but the charges against it were dropped on the grounds that the poem was judged incomprehensible, and consequently harmless.[75]

In this connection, it is worth recalling the fictitious propaganda trial against the French writer and nationalist Maurice Barrès that members of the Dada group in Paris staged in 1921. It came to play a decisive role in the movement's dispersal and gave rise to a dispute about the movement's degree of political explicitness and activism.[76] What is interesting about the Barrès case is the fact that the dispute was not based on differences of political viewpoint but on the question of how a political opinion could find its artistic expression in line with Dada principles. Especially for Tristan Tzara, the trial's straightforward and explicit addressing of a political position and its open accusation of a political adversary had little to do with Dadaist strategies, and he considered the Barrès trial to break with a Dada principle.

So, what were the factors that Dada took to be paradigmatic for its time and to which the artists were consequently required to respond to? As Dickerman suggests, "Dada was born of a moment of moral and intellectual crisis, poised between the disaster of war and the shock of an emerging modern media culture."[77] Indeed, it will prove valid to examine both the war and the emerging modern culture—although not, as I will argue, only the changing use and appearance of the media, but the changing sensorial landscape of the urban context in general—to understand Dada's conception of shock and the senseless as the appropriate responses to these twin provocations of the early twentieth century.

Irrationality and the War

Our symbol was nothingness, a vacuum, a void.
—*George Grosz,* A Little Yes and a Big No*, 1946*

We cannot conceive of Dada without the war. On a factual level, the war was the reason why Zurich became the birthplace of Dada, serving as home "to all those, which the war had thrown beyond the borders of their fatherlands."[78] Hugo Ball, Eva Hennings, Richard Huelsenbeck, and Walter Serner (alias Walter Eduard Seligmann) from Germany, the Rumanian school friends Marcel Janco and Tristan Tzara (alias Samuel Rosenstock) from an assimilated Jewish Rumanian background, Hans Arp from the Alsace, and many others, came to live in the capital of neutral Switzerland during the war years—many of them also seeking to avoid being drafted. Having started off as a warmonger who patriotically volunteered for military service but was rejected as unfit, Hugo Ball turned into a ferocious pacifist as a consequence of his unauthorized, horrifying visit to the Belgian front and the suicide of his close friend Hans Leybold, who killed himself after having been wounded at the front in fall 1914. In 1916 Ball immigrated to Zurich on a faked passport and false name. He was preceded by Walter Serner in 1914, who had forged documents for himself and others by misusing his title of doctor of law, and followed by Richard Huelsenbeck in 1916, who left Germany by virtue of a medical certificate attesting mental exhaustion. Arp, Heartfield, and Schad had pretended to be either mentally or physically disabled, and Baader, and possibly Tzara and Grosz, might have been indeed psychologically ill.[79] Others, however, such as Hans Richter, Max Ernst, George Grosz, and John Heartfield (alias Helmut Herzfelde), were called up and fought in the war. Richter was severely injured and dismissed as invalid in 1916; Ernst was wounded twice, but less severely, and served until the end of the war.[80]

Dada's early and unreserved opposition to war has at times even been considered its primary and defining characteristic,[81] all the more so considering that this attitude was unusual at the time. In profound contrast to the Futurists—as well as to the majority of the population of the warring countries—the majority of Dadaists did not hail the advent of war, nor did they share the Futurists' eulogy of the war as the "world's only hygiene" or their praise of militarism and patriotism.[82] Instead, as Max Ernst stated about himself, "Max Ernst died the 1st of August 1914. He resuscitated the 11th of November 1918."[83] George Grosz remembers,

"If we artists were the expression of anything at all, then we were the expression of the ferment of dissatisfaction and unrest."[84] The war gave rise to Dada's rejection of the social, cultural, and moral system that had failed to prevent its occurrence; and it was the war that provided the basis for the artists' dedication to the rejection of sense. Klaus Vondung writes, "The experience of senselessness [*Sinnlosigkeit*] could become . . . so overwhelming that the entire reality appeared to be utterly bare of any sense and non-sense became consequently considered the principle of existence. This was the case for the Zurich Dadaists."[85] These sentences are not taken from a publication on Dada but on World War I, in which the author investigates the various attempts to cope with and react to the incomprehensibility of the war. He finds confirmation in Hans Richter, who indicates the socio-cultural background of Dada's dedication to meaninglessness, nonsense, and the paradoxical: "The official belief in the infallibility of reason, logic and causality seemed to us senseless—as senseless as the destruction of the world and the systematic elimination of every particle of human feeling."[86] Those surviving the combat returned "in a state of stupefaction,"[87] as Max Ernst phrased it. But, as Hans Arp pointed out, a similar state of stagnation threatened those "who did not participate directly in the terrible madness of the World War," and who consequently started to act "as if they were unable to comprehend what was going on all around them. Like lost sheep they stared at the world with glazed eyes."[88]

The experience of a lack of sense and of utter incomprehensibility evolved on a factual level, given the nebulous chain of tumbling events and the lack of certainty about cause and effect on the way to war. But it also spread on the level of an impossible moral justification of the unimaginable death, violence, and suffering of a war that lacked any means of justification through military progress or victory. The artists' refusal of sense reflected their experience of the "swirling senselessness of the brooding ruined world of war,"[89] a war that had led to "the tabula rasa of all traditions, beliefs, and ideals, leaving only one imperative: to have none."[90] It initiated Dada's attack of "the foundations of the civilization responsible for the war,"[91] as Max Ernst phrased it. Tzara spoke equally explicitly about its aims: "It was no longer a question of resistance to an obsolete society: Dada took the offensive and attacked the social system in its entirety, for it regarded this system as inextricably bound up with human stupidity, the stupidity which culminated in the destruction of man by man, and in the destruction of his material and spiritual possessions."[92] Instead of attempting a change within society, Dada sought for a wholesale replacement of the current system and "aimed at the liberation of the individual from dogmas, formulas and laws."[93] More precisely, it sought for an abolition of the category of system altogether, having concluded, with Hugo Ball, that "the world of systems has fallen apart."[94] "I am against systems, the most acceptable system is on principle to have none,"[95] Tzara confirms.

The movement nicely crystallized its approach: Dada meant nothing and, as Willi Verkauf writes in his *Monograph of a Movement* from 1958, being one of the earliest art-historical publications on Dada, "To raise the question, what 'dada' really was, was usually stigmatized by them as 'undadaistic.' " Verkauf tries to summarize: "A person is Dada, provided he lives," or "Dada is a state of mind," were definitions—better than some of the others, which seemed entirely nonsensical and merely designed to shock.[96] Although Verkauf rightly links nonsensicality and shock, he might have misinterpreted his object of investigation in one aspect. The nonsensical interpretations of what the word *Dada* might signify, which were dismissed by Verkauf as "merely" designed to shock and to evade a proper answer, ranged from "rocking horse," "tail of a holy cow," or "double affirmation" to the "world's soul" or a "soap made of the milk of lilies."[97] Besides "meaning nothing," the word *Dada* thus gave way to the incessant invention of manifold potential and fictitious meanings; a possibility that had been used excessively by Dada artists. What Verkauf ignores is the fact that these optional, nonsensical, and contradictory descriptions are in fact precise manifestations (but not explanations) of Dada's primary intention. They contain the nucleus of the artists' endeavor to manifest a state exterior to meaning and rationality, and thus they do anything but evade a portrayal of what Dada is and aims for.

In a text collage from 1919, included in his magazine *Der DaDa*, Raoul Hausmann replies to the question of what Dada is by concluding tentatively: "or is it nothing, i.e., everything?" (figs. 10–12).[98] As Hausmann put it elsewhere, "The relative inexplicability of Dadaism responds to the 'factual inexplicability of the world.' "[99] And it is this inexplicability that he considered as separating Dada from Surrealism, with the latter pertaining to a request for art to be meaningful.[100] Francis Picabia agrees: "Dada itself wants nothing, nothing, nothing, it's doing something so that the public can say: 'We understand nothing, nothing, nothing.' The Dadaists are nothing, nothing, nothing—certainly they will come to nothing, nothing, nothing."[101] Huelsenbeck goes even further: "Dada . . . means

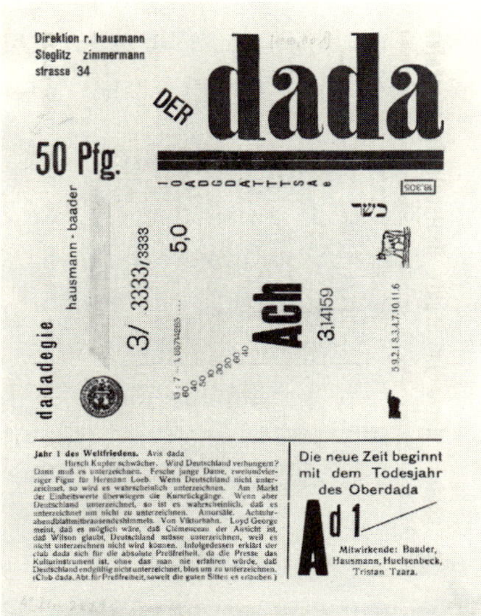

Figure 10. *Der DaDa*, no. 1, Berlin, 1919, cover page. Edited by Raoul Hausmann. Staatsbibliothek zu Berlin—Preussischer Kulturbesitz, Berlin.

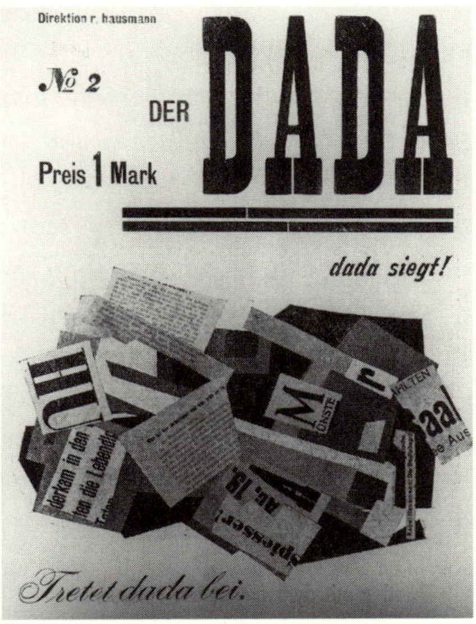

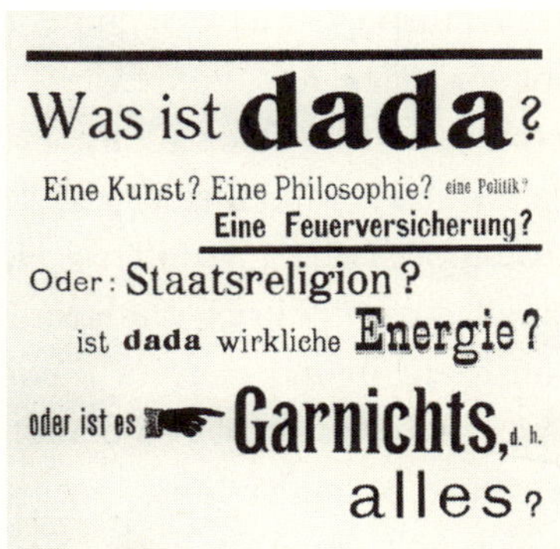
Was ist **dada**?

Eine Kunst? Eine Philosophie? eine Politik?
Eine Feuerversicherung?

Oder: Staatsreligion?
ist **dada** wirkliche **Energie**?

oder ist es ☞ **Garnichts**, d. h.
alles?

Figures 11 and 12. *Der DaDa*, no. 2, Berlin, 1919, cover page and second page. Edited by Raoul Hausmann. Staatsbibliothek zu Berlin—Preussischer Kulturbesitz, Berlin.

nothing. This is the signifying nothing, of which nothing signifies anything. We seek to change the world with nothing, we want to change poetry and painting with nothing and we intent to terminate the war with nothing.[102]

Huelsenbeck's words underline Dada's refusal to make sense as being linked to their endeavor to change something; in other words, it must be recognized as a form of critical engagement. Tzara expresses this assumption when stating that the "new transmutation that signifies nothing . . . was the most formidable protest."[103] Theo van Doesburg continued this line of thought, explaining that "the dadaists do not wish the world to be different than the way they see it, namely, dada: at once orderly and disorderly, yes and no, me and not me."[104] With this formulation van Doesburg indicates that Dada's dedication to the nonsensical and to the simultaneity of contradictions is not only an endeavor to be realized within art but an attempt to confront reality in its true state. As Hanne Bergius points out, "The loss of values was transformed into . . . the 'sanctity of senselessness.' The Dadaists turned the burden of disorientation into relief. Loss of sense was converted into the renunciation of sense, insulting the idealist tradition."[105]

This dedication to the senseless also influences Dada's production of texts, such as statements and manifestos. When Tzara proclaims that "I write a manifesto and I want nothing . . . and in principle I am against manifestos, as I am also against principles,"[106] he gives expression to Dada's intentions not so much on the level of content but rather, I would argue, through a *lack* of content. Bursting with logical contradictions, inconsistencies, and nonsense, Tzara delivers an example rather than an explanation of Dada's "organized struggle against logic,"[107] striving to demolish rational meaning and its established system of production. Focusing on Tzara's manifesto, Hanno Ehrlicher concludes that "the early manifestos of Zurich Dadaism [are] not so much [to be read] as either consistent or inconsistent theories, but as performances, which do not intend to explain but to demonstrate what they are."[108] Put differently, we have to understand Dada's manifestos not only as explaining the movement's interest in senselessness but also as manifesting the realm of the senseless, thus assuming both an explanatory and a performative function.

Confronting the audience with contradictions, Dada seeks to sabotage logic as the basis and heart of the established—bourgeois—culture. Dada understood itself as taking "hold of something that can neither be grasped nor explained within the conventional framework of 'either/or' . . . This radical attack on dualistic thought was in the very nature of the movement."[109] As Tzara explains, "I write this manifesto to show that people can perform contrary actions together";[110] or, as he states elsewhere, "If everyone says the opposite it's because he's right."[111] In proclaiming that "to be against this manifesto is to be a Dadaist!"[112] the "Collective Dada Manifesto" involved the audience in such contradictions. Claiming that "the true Dadaists were against Dada,"[113] the artists deprived the audience of any possibility of dissenting from Dada out of a belief in the dominance and value of logic.

The Dadaists thus sought to deliver a quasi-empirical proof of our accustomed need to define just one of two or more contradicting messages as correct and consequently as valuable and meaningful. The newspapers were one of Dada's preferred media to launch conflicting information by cross-posting contradictory announcements—reporting an event on one day, publishing a disclaimer or a diverging account of the supposed story the next day, and following up with yet a third differing account. The most famous example was probably the so-called Rehalp pistol duel, which reportedly took place between Tristan Tzara and Hans Arp on the Rehalp near Zurich and supposedly left Arp slightly wounded. It found coverage in over twenty newspapers in Switzerland alone.[114]

The same attempt to attack "'logic as the cement" of meaning,[115] which underlies Dada's dedicated production of the paradoxical, reappears as the basis of the artists' equally wholehearted attack on language as a means of communication, seeking to challenge the basis of the production and transportation of meaning. This intention might equally be standing behind the Dadaists writing and presentation of a large number of manifestos, parodying a manifesto's authority, still unbroken within Futurism: "By having seen through the mechanisms of the cultural system of signification, they seek to deconstruct the culture of war by help of semiotic interferences into this culture's system of signification."[116]

On this basis, the Dadaists were described as "radical semiotics,"[117] and "the first ones, who forcefully directed their attention to the sign."[118] The awareness of the close link between a culture's system of signification and its perception of the world provides the basis for Dada's approach: their critique of the system of signification is also a critique of society. This connection finds exemplary expression in Ball's praise of the Futurists' "*parole in libertà*." Upon receiving it from Marinetti, Ball exclaims joyfully: "There is no language any more . . . ; it has to be invented all over again. Disintegration right in the innermost process of creation."[119] What he finds here is the word's liberation from "the sentence frame (*the world image*) that had been thoughtlessly and automatically assigned to it."[120] It is interesting here to note Ball's equation of the "sentence frame" and a "world image." In his "Eröffnungs-Manifest" ("Opening-Manifesto") from summer 1916, Ball is explicit in his rejection of language or—more precisely—in the rejection of its established use:

> A line of poetry is a chance to get rid of all the filth that clings to this accursed language, as if put there by stockbroker's hands, hands worn smooth by coins. I want the word where it ends and where it begins. Dada is the heart of words. . . . The word, gentlemen, is a public concern of the first importance.[121]

In a diary entry written a month before this, Ball dealt with the same issue. Stating that the "plasticity of the word" is only to be achieved "at the expense of the rational, logically constructed sentence,"[122] he demands that the sentence give way to the word.[123] Ball's development of sound poems, which he characterized as "verses without words," was a consequence of this rejection of language as medium of signification and an attempt to return to the word as "meaningless" material "shorn of its burden of definitive meaning."[124] In the aforementioned "Opening-Manifesto," Ball continues: "I don't want words that other people have invented. All the words are other people's inventions. I want my own stuff [*Unfug*], my own rhythm, and vowels and consonants too, matching the rhythm and all my own."[125]

Besides Futurism and the Russian "Laboratory for the Liberation of Language," founded in 1913, there are other and earlier predecessors to which the Dadaists make reference, notably Paul Scheerbart's poem "Kikakoku Ekoralaps" from 1897, Richard Wagner's battle call of the Valkyries ("Hojotoho-ho, hojotoho-ho") from the 1870s, and the early baroque poem "Kühlpsalter" by Kuhlmann from 1684–86.[126] As Richter concludes, "words carry no meaning, apart from what has been allocated to them through habit. . . . Thus, one does better to invent a language, which isn't one at the beginning, but might turn into one eventually" (fig. 13).[127]

When Ball describes Dada's strategies of poetry as seeking to give "birth to a *new* sentence that was not limited and confined by any conventional meaning,"[128] he indicates his understanding of Dada's senselessness as such unconventional meaning. Hans Arp is even clearer: "Dada stands for art without sense. This does not mean nonsense."[129] In Theodor Less-

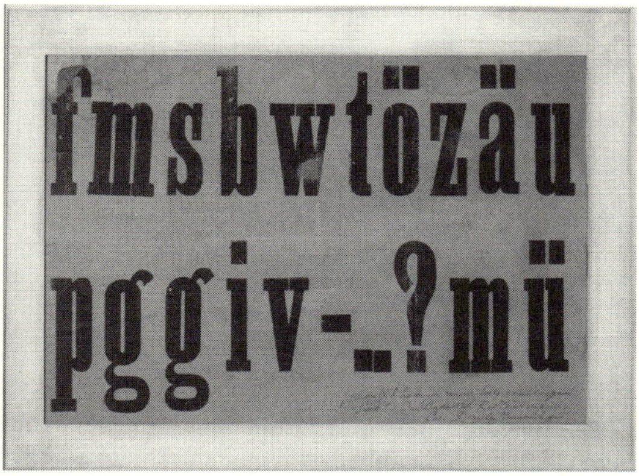

Figure 13. Raoul Hausmann, *fmsbwtözäu*, poster poem, 1918. Line block. Centre Pompidou—Musée National d'Art Moderne, Paris.

ing's *Geschichte als Sinngebung des Sinnlosen* (1919), written in response to the experience of World War I, we find the following statement: "The opposition of sense is not nonsense. Rather: On the one hand there is what is *related to sense* (*das Sinnhafte*), on the other there is what is *free of sense* (*das Sinnfreie*). The sensible, the nonsensical and the contradictory belong to the realm of that which is related to sense.[130] Lessing thus distinguishes what is related to sense from what is unrelated to sense; what is within the system and what is exterior to it. While he would probably have included Dada in his condemnation of the "hullabaloo of art, which has become an insult to any well-balanced and benign character,"[131] Lessing at the same time provides the appropriate terminology to describe the senselessness for which Dada strove. His distinction is mirrored by the notion of the "a-sensible" (*Ohnesinn*), coined by Arp in the attempt to formulate a position beyond the dualistic relationship between sense (*Sinn*) on the one hand and nonsense (*Unsinn*) on the other.[132] Hausmann agrees: "If one thought of Dada as being nothing but nonsense, one had been utterly wrong. Nonsense (*Unsinn*), in the way generally understood, does not exist. There is only "non-sense" (*Nicht-Sinn*) in opposition to what the entire world calls sense."[133] Duchamp's enigmatic credo, "In the first place, never believing in truth," can be understood on the same grounds.[134] This understanding of the meaningless as belonging to an alternative system of meaning gains relevance as an argument against Dada's much heralded relentless nihilism and the prevailing assumption that "the nihilistic tendency functioned as the primary, even solitary, psychic condition" of Dada, aiming at nothing but destruction.[135]

Thus, Dada's interest in the paradoxical as well as in a nonsignifying use of language cannot be explained solely as the result of the artists' interest in a lack of sense; rather, it is more specifically a questioning of the category of sense in the first place. With this questioning, Dada did not seek to explain what seemed senseless and inexplicable; it did not strive for the generation of new meaning. Instead, it sought to discard the unchallenged assumption that human activity and the functioning of the world had to be meaningful and comprehensible by means of the undisputed powers of reason and logic.

This approach led to the characterization of Dada as imbecilic, insane, mad. Reviewing a Dada soirée in the summer of 1916, a journalist at the *Neue Zürcher Zeitung* described Dada as "a symbol for everything. For hatred and love, for good and bad, for high- deep- dull-, and nonsense, for insanity, madness and imbecility."[136] The Dadaists would have approved of his description, seeking to go "till one goes crazy. Till one loses consciousness."[137] Another reviewer sounded rather puzzled by a Dada soirée: "One needs to have some sort of a pathological disposition, in order to read anything into this."[138] Yet another summarizes, "The audience is at a loss."[139] Dada sought to establish what Hausmann called a reign of "PURE IDIOCY."[140] Although given with different intentions, the title to the room that included Dada works at the *Entartete Kunst* exhibition in Munich in 1937 was in a way exactly what the artists intended: "Utter Madness."[141] And, as Ian Dunlop states, "The guards kept a look-out for spectators who did not appear to be shocked by the exhibits"—by that giving a sign of their understanding of these imbecilic works.[142] In a newspaper article of 1920, the neurologist Werner Leibbrand even suggested that the Dada works should rather be exhibited in the collection of the psychiatric ward of the Charité than shown to the general public.[143] Some journalist agreed: "They are men possessed, outcasts, maniacs, and all for love of their work. They turn to the public as if asking its help, placing before it the materials to diagnose their sickness."[144] A newspaper article of the time came to interpret Dada's insanity as a simulation and imitation of the many people whom the war had left shell-shocked.[145] Leah Dickerman arrives at a similar connection: "Dada was envisioned as a shock tactic, analogous to the electric shock therapy used to treat shell shock, breaking through a protective mental buffer to consciousness."[146] In her analysis of the traumatophilic character of Dada montage, Brigid Doherty agrees with Dickerman, defining it as "a technique for the materialization of traumatic shock."[147] She continues: "It was those physical and psychical symptoms of shock that Berlin dada simulated by employing the technique of montage.[148] Dada montage, she states, "aimed to be mimetic of traumatic shock in such a way that the materialization of shock experiences would be effected in the bodies of both the maker and the beholder of the dada object. . . . Both the making and the viewing of montage should themselves be seen as traumatophilic."[149]

However, I would argue that Dada did not, as Doherty suggests, strive to imitate the insanity of the shell-shocked and their symptoms, but rather the conditions that left them shell-shocked: the insanity, imbecility, and incomprehensibility of the age, and notably of those who apparently kept their sanity and continued to consider everything normal and coherent. Turning to a comparison of Dada shock and hysteria, Elizabeth Allen Chabert comes to consider Dada as "less the dance of the epileptic than the mimicry of that dance."[150] I would go yet a step further, arguing that Dada does not mimic that dance but the reasons for it, or—to put it differently—it mimics the etiological conditions rather than their effect. Dada is not or not primarily directed at imitating the shocked, but the conditions that produce shock.

Senselessness and the Metropolis

> I am like a child in a thousand amusement parks
> And in narrow bands, film
> Twist around red and yellow
> . . . .
> And notes like shrapnel throw little holes into my brain.
> . . . .
> I am a machine whose pressure gauge has gone to pieces!
> And all the cylinders run in a circle—
> See: we are all neurasthenics![151]

In her essay entitled with the last line of George Grosz's poem "Kaffeehaus," Brigid Doherty suggests that "the shock of the trenches are simulated by the shocks of the metropolis,"[152] conceiving of the latter as generating a repetition of the shocking experiences of the war. However, as I will argue, the metropolis represents a shocking potential of its own and distinct from the experiences of the war. In my preceding analysis of the war's irrationality as the breeding ground for Dada's refusal to make sense—defined as an interest in the "a-sensical" rather than in the nonsensical—the absence of meaning has so far been examined as an experience of the intellect. With regard to Dada's pursuit of the paradox and of a nonsignifying use of language, the failure to allocate meaning evolves on the level of intellectual reception. As I have argued, this interest in the a-sensical can be understood as a renunciation of the dominance and unquestioned reliability of rationality and logic. Their rejection is an expression of Dada's discontent with contemporary society—a discontent that can ultimately be traced back to the artists' opposition to the war, and in particular to the war's incomprehensible and unjustifiable nature.

In the following, however, I will turn to an examination of the senseless as evolving on a level other than the intellectual, both mimicking and culminating in an experience of senselessness. As exemplified in the movement's rejection of Expressionism, Dada perceived the new scope of impulses of the urban environment as paradigmatic for the time to the extent that artistic creation should be required to respond to this changed situation. As Bergius explains: "The behavioral attitudes of the city-nomad and ragtime-dancer also were taken on by the forms of expression and presentation of his artistry: the erratic, the broken-up and broken-off, the departure, the migratory, the associative, the sudden affinity, the observing distance, the coincidental, the multiperspective, the cosmopolitan."[153] The Dadaist's soul, as Huelsenbeck stated, was "not to be found in books, but in the screeching of the brakes and in the curves, made by the swing boats at the funfair."[154] The reality to which Dada reacts is experienced as brutal on a sensuous level, loaded with new sensorial challenges, partly though not exclusively as a consequence of the war.

> The highest art will be that which in its conscious content presents the thousandfold problems of the day, the art which has been visibly shattered by the explosions of last week, which is forever trying to collect its limbs after yesterday's crash. The best and most extraordinary artists will be those who every hour snatch their bodies out of the frenzied cataract of life, who, with bleeding hands and hearts, hold fast to the intelligence of their time.[155]

The "thousandfold problems of the day," "last week's explosions," and "yesterday's crash" refer not just to the experiential realm of the soldier but to the ubiquitous potential experiences in modern cities. They are examples of the violence of simultaneous, heterogeneous, and rapid sensory impulses generated by everyday urban life that attack the individual's sensory perception. In the "Collective Dada Manifesto," Huelsenbeck characterized life "as a simultaneous muddle of noises, colors and spiritual rhythms, which is taken unmodified into Dadaist art, with all the sensational screams and fevers of its reckless everyday psyche and with all its brutal reality."[156] In the text "Synthetisches Cino der Malerei" of the same year, Hausmann correspondingly states: "Initially, life appears to us entirely a monstrous noise, tension within collapses, expressions, which are never unmistakably directed, an (after all) relevant swelling of profound irrelevance taking shape without ethical somersaults on a small base."[157]

Both Simmel and Benjamin characterized modern urban life as defined by an overload of heterogeneous sensory impulses, exceeding the individual's capacity to fully register and make sense of them. Dada's experience of meaninglessness based on the disparity and disorder of sensorial impressions corresponds explicitly with Benjamin's own approach, conceiving modern life as shaped by the experience of a lack both of meaning and of the capacity to construct meaning.

Earlier, I explored Dada's artistic rejection of the society that gave rise to war via its exploitation of the paradox. To examine Dada's artistic response to the changed sensorial landscape I will discuss its use of Simultaneist and Bruitist poetry. However, this aspect of Dada also finds its expression in the overall dramaturgy of their soirées composed of incongruous, overlapping, and chaotic presentations, as well as in the techniques of collage and montage with their combination and juxtaposition of heterogeneous material. The collage *Leben und Treiben in Universal City, 12 Uhr 5 Mittags* (*Life and Activity in Universal City at 12:05 Midday*, 1919–20, fig. 14) by John Heartfield and George Grosz, as well as Raoul Hausmann's *ABCD, oder das Portrait des Künstlers* (*ABCD, or the Portrait of the Artist*, 1923–24, fig. 15) are exemplary artistic realizations of the lauded simultaneity of events and impressions. Here, Dada transposes mimesis from the visual level of depiction onto the more immediate sensorial experience. Or, to put it differently, the recipient's experience of being overstrained by the abundance of disjunct impulses is here not an intellectual but a sensorial one.

With their use of the techniques of collage and montage, the Dada artists achieve on a visual level what a Simultaneist poem seeks to capture on the level of language. Analogous to collage and montage, "the Simultaneist poem teaches a sense of the merrygoround of all things."[158] Simultaneist and Bruitist poetry can be examined as two forms of artistic reactions to and illustrations of the "sensorial meaninglessness" experienced within the framework of modern urban life.[159] Presented by Huelsenbeck, Tzara,

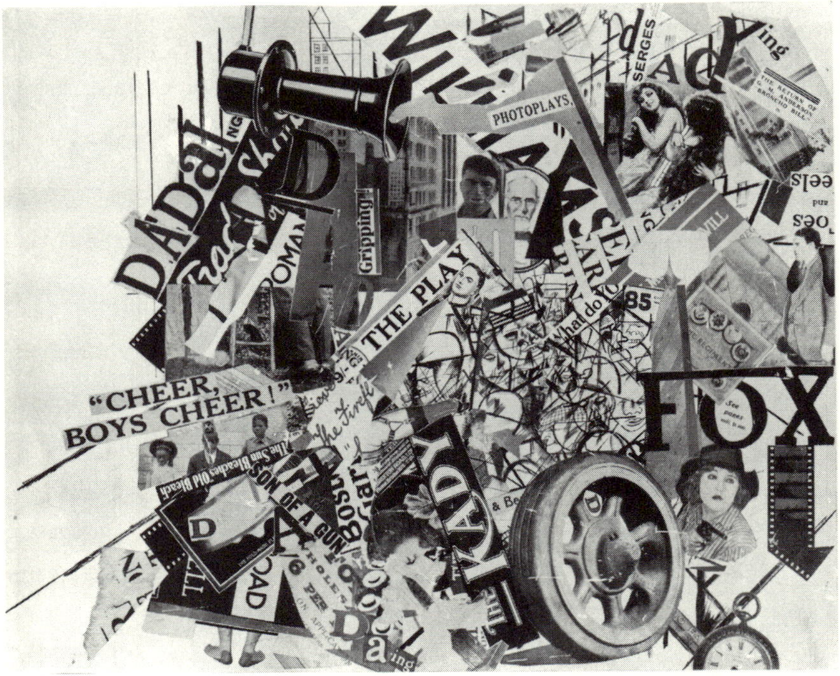

Figure 14. John Heartfield (and George Grosz), *Life and Activity in Universal City at 12:05 Midday*, 1919–20. Original test print of photomontage with photo and text elements and a drawing by Grosz (photomontage since lost). Photo by Markus Hawlik. Akademie der Künste, Berlin.

and Janco, and consisting in simultaneous recitations, "L'admiral cherche une maison à louer" ("The Admiral Looks for a House to Rent"),[160] was the first Simultaneist poem to be performed early in 1916. It consisted of three separate texts, each of a different language (French, German, English), that were recited simultaneously, with parts of it consisting simply of rhythmic noise and accompanied by percussive musical instruments. It sought to present life as "an almighty and attractive mess."[161] Simultaneity, an issue of relevance in painting already since the 1910s, was used, as Huelsenbeck explains, as "a term for the concomitance of dissimilar incidents" and conceived as "a direct reference to life."[162] In a letter to Otto Schmalhausen, Grosz apostrophizes:

> Oh sacred simultaneity: streets rushing onto the paper; the starry sky circles above the red head; the tram bursts into the picture; the telephones ring; women scream in childbirth; whilst knuckle-dusters and steel knife rest peacefully in the hot trouserpocket of the pimp: the labyrinths of mirrors; the magic street gardens where Circe transforms men into swine.[163]

Describing the interlacing and superposition of impressions as both a visual and acoustic experience, Grosz seems to deliver both a description of the Simultaneist poem and of the collage, both responding to the violent confrontation with multilayered, unstructured, and excessive sensorial impulses. As Georges Hugnet explains in his *Dictionnaire du Dadaïsme*, a Simultaneist poem was "understood to give an aesthetic expression to plurality instead of unity, to the plural instead of the singular and to the dynamism of modern times."[164] It was a mimetic response to the world and a repetition of its characteristic feature, being grounded "upon an imitative and stylised mode of expression and upon a naturalist acceptation of the modern world and its movement," with the various voices no longer attempting "to harmonise with each other, neither on the level of sense, nor on that of sound."[165] As a newspaper article concluded, "Right now mayhem is the sign of the times, it is the age of Dadaist stammering."[166] As Hausmann stated, "Man is simultaneous, a monster of what is his own and what is foreign, now, before, after and at the same time."[167] The artist conceives of the "non-sense of Dada . . . [as] the sense of all senses simultaneously,"[168] and asks for the use of simultaneous expression as a consequence of the experienced reality. "We request

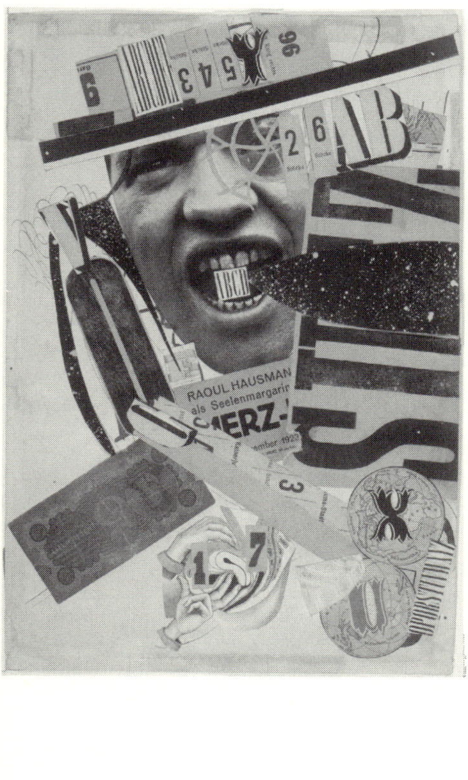

Figure 15. Raoul Hausmann, *ABCD, or the Portrait of the Artist*, 1923–24. Photo collage. Centre Pompidou—Musée National d'Art Moderne, Paris.

the enhancement and mastership of all our senses! We want to blast all limits hitherto existing!!"[169]

In this, Dada's demand for simultaneity, perceived as a necessary and inevitable feature of the individual's receptive disposition and developed as mimicking reality's unstructured mixture of chaotic and heterogeneous events, differs from that of Futurism, which instead focused on the simultaneous execution of activities for the sake of economizing time (as expressed, for example, by Fedele Azari).[170] Discussing the Simultaneist poem "The Admiral Looks for a House to Rent," Hanno Ehrlicher states that "the audience had no other way than to interpret" this poem "as the deprivation of the possibility to apprehend meaning."[171] To my mind, Ehrlicher's formulation exceeds Dada's own intentions insofar as it implies that the audience interprets and thus conceptualizes the Dadaists doings. Dada did not aim at the audience's intellectual understanding of their engagement with the meaningless but at delivering the experience of meaninglessness itself.

Having outlined Dada's shift from an intellectual level of reception to the perceptive level of experience as a reaction to the observed conditions of modern life, we might equally interpret its use of Bruitist poetry as a response to yet another dominant feature of that environment. Instead of focusing on the simultaneity and heterogeneity of sensorial impressions, Bruitism reacts to the increasing relevance of noise. "The Bruitist poem represents a streetcar as it is, the essence of the streetcar with the yawning of Schulze, the cuppon clipper, and the screeching of the brakes,"[172] wrote Huelsenbeck in 1920. The focus on the reproduction of a particular soundscape might include the production of actual noise: "I introduce real noise in order to aggravate and accentuate the poem. In this sense, objective reality is let into the poem for the first time, corresponding to a reality, which the cubists equally apply in their pictures."[173] Hausmann correspondingly requested the use of real or concrete material—as Fluxus would later describe it—such as wire, glass, cardboard, and fabric, expecting a unique "punch" to result from the use of such kind of material.[174] As Huelsenbeck states, "Bruitism is life itself, which cannot be judged upon like a book but is rather part of our personality and attacks us, chases us and tears us to tatters";[175] it is "the direct pointer to action":[176]

> Whatever way you look at it, music is a matter of harmony. It is an art, an activity of reason. Bruitism is life itself and as such it can't be assessed. Wagner has demonstrated the utter mendacity of a lofty abstraction—at least the

> screech of a brake can induce toothache. The same tendency that made tap dance and rag-time the national music of the United States was in Europe a cramp and tendency towards "bruit" and noise.[177]

As Isaac Goldberg put it in the title of an article in the *Boston Evening Transcript*, "Dada [is] Putting the Jazz into Modern Verse."[178] In opposition to music, noise is appreciated as immediately related to the activity from which it emerges, without being processed through the mechanisms of consciousness and control. As a consequence, noise is considered to have the capacity of directly affecting the individual, that is, on a physical rather than an intellectual level. Huelsenbeck's preference for "unconscious" noise instead of "conscious" music follows from his contention that any "harmonious range of forms richly melodious has lost any direct relevance for our time."[179] Consistency and harmony no longer correspond with the contemporary experiences of daily life, as Ball's description of Huelsenbeck's poetry makes clear: "His poetry is an attempt to capture in a clear melody the totality of this unutterable age, with all its cracks and fissures, with all its wicked and lunatic genialities, with all its noise and hollow din. The Gorgon's head of a boundless terror smiles out of the fantastic destruction."[180]

As this account of Simultaneist and Bruitist poetry shows, Dada artists did not abandon the traditional artistic endeavor of a mimetic reproduction of the world, but sought for its actualization in order to do justice to the changed features of this world. By repeating a particular sense perception with artistic means, Dada remained well within the art-historical tradition of mimesis, but no longer focused on the rendition of a visual experience with the means of painting, sculpture, or narration. "Who would be trying to represent the impressions of today's man, the endless change of lit metropolitan streets, with these means?"[181] asks Hausmann in 1921, continuing a thought he had already expressed in 1918, discussing the limitations of traditional, visual modes of representation: "Cubism and Futurism—means to express with visual intellectuality and with the great gesture of a breakthrough to the fourth dimension, remain attempts to extend perception on the level of optical chemotropism."[182]

As Dada is convinced, such attempts must necessarily fail, since they operate on the wrong level. The outstanding achievement of Dada—and this is precisely what Walter Benjamin appreciated in the movement—was the transferral of mimesis from an optical onto a tactile level. This observation is unrelated to the fact of whether we are speaking about visual (pictorial) or acoustic (linguistic) means of reproduction: both Simultaneist and Bruitist poetry represent modes "of imitative expression" developed as part of the endeavor to respond to the "absent-mindedness" of the time.[183] By transferring artistic mimesis from an "optical" to a "tactile" level, Dada fulfils both its own as well as Benjamin's request for art to react to what was considered paradigmatic about the given context.

Having analyzed the relevance of senselessness as the response of (and repetition by) Dada artists to their experience of their sociocultural context, it remains to research the link between senselessness and shock. It will then become apparent that Dada's interest in the experience of shock is an equally integral and crucial part of its striving for an appropriate artistic response to contemporary life.

Senselessness, the New, and the "Shock of the Unintelligible"

> Artistically people can only be reached any longer by the shock that imparts a blow to what pseudo-scientific ideology calls communication; for its part art is integral only when it refuses to play along with communication.[184]

Adorno's rejection of established mechanisms of communication and his call for them to be subverted suggest that, for him, the validity and vitality of art consists in its development of new and, as I will argue, "senseless" ways of reaching the recipient. Rejecting works of art that "silently acknowledge the flourishing establishment of communication,"[185] Adorno asks that art overthrow and renew visual and linguistic forms of communication.

> The more art expels the preestablished, the more it is thrown back on what purports to get by, as it where, without borrowing from what has become distant and foreign. . . . The contraction of the accessible, the totality of refusal, terminates in complete impoverishment: the scream of the destitute, powerless gesture, literally the syllables "da-da."[186]

Adorno's request for art to expel the preestablished can be rephrased as a call for the new. "The new is a blind spot";[187] it is an equation "with the unknown, with the hidden telos, as well as with what is monstrous by virtue of its incommensurability."[188] It is necessarily abstract, not in terms of its formal qualities but due to its refusal to be understandable.[189] In exemplary manner, Adorno thus accounts for the crucial and inseparable union between the new and the senseless. The new *is* the senseless or, more precisely, the new is received as senseless by appearing disconnected from any established system of constructing and revealing meaning. By appearing unrelated to anything existing and known, the new exceeds the established system of sense making and, it could be argued, demands an alternative system of evaluation—a system that is not (yet) established and whose values of evaluation are not (yet) recognized. Henri Bergson approached the same relationship between the new and the senseless by focusing on the difficulty of an intellectual appropriation of the new: "Precisely because it is always trying to reconstitute, and to reconstitute with what is given, the intellect lets what is *new* in each moment of a history escape. It does not admit the unforeseeable . . . [and fails to] admit complete novelty."[190] The new does not make sense.

The relevance of all this for Dada's intentions is that the relationship between the new and the senseless is not optional but inevitable: it is a conceptual given. Lenin, who lived opposite the Club Voltaire in the Spiegelgasse in Zürich, is reported to have said, "I don't like modern movements [of art] because I am unable to comprehend them."[191] The urge for new means of artistic expression and artistic communication can be shown to occupy a central position within Dada and refers us back to the link, outlined earlier, between the shock of the new and the shock of the senseless. "We want something new at any rate,"[192] Huelsenbeck proclaimed, stating elsewhere that "Dadaism is something that has superseded the elements of Futurism or the theorems of Cubism. It is necessarily something new."[193] As Alexander Partens claims in the *Dada Almanach* (*Dada Almanac*), Dada developed itself "right from scratch," creating "works from a new powerful and genuine feeling for life."[194] This corresponds with Hausmann's request for the "new human" to have the courage to be new indeed.[195]

Patrick Waldenberg explains the structural difference between Dada and other artistic movements at the beginning of the twentieth century with its distinctly different understanding of the notions of the new and of renewal: whereas other contemporary movements "remained in a tradition of thought accessible to the attacks of their opponents, Dada assailed the foundations of thinking themselves, by putting language, coherence and the principle of identity at stake and by questioning the support and vehicles of art."[196] For our interest in the conceptual linkage between the notions of shock, senselessness, and the new, the question of whether Dada actually fulfils what Waldenberg postulates is of secondary importance and does not diminish the conceptual relevance of this endeavor. Quite evidently with regard to Futurism, but also to Expressionism and Cubism, Dada's claim to be utterly separate is dubitable in its strictness. However, Dada's fierce rejection of any connection with preceding artistic movements is based on its declared unwillingness to further existing values and to thus feed into the notion of progress, which belongs to the system it rejects. This unwillingness finds expression in Ribemont-Dessaignes's enigmatic phrase that a "successful revolution signifies an undertaking that has failed."[197] In Tzara's proclamation that Dada is "definitely against the future,"[198] we see the movement's desire to create something categorically rather than comparatively new and its attempt to sever any connection with preceding avant-garde movements.[199] Dada sought to achieve the new not by modifying tradition but by transgressing it, wanting to attack the very foundations of our thinking. This striving for the new was both noted as well as criticized at the time. As Ernesto de Fiori remarked skeptically in view of Dada's activities in Zurich: "'New' makes only sense in connection to 'old.' What would it mean to fully break any connection with the old? Senselessness—but this, again, is nothing new at all."[200]

But returning to Waldenberg's words, we can apply them to the distinction between the different and the new, borrowing from Boris Groys's account of Kierkegaard. Whereas "the different" is defined by its being different from something else, "the new is a difference without difference—a difference which we are unable to recognise because it is not related to any pregiven cultural code."[201] This distinction reappears in Bürger's summary of Adorno's definition of the new as "a category of modern art as something distinct from the renewal of themes, motifs, and artistic techniques that also marked the development of art before the advent of Modernism."[202] Bürger goes on to describe this difference as a shift away from understanding the new as an advance to understanding it as a transgression. Whereas previous phases of change and renewal did in fact continue with tradition through change, the relevant positions at the beginning of the twentieth century aim for disruption and discontinuation. As Adorno wrote of modern art, "It is more the negation of what no longer holds than a positive slogan. It does not, however, negate previous artistic practices, as styles have done throughout the ages, but rather tradition itself."[203] Karl Heinz Bohrer describes this distinction as a difference in the breaking of established rules. What is irritating is not so much the breaking of a rule in itself, but rather "the way this rule gets broken":

it "is not refuted from within the system of rules; rather, it is just ignored and simply passed over."[204]

I will largely refrain from recapitulating the differing definitions of *modernism* on the one hand and the *avant-garde* on the other—terms that are at times used interchangeably.[205] However, it is undisputed that Dadaism is a distinctly avant-garde movement, representing the "archetypical trait[s] of the avant-garde"[206] in the urge for the new, understood as a fundamental separation from the past and thus frequently read as an expression of nihilism. But it is, as Hugo Ball outlines, not only an inevitable but also a productive nihilism: "Art cannot have any respect for the existing view of the world unless it renounces itself. Art enlarges the world by negating the aspects that were known and in operation up to now, and putting new ones in their place. That is the power of modern aesthetics; one cannot be an artist and believe in history."[207] The urge to "make it new,"[208] as Ezra Pound stated, becomes a conceptual prerequisite and represents itself as an indispensable instead of an optional element of artistic creation in the avant-garde, which became defined as "a small, self-conscious group of artists who undertake . . . to 'make new.' "[209] Thus, the relevance of the new within the avant-garde cannot simply be seen as having increased in quantity, but as having changed in its quality. As Rosalind Krauss states, "More than a rejection or dissolution of the past, avant-garde originality is conceived as a literal origin, a beginning from ground zero, a birth."[210]

But the conceptual link between the new and the senseless does not terminate at this point: as indicated earlier, Adorno goes even further. Having established the interrelation between the new and the senseless, Adorno goes on to consider the effects on the recipient of such avant-garde manifestations. The new appears to the recipient as necessarily nonsensical, but this encounter with the senseless—or, to put it another way, with something intellectually inaccessible—is not considered as emotionally neutral but as violent.[211] The new, as Adorno states, has the capacity to trigger a "blow,"[212] or a "shudder."[213] This shudder "is a reaction to the cryptically shut, which is a function of that element of indeterminacy."[214] In his much earlier essay "Über Jazz" (1935), Adorno specifies this shudder as the "shock of the unintelligible [*Schock des Unverstandenen*]";[215] a notion that will prove crucial in this context and that I will explore further at a later point. As Bürger paraphrases Adorno, the "refusal to provide meaning is experienced as shock by the recipient."[216] What potentially shocks us within the new is its appearance as something incomprehensible, something that eludes our intellectual grasp. "When artists provoke in this way," writes Karl Heinz Bohrer, "they use their words not as a vehicle of communication but as a means of alienation."[217] He continues later, "Shock is disturbing not only because it provokes us, but also because of the up to now unknown aspect of what it expresses, an aspect that confuses us."[218]

Being new, unexpected, and incomprehensible, the experience of shock results from an encounter that takes us by surprise and eludes our intellectual seizure, an encounter that lacks contextualization and appears without connection to the experiential realm we are familiar with. Dada is well aware of this correlation between the lack of connection (i.e., the corresponding lack of anticipation, as Freud underlined) and shock. Hausmann states that "the 'audience' is generally unable to support the new, although it finds itself attracted to the unknown by a craving for sensation. New ideas might just about to be possible, but a new optic, a new mode of seeing—nothing enrages the bourgeois more than an unaccustomed sight."[219]

This ambivalence, of being repulsed and shocked on the one hand yet attracted on the other, is proved by the heavily booked and at times utterly overcrowded Dada soirées. Although it might be wise not to believe the actual numbers, both Tzara and Hausmann mutually purport that 1,200 people had to be turned away from a Dada soirée in Paris in March 1920 due to congestion, and another event in Dresden is said to have attracted 2,000 visitors.[220] "People were aroused against us. They could not understand a movement that made so little sense."[221] With this quote, Grosz states Dada's interest in questioning and challenging the audience's inevitable expectation of a continually meaningful artistic production. This distinct predilection for the production of the senseless constitutes a divergence from Surrealism, which, while shifting it to uncontrollable and unconscious regions, still adhered to the idea of meaning. In his memoirs *Die Fackel im Ohr* (*The Torch in My Ear*), published in 1980, Elias Canetti recalls how the artist John Heartfield was only affected by what he conceived as new and "learned only from things that he regarded as attacks; and in order to experience something new, he had to regard it as an attack";[222] or, to phrase it the other way around, what is new presents itself as an attack. Both the new and the experience of shock constitute a discontinuity, an interruption in the continuous flow of time and meaning, manifesting themselves as a "bloody rift in the present moment."[223]

Having outlined the triangular relationship between *shock*, *meaning-*

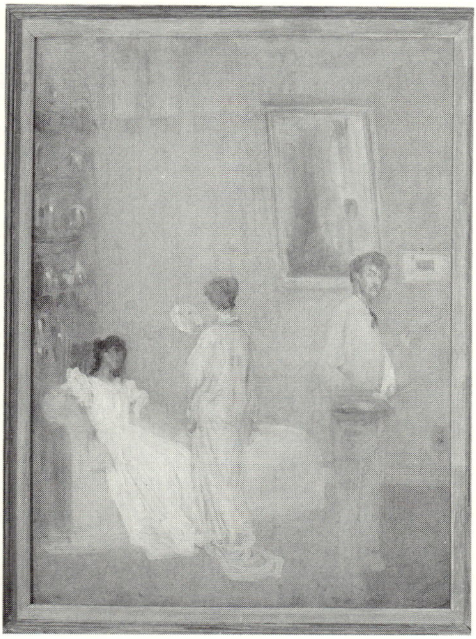

Figure 16. James McNeill Whistler, *The Artist in His Studio*, 1865–66. Oil on paper, mounted on panel. The Art Institute of Chicago, Friends of American Art Collection, Chicago.

lessness, and *the new* as three terms not only central to Dada but as conceptually interrelated, the primary reasons for Dada's interest in shock can be summarized. First and foremost, the relevance of shock within artistic expression became apparent as a response to the paradigmatic relevance of shock within the artists' own range of experience. This relevance was produced by the specific sociocultural situation in the early twentieth century and appeared connected to a lack of sense, resulting from a pervasive exposure to experiences of an utterly new range. This experience of senselessness was described as evolving on both the level of sense perception and intellectual reception. The ensuing relevance of shock for Dada's artistic production was based on their sense of the duty of art to respond to the specifics of the given sociocultural situation. They concluded that the appropriate response was a repetition of the senseless, figured as the dominant source of shock.

Although Dada can be considered the first movement to use the shock of the senseless to a significant degree and in a conceptualized manner, there were of course earlier artistic approaches that anticipated it. A less prominent case is to be found in James McNeill Whistler's works such as *Symphony in White, No. 1: The White Girl* from 1862 or *The Artist in His Studio* from 1865–66 (fig. 16). At the time of their creation, the almost monochromic white paintings of pale-colored figures in front of equally colorless backdrops had been received as an artistic affront due to their lack of any apparent formal dramaturgy and composition. Whistler "was not simply trying to give his audience a frisson," Nicholas Daly concludes: "There was a serious artistic purpose to his shock techniques: he wished to jolt the viewer out of a comfortable and contemplative relation to the work, and to confront him or her with both its hereness and nowness, and its material medium specificity, its nature as paint on canvas."[224]

The lack of a meaningful and visibly deliberate composition of color—as of a meaningful subject matter—might thus be seen as a precursor to the later development of senselessness as a strategy of shock in the early twentieth century, although it would manifest itself in a quite different manner.

The Senseless in Walter Benjamin's Concept of Shock

The preceding investigation into Dada's concept of shock and its inherent link to the notions of the senseless and the new makes it necessary to return to Walter Benjamin. This necessity emerges from an apparent discrepancy between the two approaches. Although Dada serves as one of Benjamin's primary examples within his investigation into shock, we find no corresponding discussion of the role of senselessness within his account. How can we explain Benjamin's interest in Dada and, more precisely, his interest in the movement's use of shock on the one hand and the simultaneous neglect of the movement's interest in the abolition of meaning on the other? This discrepancy between my own examination and Benjamin's approach requires an investigation into the latter's understanding of shock in its relation to the notion of the senseless. Is senselessness relevant to Dada's concept of shock but irrelevant to Benjamin's? Is it considered a possible source of shock in Benjamin's approach, or does it make no considerable appearance at all? Ultimately, the answering of these questions will not only shed further light on Benjamin's concept of shock, but will also specify Dada's use of the senseless as an approach to trigger this experience.

Once again, a route into this field is provided by Adorno, Benjamin's mentor at the Institut für Sozialforschung. As outlined earlier, Adorno coined the phrase "shock of the unintelligible" in his essay "Über Jazz," written during 1935 and thus precisely at the time when Benjamin was working on his "Artwork Essay." Adorno developed this notion of shock as part of his reflections on the effect of syncopated rhythms upon the listener. In his first letter to Adorno after having received the blueprints of the "Jazz Essay," Benjamin replies with the following lines: "In view of our upcoming meeting, I will refrain from commenting on individual aspects of your work. However, I simply can't put off telling you how much my thoughts about the shock effect within film have been elucidated by your description of the syncope within jazz."[225] This quote is striking for a number of reasons. Although Adorno had repeatedly envisioned the potential for affinities between the two texts throughout their production, the parallels are less obvious when we actually compare the works. Though both are based on a sociological analysis of artistic phenomena generated by and accommodated within the sociocultural situation of the time, Adorno's elaboration of shock does not play a dominant role in his essay, which focuses on a sociological positioning and critique of jazz. In fact, the term *shock* itself appears only twice.[226] Furthermore, Adorno limits himself to a specific definition of shock: by defining it as the shock of the unintelligible, he outlines the connection between shock and unintelligibility that is of interest to us in the context of this thesis. In other words, Adorno relates the experience of shock to a failure in the intellectual appropriation of a particular experience. In a letter to the composer Ernst Krenek from 1931, Adorno recalls the debut performance of Krenek's Symphony No. 2 and reports of the shock it had effected in him.[227] With regard to syncopation, he considers its shocking effect as inseparably linked to its occurrence exterior to a known and appropriated rhythmical system. More specifically, to an audience not yet familiar with the compositional and rhythmic structures of jazz, the syncope does not merely appear unpredicted but seems in principle unpredictable. In other words, the shocking effect of a particular experience results from this experience's apparent lawlessness, which thwarts its anticipation and the recipient's consequent preparation, placing it beyond the realm of the listener's "control."

As Adorno's analysis of jazz exemplifies, the unpredictability of a specific experience is not a constant and timeless attribute but changes over time. In the case of jazz, for example, the rules behind the syncope's occurrence were not yet appropriated by the recipient, nor had he become used to this musical experience. In other words, what is experienced as lawless, unpredictable, and new, and thus as potentially shocking, depends of course on a particular time and context. Jazz music's correspondence with the sociocultural context of the early twentieth century has been stated repeatedly, being perceived as a significant and fitting artistic reaction to this very context. The analogy between the music's rhythmical raggedness and the raggedness of the individual's living experience is reflected in the terms that were used as synonyms to the term *jazz* during the early decades of the twentieth century, *ragtime* and *syncopated music*. They referred explicitly to the experience of a ragging of time inherent to this new form of musical expression. This is what Adorno had in mind when describing the syncope as a "laceration of time."[228] Used within musicology to describe a shift of stress onto the unstressed part of the beat,[229] the term was transferred to the field of poetry, describing deliberate irregularities and omissions within the metric structure of a verse. We can thus define the notion of the syncope as a rhythmical or metrical discontinuity;[230] an understanding, by the way, that is reflected in yet another definition of the term as a "loss of consciousness," a "blackout." In his essay "Über reimlose Lyrik mit unregelmässigen Rhythmen" ("On Unrhymed Lyrics in Irregular Rhythms") of 1939, Bertolt Brecht reflects upon the challenge posed to the recipient by irregular rhythms, coming to perceive this challenge as specific to the given time and sociocultural context:

> It must be further admitted that the reading of irregular rhythms at first offers several difficulties. . . . The ear is undoubtedly going through a physiological transformation. Our acoustical environment has changed tremendously. There was a scene in an American movie in which Fred Astaire did a tap dance to the noises of an engine room; the tap rhythm showed the startling similarity between the new noises and jazz.[231]

Of further interest to us is the similarity, noticed by Brecht, of ragged music or poetry and the paradigms of the modern environment to which they were the artistic response. Ragging metrical continuity by a-rhythmical gaps—"syncopated language," as Brecht phrased it—resembles "the panting of the runner."[232] For a Dada soirée in Berlin in 1918, George Grosz announced the presentation of "Sincopations," verses that the press described variously as "Niggersongs," "abrasive exhibitionist verses," and "bruitist" poems.[233] Besides referring to fragmented metrical rhythms, Grosz—who was a keen listener of jazz—also used words taken from the realm of jazz, ragtime, or cakewalk.[234] Reviewing Walter Mehring's chansons, which the Dadaist himself described as "Language-Rag-Time," and of which one was entitled *Tempo-Synkopen*, Frank Hellberg observes that "the music from North America . . . with its propelling rhythm . . . fitted well into the hectic and fast moving goings of the European metropolis."[235] On this account, it is worth recalling Hausmann's dismissal of

Expressionist painting because it failed to create a rhythm that "grabs," "drops out," and creates a "staccato."[236]

These definitions of the characteristics of modern life via the notions of rhythm and a-rhythmicity remind us of our earlier account of Walter Benjamin's characterization of the modern metropolis from the point of view of its rhythm and rhythmic disturbances. Besides the rhythmical irregularities of jazz being transposed into the metric irregularities of poetry, and besides explicit references to jazz in the lyrics or titles of Dada works, Eugen Egger found yet a third analogy with Dadaist poems in the so-called "scat" or "bob-vocals" developed in jazz since the 1920s: vocalizations consisting of meaningless syllables, sung in the place of proper lyrics and used as an additional level of sound and rhythm but void of decipherable meaning.[237]

Based on these reflections on the syncope as an unexpected rhythmic discontinuity and on jazz as an appropriate musical reaction to sensorial features considered as paradigmatic for the given time, we can now return to Adorno's notion of the shock of the unintelligible and suggest an alternative phrasing: the shock of the unexpected, or, more precisely, the shock of that which is received as *unexpectable*. This rephrasing does not necessarily pay more justice to Adorno's own endeavor, but is helpful insofar as it renders more perceptible the affinity between Adorno's and Benjamin's approach to shock and helps to locate the notion and role of the senseless within the latter. The authors' differences do not lie in a divergent understanding of shock as such, but derive from the fact that they focus on different levels involved in enabling an experience of shock. As has been shown, Adorno investigates the predispositions of shock on the level of intellectual activity and focuses on the possibility of an incident's intellectual appropriation and anticipation. For him, the impossibility of understanding a particular experience coincides with the inability to anticipate this experience, as the recipient is not aware of the rules according to which this experience occurs.

In contrast to this, Benjamin's approach is centered not on intellectual but on perceptional reception. Whereas Adorno focuses on the process of understanding what has been perceived, Benjamin investigates the sheer possibility of hearing or seeing something consciously. As shown in my examination of Benjamin's concept of shock, his notion of tactility explores the gray zone of sensory perception that takes place exterior to the complete conscious registering of sensory impulses. It is considered as an indispensable mode of reception for coping with the considerable quantitative increase and qualitative change in sensorial impulses generated by the modern environment. It became equally apparent that Benjamin's focus on the sensual perception of impulses and not on their consequent intellectual processing is not to be understood as merely a personal predilection: it is the consequence of Benjamin's assumption that the quantity and type of sensually perceived impulses in the modern environment exceeds our ability to absorb them intellectually. The mode of tactile perception therefore presented itself as essential for meeting the new challenge to individuals' capacities of sense perception. However, although tactility was essential in order to cope with the range of sense impressions, it also made it more likely that one would experience shock. This modern dilemma derived from the fact that tactility referred to a mode of perception prior and exterior to a conscious registration of the perceived, which might consequently elude its anticipation, control, and assimilation into structures of meaning.

Whereas Adorno's interest is largely in the possibility or impossibility of an intellectual anticipation of an occurrence, Benjamin focuses on the sensory level of experience rather than on its intellectual appropriation. The distinction between something being meaningful or meaningless is transposed onto the question of something being perceived consciously or unconsciously—or, to use another distinction, something perceived with attentiveness or within a mode of distraction. Tactility thus becomes describable as meaningless sense perception or, more briefly, as senseless perception. We can thus argue that the notion of senselessness plays no considerable role within Benjamin's concept of shock because notions of tactility and tactile perception have taken its place. Meaninglessness on the level of intellectual reception is paralleled by tactility on the level of sense perception.

We can therefore see how the apparent departure of Benjamin's reflections on shock does not stem from an understanding of shock utterly different from Adorno's or Dada's, nor does it result from an account of Dada profoundly different from my own. Benjamin's preference for the notion of tactility—and the need to use this new term—is a consequence of his focus on sense perception and thus on a level prior to the intellectual processing of an incoming impulse. In contrast to the Futurists—and notably to Marinetti's "Manifesto del Tattilismo" ("Manifesto of Tactilism") of 1921—and in concord with Benjamin, Dada did not herald a refinement and training of the sense of touch but of a tactile mode of perception independent of any specific sensory organ. Dada, as Benjamin famously praised, "turned the artwork into a missile . . . [that] jolted the viewer, taking on a tactile quality."[238] Quite strikingly, a similar comparison between a missile and the artwork's impact is to be found in an early declaration by Huelsenbeck, as he welcomed the audience to a Dada soirée at the Cabaret Voltaire: "I have to make a statement today, which will give you a shudder. I hope, however, that no physical harm will befall you, but what I have to tell you now, will hit you like a bullet."[239]

I do not intend to replace Dada's drive for the senseless with Benjamin's notion of tactility. It is brought in in order to elucidate the two levels on which Dada's experience and pursuit of senselessness takes place. As I set out to show, Dada's preoccupation with a lack of meaning evolves on the level of intellectual reception, outlined in its parallel with Adorno, as well as on that of sense perception, elucidated in its reference to Benjamin. Whereas the first appeared as notably developed in response to a critique of society ignited by the occurrence of the war, the latter can rather be seen as response to and repetition of the sensorial challenges of the modern urban life. Here, senselessness is perceived as something occurring on a physiological level. Dada does not see the changes in the sociocultural environment (such as technological developments) as merely external or as only posing an intellectual challenge to the individual. It considers them as influencing and changing the individual's physical and psychological condition by transforming the landscape of experience: "The human being has changed utterly in our awareness, not only because we possess the telephone and the airplane, the electric piano and the turret lathe, but because our entire psychophysical condition is transformed on the grounds of this experience."[240] The experience of shock and the senseless play a crucial part in this transformation.

Both manifestations of senselessness relevant to Dada—on the level of the intellect and of sense perception—can be characterized as a *rejection* of society on the one hand and a *reaction* to society on the other. These two positions toward the sociocultural context are not contradictory but interlinked. As Dada's critique of Expressionism shows, their *rejection* of society involves rejecting all prevailing artistic *reactions* to this society. Being grounded upon the conviction that contemporary society fails to recognize its true state, Dada consequently refuses to create art that represents society to its own satisfaction. In simplified terms, a society perceived as meaningless, idiotic, imbecilic, and insensible wrongly holds fast to meaningful means of representation, to that which is coherent, homogeneous, and decipherable. It is to this imbalance that Dada responds.

4 Shock and the Senseless in Fluxus

> As one of historical Dada's most direct descendants (and having, in its own right, captured the imagination of our present), perhaps it is time for Fluxus to rethink its initial anxiety about openly acknowledging its familial relationship to its venerated progenitor.[1]

Estera Milman's request for Fluxus to reconsider its at times dismissive attitude toward Dada might with even more justification be made of art historians. While readily acknowledging the affinities between Dada and Fluxus, considering Dada as Fluxus's "historic paragon,"[2] the scope and implications of these affinities, as well as of the differences, have hardly been analyzed in any depth. What did Fluxus learn from Dada? Why did it choose to continue certain strategies and disavow others? What are the reasons behind their similarities and divergences? These are questions that have yet to be fully investigated. It is not my aim to try to answer them in general. Rather, my interest in comparing Dada and Fluxus is guided by a range of more specific enquiries: Does Fluxus continue with Dada's concept of shock and thus with its distinct relationship to the senseless? In what way does it modify the artistic methods used by Dada to reach a reaction of shock, and to what extent have the intentions and motivations changed? Finally, what is the sociocultural and artistic context and background by which we can try to understand this continuation or change? I thus intend to investigate Fluxus as "one of historical Dada's most direct descendants" by focusing on the movement's concept and use of shock and on the notion of the senseless.

Indeed, comparing press reviews on Dada soirées from the late 1910s with those of Fluxus concert evenings from the early 1960s, we can observe a striking similarity, both with regard to the type and structure of the performances as well as to the audience's and the reviewers' reactions to those performances. The account of a "young lady" who "fired two pistol shots, smashed window glass with a hammer and smacked and punched a man Friday night at the Museum College of Art" might just as easily have been that of a Dada soirée as a Fluxus concert evening. In this case, the journalist was in fact writing about a concert evening by Nam June Paik and performed by Charlotte Moorman: "It wasn't a riot. It was a concert. The young lady also jumped into a tank of water in the middle of one number, read advertisements, screamed, banged on garbage can lids with a hammer."[3] An account of one of the earliest Fluxus concerts, *Neo-Dada in der Musik*, which took place at the Kammerspiele in Düsseldorf on June 16, 1962,[4] reads just like a reenactment of a Dada soirée:

> Fresh eggs were thrown into the audience. The boss smeared tomato puree on his face and had a mannequin dismantled, which was suspended head first. Following the recitation of senseless sentences and scraps of words, there was a five minute reading of postcodes and corresponding city names, until the visitors—including sundry notables—revolted.[5]

Where the confusion, incongruity, simultaneity, and senselessness of the performance met the level of a Dada soirée, the audience did the same, using not only verbal but material means to express discontent (e.g., throwing eggs onto the stage) and, like Dada, creating an "unbelievable kerfuffle of whistling, laughter and outrage."[6] The reviewer's verdicts had progressed little, condemning Fluxus concerts as "escapades of manifested nonsense."[7] In the case of both Dada and Fluxus, the audience reactions were dominated by shock, repulsion, and incomprehension, and both movements were known for stirring scandal. As the Fluxus founder George Maciunas reported bluntly after the first Fluxus concerts, "Wiesbaden was shocked."[8] Emmett Williams, who had met Tristan Tzara back in 1949,[9] described Maciunas as behaving like "a tyrant, in the style of Tzara and Breton."[10] He recalls his appearance during Fluxus festivals to have been "like a reincarnation of Tristan Tzara in his prime, complete with bowler hat, monocle, high collar and black tie."[11] Robert Filliou recalls correspondingly: "George, do you remember the exact day and place where we met? . . . You wore a bowler hat" (figs. 17–20).[12]

However, before making a closer comparison of Dada and Fluxus with a specific focus on their interest in shock and the senseless, it is worth

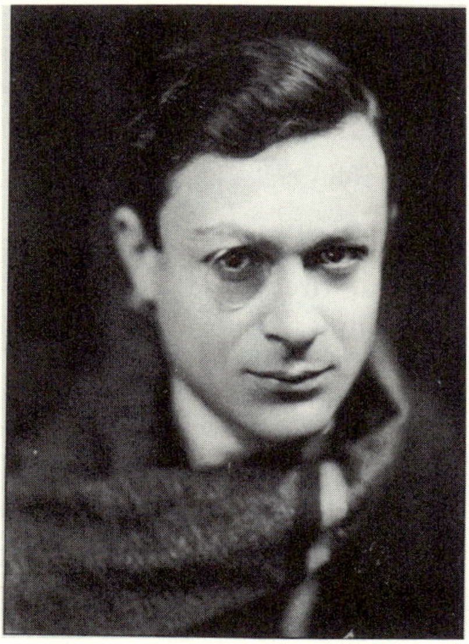

Figure 17. Tristan Tzara, *Self-Portrait*, undated. Black-and-white photograph.

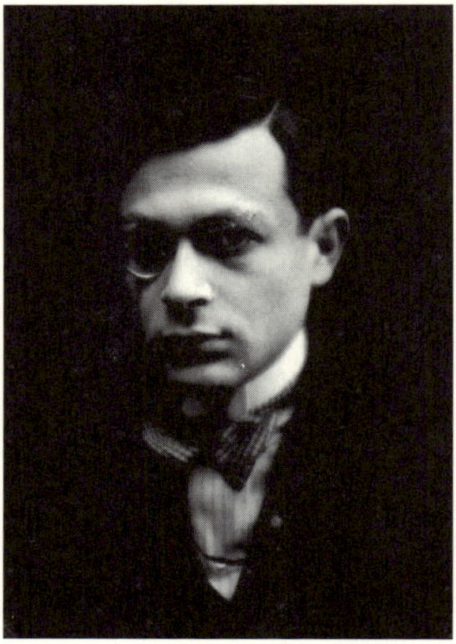

Figure 18. Tristan Tzara, *Self-Portrait*, undated. Black-and-white photograph.

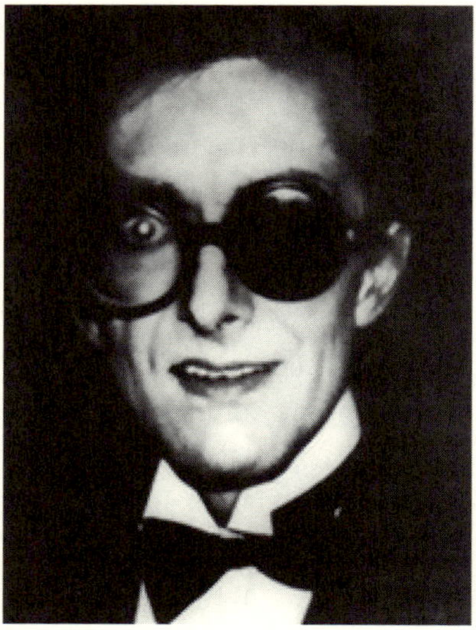

Figure 19. George Maciunas, *Self-Portrait*, undated. Black-and-white photograph.

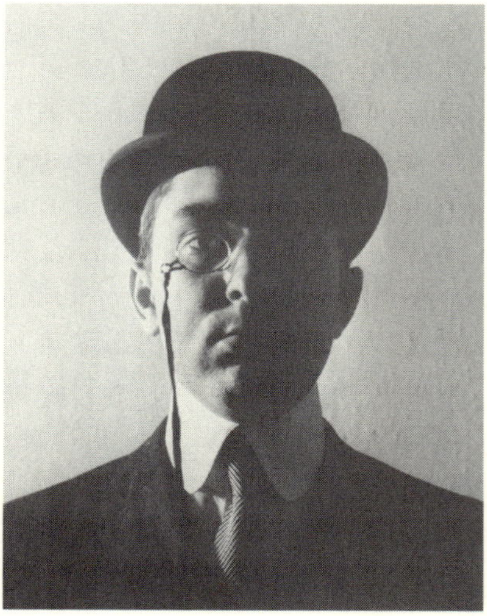

Figure 20. George Maciunas, *Self-Portrait*, 1961. Black-and-white photograph.

casting an eye over the artistic climate of the late 1950s and early 1960s in order to understand the context of Fluxus's reference to Dada, which was far from unique at the time. Rather, artistic and art-historical interest in Dada experienced a strong and sudden rise in the late 1950s and early 1960s, going far beyond the specific case of Fluxus and giving birth to a wider artistic reconnection with the historical avant-garde, which became labeled as neo-avant-garde or even as neo-Dada. Hal Foster distinguished "at least two moments in the initial neo-avant-garde": the first, including Robert Rauschenberg and Allan Kaprow, located in the 1950s and centered around a reference to Dada; the second, located in the 1960s and exemplified by Daniel Buren and Michael Asher, focused on a resuscitation of the institutional critique.[13] As a 1958 newspaper article entitled "Trend to the 'Anti-Art' " states more generally and with alarm, the newly emerging artistic tendencies inaugurate "a throwback on an old movement which shocked Europe 40 years ago."[14]

Pop Art, Nouveau Réalistes, the Wiener Gruppe, and the Internationale Situationiste were among the movements of the time that either established a reference to Dada themselves or were labeled as neo-Dada by critics or art historians. As Richard Hamilton states in 1961 with regard to Pop Art, a "new generation of Dadaists has emerged today, but the Son of Dada is accepted."[15] Also, individual artists—for example, Bruce Nauman—started to name Dada as a point of reference.[16] Maria Müller even considers it possible "to examine most of the artistic tendencies of the 1960s with regard to their references to Dadaism—and most notably to Marcel Duchamp."[17] While it is questionable to subsume Duchamp unanimously within Dada, as he had never been a declared member of the group, Müller's assumption does express the omnipresence of their joint inheritance in these years as well as Duchamp's prevalent characterization as "the personification of Dada's refusal to distinguish between "art" and "life.' "[18] About two decades later, neo-Dada tendencies would reappear in quite a different area of cultural production, in popular music—or non-popular music in that matter—punk.[19] It is a parallel Dada might have favored in the attempt to escape the inevitable elitism of the art world.

Developing in correspondence with this trend, a range of exhibitions started to illustrate the links between Dada and various artistic tendencies of the late 1950s and early 1960s. The MoMA exhibition *The Art of Assemblage* from 1961, traveling to Dallas and San Francisco, emphasized the relationship between Dadaist collage and postwar assemblage, combining Kurt Schwitters, Man Ray, and Marcel Duchamp with Jean Dubuffet, Robert Rauschenberg, and others. It was a concept, by the way, that Tzara rejected as "particularly stupid."[20] (Hausmann agreed and complained in turn, "There is no protest and no revolution and hardly any 'épater le bourgeois.'"[21]) *A 40° au-dessus de Dada* at the Galerie J in Paris in 1961, entitled after Pierre Restany's first manifesto on *Les Nouveaux Réalistes* (April 1960), and the anniversary show *Mouvement Dada 1916–1966* at the Galleria Schwarz in Milan,[22] fostered the link between Dada and the French and Italian Nouveau Réalistes. Following its earlier show, MoMA opened an exhibition on *Dada, Surrealism and Today* in 1967, focusing on the triangular relationship between Dada, American Pop Art, and Nouveau Réalisme. (The same focus provided the basis for the more recent exhibition on *Neo-Dada: Redefining Art, 1958–1962*, organized as a touring exhibition by the American Federation of Arts in 1994–95.) These few examples are sufficient to indicate the vagueness with which the name "neo-Dada" was applied. At times, the terms *Pop Art*, *neo-Dada*, and *Nouveau Réalisme* were even used as synonyms, as illustrated by Hilton Kramer, who announced his presentation at the high-profile *Symposium on Pop-Art* at MoMA in December 1962 as some "remarks on the phenomenon of pop-art, neo-Dada, New Realism, or whatever we finally agree to call it."[23]

The sudden increase in artists' references to Dada was complemented by a rise in art-historical interest in the avant-garde predecessor and an increase in exhibitions on the movement. The *Centre du XXe Siècle* at the Université de Nice, founded in 1968 and explicitly dedicated to the research and promotion of the literary and artistic avant-gardes of the last century, lists one single exhibition on Dada in the 1930s,[24] and only two in the 1940s (even including monographic shows of individual artists). In the succeeding decade this number rises to thirteen, before experiencing a significant increase to a total of forty-one exhibitions between 1960 and 1970, comprising group shows on Dada in museums, exhibition spaces, and private galleries. In 1966–67, to name an example, the Kunsthaus Zurich and the Musée d'Art Moderne in Paris commemorated the fiftieth anniversary of Dadaism, and a group show at the Moderna Museet in Stockholm followed in 1968.

These exhibitions, and most notably a retrospective show in Düsseldorf in 1958, which later traveled to Frankfurt, proved seminal for a new generation of artists, as they represented "an impressive turn,"[25] as Wolf Vostell remembers. "For the first time in my life, I saw my own artistic ideas as having begun in an earlier tendency."[26] This exhibition helped put an end to the preceding ignorance in "post-war Europe [where] . . . Dada was hardly taught or talked about."[27] As Emmett Williams remembers, "In 1949, Dada didn't have the aura that it attained through the years, and they didn't influence me at all—at least not then."[28] Indeed, compared to other contemporary movements, such as Expressionism, whose works increased tenfold in value already in the early 1920s, Dada's reception and appreciation developed somewhat belatedly. Its weak presence in museum collections at the time also might have been the reason for Dada's comparatively minor appearance in the Munich exhibition *Entartete Kunst* in 1937.[29] Gerhard Rühm, founding member of the Wiener Gruppe, states in a letter to Hausmann:

> We only got to know about Dada on the occasion of its first exhibition in Düsseldorf 1958. . . . In New York I was able to observe that the young American Pop-Art artists had been able to widely profit from European Dadaism. As a matter of fact, it had been easier for them to establish connexions after the war.[30]

Indeed, the first seminal anthology on Dada, Robert Motherwell's *The Dada Painters and Poets*,[31] was published in America in 1951 and proved to be especially influential on the reception of Dada in the United States. It was, however, only the beginning of a sudden rise of art-historical publications on the movement,[32] to which the Dadaists responded by resuming their own and previously rich production of texts, résumés, and manifestos, which had largely ceased after 1920, the year of Walter Serner's *Letzte Lockerung* (*Last Loosening*) and of the two books by Richard Huelsenbeck, *Dada Almanac* and *En-avant Dada*.[33] After a pause of more than three decades, 1957 saw the launch of two publications by Dadaists: Hans Arp, Richard Huelsenbeck, and Tristan Tzara jointly contributed to Peter Schifferli's *Die Geburt des Dada . . . Dichtung und Chronik der Gründer*, and Richard Huelsenbeck's *Mit Witz, Licht und Grütze: Auf den Spuren des Dadaismus* reflected explicitly upon the possibility of Dada members launching a neo-Dada group.[34] Walter Mehring's *Berlin Dada: Eine Chronik mit Photos und Dokumenten* was printed in 1959, and *Dada: Eine literarische Dokumentation*, edited by Huelsenbeck, was published in 1964, the same year as Hans Richter's *Kunst und Anti-Kunst: Der Beitrag Dadas zur Kunst des 20. Jahrhunderts*.[35] Richter's book was a crucial contribution toward relativizing the dichotomy between an apparently a-political Dada movement in Zurich and a political movement in Berlin—an idea forcefully promoted by Huelsenbeck.

Unlike some of the other Neo-Dada movements, Fluxus's link with Dada was not (or not only) the verdict of the critics at the time and was far from being the retrospective find of art historians. Instead, it is a connection that had been established by the founding members of Fluxus at the very point of the movement's emergence. The first manifestations of what was yet to be named Fluxus were explicitly announced as "neo-Dada." At the *Kleines Sommerfest: Après John Cage*, a concert evening that came to mark the beginning of the movement and that took place at Rolf Jährling's Galerie Parnass in Wuppertal on June 9, 1962, George Maciunas presented an inaugural speech entitled "Neo-Dada in Music, Theater, Poetry, Art,"[36] announced in the evening's program as introduction to "Neodada in New York."[37] In the speech, Maciunas introduced "what one might call neo-Dada in the United States, or what in any case we would like to view as such renewed Dadaism."[38] Subsequently, some reprints of the text came to carry the alternative title "Neo-Dada in the United States." Only a week later, on June 16, 1962, Maciunas and Paik organized the aforementioned concert evening at the Kammerspiele in Düsseldorf, entitled *Neo-Dada in der Musik*.

Although Maciunas had not explicitly planned to come to Germany in order to bring Fluxus into existence, he was certainly aware of its being—among other places—the factual and spiritual home of Dada. Prior to the event in Wuppertal, Maciunas had tried to organize a similar evening in Berlin, but proved unable to do so. As Jon Hendricks (brother of the Fluxus artist Geoffrey Hendricks, curator of the Silverman Collection, and loosely connected to the Judson Dance Company) observes, "The desire to launch Fluxus in Berlin mirrors the appreciation for the radical Berlin Dada movement."[39] It was only after the first manifestations of the new movement in Germany that the term *Fluxus*, used since 1960 as title for a magazine projected by Maciunas and his friend Almus Salcius, was adopted for the group's performative activities. As Higgins remembers, "In the autumn of 1962, *fluxus* became *FLUXUS*, and the press decided to call us the "Fluxus-Leute" (Fluxus-people)."[40]

At around the same time, the Dadaists Hausmann, Tzara, Huelsenbeck, and Richter unequivocally proclaimed that "neodadaism does not exist."[41] In a letter to Tzara of September 9, 1962, Hausmann announced plans to write a book on "Neodadaism," in which he intended "to show the true origins of dada and its possible links with the new 'flux.'"[42]

Indeed, in the same year, Hausmann wrote a long manuscript entitled "Aussichten oder Ende des Neodadaismus" (1962), including in it earlier writings of his own as well as a copy of Fluxus's foundation text "Neo-Dada in Music, Theater, Poetry, Art" in German translation. The manuscript was only published in its entirety in 1994 as part of a monograph on Hausmann.[43] Though Hausmann's phrasing here is neutral, the draft of the book leaves no doubt about the Dadaist's refusal to consider neo-Dada in general and Fluxus in particular as inheriting the Dada spirit. With Fluxus specifically in mind, Hausmann asks his fellow Dada artists "to oppose Neo-Dadaism, which neither searches for nor finds something new. Thoughtlessly, it appropriates an outdated attitude."[44] Addressing the Fluxus artists, Hausmann requests: "Don't call your self a Neodadaist. Neo is always NO. Call your self as you like, but don't go on copying an event as dada was, because it was a single one singularly."[45] Dada was a unique and "inimitable psycho-morphological gesture."[46] Notwithstanding this uniqueness, Huelsenbeck reports that Janco, Richter, Duchamp, and he discussed in 1955 the possibility of inaugurating some sort of neo-Dadaism themselves.[47]

Among the various statements made by Fluxus artists, one can find negative and affirmative evaluations of the relationship with Dada alongside each other. However, they tend to differ regarding the extent of the relationship rather than denying an affinity altogether. Ben Vautier proclaims that "Fluxus would not exist . . . without Cage, Marcel Duchamp, and Dada,"[48] corresponding with Kate Millett, who defines Fluxus as "a political art movement out of Dada."[49] Huelsenbeck, as Wolf Vostell adds, "represented for us Fluxus composers some sort of antipope to Marcel Duchamp."[50] In Maciunas's meticulous charts dedicated to the genealogy of Fluxus, Dada is listed without exception among the numerous influences and inheritances perceived by the Fluxus founder.[51] Assuming instead a more skeptical position, Ken Friedman argues that "the seeming relationship between Fluxus and Dada is more a matter of appearance than deep structure."[52] Dick Higgins agrees that the alleged affinity between the two movements is "extremely annoying and embarrassing to those of us who knew what Dada was or had been."[53] Looking back at the early use of the label "neo-Dada," Higgins comes to describe it as "ill-named, because there was really little in common between what we were doing and Dada."[54] However, both Friedman and Higgins do not go into more detail in outlining the difference.[55]

. . .

This rise in interest in Dada in the late 1950s and early 1960s leads us to look for the reasons behind it. Although my investigation concerns Fluxus in particular, it might implicitly touch upon other neo-Dada tendencies in an American context. Fluxus's initially overt reference to Dada and thus to a notably European art movement appears as surprising and paradoxical when taking into account Fluxus's equally explicit rejection of European culture. In a manifesto from 1963, Maciunas exhorts his readers to "purge the world of Europeanism," in other words of "bourgeois sickness, intellectual, professional, commercial culture" (fig. 21). He seeks liberation from "dead art, imitation, artificial, abstract art, serial art etc. etc." (Seven years later, Joseph Beuys reissued the manifesto in a modified version, replacing the word "Europeanism" with "Americanism," thus transforming the document into an anti-American pamphlet without modifying the reasons for such a rejection.) In a letter to Tomas Schmit, Maciunas explains the rejection of Europe with its "being the place supporting most strongly—& even originating the idea of—professional artist, art-for art ideology, expression of artists ego through art etc., etc."[56]

Considering these specifications, Fluxus's anti-Europeanism becomes apparent as the locus for the rejection of a specific set of cultural values and of a cultural tradition that Fluxus perceives to be of distinctly European origin. "All in all," Maciunas summarizes in a letter to Vostell, "we can say that Fluxus opposes to serious art and culture, as well as to their institutions, against Europeanism."[57] The polarity of Europeanism and anti-Europeanism epitomized by Fluxus can thus be read as a short-hand reference to two different art-historical genealogies, with Fluxus integrating itself into an artistic lineage deriving from Zurich and Berlin rather than from Paris or Munich and defining itself as of countercultural inclination. Here, I am not ignoring the fact that there have equally been Dada groups in Paris and New York at a slightly later date. But it was in its earliest formations that the movement found its most pronounced formulation. On similar grounds, Hausmann argued that Paris Dada did not truly exist, since it was infiltrated from the outset by the emerging movement of Surrealism.[58] And a parallel argument could be brought up in view of New York Dada, centered exclusively on the solitary figure of Duchamp and the later Surrealist Man Ray. "Against the codified high-rise modernity of the 1950s, the American postmodernism of the following decade attempted to resuscitate the strategies

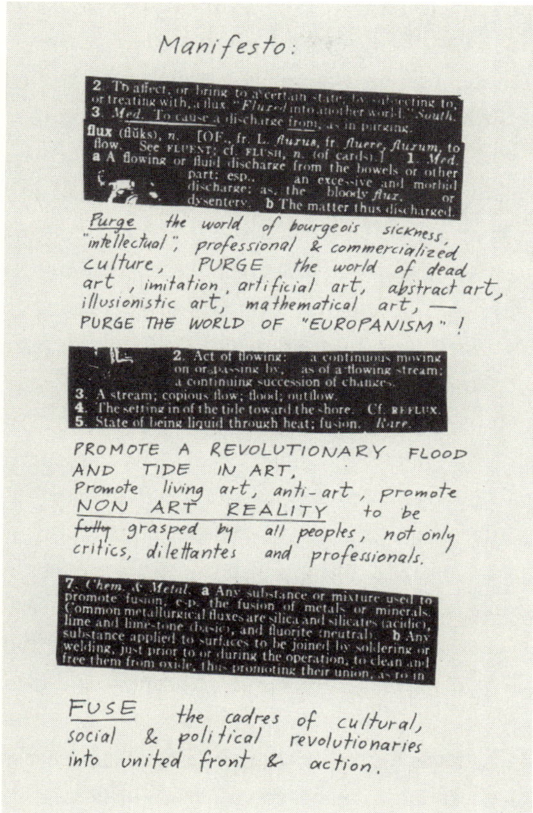

Manifesto:

2. To affect, or bring to a certain state, by subjecting to, or treating with, a flux. "*Fluxed* into another world." *South.* 3. *Med.* To cause a discharge from, as in purging.

flux (flŭks), *n.* [OF., fr. L. *fluxus*, fr. *fluere*, *fluxum*, to flow. See FLUENT; cf. FLUSH, *n.* (of cards).] 1. *Med.* a A flowing or fluid discharge from the bowels or other part; esp., an excessive and morbid discharge: as, the bloody *flux*, or dysentery. b The matter thus discharged.

Purge the world of bourgeois sickness, "intellectual", professional & commercialized culture, PURGE the world of dead art, imitation, artificial art, abstract art, illusionistic art, mathematical art, — PURGE THE WORLD OF "EUROPANISM"!

2. Act of flowing: a continuous moving on or passing by, as of a flowing stream; a continuing succession of changes. 3. A stream; copious flow; flood; outflow. 4. The setting in of the tide toward the shore. Cf. REFLUX. 5. State of being liquid through heat; fusion. *Rare.*

PROMOTE A REVOLUTIONARY FLOOD AND TIDE IN ART,
Promote living art, anti-art, promote NON ART REALITY to be ~~fully~~ grasped by all peoples, not only critics, dilettantes and professionals.

7. *Chem. & Metal.* a Any substance or mixture used to promote fusion, e.g. the fusion of metals or minerals. Common metallurgical fluxes are silica and silicates (acidic), lime and limestone (basic), and fluorite (neutral). b Any substance applied to surfaces to be joined by soldering or welding, just prior to or during the operation, to clean and free them from oxide, thus promoting their union, as to in

FUSE the cadres of cultural, social & political revolutionaries into united front & action.

Figure 21. George Maciunas, *Fluxus Manifesto (Purge the World)*, 1963.

and techniques of the European iconoclastic Avant-garde, adding to it an American perspective, something along the axis Dada—Duchamp—Warhol—Cage—Burroughs."[59] A lineage similar to the one outlined here by Andreas Huyssen is indicated in Maciunas's charts, notably the one outlining Fluxus's "Historical Development and Relationship to Avant-garde Movements."[60] In other words, the much-discussed distinction between modernism and avant-garde proves not only useful for describing the heterogeneous artistic situation prior to World War II, but appears of help in positioning the artistic tendencies of the 1950s and 1960s with regard to their art-historical references.

On the same grounds on which we can explain Fluxus's interest in Dada and its simultaneous rejection of Europeanism, we can understand its equally explicit rejection of Abstract Expressionism and thus of an artistic movement celebrated as distinctly American, that is, non-European. Fluxus artists would probably have agreed that Abstract Expressionism had found a new style and form of expression and had indeed achieved a shift of focus from Paris to New York and thus from Europe to America—but they would not abide the dominant perception of Abstract Expressionism as "an indigenous American artistic Avant-garde" and as "significantly new and non-European."[61] Instead, Fluxus would rather argue that Abstract Expressionism had not led to a replacement of historically European values of high culture and had not abandoned the established social rank of either art or of artist. It represented instead a late manifestation of artistic values and a concept of art belonging to European modernism. Thus, Fluxus's condemnation of Europeanism, its rejection of Abstract Expressionism, and its reference to Dada are all part of a desire to prioritize particular cultural values and notably a particular concept of art over another more dominant one, which Fluxus came to label "European" and which Dada had defined as "bourgeois." As David Doris outlines, the emerging neo-Dada tendencies sought "to stake out their own place within an alternative lineage of artistic production, a marginalized history that stood outside and against the mainstream."[62] Ken Friedman, who joined Fluxus in 1966, concludes: "This century saw two arts and two cultures growing side by side. One was public, heroic and national in inclination. The other was intellectual, hermetic and global in tone."[63]

These hermetic approaches, reemerging in the late 1950s and early 1960s, might be described as centered on a shared cause: an understanding of art as capable of initiating social or political change. Conceiving of a connection between art and life, they reanimate and continue the avant-garde's attempt to destabilize and question the dominant cultural values and institutionalized codes of practice and evaluation. As Jon Hendricks observes, both Dada and Fluxus "sought to unnerve a complacent, militaristic, decadent society by bringing art into direct confrontation with triviality and aesthetics."[64] On the basis of this shared endeavor, we can show that Fluxus's use of shock is a continuation of Dada's insofar as it functions both as expression and tool in the attempt to exert an influence upon life. More precisely, the interest in the senseless as a means to trigger shock belongs to an artistic genealogy of which both Dada and Fluxus are part.

The Sociocultural Context of Fluxus

The beginning of Fluxus is difficult to mark and rather occurred "in flux." When Fluxus emerged as a group in Wiesbaden in the summer of 1962, notably at the concert evening *Kleines Sommerfest: Après John Cage* mentioned earlier, some of the participants had already been doing work in the Fluxus spirit for several years. George Brecht, for example, had developed the "event" in 1959, inspired by John Cage's courses in experimental composition at the New School for Social Research in the late 1950s, to which Brecht had been invited by Cage.[65] La Monte Young had worked on compositions consisting of written instructions since 1959 and Jackson Mac Low had been interested in chance operations since the late 1950s. In Cage's *Music for Changes* from 1951 the decision about which notes were played and when they should sound was determined by consulting the *I Ching—Book of Changes*, which had only been translated into English the previous year. It was a proceeding Paik used for several of his compositions,[66] and it was resumed by Jackson Mac Low in *The Marrying Maiden* from 1958, where words and phrases were taken from the *I Ching*, chosen by systematic chance operations, and were accompanied by a score by Cage, the use of which was determined by the throwing of dice. With her *Lighting Piece* (light a match and watch it till it goes out), Yoko Ono had produced an event score as early as 1955, and Nam June Paik had performed pieces of "action music" since 1959. The first seminal publication to be considered a Fluxus work, *An Anthology of Chance Operations* (which included Henry Flynt's seminal text on concept art), was ready for printing in 1961, but only appeared in 1963 for financial reasons. Thus Fluxus had been under way for several years before its supposed 1962 starting date. Even more difficult to determine, however, is the end of Fluxus. Although some mark it by the death of Maciunas in April 1979, the other artists were "still as much of a group as we ever were," as Dick Higgins stated in 1982,[67] and continued doing Fluxus artworks, although not necessarily exclusively.

Just as complex as the group's time frame is its geographical and cultural positioning, thus raising the question of Fluxus's national allegiances. For an answer, one should distinguish between the movement's national makeup and its cultural context. Consisting of a heterogeneous international group of artists, Fluxus included individuals from Europe, America, and Asia (notably from Japan, with some artists of the group Hi Red Centre being involved in Fluxus activities),[68] many of whom did not live in their home country. A quick survey of the biographies of some of the core Fluxus artists illustrates both the movement's international composition and the nomadic lifestyle of its members. In both these aspects Fluxus resembles Dada, and for both movements this factor was more than merely circumstantial, becoming part of their self-understanding as having a global nature. As Geoffrey Hendricks writes, "Fluxus is about internationalism, the idea that in a certain way we are nomads."[69] With his plan to circumnavigate the world in a 145-foot converted minesweeper with a team of Fluxus artists, Maciunas strove to integrate this nomadism into their artistic practice.[70] Furthermore, the diversity extended beyond the movement's national composition. "Fluxus is the first or maybe even the only major movement to have members who are black, white, Asian, Hispanic, male gay and straight, female gay and straight," as Hanna Higgins, daughter of Dick Higgins, observes.[71]

To name a few examples, the movement's founder, head, and principal organizer, George Maciunas, was of Lithuanian origin, having been born in Kaunas in 1931.[72] Together with thousands of Lithuanians, his family fled the Russian army to Germany in 1944 and moved to New York in 1948, where he continued to live, with the exception of a stay in Germany between 1961 and 1963 and his move to a run-down farmhouse in Massachusetts shortly before his death. (He had bought this place as a potential site of a commune for Fluxus artists to live and work.) It was in those two years in Germany, while working as graphic designer for the U.S. Army, that Fluxus started to manifest itself as an artistic group. When Maciunas returned to New York early in 1963, having lost his position due to poor health, he was joined by many of the artists who had participated in the first Fluxus concerts in Germany. One of them was Nam June Paik, who had met Maciunas in 1961 and moved to New York in 1964, living there for several years.

Born in Seoul in 1932, Paik and his family fled the Korean War in 1950, moving first to Hong Kong and then to Tokyo, where he began to study. Having worked on composer Arnold Schönberg at Tokyo University, Paik resumed his studies in musicology and composition at the University of Munich and the Conservatoire in Freiburg between 1956 and 1958. Paik met Karlheinz Stockhausen in 1957 and joined the "Internationale Ferienkurse für Neue Musik" (International Summer Course for New Music) in Darmstadt in 1958, an annual event that had been launched in 1946 in order to compensate for the artistic backwardness fostered by the Nazi regime. Here, Paik attended a course and performances by John Cage, who also gave three papers on "Changes," "Indeterminacy," and "Communication." Paik thus made contact with the two individuals at the heart of vanguard music in the United States and in Germany, one of whom (Cage) was to become the "godfather" of Fluxus,[73] its primary teacher, and influential to the extent that Paik jokingly redefined BC as "Before Cage."[74] Together with Stockhausen, who eventually became its director, Paik worked at the groundbreaking Studio for Electronic Music at the broadcasting house of the WDR (Westdeutscher Rundfunk) in Cologne between 1958 and 1963. It was soon followed by the WDR Studio Acoustic Art, opening in January 1963.

Living in Cologne at the time, Paik also attended the landmark "Counter-festivals" in the studio of the painter Mary Bauermeister, who was to become Stockhausen's second wife.[75] He was joined there by Benjamin Patterson, another Fluxus artist-to-be, who also resided in Cologne between 1960 and 1962, taking active part in the thriving scene for contemporary music, before moving to New York in 1963. Born in Pittsburgh in 1934, Patterson had come to Germany in 1956, playing double bass in the Seventh U.S. Army Symphony Orchestra in Stuttgart until 1959. Emmett Williams, born in South Carolina in 1925, was yet another American artist who lived in Germany as an employee of the U.S. Army, working as a journalist for the army's newspaper *The Stars and Stripes* between 1955 and 1964, following a first visit to Germany in 1949. He returned to New York in 1966, functioning as editor-in-chief for Dick Higgins's Something Else Press until 1970. Dick Higgins himself was born in the United Kingdom but had moved to New York in the 1950s. Similarly, Yoko Ono, born in Tokyo in 1933, first moved with her family to San Francisco and then to Scarsdale, before she settled in New York, making her Soho loft a location for proto-Fluxus and Fluxus activities, like Bauermeister's studio in Cologne.

As this summary shows, the prevalent characterization of Fluxus as an American movement is based less on the nationality of its members than on the sociocultural context by which it is dominated. As Andreas Huyssen suggested, the postwar revival of artistic strategies and techniques of the avant-garde can be considered as a notably American appropriation and continuation of a European artistic tradition.[76] In the attempt to defend Charlotte Moorman's seminude performance of his *Opera Sextronique* in New York in 1967 (which ended with the arrest of both artists), Nam June Paik made a photocopied collage, in which he emphasized the performance as "advanced american [*sic*] avantgarde art,"[77] protesting against Charlotte Moorman's and his own arrest during the performance of the piece at the Cinematheque in New York on February 9, 1967. On the occasion of its first manifestations in West Germany and introducing itself as a "new way of life, coming from the United States,"[78] Fluxus appeared before the public by announcing itself as "Neo-Dada in the United States," being "born and nurtured in New York City."[79] Thus, New York was not so much the birthplace but the place of residence for many of the Fluxus artists, and notably for its initiator; Soho in particular became a primary base for Fluxus, the site of its headquarters and the focus of its activities. Already in 1966 Maciunas had tried to establish the Fluxhouse Cooperative, Inc., an artists' condominium in Soho, which he envisioned as a communal living and work space.

This positioning of Fluxus within a specific sociocultural context is important, as Fluxus reacts to this context. As much as the movement can be shown to be influenced by an Asian spirituality and a European artistic tradition, the sociocultural values it reacts to and opposes derive notably from an American context. Sharing Dada's urge for art to reconnect with society and be influenced by as well as influence life, Fluxus continued the historical avant-garde's "combination of radical aesthetic innovations with the attempt of revolutionizing not only artistic practice, but society as a whole."[80] In parallel with Dada, Fluxus's response can be shown to evolve on both an intellectual and a sensorial level and its interest in the renunciation of sense and triggering shock forms an integral part of this response.

We must therefore examine the specific qualities of the sociocultural situation in America as the 1950s became the 1960s in order to perceive what it is that Fluxus reacts to. Unlike Dada, whose members were in their early thirties at the outbreak of World War I (Hugo Ball, Raoul Hausmann, Tristan Tzara, and Hans Arp all born in 1886, Hans Richter in 1880, Kurt Schwitters in 1887, Walter Serner and Hannah Höch in 1889, and Richard Huelsenbeck in 1892) and whose biographies as well as artistic production were directly influenced by the experience of the war, Fluxus reacted rather to a postwar reality. With the majority of the artists being born at the beginning of the 1930s, they were only entering their teens when World War II began, and hardly any of them lived in Europe during wartime. Only the oldest among them, notably Emmett Williams (from 1943 to 1946) and George Brecht (from 1943 to 1945), served in the U.S. Army. As we have seen, Maciunas's move to Germany and then to New York was a consequence of the Red Army's reoccupation of Lithuania, and Paik's move away from South Korea was caused by its Soviet invasion—both occurrences in the aftermath of World War II. However, in comparison with the Dadaists, the Fluxus artists' biographies and, more specifically, their artistic orientation were not influenced by the war to a comparable degree. One prolific exception is Joseph Beuys, who served as radio operator and aviator in the German army and became a prisoner of war in 1945. His experiences of the war, and notably of crashing his bomber over the Crimea (which left him critically wounded and—according to his own account—in the healing hands of nomadic Tartars), have been extensively considered in relation to his work. It might be of interest to examine the relationship between his wartime activities and his maverick existence within Fluxus. But the context dominating Fluxus in general was not so much World War II as the Cold War. When Ralph Burmeister thus states that "Fluxus too responded to a post-war reality, that of the second world war and of the holocaust," I would agree with him with regard to Fluxus but would disagree concerning Dada.[81]

The postwar climate in the United States was dominated by a strong ideological dualism, exemplified in the political and ideological tensions between the United States and the Soviet Union. It culminated in the "shock of the century,"[82] when, by launching the first satellite into space, the United States' principal enemy, hitherto considered technologically and scientifically inferior, jolted an entire nation. The prevailing ideological dualism was not just the battle between communism and capitalism, but more fundamentally that between ideology and "no ideology." As the sociologist C. Wright Mills argued in his influential book on white-collar postwar American society, published in 1951 (the same year as Motherwell's seminal anthology on Dada), the prevailing political attitude of American society around 1950 was one of indifference.

Mills conceived this attitude as endorsed by the recent confrontation with ideological extremes and as being socially and economically supported by a climate of personal affluence and security.[83] "They are not radical, not liberal, not conservative, not reactionary; they are inactionary; they are out of it."[84] Interpreting the situation as a consequence of the preceding decades of depression and war, Arthur M. Schlesinger wrote in 1960: "We were tired of subordinating the reality of our daily lives to remote and abstract national objectives. We wanted a vacation from public responsibilities. . . . Lull was the natural and predictable result."[85] Lisa Phillips retrospectively portrays this "lull" in a more positive light, writing in the exhibition catalog on *The American Century* that "under Eisenhower's paternalistic leadership, stability and complacency reigned."[86] American society of the 1950s was centered on a white, affluent, middle class of conservative and conformist orientation.

In his book *The Lonely Crowd*, which became an immediate bestseller when published in 1950, David Riesman concurs with Mills, detecting a new form of political indifference that was far from being based on a lack of education and information. Instead, it spread among a well-educated, socially and economically secure class. It was furthermore this social class that expanded considerably in the decade in question. By 1956 the number of white-collar workers exceeded the combined number of blue-collar and agricultural workers.[87] Looking back at the 1950s in 1968, Ronald Berman wrote: "The liberal mainstream of American life had become solidified. If the tradition of the new proved unattractive that was true, in part, because the liberal community was satisfied with its status."[88]Apart from the lack of an immediate personal necessity for change and emendation, this indifference toward political matters was explained by Riesman with reference to the earlier ideological excesses, as a form of detachment: "This apathy cuts two ways. It deprives them of the capacity for enthusiasm and for genuine political involvement, but it also helps protect them from falling for many of the fairy tales about politics that have mobilized people in the past for political adventures."[89]

The political indifference and lack of social engagement did not, however, necessarily imply a weakening of this context's influence upon the artistic production of the time. Quite the contrary, as Klaus von Beyme observes with regard to Abstract Expressionism of the late 1940s and 1950s: "Never before—apart from the WWI and dictatorial systems—has the influence of political occurrences upon the development of painting been as strong as in the times of the Cold War."[90] He continues by specifying this influence: "The world's liberation from a fascist dictatorship and the overcoming of previous pro-communist sympathies amongst radical American artists left art free from political imperatives."[91] The rise of political neutrality, or rather passivity—in other words a "new liberalism powerfully situated midway between fascism and communism"[92]—unusually included both intellectuals and artists. Artistic and political engagement were conceived as distinctly separate issues.[93] Describing the artist as an autonomous, self-focused subject, creating works on the basis of introspection and subjective experience rather than by reacting to the external world, Samuel Kootz presents an unmistakable paradigm of the Abstract Expressionist:"The intrasubjective artist invents from personal experience; creates from an internal world rather than an external one. He makes no attempt to chronicle the American scene, exploit momentary political struggles, or stimulate nostalgia through familiar objects;

he deals, instead, with inward emotions and experiences."[94] In fact, the movement's abstinence from socio-critical and political issues was considered part of its dedication to abstraction. "To put it crudely (and in the confrontational Cold War climate it often was), realism tended to be seen as 'political' and abstraction as nonpolitical or 'pure' art," as Christine Lindey put it.[95] "Instead of making *cathedrals* out of Christ, man or 'life,' we are making . . . [them] out of ourselves, out of our own feelings,"[96] Barnett Newman confirms in his famous text "The Sublime Is Now" (1949), formulating an implicit reference to Kurt Schwitters's famous description of a column in his *Merzbau* as "cathedral of erotic misery." He thus solidifies the observation that the search for self became art's and the artist's central idea. As Jon Hendricks states in the foreword to the *Fluxus Codex*, the 1950s were "a time of political conservatism. A period in art of abstraction, individualism, and nationalism."[97]

However, Abstract Expressionism's political neutrality did not render it politically unusable within the ideological dispute of the Cold War—far from it. It was precisely Abstract Expressionism's political and ideological abstinence and its turn toward introspection and subjectivism that encouraged its co-option to promote the American ideal of "ideological liberty," as Serge Gilbaut convincingly argues,[98] and to be seen as the appropriate expression of the "free world." This rise of individualism is said to have emerged in conjunction with the United States' profound condemnation of communism; neither of these developed in Europe to a like degree. In Europe, the artist group CoBrA, for example, developed a mode of painting that showed stylistic affinities with Abstract Expressionism, but used art distinctly not only to stimulate "a new and fantastic way of seeing," as the CoBrA manifesto from 1948 states, but to show a clear commitment to communist ideology, aiming for a liberation of creativity from conventional, bourgeois culture.[99] (The failure of CoBrA to communicate its aims and achieve them might have been in fact a consequence of its stylistic affinities with Abstract Expressionism, which concealed their ideological differences.)[100]

Having discussed the Cold War's intense influence on the artistic production of Abstract Expressionism, what differed for the Fluxus artists was not the intensity of this influence but the form their artistic reaction took. We can conceive of Fluxus as in opposition not only to the leading art of its time, but also to the sociocultural context in which it was embedded, and, more specifically, to the artists' reaction to this context, thus showing a structural similarity with Dada and its rejection of Expressionism. Fluxus forms part of and contributes toward a change from the 1950s to the 1960s that was less a seamless shift than a rupture. On the part of the arts, this rupture was inaugurated by the decline of Abstract Expressionism; on the part of politics it started with the downturn of Joseph McCarthy's strong anticommunism. "Isolationism was temporarily dissolving in the mist of a new internationalism, the world was preparing for the 1960s, which, in retrospect, appeared as one of the most tumultuous, creative, and vibrant periods that Western culture has ever seen, certainly rivalling the first decades of the twentieth century in Europe."[101] In "The New Mood in Politics," Schlesinger delivers a detailed account of the shift underway and of the expectations at the dawn of the new decade:

> At periodic moments in our history, our country has paused on the threshold of a new epoch in our national life, unable for a moment to open the door, but aware that it must advance if it is to preserve its national vitality and identity. One feels that we are approaching such a moment now—that the mood which has dominated the nation for decades is beginning to seem thin and irrelevant; that it no longer interprets our desires and needs as people. . . . The Eisenhower epoch—the present period of passivity and acquiescence in our national life—is drawing to a natural end. . . . As we commit ourselves to this vast challenge, we will cross the threshold into what promises to be one of the exciting and creative epochs in our history.[102]

Schlesinger thus expresses the hope for a shift away from the passivity, self-indulgence, and introspection of the 1950s, where people had been "largely absorbed in themselves—in their own careers, their own lives, their own interests," and where "the badge of our self-indulgence has been the contemporary orgy of consumer goods."[103] Expressing his vision for the coming decade, he writes, "The hallmark of the '60's might well be the revival of a sense of supremacy of the public interest";[104] a tendency that would eventually culminate in the sociocultural agitation of 1968.[105]

With Schlesinger's vivid description of this turning point in the American sociocultural disposition at the very moment when Fluxus emerges, we can begin to understand the movement as part of this change, and locate it, as Jon Hendricks suggested, "in the centre of this maelstrom."[106] However, the spreading passivity was deplored not only on the level of a critical and intellectual engagement, but also more profoundly on the level of perceptive activity in general. Having become the wealthiest nation on earth, the United States in the 1950s "became trapped by its own affluence,"[107] spending more on advertising than on education.[108] Based on the unquestioned belief in a relentless expansion and the permanence of "the affluent society"—also the title of John Kenneth Galbraith's skeptical and much discussed book of 1958—the economy ignored the possibility and prediction of stagnation. And, indeed, consumption flourished: whereas in 1950 only 9 per cent of households in the United States owned a television set, this number rose to 87 per cent in 1960 and to 95 per cent by 1967,[109] and by the late 1960s, the average American citizen would spend more time in front of the TV than at work.[110] But the soaring influence of television is just one aspect of the enormous spreading of a "consumerist" attitude of what we might call the "passive receiver." This attitude can be described as consisting in an imbalance between production and reception. Whether we think of the purchase of goods or the consuming of televised information and entertainment, the consumers, users, and audiences found themselves increasingly confined to the role of the recipient, the receiver, becoming accustomed to an increasingly passive role with neither the possibility nor the desire for interaction, response, and reciprocal creativity. "Direct engagement yielded to vicarious involvement, and interpersonal, active communication was replaced by an impersonal, passive receptivity."[111]

This situation and its effects enable us to understand Fluxus as an artistic reaction to a prevailing mode of passive reception, and it helps to explain the attention that these artists gave to processes of sense perception. We will come to see the movement's attempt to reactivate the recipient's attitude as standing at the heart of Fluxus's endeavor to trigger an experience of shock and to irritate an established receptive situation. As I will argue, we can consider Fluxus's artistic undertaking as a response to the outlined sociocultural climate and, more specifically, to the dominance of a passive attitude manifesting itself on the two levels outlined earlier.

From Politics to a Worldview: Transforming the Senseless

The Fluxus artists' varying political opinions and activities can be shown to feed into a concept of art that is understandable not only as opposition and alternative to a dominating bourgeois or "European" tradition but also as a transposition of basic Marxist principles into the realm of art, containing a critique of capitalism and consumer culture. But Fluxus's criticism of the political and cultural structure in which it finds itself does more than take refuge in another set of political and cultural values. A deeper level of opposition is apparent, and of interest here, as it enables a better understanding of Fluxus's engagement with the senseless.

A first act of opposition can be found in the artists' resumption of a critical agenda for artistic production. In utter contrast to the prevailing climate of political indifference, Fluxus's leader took an overtly political stand from the outset, offending American society by explicitly sympathizing with communism, although never subscribing to a communist party himself.[112] Maciunas, whose mother had been secretary to Stalin's daughter,[113] made no secret of his sympathy with communism, which eventually led to his split from the Lithuanian community of Long Island, the members of which had recently escaped such political system by emigrating from the newly founded Lithuanian Soviet Socialist Republic. This distancing found expression in Maciunas's decision to change his first name from the Lithuanian Yurgis to the English equivalent George in 1961—an ironic move, given the fact that the slightest sympathy with communism at that time was at least as confrontational to U.S. citizens as it was to immigrants from Eastern Europe. "Emmett. I have to know how you feel about involving Fluxus politically with the party (you know which one)," asks Maciunas in a letter to Emmett Williams, whose answer to this question turned out to be distinctly negative.[114] Maciunas explains: "Our activities loose [*sic*] all significances if divorced from socio-political struggle going on now. We must coordinate our activities or we shall become another "new wave," another dada club, comming [*sic*] and going."[115]

The reference to Dada Berlin bears interesting implications when recalling what has been said earlier about its communist affiliations. Maciunas's desired demarcation from Dada Berlin is thus not based on a lack of communist sympathies in Dada but on the desire for a closer coordination of artistic production and party political activities. As Maciunas and Henry Flynt (philosopher, musician, communist, and "anti-art activist") demand in a manifesto from 1965, "communists must give revolutionary leadership in culture."[116] In an undated draft of a letter to an unnamed recipient, held in the Sohm-Archive in Stuttgart, Maciunas announces "the prime objective of promoting fusion and unity between the revolutionary-realist society of USSR and the revolutionary-realist artists of the world" (fig. 22).[117] In this letter, Maciunas expresses his intention to "commence coordinating our efforts with the socio-political aims

We wish to seek your esteemed auspices in regards to two projects we are embarking upon with the prime objective of promoting fusion and unity between the revolutionary-realist society of USSR and the revolutionary-realist artists of the world. Plans for this programme under the name of FLUXUS commenced shortly after a letter was sent by the undersigned to the Chairman of the Presidium, a copy of which is enclosed. Since then considerable support was obtained from all important cadres of new concretist art gaining for the movement increasing momentum and new adherents. In consideration to our original and primary objective and the revolutionary political orientation of the adherents, it was important in our belief, that we should commence coordinating our efforts with the socio-political aims of your party leadership.

The first part of the programme consists of publishing a periodical in bilingual editions, each issue being edited and assemblied in a separate country or region. It is by way of these publications that we would be able to express in most articulate terms: (1) our desire for purging the sickness of the bourgeois world, (2) our desire for continuous moving forward of arts, music and philosophy towards concretism-realism and (3) our desire for reapproachement and unity between concretist artists of the world and the concretist society which exists in USSR. All these objectives are best summarized in the very meaning of flux and fluxus. The enclosed prospectus outlines our planned contents of each forthcomming issue.

The second part of the FLUXUS programme consists of organizing a world-wide concretist art and music festival,extending and centering in the socialist states, during which newest and most progressive realist-concretist visual and aural art, compositions from all parts of the world could be presented in the light of discussions regarding their concretism and their consistency to the Materialist concepts. We would like to propose a 3 to 4 month long "exhibit-tour" throughout USSR (in most European and Siberian Republics), during which it would be offered free to the public at any town or village the tour route would lead us through. We firmly believe that such an extensive exhibit-tour would promote the fusion between the revolutionary society and the international community of the revolutionary artists, composers, writers and philosophers.

In connection to these two projects, we wish to seek your esteemed auspices specifically in: (1) promoting cooperation of the most revolutionary and concretist artists in USSR with the FLUXUS programme of action (2) providing political leadership to the FLUXUS movement, (3) providing support to us in our plans of extending and centering the festival series of new concretist art in USSR and (4) possibly permitting us to establish the directive and operational headquarters for all FLUXUS activities (publications & concert-exhibits) anywhere within the USSR. We believe such a move would greatly increase the success of our objectives to promote concretist art in USSR, strengthen the allegiance of the avant-garde of the world towards USSR and finally to help implant again in USSR the leadership of revolutionary arts.

Hoping our plans will receive favourable consideration we remain yours very respectfully,

Figure 22. Letter by George Maciunas, undated. Typewritten draft or transcript. Archiv Sohm, Staatsgalerie Stuttgart.

of your party leadership," and pleads for the USSR's active support of "concrete art," in the attempt to foster "unity between concretist artists of the world and the concretist society which exists in USSR." Maciunas asks for the addressee's "esteemed auspices . . . [in] providing political leadership to the FLUXUS movement . . . and possibly permitting us to establish the directive and operational headquarters for all FLUXUS activities . . . anywhere within the USSR." This document is most likely a draft or copy of the letter Maciunas is said to have written to Nikita Khrushchev, first secretary of the Soviet Communist Party (1953–1964) and prime minister of the Soviet Union (1958–1964), in the attempt to pave the ground for an extensive Fluxus tour through the country, which he considered "a good possibility . . . for summer 1964 or more likely 1965" and for which he had been granted "one freight car attached to freight trains," as well as the possibility of giving "free concerts in freight yards whenever and wherever train stops."[118] As Mac Low remembers, Maciunas "once showed me a very long letter he'd just sent to Premier Khrushchev in which he urged the Soviet ruler to encourage 'realistic art' . . . as being more consonant with 'a realistic economic system' such as that of the Soviet Union than the old-fashioned 'socialist-realist' art then in favour."[119]

Maciunas's fierce response to an independent series of performances in various cities in the USSR undertaken by Eric Andersen, Andersen's brother, and (which turned out to be a joke) Emmett Williams, Tomas Schmit, and Addi Køpcke, gives expression to the importance to Maciunas of a successful anchoring of Fluxus in the USSR. As Andersen remembers later, "We told him [incorrectly] that we . . . had just performed Nam June Paik's *Pissing Contest* at Red Square in Moscow in front of tens of thousands of happy communists."[120] Maciunas reacted by "denouncing these . . . renegades and impostors most emphatically,"[121] excluding from Fluxus everyone whom he believed to have taken part in this tour. He condemned the provocation of such "vulgar shock" as a "sabotage of Fluxus" and notably of its plans to take root in the USSR (fig. 23).[122]

Maciunas's strong desire for a joint venture between party politics and artistic production—and, more specifically, between communism and Fluxus—also finds expression in the ideological link he draws between Fluxus and the Left Front of Art (LEF) of the early 1920s. A distinctly political artistic gathering in a communist context, the LEF had fought against an aestheticism freed from any political agenda, disqualifying it as a "passive reaction to reality." [123] Reality, as Sergej Tretjakov put it, becomes paralyzed when translated "into the language of aesthetic illusions."[124] LEF consequently sought to dissolve the demarcation between art and life, similar not only to Fluxus but also to Dada. Indeed, when Boris Arvatov announces the need to declare war on the bourgeoisie by attacking its values and conventions, LEF appears distinctly akin to Dada.[125] (Majakowskij, founder of LEF, was acquainted with both Wieland Herzfelde, founder of the communist Malik-Verlag, and his brother John Heartfield.[126])

However, returning to Maciunas, we should not forget that neither his

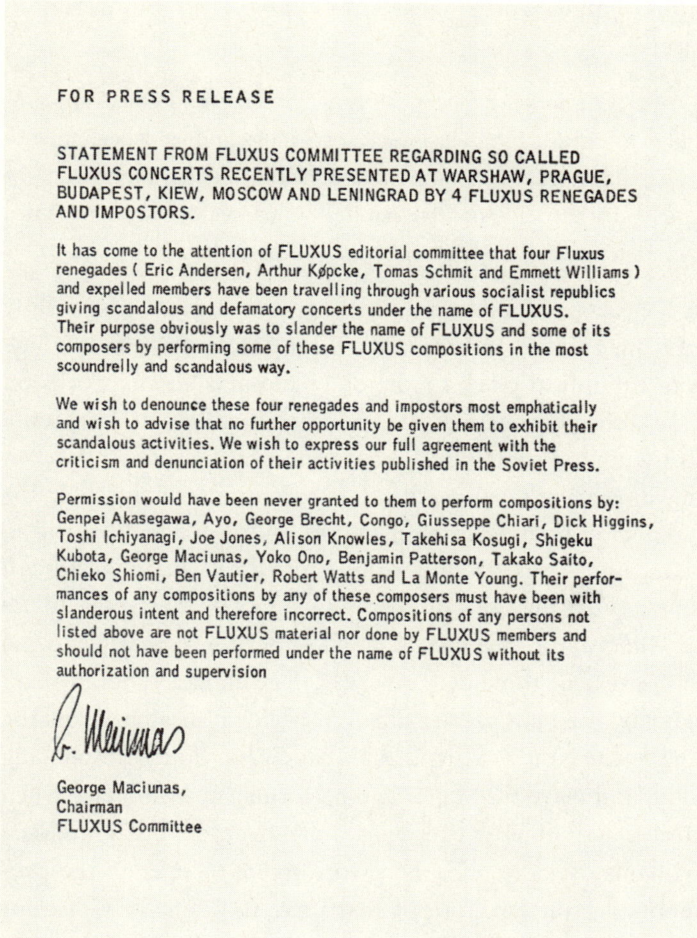

FOR PRESS RELEASE

STATEMENT FROM FLUXUS COMMITTEE REGARDING SO CALLED FLUXUS CONCERTS RECENTLY PRESENTED AT WARSHAW, PRAGUE, BUDAPEST, KIEW, MOSCOW AND LENINGRAD BY 4 FLUXUS RENEGADES AND IMPOSTORS.

It has come to the attention of FLUXUS editorial committee that four Fluxus renegades (Eric Andersen, Arthur Køpcke, Tomas Schmit and Emmett Williams) and expelled members have been travelling through various socialist republics giving scandalous and defamatory concerts under the name of FLUXUS. Their purpose obviously was to slander the name of FLUXUS and some of its composers by performing some of these FLUXUS compositions in the most scoundrelly and scandalous way.

We wish to denounce these four renegades and impostors most emphatically and wish to advise that no further opportunity be given them to exhibit their scandalous activities. We wish to express our full agreement with the criticism and denunciation of their activities published in the Soviet Press.

Permission would have been never granted to them to perform compositions by: Genpei Akasegawa, Ayo, George Brecht, Congo, Giusseppe Chiari, Dick Higgins, Toshi Ichiyanagi, Joe Jones, Alison Knowles, Takehisa Kosugi, Shigeku Kubota, George Maciunas, Yoko Ono, Benjamin Patterson, Takako Saito, Chieko Shiomi, Ben Vautier, Robert Watts and La Monte Young. Their performances of any compositions by any of these composers must have been with slanderous intent and therefore incorrect. Compositions of any persons not listed above are not FLUXUS material nor done by FLUXUS members and should not have been performed under the name of FLUXUS without its authorization and supervision

G. Maciunas

George Maciunas,
Chairman
FLUXUS Committee

Figure 23. Press release by George Maciunas, undated. Typewritten draft or transcript. Archiv Sohm, Staatsgalerie Stuttgart.

reference to LEF nor the desire to establish a Fluxus headquarters in the USSR found any consensus within the group of Fluxus artists. Maciunas's rather utopian concept of communism was hardly shared by any of the others,[127] with the exception of Henry Flynt, whose affiliation to Fluxus was based not on his artistic work but his political views. As Flynt himself states in a letter to Harry Ruhé from 1976, he "never had any connection with Fluxus. I did work with George Maciunas on a series of projects that no other publisher would support at that time."[128] Reminiscent of Dada and notably of the dispute around the Barrès trial, the heterogeneous Fluxus group disagreed about the level of political activism acceptable within Fluxus works. Jackson Mac Low gives an illustration of this variance:

> On April 6, 1963, at a time when some of us were engaged in practical political work and demonstrations against nuclear weapons and were beginning to protest U.S. activities against the Vietnamese people, George proposed . . . a series of bizarre, disruptive, antisocial manifestations, such as breaking down trucks in the tunnels under the Hudson River to stop traffic.[129]

As the many negative responses to this proposal indicate (Mac Low even resigned from Fluxus), the majority of the artists drew a clear line between practical political work on the one hand and Fluxus works on the other.[130] As a consequence, Maciunas criticized Brecht, La Monte Young, Mac Low, and in particular Daniel Spoerri as apolitical.[131]

Indeed, the movement's socio-critical interventions rarely took the shape of an explicitly political subject matter and message, as it did in a poster by Maciunas from around 1967 entitled *U.S.A. Surpasses All the Genocide Records!* (fig. 24). Emmett Williams's performance *White for Governor Wallace*, for example, is much rather representative of the movement. It consists of three performers each reading a random book silently on stage by the light of a candle. If a performer came across the word *white*, he or she would extinguish his candle, without pronouncing the word aloud, and leave the stage. The performance would end when the last performer had gone.[132] Stopping short of an explicitly political statement, Williams uses the unspoken word *white* to refer to the pro-segregation politics of the governor of Alabama. As *White for Governor Wallace* suggests, and as was indicated earlier through Maciunas's paralleling of artistic and political "concretism," subtler levels were found to express a socio-critical intention or political orientation.

It is worth examining Fluxus's concept of art and, more specifically, its conception of the art object and the artist, in this regard, as they can be seen as a transposition of Marxist values. The artists' ferocious rejection of an understanding of art as the creation of unique, extraordinary, and highly valuable objects created by an exclusive group of people and to be owned by an economic and social elite can be understood in this manner. Describing its activities as "art-amusement" in the tradition of the circus and of Vaudeville, Maciunas defines Fluxus through its oppositions to "high art."[133] (Indeed, games and game structures played a frequent part within Fluxus works, culminating in a several-day-long Fluxus game

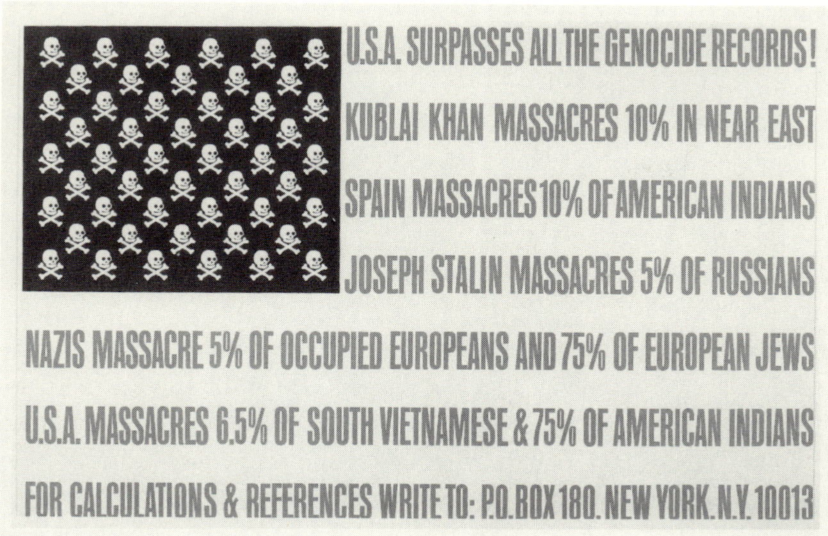

Figure 24. George Maciunas, *U.S.A. Surpasses All the Genocide Records!*, 1967. Poster.

party, in New York in May 1973.) More laconically, Ben Vautier proclaimed, "Fluxus is a pain in art's ass."[134]

The deliberate rejection of the value and rarity of the art object finds its counterpart in the reduction of the rank of the artist. Maciunas in particular requested the irrelevance of the artist's ego and strove for anti-individualism, collective production, and collective authorship, features that were all listed in a letter by him to Tomas Schmit from January 1964.[135] And we can find Nam June Paik stating that "I was never really anti-art, but I was anti-ego. Post-industrial society will be a kind of egoless society is what I think."[136] In expanding Marx's appeal for public ownership of all means of production, Nam June Paik also asked for public ownership of the means of distribution. Fluxus conceived of art as something ideally made, distributed, and owned by everybody, aiming at the creation of works that were cheap and easy to produce, and were consequently available without limit and economically worthless. Pursuing its concept of anti-art, Fluxus opposed "the purposefulness, formfulness and meaningfulness of art; Anti-art is life, is nature, is true reality—it is one and all."[137] It was, as Vautier outlined, "an attitude rather than a product."[138]

Fluxus's affinity with basic Marxist values and their transposition of them onto the realm of art means Fluxus can be seen as simultaneously formulating an artistic critique of consumerism and capitalism. The immateriality of many of the Fluxus works, which culminates in the "artist's exertion of nothingness,"[139] can be understood as both a reaction to and rejection of "a society where a commercial meaning will be the prime one to be attached to almost anything."[140] Upon this backdrop, as Victor Musgrave suggests, "one might say that the truly worthwhile work of art will be the one that is completely meaningless."[141] A meaningless—and consequently worthless—artistic production undermines the commercial dynamics of capitalist economy in general and the art market in particular. In this vein, Paik planned to place an advertisement in a New York newspaper seeking for a "member of the club for nothing, of nothing, by nothing, between nothing, after nothing, beyond nothing."[142]

Like Dada, Fluxus strove to strip artistic expression of its significance and sensible qualities as part of a questioning of the established system of constructing and evaluating meaning. Modifying the early twentieth-century writer Ryunosuke Akutagawas's conviction that "the perpetual evolution is the perpetual UNsatisfaction,"[143] Paik stated correspondingly that "the sole achievement of dialectics consisted in its proving that constant development corresponds with constant dissatisfaction."[144] In this, he gives expression to a skepticism concerning Western notions of rationality, progress, and teleology very close to Dada. "Why do you need this meticulous proceeding in dualist[ic] terms?," asks Paik,[145] and Joseph Beuys states correspondingly: "For many people, causal meaning is perceived in opposition to acausal meaning—non-sense. However, if a mode of thinking is to do justice to reality, it has to include both modes of thinking. Of course, actual non-sense does exist."[146]

We only have to repeat Hans Richter's explanation that "Dada took hold of something that can neither be grasped nor explained within the conventional framework of "either/or,"[147] or quote Hans Arp's postulation that "dada is for the senseless which does not mean nonsense,"[148] to perceive the similarity.

In the case of both movements, the rejection of meaningful sense making can be interpreted as the attempt to step outside the established system of defining what is and what is not meaningful, to question the established criteria on the basis of which meaning is established, and to propose alternative possibilities. When Owen Smith consequently focuses on Fluxus's process of meaning making as "the continuous deconstruction of established meaning and the projection of new possibilities,"[149] his observation is crucial to our concern, as it indicates the simultaneous destruction and production of sense. Similar to Dada, Fluxus's notion of new meaning incorporates guidelines conventionally considered as senseless or, to choose a different word, irrational.

> The goal or aspiration of much of the tradition of Western thought has been directed towards the establishment of meaning and presence as an outgrowth of fixed abstract essences or higher conceptual ideals. . . . [Fluxus] rejects this tradition and posits instead a view of the world and its operations which celebrates an absence of a higher meaning or an unified conceptual framework. . . . If there is an end or goal in the Fluxus world view it is to have no fixed end or goal.[150]

This conclusion by Smith resonates with Tzara's proclamation that "the most acceptable system is on principle to have none."[151] Like Dada, Fluxus activities set out to challenge the construction of meaning and the definition of significance according to the established value system.

Unlike Dada, however, Fluxus integrated this endeavor into a specific philosophical tradition, to which Smith alludes when describing Fluxus's opposition to "the tradition of Western thought," thus implying an affiliation with non-Western traditions of thinking. This interpretation is hardly surprising or far-fetched—rather, Smith's is just one of the many references to Zen Buddhism made not only by scholars (the most extensive one being David Doris's text "Zen Vaudeville") but by Fluxus artists themselves.[152] Ken Friedman had become interested in Zen and Buddhist literature around 1959 and thus even prior to his engagement with Fluxus, and Emmett Williams, though he remained skeptical about the mixing of Fluxus and Zen,[153] went to live with a Soto Zen master at the Ryodenji Temple for two months in 1976, after having toured Japan with his Fluxus colleague Ay-O. Also, Robert Fillou became a Tibetan Buddhist after Fluxus had come to an end. As regards Zen theory, Fluxus artists were notably influenced by Daisetz Taitaro Suzuki, whose extensive writings provided the most important and influential basis not only for them but for the rising Western interest in Zen more generally. This interest experienced a considerable boom in America through the Beat lifestyle and literature toward the end of the 1950s, initiated, for example, by Jack Kerouac's 1958 novel *Dharma Bums*.[154] It is a boom that might be attributed to a reemerging need for spiritual or religious direction, with the late 1950s having entered, in Arthur Schlesinger's terms, a "phase of psychological restlessness and spiritual discontent."[155] In the case of Fluxus, however, the interest in Zen derived notably from John Cage, who attended lectures by Suzuki in New York in the late 1940s and early 1950s, as did Mac Low, Paik, and quite likely George Brecht.[156] This functioning of Cage as a link between Zen and Fluxus brought Emmett Williams to consider it more accurate that "Fluxus has a direct connection with John Cage" than "a direct connection with Zen."[157] Cage, as Ben Vautier agrees, "has done two brainwashings. The first, at the level of contemporary music by the notion of indeterminateness, the other, by his teaching through the spirit of Zen and his will to depersonalise art."[158] In a 1963 issue of the German magazine *Magnum*, the "demonstrations and manifestations" of Fluxus were described as intending "to enmesh life, which they perceive as nonsensical and absurd, with nonsensical and absurd activities, gestures, words and sounds—in order to make it liveable. . . . Dadaism serves as their paragon—if denied. . . . Zen Buddhism delivers the basis of their world-view."[159] Indeed, in his last interview, Maciunas described Fluxus "as being more like Zen than Dada."[160] His preference of Zen over Dada is understandable, as it implies the movement's integration into a history of ideas rather than into an art-historical development, which would contradict Fluxus's claim for anti-art as much as it did for Dada.

This link with Zen can provide us with a useful terminology for describing Fluxus's artistic endeavors. Fluxus's concept of the senseless, in particular, can be defined with reference to the Zen distinction between discursive and intuitive knowledge.[161] Zen considers discursive knowledge to be based on "the self-identification of contradictions and not the unification or synthesizing of opposites," whereas intuitive knowledge encompasses "the Buddhist logic of self-identity."[162] It is no longer confined to the limits of dualisms. "When we say a thing is, it is an affirmation; when we say it is not, it is a negation. This is true in the world of distinction, it is the very nature of distinction that it is so; negation and affirmation cannot be together all at once."[163]

We can understand Fluxus as striving for the momentary manifestation of intuitive knowledge, defined as nondiscriminative, void of concepts, and based on dissolving the distinction between subject and object. Its enterprise could be described as the temporary suspension of the ever-dominant discursive approach, continuing with the Zen attempt to "foster a direct, unmediated relationship between the mind and reality."[164] As we saw earlier, it was this discursive knowledge based on rationality and dualisms to which Dada had been opposed, since it likewise sought to redefine meaning in a way that could include rather than exclude oppositions. Reminiscent of Dada, "the inconsistencies of Fluxus add up to a logic of their own, anti-rational in the same way that Zen uses anti-reason to produce the blinding flash of understanding."[165] Clearly, the new "logic" is illogical if evaluated according to the prevalent understanding of logic.

Art as Perception

Fluxus's renunciation of meaning and sense as a means of questioning the principles by which they are defined and established—which it shares with Dada—led it to use shock in a comparable way. As especially exemplified in the works and intentions of Nam June Paik, called a "cultural terrorist,"[166] Fluxus's triggering of shock emerges from the transgression of what had hitherto been conceived as artistic expression. Paik, who developed his performances described as action music in "reaction to the society in which he live[d]," as he states himself,[167] caused shock frequently and intentionally by confronting the recipient with utterly unexpected occurrences. Forcing the recipient into a state of insecurity and a lack of understanding initiated by something perceived as utterly senseless and distinctly nonartistic, Fluxus intended not to amuse but to irritate and ultimately to generate shock, as with Dada's excess of heterogeneous impulses and simultaneous manifestations. In George Brecht's *For a drummer, variation 1, 2, 3, 4*, for example, "all variations [are to be] performed simultaneously."[168] Paik himself describes his "sosaid action music" as an explicit attack on the audience.[169] Paik and his fellow artists sought to introduce "aggression into music" (figs. 25–27).[170] Entering the stage in silence, Paik "tended to shock the audience by dint of "as quick as a flash" activities," as Karlheinz Stockhausen remembers.[171] Allan Kaprow recalls that Paik "shocked his musical audience" by "sudden rippings of others' neckties" (Paik had spontaneously cut off Cage's necktie during a concert of his in Cologne in 1960), by "his soap-lathered head plunging, screaming into a washtub, nearly drowning," or by "his demolitions of pianos."[172] Cage attests that "Paik's work, conversation, performances, daily doings never cease by turn to amaze, delight, shock and sometimes terrify me."[173]

The destruction of coherent meaning and the production of something new and unexpected have not lost their ability to shock. In a manner typical of Fluxus, Paik combines disparate and inhomogeneous elements to produce new and unexpected meanings and to jolt the audience. The violent destruction of musical instruments, repeatedly used by Paik and

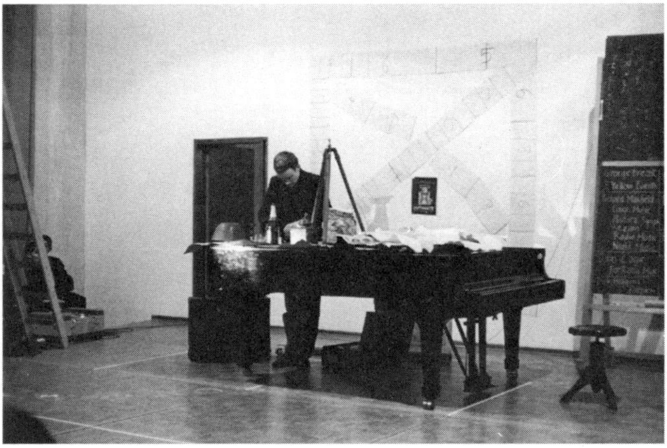

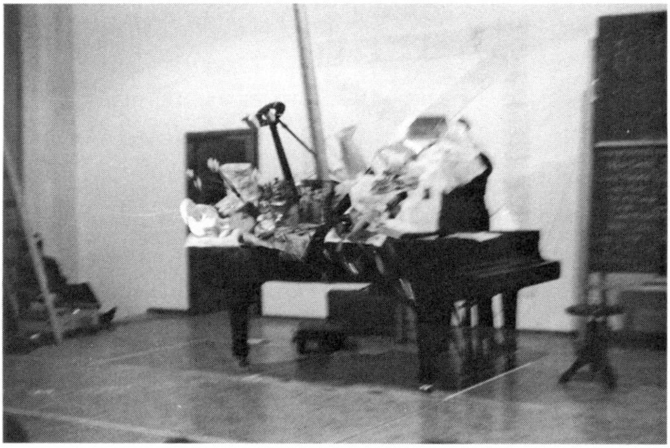

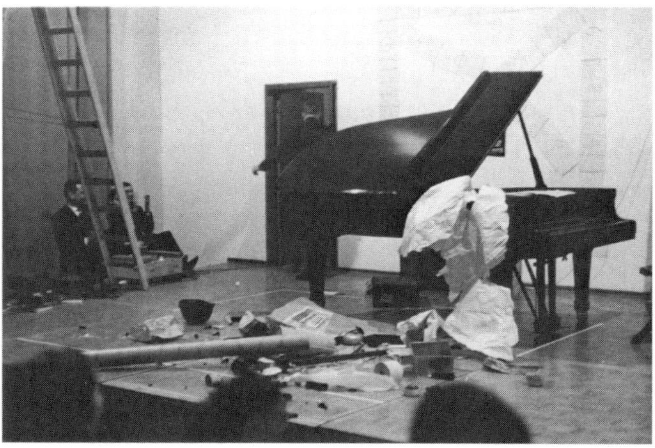

Figures 25–27. Tomas Schmit, *Three Piano Pieces for George Maciunas*, 1962. Performed at Fluxusfestival, Kunstakademie Düsseldorf, 1963. Black-and-white photographs. Photos by Manfred Leve.

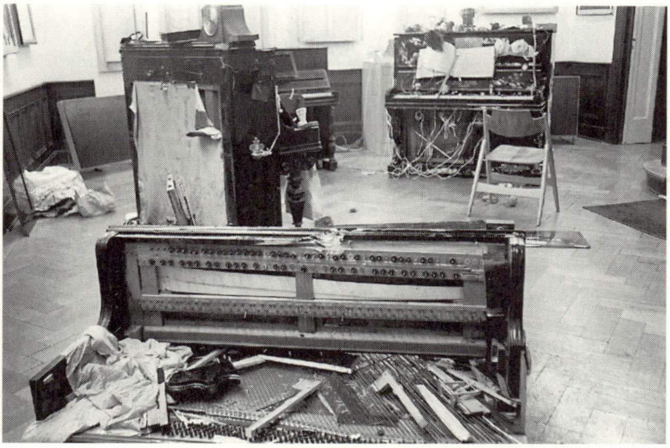

Figure 28. Nam June Paik, *Exposition of Music—Electronic Television*, exhibition view, 1963. Black-and-white photograph. Photo by Manfred Montwé. Museum Moderner Kunst Stiftung Ludwig Wien, Vienna.

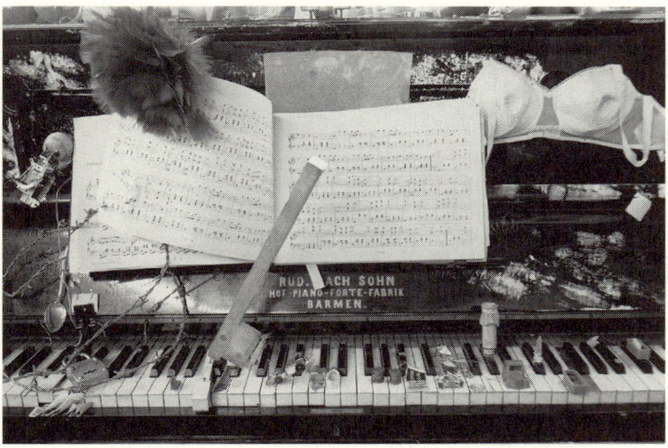

Figure 29. Nam June Paik, *Klavier Intégral* (detail), in *Exposition of Music—Electronic Television*, 1963. Black-and-white photograph. Photo by Manfred Montwé. Museum Moderner Kunst Stiftung Ludwig Wien, Vienna.

others, was one such unexpected and irritating activity and openly attacked the established notion of high art and the expectations brought to acts of artistic production. "The piano is a taboo. It needs to be destroyed,"[174] Paik states, seeking to smash "everything . . . in the music tradition" (figs. 28–29).[175] In Paik's famous piece of action music, *One for Violin* (1962), the performer raises the violin slowly above his head, before crashing it down on the table, thus smashing the instrument into pieces. And in *Zen for Walking*, Paik trailed his *Violin on a String* behind him on the floor (fig. 30). When Robin Page performed his *Guitar Piece*, consisting of the artist kicking a violin off the stage, out of the room, out of the building, and around the block, at the ICA in late October 1962, it "thoroughly shocked the Londoners, gentle as it was, and turned off Britain to Fluxus for another ten years."[176] (In this, however, the reaction of the British audience was not so different from the German one, as Maciu-

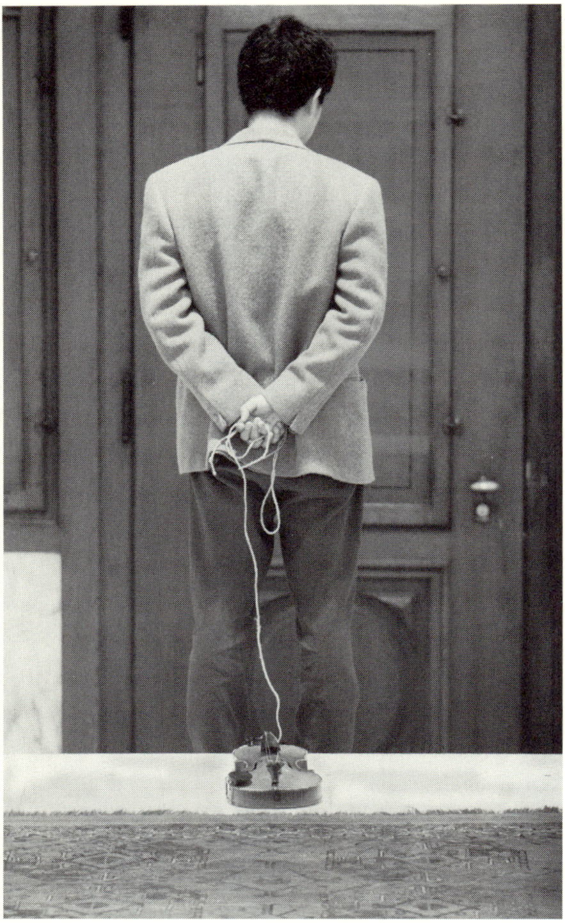

Figure 30. Nam June Paik, *Zen for Walking* (*Action with Violin with String*), 1961. Black-and-white photograph. Photo by Manfred Montwé. Museum Moderner Kunst Stiftung Ludwig Wien, Vienna.

nas recalls in a letter to La Monte Young in 1963: "German sentiments about this "instrument" . . . were hurt and they made a row about it."[177]) The event was part of a Fluxus concert at the ICA on October 21, 1962, during the dramatic climax of the conflict between Kennedy and Khrushchev over Cuba. The audience's reactions were hardly much different elsewhere. "How can this be explained?" wondered a journalist reviewing Paik's *Exposition of Music—Electronic Television* at the Galerie Parnass in Wuppertal in 1963. "In Germany there is an explanation for everything,"[178] he continued, admitting no place for a merely meaningless activity.

However, Fluxus's interest in shock is not only linked to a questioning of sense, with shock being a reaction to its destruction and withdrawal. It also has a function on a sensory level, a function resulting from the capacity of shock to jolt the audience and break open the established structures of reception, achieving the recipient's forceful and possibly violent awakening from a perceptive lethargy furthered by habit. "People who come to my concerts or see my objects need to be transferred into another state of consciousness. They have to be high. And in order to put them into this state of highness, a little shock is required. . . . Anyone who came to my exhibition saw the head and was high."[179] Here, Paik refers to his exhibition in Wuppertal, in which the truncated head of a cow was suspended from the ceiling, greeting—and possibly shocking—the visitor (fig. 31). In his piece *Dragging Suite* (date unknown), Paik imagines a similarly grueling scenario: "naked or clothed dolls, broken, bloody or new dolls, real man or woman, musical instruments, etc." to be dragged "by a string along the streets, stairs, floors."[180] Returning to Paik's Wuppertal exhibition, the severed head was deliberately intended to shock the audience.

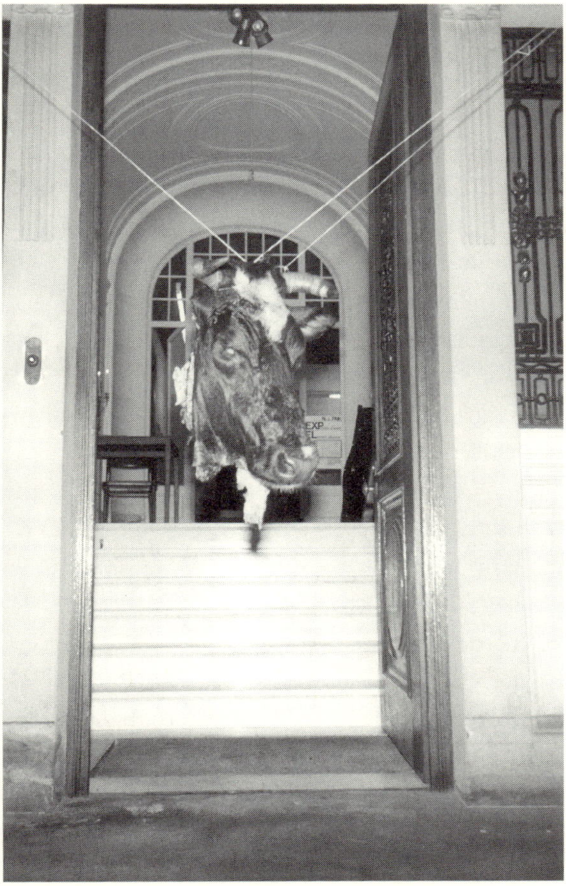

Figure 31. Nam June Paik, *Cow's Head,* in entrance to exhibition *Exposition of Music—Electronic Television*, Wuppertal, 1963. Black-and-white photograph. Photo by Rolf Jährling. The Museum of Modern Art, New York. The Gilbert and Lila Silverman Fluxus Collection Gift, 2008.

Effected by the suspended head of a cow or by the sudden destruction of an instrument, the occurrence of shock is connected to the disruption of an expected experience. It defines a moment when "thinking suddenly stops in a configuration pregnant with tensions,"[181] as Walter Benjamin phrased it. As a moment of irritation and nonunderstanding, it establishes a fundamental rupture, an uncompromising discontinuity that runs "right through the middle of the lived Now," as Ernst Bloch described what he called the "unbearable moment."[182]

The reasons for Fluxus's determination to push the audience out of its lethargy and end its attitude of passive reception are found in what was said earlier about the sociocultural context of Fluxus. With his groundbreaking appropriation of the television both as an object and technique for his own creative work, Nam June Paik is certainly the clearest example of Fluxus's reaction to this observed spreading of the passive recipient. With his famous slogan "Television has attacked us for a lifetime, now we strike back"—which was also the title of the first footage Paik recorded with his new video-camera in 1965[183]—he gives explicit expression to the attempt to reawaken the recipient's disposition, seeking "to humanize the technology"[184] and to reactivate the role of the recipient. "Communication means two-way communication. One-way communication is nothing but indoctrination,"[185] said Paik, and he set out to deprive television of the flood of impulses and thus of the information and meaning it generally delivers, turning it into an "empty" medium, subverting both the TV's role and the viewer's expectations (fig. 32). Allan Kaprow, who was equally interested in the activation of the recipient,[186] said of Paik: "He shook up the habits of our minds in the past, he shakes up the electrical pathways in the television brain. If only to clear the air for wonderment and positive action. Once cleared, work begins."[187]

However, Fluxus's endeavor cannot be confined to a critique of the mass media, but pursues the ferocious rejection of the passive receiver on a more general level. The many Fluxus statements outlining the centrality of the senses also indicate an intent to modify sense perception. As Ben Vautier states, "Fluxus is the major part of the education as to John Cage, Dadaism and Zen."[188] By stating this lineage, he not only implicitly expresses the relevance of sense perception, standing equally at the core of Cage, Dada, and Zen, but also indicates the educational interest attached to this endeavor. Responding to Gilbert Silverman's request to characterize the "philosophy, attitudes, influences and purposes" of Fluxus with a maximum of ten words (a request with which Silverman

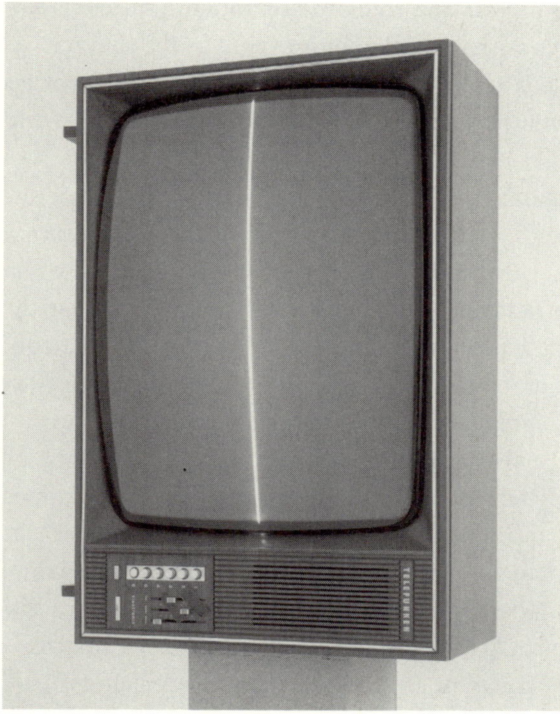

Figure 32. Nam June Paik, *Zen for TV*, 1963 (authorized version, 2006). TV monitor. Photo by Jens Ziehe. Nationalgalerie im Hamburger Bahnhof—Museum für Gegenwort, Staatliche Museen zu Berlin.

approached about forty-five former Fluxus artists in 1981), Mieko Shiomi defined Fluxus as: "How to view and feel the world with innovated perception."[189] On another occasion, Patterson explained the purpose of his works as an attempt to perform a "momentous step into a new field of experience."[190] Correspondingly, Paik described his compositions not as objects, but as "possibilities of experience" [*Erfahrungsmöglichkeiten*].[191] Many Fluxus works can indeed be understood as providing "a frame for perception and the experience of looking,"[192] as Bracken Hendricks (son of Geoffrey Hendricks) outlines.

The same endeavor to influence, modify, and ameliorate the level of sense perception within the receptive process has been observed in Dada, also a response to the prevailing sensorial situation generated by the sociocultural climate. However, since the context had changed, the two movements actually strive in contrary directions with regard to the receptive attitude that they seek to initiate in their audience. Dada's interest in creating an overload of incongruous, concurrent sensual impulses was analyzed earlier as part of the endeavor to imitate reality *appropriately*. "The non-sense of Dada," as Hausmann had outlined, "was the sense of all senses simultaneously."[193] Having recognized a tumultuous conglomerate of simultaneous, inconsistent sensual impressions as the characteristic feature of the time, Dada replaced the artistic imitation of the world's visual appearance by an imitation of the ways in which the modern world presented itself to all senses in a simultaneous muddle.

Applying Walter Benjamin's terminology to Dada, I described the movement as having sought to implement a mode of *tactile perception* in the reception of art, seeking to introduce a mode of *reception in distraction*. Dada thus contradicted the conventional assumption that the reception of art has to take place in a mode of contemplation and concentration. Or, more accurately, the impossibility of contemplation was one manifestation of the intended abolition of art, here taking shape on the level of reception. The sensuous impressions of daily life, defined by excess and incongruity, determined and shaped the sensual impressions intentionally generated by Dada works. Consequently, the recipient was given no other option than to perceive them in a mode of distraction, lack of awareness, and impossibility of contemplation—and thus in a distinctly nonaesthetic manner. Dada's interest in the senseless as an artistic strategy of shock became apparent as based on these very grounds.

Fluxus, on the other hand, while it continues with the increasing obliteration of artistic and nonartistic expression, has the objective of reactivating perceptive activity and perceptive precision. As such, it seeks to transfer the highly attentive attitude of perception that is traditionally adopted when receiving works of art to impulses that are ultimately indistinguishable from those generated by daily life. As Vostell proclaims, Duchamp had made "the mistake of declaring the urinal to be a sculpture but not to consider that using the urinal was an equally artistic activity. Or to place a bicycle wheel on a pedestal, without declaring the act of cycling . . . an artwork on its own."[194] Vostell's declaration implies that both artistic and nonartistic activities—or, to choose a different phrasing, intentionally and unintentionally generated impulses—deserve to be received with the same level of attention.

John Cage's legendary pre-Fluxus composition *4'33"* of 1952 gives exemplary expression to the conviction that there is no qualitative and thus hieratic difference between artistic music and nonartistic noise. His instruction to the piece reads as follows:

> The title of this work is the total length in minutes and seconds of its performance. At Woodstock, N.Y., August 29, 1962, the title was 4'33" and the three

> parts were 33," 2'40, " and 1'20." It was performed by David Tudor, pianist, who indicted the beginnings of parts by closing, the endings by opening the keyboard lid. However, the work may be performed by any instrumentalist and last any length of time.[195]

With this piece, Cage strove for the abolition of any divergence in the receptive attitude with which artistic and nonartistic impulses are conventionally perceived. "During silences when you, as a performer, don't do anything for a while," Mac Low observes, "other things that are happening become part of the piece."[196]

Fluxus seeks to promote an increased level of alertness and to cultivate attentiveness for the richness and range of sensory impressions unrelated to their artistic or nonartistic nature. However, this request for art to become visually or acoustically indistinguishable from life does not mean that the receptive attitude should align itself with that of daily life, but vice versa. Tomas Schmit describes this intention as being about the following:

> TO DO SOMETHING . . . WITHOUT delivering something that could distract the people from REALITY; something, which were different from reality; something, which people could seize as their "art," as their "opposition to daily life."[197]

Fluxus works not only do not intend to distract from reality, they seek to draw attention to it. "Most of us wanted to make art that turned people's attention to the actual phenomena of the world rather than to the thoughts or emotions of the artists."[198] With this in mind, it is worth recalling the famous statement in which Duchamp described the achievement of R. Mutt, his *alter ego*, who signed *Fountain*, as having taken "an ordinary article of life, placed it so that its useful significance disappeared under the new title and point of view—created a new thought for that object."[199] Fluxus extended the concept of the ready-made from objects to fields of activity and expression, fulfilling Duchamp's intention to create something new. But instead of aiming at a new thought for an activity or expression, Fluxus aims at a new quality in perceiving it. This new quality coincides with a shift of the notion of sensibility from the level of the intellect to that of sense perception. Fluxus seeks to deliver an experience that could be described as meaningless but sensible.

Walter De Maria's instruction for meaningless work, included in the early Fluxus publication *An Anthology of Chance Operations Concept*

Art Anti-Art Indeterminacy Improvisation Meaningless Work Natural Disasters Plans of Action Stories Diagrams Music Poetry Essays Dance Constructions Mathematics Compositions,[200] is a classic example of Fluxus's extension of the ready-made and the motives behind it. It proposes a purposeless physical work, done exclusively for the sake of the individual's experience of doing this work and perceived as delivering an "aesthetic feeling."[201] As De Maria concludes, "Meaningless work is obviously the most important and significant art form today."[202] A second difference to the Dadaist ready-made consists in the function of the institution. Whereas Duchamp sought to generate a new concept for a found object by transferring it into the context of the museum, Fluxus seeks to facilitate an aesthetic perception of any object or activity without transferring it into a different (i.e., artistic) context.

To summarize what has been said so far, Fluxus's endeavor to "ameliorate" sense perception can be described as aiming at its transformation from an activity of half-conscious recognition of something known and previously experienced into a genuine encounter, potentially new and different at each moment. "The need that is perceived in helping us to develop unusual or new disciplines of attention is one which has to do with how difficult it is to recognize the startling quality of everyday things."[203] Consequently, Fluxus's attempt to recharge sense perception with a new quantity and quality of awareness was sought not by producing new types of sensory impulses, but by focusing one's attention on highly familiar impressions. As Maciunas put it, "If man could experience the world, the concrete world surrounding him, . . . in the same way he experiences art, there would be no need for art, artists and similar "non-productive" elements.[204] This can be read as a continuation of Tristan Tzara's conviction of 1922, that "art is not the most precious manifestation of life. . . . Life is far more interesting."[205] But Fluxus does *not* apply Tzara's assumption to the *receptive attitude* it seeks to foster. Although it abolishes the art object, Fluxus does not abolish an aesthetic attitude of reception. The disappearance of art as an external manifestation coincides with its emergence as a particular state of reception. Ideally, this receptive attitude should not require an artistic expression to be invoked. Once this capacity is achieved, the artwork becomes superfluous. Fluxus concerts, as Maciunas underlines, "serve only as educational means to convert the audiences to such non-art experiences in their daily lives."[206] Fluxus's notion of "anti-art" or "art-nihilism" and the related request for art's dissolution into life is thus not to be understood as the actual termination of art but as its thorough redefinition. Instead of ceasing to exist, it rather becomes potentially omnipresent. "Fluxus people," as Maciunas requests, "must obtain their 'art' experience from everyday experiences, eating, working, etc."[207] Choosing it as the title of an exhibition, Ben Vautier formulated that *Absolutely Anything Is Art.*[208] We might explicate further: absolutely anything can be (perceived as) art. Once this state of reception is attained, "all other work would become transformed to the artistic dimension."[209]

As people are thus asked to perceive any occurrences, any stimulation of life, optionally as art, Fluxus shifts the responsibility of assuming the necessary receptive attitude and ultimately the responsibility for "creating" a work of art from the artist to the audience. One can thus consider interactive works such as the *Fluxlabyrinth* at the Akademie der Künste Berlin in 1976 as a tool toward this achievement. Another training ground is to be found in the many Fluxus events that consist in mundane, utterly unspectacular, and certainly inartistic activities, such as the switching on and off of a lamp in George Brecht's *Three Lamp Events* from 1961 (with the score reading "On.Off. / Lamp / Off.On."), a variety of potential daily activities around the notion of "exit" in Brecht's *Word Event* from the same year (with the score reading "Exit"), or the pouring of water from bottle to bottle in Tomas Schmit's *Cycle for Buckets (or Bottles)* from 1962. Often describing an activity regularly done in daily life, the realization of a Fluxus event is considered to occur every time the activity specified in the event's score is performed, whether in the context of art or not. It is thus not Fluxus's objective to stage this activity in a context other than daily life and to declare it as artistic. Instead, it seeks to modify the performer's/recipient's perception of this daily activity by activating his attention for this activity. Locating artistic production within the act of reception implies an ultimate availability of the means of artistic production by shifting the creative act from the artist to the recipient and by requiring no material possessions. It can thus be understood as another step in the communal and communist spirit integral to Fluxus's concept of art.

The perceptive awareness that Fluxus seeks to achieve is far from being limited to a specific sense or senses, but pursues a comprehensive approach and encompasses the idea of synesthetic perception. "Isn't it wonderful if someone listens to something he is ordinarily supposed to look at?" La Monte Young points out, and thus resonates a famous Zen anecdote in which the master raises his hand in front of his students and asks them to listen to its sound.[210] Consequently, Fluxus's notion of the "Gesamtkunstwerk" not only envisions the integration—a being "in flux"—of all media and genres, but the integration of all senses, aiming at "the total, multisensory experience."[211] The largest of Maciunas's many charts, somewhat the ultimate Fluxus chronicle, carries the title *Diagram of Historical Development of Fluxus and Other 4 Dimensional, Aural, Optic, Olfactory, Epithelial and Tactile Art Forms.*

But Fluxus's interest in shock is not fully explained by its capacity to jolt and thus to awake the recipient from his habitual receptive disposition. It also assumes a function in the attempt to achieve a change in consciousness. In a manuscript recalling the exhibition at the Galerie Parnass in 1963, Paik not only requests that the "see-er should '*learn to see*,' "[212] but emphasizes that this process is connected to a change in the recipient's state of consciousness to expand their perceptive capacities. As Paik explains, shock is used in the attempt "to get the audience into an artistic mind of *oneness of consciousness* so they could perceive more."[213] He thus formulates two crucial aspects: First, he defines the desired state of mind as of artistic nature, corresponding with our earlier observation of Fluxus's striving toward an artistic or aesthetic attitude of perception. Second, Paik indicates that a shift in perception coincides with a shift in consciousness. This intended shift in consciousness initiated by shock and of which the perceptive alertness, outlined earlier, forms a part, is worth examining further.

Shock and Boredom: Fluxus's "Senseless Perception"

Comparing Dada and Fluxus, Ralf Burmeister comes to conclude that the incitement of Fluxus corresponded with that of Dada's "breaking open of mental as well as social incrustations by way of massively undermining established values and styles or, in short, the bourgeois practice of art. Here and there: revolt against any torpor of time with an amalgamation of shock and humour."[214] Although Burmeister is clearly right in outlining the continuing relevance of shock, we need to specify that in Fluxus it has lost the dominant and unique position it held for Dada. Instead, it is joined by another equally central and rather contradictory feature, namely boredom.

"More often than not, they use one of two approaches—shock treatment or gentle persuasion,"[215] Victor Musgrave states in his 1972 article on "The Unknown Art Movement," thus correctly distinguishing two dominating strategies. Shock, suddenness, surprise, "explosive humour,"[216] and "uninhibited laughter"[217] describe just one dominant quality of Fluxus. On the other side are works better described as dull, slow, repetitive, uneventful, empty, and, ultimately, boring. These two strands were already visible in our brief reference to Nam June Paik's pieces of action music on the one hand, deliberately aiming at a reaction of shock, and his use of "emptied" television on the other, likely to raise boredom. The latter insinuated a form of meditative contemplation, inactivity, and complete lack of input, confronting the audience, as a critic remarked, with the "flow of empty temporality for hours."[218] It is worth recalling that Paik admired Cage's *Music of Changes* (1951) "first of all because it is Cage's most tedious composition,"[219] planning himself a concert evening as part of the series *So langweilig wie möglich* (*As Boring as Possible*) in July 1966.[220] Williams's performance *White for Governor Wallace* is another of the many examples of this reduction of impulses, offering nothing to the audience but the sight of three performers reading in silence. Similarly uneventful and tedious is Tomas Schmit's previously mentioned *Cycle for Buckets (or Bottles)*, in which the performer crouches in the center of a circle of containers, only one of which is filled with water, pouring the contents from one vessel into to next "till all the water is spilled or evaporated," as the score reads (figs. 33–35).

The reasons for the diminished dominance of shock for Fluxus clearly need addressing here. In the case of Dada, the artists' strong interest in shock was shown to be a reaction to the paradigmatic position that the experience of shock occupied within modern society. Dada's use of excessive sensory impulses—and the experience of shock as a consequence of this use—became understandable as a new and actualized form of artistic mimesis, having abandoned the limitations of visual reproduction. As our investigation into contemporaneous psychoanalytical, sociological, and socio-philosophical research showed, the paradigmatic character of shock was by no means an insight unique to Dada artists but was a prevalent attitude at the time. This is where the differences begin.

America in the early 1960s did not share this awareness for the widespread sociocultural relevance of the experience of shock. This was not necessarily due to an actual reduction of the impulses attacking the recipient and a decrease in potentially shocking experiences. Instead, as Karl Heinz Bohrer outlined in 1969, "Today, terror no longer constitutes a state of emergency, but of everyday life."[221] What had evolved was the

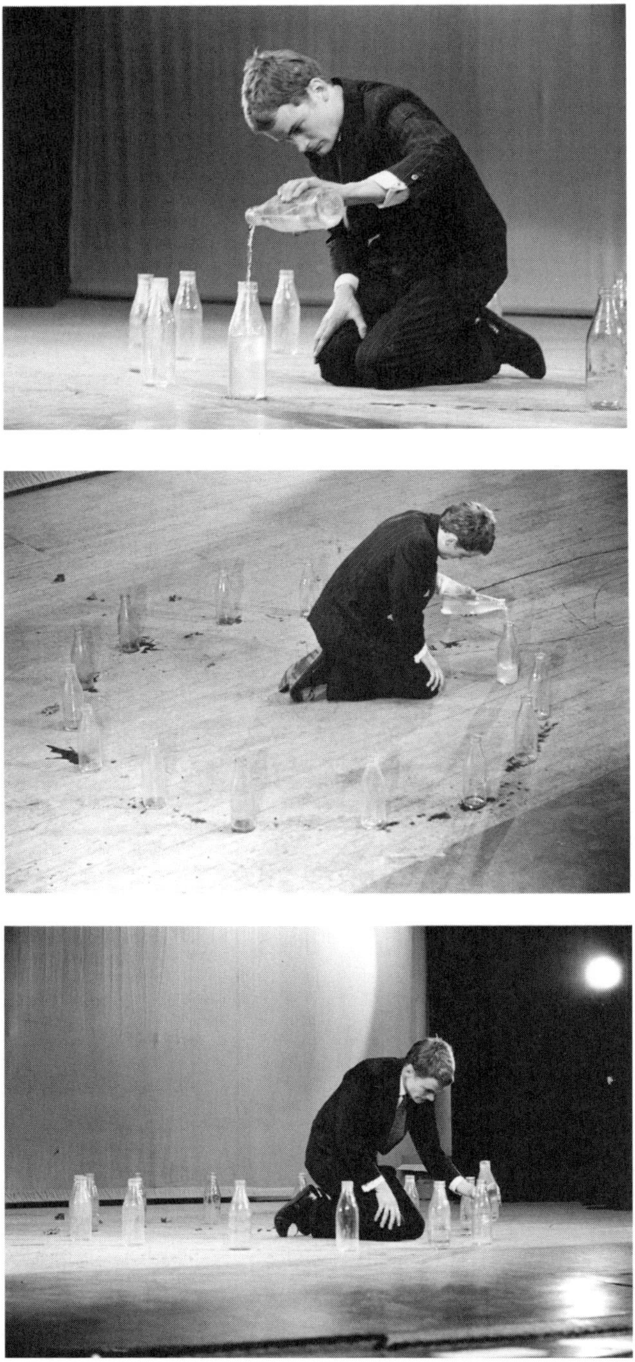

Figures 33–35. Tomas Schmit, *Cycle for Buckets (or Bottles)*, 1962. Black-and-white photographs. Photos by Dorine van der Klei.

recipient's heightened capacity for passive reception. It is this changed situation to which Fluxus reacts. By deliberately producing impulses that can be characterized as either unexpectedly strong or unexpectedly weak, Fluxus works attempt to resist their casual or incidental reception through the one or the other extreme. As Albrecht Riethmüller concluded with regard to music, an effect of shock consists in "a work having too strong an effect upon the listener."[222] Boredom results from the opposite, arising from a work's having too weak an effect upon the recipient. Since both shock and boredom run counter to the audience's expectations, both were legitimate means for Fluxus artists either to jolt or drag the recipient into a mode of productive or engaged reception through a moment of irritation. As Paik stated, "irritation is a defence against fossilisation."[223] Planning a book on *Comparative Aesthetics—Cybernetics of Art*, Paik envisioned a long multipart chapter dedicated to the "Aesthetics of boredom," including Indian, European, and American approaches to this concept and experience.[224] In his work *Zen for Film* (1964)—somewhat the visual equivalent to Cage's *4'33"*—the audience is shown the projection of a transparent 16 mm filmstrip in an infinite loop.

Within the heterogeneous group of Fluxus artists, individuals are inclined to pursue either boredom or shock. But both approaches try to provoke irritation and use it as a means to combat "fossilization." And when Paik describes his aim to use shock to achieve a oneness of consciousness, the same intention can be shown to motivate Fluxus's use of boredom. Whereas shock achieves a sudden and momentous transformation in consciousness, boredom has the effect of doing so slowly and in several stages. My analysis of the intended shift of consciousness behind Fluxus's interest in irritation will therefore focus first on the example of boredom and will apply its outcomes toward a better understanding of Fluxus's use of shock.

In her essay "Stuplimity: Boredom and Shock in Twentieth-Century Aesthetics," Sianne Ngai describes boredom as confronting us "with the limitations of our capacity for responding in general,"[225] a description that is justified when one considers the two premises of boredom. First, it is caused by an insufficiency or lack of stimuli; second, this lack of stimuli manifests itself in a decline in or absence of the recipient's engagement with these stimuli. Together, these two aspects give rise to an experience of boredom. It is on this understanding of boredom as a manifestation of the recipient's limits of engagement that Ngai builds her comparison of boredom and shock: "The sudden excitation of 'shock,' and the desensitization we associate with 'boredom' though diametrically opposed and seemingly mutually exclusive, are both responses that confront us with the limitations of our capacity for responding in general."[226] Ngai considers both shock and boredom to be grounded on the recipient's experienced incapacity for engagement, or, to put it another way, in the incapacity to allocate meaning and significance to an experience. Thus, Ngai's consideration of shock and the incapacity to engage with an impulse corresponds with my earlier analysis of Dada, where shock resulted from an encounter with something that was received as profoundly senseless and inexplicable.

The Fluxus works described earlier triggered boredom by a reduction of impulses and by their prolongation or repetition. In numerous examples—notably in the format of the Fluxus event, characterized by "brevity, minimalism, immediacy, concretism, gesture, [and] exiguous action"[227]—impulses are reduced as much as possible. Most often, a Fluxus event consists of a simple, monostructural act that does not form part of a larger narrative structure but might be repeated over and over. Recalling a performance of Emmett Williams's opera *Ja, es war noch da* (*Yes, it was still there*) from 1960, Higgins describes it as "the longest three-quarters of an hour I have ever spent, since it is mostly tapping on a pan in regular rhythms a prescribed number of times." [228] The press was equally perceptive to the related experience of boredom, if less patient. It condemned the reading of "a horribly stupid text with several voices," which "was interrupted by a monotonous rattling onto an old tin pot for an infinitely long time."[229] The journalist thus gives expression to the generation and the effects of deprivation. In many Fluxus works these processes of reduction and the event's simplicity are combined with extreme duration and repetition. Jackson Mac Low's concept for a *Tree* Movie* from 1961, for example, envisages a film consisting of a single and uncut shot of a tree filmed (and consequently watched) for an undetermined number of hours. The full description of the work reads as follows:

> Set up and focus a movie camera so that the tree* fills most of the picture. Turn on the camera and leave it on without moving it for any number of hours. If the camera is about to run out of film, substitute a camera with fresh film. The two cameras may be alternated in this way any number of times. Sound recording equipment may be turned on simultaneously with movie cameras. Beginning at any point in the film, any length of it may be projected

at a showing. For the word "tree," one might substitute "mountain," "see," "flower," "lake," etc.[230]

Although Mac Low's given examples are objects of contemplation within nature, what matters is not so much the filmed object as the duration and activity of watching it. "Emptiness is of essence,"[231] said Cage in an interview with Joan Retallack, agreeing with her specification of "emptiness as receptivity."[232] When Henry Geldzahler writes of Andy Warhol's *Sleep* "that the more that is eliminated the greater concentration is possible on the spare remaining essentials,"[233] he could equally be describing Mac Low's *Tree* Movie*. This affinity is not surprising considering the repeated assumptions that it was Mac Low's film concept, published in the new magazine *ccV TRE* in January 1964 (to become the principal Fluxus organ) that caught Warhol's attention and inspired his various static movies, such as *Sleep* (made in April of that year).[234] As Geldzahler rightly remarked, the reduction of visual and acoustic impulses and the absence of meaningful and informative activities are means of focusing the audience's attention. But they might have the opposite effect just as well, risking loss of the audience's attention by offering too little.

In a way, Fluxus can be said to engage with this turning point at which focused attention flips over into a lack of attention and vice versa. The artists seek to train the diligence, precision, and endurance of the viewer's receptive capacity *via* boredom. "If we think things are being repeated, it is generally because we don't pay attention to all the details. . . . There is no such thing as repetition,"[235] said Cage. It was Cage, after all, who organized the first complete performance of Eric Satie's *Vexations* (1893–95) at the Pocket Theatre in New York in 1963. The composition consists of 180 notes repeated 840 times. Andy Warhol, who was in the audience, was enthused by the experience and stayed for the performance's entire duration of just under nineteen hours.[236] The piece's first performance in Europe took place in Berlin in July 1966, appropriately forming part of Paik's concert series *As Boring as Possible*. In a frequently quoted adaptation of a famous Zen parable about perception, Cage requests the audience to behave as follows: "If something is boring after two minutes, try it for four. If still boring, try it for eight, sixteen, thirty-two, and so on. Eventually one discovers that it's not boring but very interesting."[237] This request, which clearly informed works such as Mac Low's *Tree* Movie*, is crucial insofar as it indicates a state that comes *after* boredom. As will become apparent in the following, Fluxus is not interested in boredom as such but in its transgression. This is the shift that Fluxus seeks to reach with its strategy of gentle persuasion, achieved through an insufficiency of impulses. It is here that the desired shift in the recipient's state of consciousness takes place and where we will perceive an analogy to the functioning of shock.

In his 1966 essay "Boredom and Danger," Dick Higgins comes to consider Mac Low's *Tree* Movie* and answers the inevitable question "Boring?" as follows: "Of course; if one were to ignore the more intense activity . . . which took one beyond the initial level of simple boredom."[238] Defining this second level as "super-boredom," Higgins describes it as a "dialectic between boredom and intensity."[239] However, this specification doesn't get us very far in terms of understanding the indicated level of intense boredom, which Paik (also thinking of Mac Low's film project) described alternatively as "more meaningful boredom."[240] Elsewhere, Paik distinguished between "good and boring" and "bad and boring,"[241] and devised a Fluxus concert evening with the title "Towards More *Sensible* Boredom."[242]

Recalling Ngai's definition of boredom as proof and consequence of the recipient's incapacity for engagement, we might assume that "more meaningful boredom" could consist in a reactivation of the recipient's engagement. But then, how would it differ from any other nonboring experience? For a start, the termination of an experience of boredom generally implies a change in the quantity or quality of the incoming impulses. In contrast to this, Fluxus envisions the transgression from boredom to super-boredom not as based on either a change or increase of impulses but precisely on their continuation. Put differently, it is to be achieved by a change in the reception of the very same impulses; it is not the impulses that change but the recipient's reception of those impulses. Recalling his own experience of the performance of *Vexations*, Cage states that it had set something "into motion that changed me. I wasn't the same after that performance as I was before. The world seemed to have changed."[243] Given that Cage had arrived at that level of experience Higgins named super-boredom, we can conclude from his report that this state comprises a change in the subject's perception of itself and of its environment. On this basis, super-boredom would consist in the reactivation of engagement based on a shift in consciousness.

From this we can conclude that the change between the two levels of boredom results from a shift in consciousness effected through extended exposure to the same continuous or repetitive impulses. This continuation or repetition can be shown to achieve the intended shift through a moment of estrangement. Once again, Mac Low's *Tree* Movie*, or rather its presentation at the Anthology Film Archives in New York in 1975, can serve as an example, employing both continuation and repetition. Accompanying the simultaneous projection of three four-hour-long realizations of the movie, showing steady footage of three different trees (a mimosa, a sugar maple, and some random tree in Central Park), the artist repeated the word "tree" endlessly throughout the entire screening.[244] Starting by recording his voice on tape, there were eventually three tape recorders, which multiplied his voice, creating an endless cacophony of the word "tree."[245] In doing this, Mac Low repeats on the level of language the endeavor he pursued on the level of visual representation. "What happens if a word is repeated to the point, at which its meaningful, semantic entity collapses and only an alignment of independent phonemes remains?" Kathryn Chiong answers her own question: "The result is not simply some mumbling, rather such excess signals its own presence."[246] Once a word becomes perceptible as a sound figure separate from what it signifies, it gains a presence independent of its signifying function. Joseph Byrd's *Homage to Jackson Mac Low: A Poem for Readers by Joseph Byrd* consists of the instruction to read each word of the title "as though it were not an entity but a sequence of separate vowels and consonants,"[247] thereby liberating each word from the expression of meaning.

Through such processes, visual or linguistic signification is eventually pushed toward losing any signifying function. Through the recipient's extended exposure to the same image or word, Fluxus aims at a moment of irritation by estranging that which seems banal and familiar. Such disruption of the automated processes of perception and interpretation is considered as triggering "a new attitude of experience," as Christian Kellerer states in his thoughts about the objet trouvé:

> [This] new attitude of experience . . . [is] precisely the kind of mindset from which a new and thoroughly experienced understanding, instead of merely a known one, can emerge from behind our linguistic, logical, and representational modes of thought. This hidden understanding is far from mystical, and is in fact (under certain conditions) perfectly accessible to our conscious experience. These conditions can be described as a distancing from the one-dimensional concepts within which our imagination and perception are constrained due to their partial usage.[248]

Higgins refers to the same partial and incomplete perception, when reminding us that "[w]e can talk about a thing, but we cannot talk a thing. It is always something else."[249] Having mentioned Fluxus's affinity with Zen regarding its concept of the senseless, we can now draw attention to another parallel concerning their mutual approach to language. As Daisetz Taitaro Suzuki phrased it, language "has been associated too long with ideation, and has lost direction or being by itself. As soon as words are used, they express meaning, reasoning; they represent something not belonging to themselves."[250] Elsewhere, he writes, "To one who has not yet studied Zen, a mountain is a mountain; when he begins to know something of Zen, a mountain is not a mountain; but once he thoroughly masters Zen, a mountain is again a mountain.[251] We might be able to understand Mac Low's intention behind his presentation of a tree over several hours accompanied by the repetition of its name as the first step within this process, seeking to trigger that moment when the tree stops being perceived as a tree, or at least when its perception as a manifestation of the concept "tree" no longer appears as the only possible approach. "When I look at a picture the senses perceive it without the medium of a concept,"[252] writes Suzuki, expressing the wish to overcome what Kellerer described as "conceptual thinking with its dualistic differentiation."[253]

In the previously mentioned essay "Stuplimity: Boredom and Shock in Twentieth-Century Aesthetics," Ngai recalls an anecdote used by Jacques Lacan as an example of sublimation. Lacan recollects a visit at Jacques Prévert's home in southern France, where he finds himself impressed by the friend's collection of matchboxes, or—more precisely—by the way in which they are presented. With their drawers pulled out slightly, the boxes were made to cling to each other and consequently formed a long lineup of identical boxes running along the mantelpiece. Prévert's repetitive, unusual and pointless presentation of matchboxes enabled a new and unusual perception of these familiar objects.[254]

Either by an instantaneous (shocking) or a gradual (boring) irritation, Fluxus seeks to delay and unhinge the automatic paring of a sensory impression with a concept of what it stands for. Thus, Zen's endeavor finds its counterpart in Fluxus's striving for what we might describe as "senseless perception" (an artistic attempt not utterly unprecedented if one thinks, for example, of John Ruskin's 1857 request to recover "the innocence of the eye" and to regain a separation of perception and cognition[255]). Fluxus appears to share the Zen conviction that "sense perception does not require any mediating agency" but is capable of seeing things "as they are"[256]—a conviction equally central to the notion of "intuitive knowledge." Pursuing an attempt similar to Dada's endeavor to regain a purified and original use of language, Fluxus seeks to hinder the habitual and automated interaction between sense perception and its immediate identification with the concept or idea that it signifies. As the score for Emmett Williams's event *The Gift of Tongues* (1962) reads, "Sing meaningfully in a language made up on the spot,"[257] thus reminding us of Hugo Ball's ferocious rejection of "words that other people have invented," claiming: "I want my own stuff, my own rhythm, and vowels and consonants too."

The common denominator between an experience of shock and an experience of super-boredom, as envisioned by Fluxus, is an absence of the level of reflection. Put more simply, it can be described as a state of immersion and can be shown to be a different phrasing of Paik's oneness of consciousness. Of Satie's *Vexations,* Higgins writes, "By the time the piece is over the silence is absolutely numbing, so much of an environment has the piece become. . . . The environment would become part of the piece and vice versa.[258] Evidently, what Higgins describes here is not a factual shift within the relationship between artwork and environment, but a shift within the recipient's subjective experience of this relationship. This perceived merging of artwork and environment is conceived as affecting and altering the self-perception of the recipient. As Ina Blom concludes in her essay "Boredom and Oblivion," "the work will disappear into the surroundings, and the spectator will disappear into the work,"[259] finding himself in a state of "oblivion or unknowing."[260] The vanishing separation between the subject and the surrounding world is a result of the recipient's immersion within the receptive process and was described by Paik as leading to an experience of "absolute void"—as he describes his own experience of listening to a concert by Cage.[261]

In this lack of distinction between the subject and the object (in other words the subject's surroundings), we reencounter Paik's notion of a oneness of consciousness, which he considered as caused by shock, and which appears as the goal of the recipient's exposure to both an insufficiency and an excess of impulses. The desired effect of shock, as expressed by Paik, can also be shown to motivate Fluxus's interest in boredom. Unlike ordinary boredom, the indifference peculiar to super-boredom does not coincide with an insufficient engagement but an excessive one. Although thus implying a reactivation of engagement, this engagement cannot be described as of rational nature and does not consist in a critical reception of what is perceived. It is about achieving, as Cage described it, "an active and curious but empty consciousness."[262] By aiming to generate an experience of immersion, Fluxus seeks the dissolution of any distinction between subject and object on the level of experience, achieving what Cage called "a sense of at-oneness with whatever"[263]—or, to use a Zen phrasing, "I am the flower and the flower is me."[264]

Thus, we can conclude that Fluxus's use of its two dominant means of irritation is aimed at a shift in consciousness: It strives for the temporary suspension of the ever-dominant discursive approach. The experiences of shock and of super-boredom manifest the suspension of the rational approach to the world, which is based on the indispensable distinction between subject and object. Both shock and super-boredom are thought to enable the recipient to experience an immediate access to things and to "forgo all systems of objective and subjective analysis, to become sensitized to the world and to unmediated experience."[265]

Coming from this angle, we can recognize Fluxus's approach as a continuation of the purpose of art as defined by Viktor Shklovsky in his famous text "Art as Technique" from 1917, written in the context of Russian Formalism and discussing strategies of defamiliarization within methods of narration. Fluxus complies with the linguist's request for art "to impart the sensation of things as they are perceived and not as they are known. The technique of art is to make objects 'unfamiliar,' "[266] rendering automated perception impossible. Fluxus's drive to generate shock or excessive boredom becomes understandable as the extreme end of the concept of defamiliarization, being the artistic act of making the familiar seem strange. Fluxus plays on art's capacity to increase either the difficulty (shock) or the length (boredom) of perception, complying with Shklovsky's conviction that "the process of perception is an aesthetic end in itself and must be prolonged."[267] As Shklovsky famously put it, "Only the creation of new forms of art can restore to man sensation of the world, can resurrect things"[268] and "make the stone stony."[269]

Continuing with the concept of defamiliarization as developed by Russian Formalism, the Constance School of Reception Aesthetics around Wolfgang Iser and Hans Robert Jauss described this aim as the "deautomation of perception," attempting "to defamiliarize the conventionalized forms of perception, so that teleological inspired constructions of reality are not confused with reality itself."[270] When Iser formulates art's capacity to act against "solidified perception,"[271] he formulates a request not unlike Paik's assumption that an instance of irritation is a protection against fossilization. Both describe the purpose of art as to startle, irritate, and ultimately shock the recipient, leading to the interruption of a habitual receptive attitude.

5 Conclusion: Communicating the Void

A rift has no content of its own.
—Ernst Bloch, "The Unbearable Moment," 1965

As outlined in this book, Dada's and Fluxus's wish for art to have an effect upon life is the ultimate motivation for both movements' interest in shock. But it is a connection that is not restricted to Dada and Fluxus. When Andrei Nakov observes of Dada that "only constant provocation could create any real sense of communication,"[1] he points at a connection that exceeds the avant-garde movement and that can be shown to dominate a more general artistic interest in shock. As I will argue, it is the communicative capacity of shock on which this wider artistic interest is based.

In the realm of art, the experience of shock is effected by an artwork and experienced by the recipient. By thus evolving between the work and the viewer, shock can be seen as a particular link between the two or, more precisely, between the artist and the recipient via the mediation of the artwork. This capacity of shock to function as a tool in establishing a link between the artist and the recipient appears to be the principle motive for the use of shock within art and exceeds the specific cases of Dada and Fluxus. "A shock of surprise is one of the most effective methods of arousing attention,"[2] John Dewey stated in 1887. Much later, the same conviction was expressed in Roland Barthes's demand for shock to "disorganize" us,[3] and caused the artist Marc Quinn to distance himself from "shock artists," who use shock "for no other reason but to use it, whereas I would use it to make the work communicate a different idea more directly."[4] Wolfgang Flatz points in a similar direction when stating that "an experience of shock" functions as a means to find immediate "access to a person" and is consequently "capable to set something going, to make an existing world view tremble, to set awareness rolling or to ignite irritation."[5] As Flatz continues, "this is the first step towards change and it makes destruction a constructive element."[6]

Of course, this initiating potency of shock is not limited to the realm of art. Numerable studies of advertising strategies and theories of communication address the efficiency of shock as a means of arousing attention and starting communication. Once again, Toscani's Benetton campaign only provides the most prominent of examples in this matter. An empirical study launched by the Swiss government to examine the efficiency of promoting health care, for example, attests the efficiency of negative messages, as they are most likely to trigger attention. This efficiency lasts for more than a moment: The higher the level of excitation—in both a positive as a negative direction—the better a message is remembered. Hardly surprising, unsettling messages are more easily kept in mind than neutral ones.[7]

Ultimately grounded upon the conviction that our psychic life can be "'touched' or affected only when 'struck' or hit,"[8] as Richard Shiff reflects upon Walter Benjamin, this perceived potency of shock as a means of communication explains its attraction for artists, but appears to generate a reason for restricting its use. Since shock has such a high communicative capacity, the use of shock appears to be acceptable only when communicating some worthy subject matter. In fact, the failure to comply with this request was the major criticism of works of the Young British Artists, as of Toscani's advertisement. A considerable part of the uproar triggered by the latter's photographs was caused not by the images themselves but by the perceived lack of a legitimate use for them.

Many debates on shocking artworks and censorship can be understood as a disagreement over the importance and legitimacy of what is communicated. In other words, there is an implicit distinction between an acceptable and an unacceptable use of shock—a distinction that culminates in the prevailing condemnation of a *shock for shock's sake*: an unwarranted use of shock, triggered for the mere sake of drawing attention to a work for its own publicity. "The aim of art is a transformation of consciousness, and sometimes we do need a shock to the system. . . . I do not, however, like shock for shock's sake,"[9] as Jean Paul Caponigro reiterates a prevailing conviction. "Shock tactics," as Howard Brenton underlines, "are not enough on their own";[10] and J. G. Ballard writes, "People are searching for truth through trying to shock."[11] As was said about Allan Kaprow, it is "through provocation [that] he intends to find new positive aesthetical or ethical answers."[12] In his book *Transgressions*, Anthony Julius considers shock as supporting art's capacity to teach,[13] and recalls an argument brought forward to defend the artistic approach of Andres Serrano: "It is the job of art to shock us into grasping some truth about ourselves, or about the world, or about art itself, and . . . one way in which it does this is to alienate us from our preconceptions, by making the familiar strange and the unquestioned problematic.[14] Serrano's aesthetically pleasing photograph *Immersions (Madonna and Child II)* from 1989, showing a beautifully lit sculpture of Virgin Mary immersed in a yellowish liquid that—if we believe the artist's suggestion—can be identified as urine, might "shock the viewer into a reconsideration of the image and its true meaning" (fig. 36).[15] Norman Rosenthal, cocurator of the exhibition *Apocalypse* at the Royal Academy of Arts in London in 2000, expressed his hope that it "will be a cathartic experience for people who come and engage with the work[s], rather than those who come," as many press reviews suggest, only "to gawp and be shocked."[16] All these various formulations give expression to an understanding of shock as a transitory experience, leading beyond the immediate encounter to something else, and initiating a "reconsideration of the image" or some cathartic process.

Bearing in mind shock's use within art as a means of estranging us from what we usually take for granted, "to overthrow our sense of the familiar, to sabotage our habits, [and] to put the real world on trial,"[17] let us return to Dada and Fluxus. To what extent do these two movements conform to this assumption dominating the artistic use of shock? To put it another way, do Dada and Fluxus use shock for its communicative capacities, and, if so, what is it that the shock of the senseless and the consequent absence of any intelligible content matter seeks to communicate? On a structural level, we are asking whether Dada and Fluxus use shock as a means to a certain end, to have a certain effect. As outlined in this volume, both Dada and Fluxus conceived of art as a means of interacting with life and of having a discernible effect on society. What function does shock assume within this attempt?

As a first step toward an answer, we need to summarize the relationship between shock and the notion of the senseless. Starting with Dada, this relationship has been outlined as one of cause and effect. The withdrawal and destruction of sense and a deliberately nonsensical artistic production were shown to function as a source of shock. What remains to be determined is whether Fluxus carries on with this causal correla-

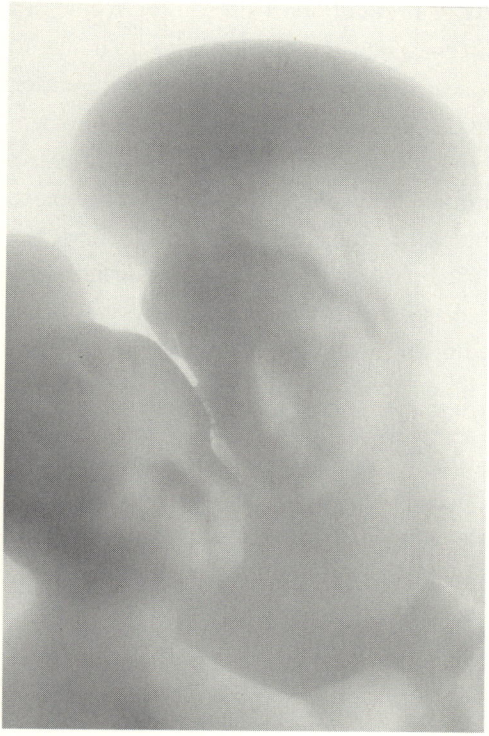

Figure 36. Andres Serrano, *Madonna and Child II*, 1989. Silver dye bleach (Cibachrome) print. Corcoran Gallery of Art, Washington, D.C. Gift of Carolyn S. Alpers.

tion. Does the recipient's exposure to something utterly insensible continue to function as a possible trigger of shock?

Recalling our explorations of Fluxus's interest in irritating the recipient, it appears necessary to distinguish two levels of senselessness or, more specifically, two ways of receiving that which makes no sense. Using the terminology established earlier and deriving from Zen, one can describe the first level as a lack of sense according to the system of discursive knowledge, and the second as senseless according to the system of intuitive knowledge. Examples of the first type of senselessness are Paik's pieces of action music, in which the artist's doings surprise the audience by appearing to them as utterly senseless, nonartistic, stupid, and ridiculous. As Paik made clear, these actions were explicitly designed to induce a reaction of shock, and thus they show an unmistakeable affinity to works and performances typical of Dada. Received within the parameters of discursive knowledge, a confrontation with what is senseless, incongruous, and unexpected does indeed continue to function as a trigger of shock. In this, Fluxus carries on the Dadaist tradition. But our examination of Fluxus's interest in irritation has furthermore outlined the aim of this irritation, namely to bring about a shift in the recipient's state of consciousness. This shift was said to coincide with a change in the understanding and evaluation of sense or senselessness in that matter. As I concluded, the irritation Fluxus inflicted on habitual modes of reception and thus on a habitual approach to the world was intended to effect a transfer from discursive to intuitive knowledge, the latter, according to Zen, being nondiscriminative and nonrational.

With this in mind, Fluxus's use of shock can be understood not only as set off by senselessness but also as a strategy *toward* senselessness, that is, toward a changed understanding of meaning. This mirroring gives expression to the transitory role Fluxus allocates to shock, which is distinct from the use of shock within Dada. Shock appears here as the interface, or the point of transition, from one level of senselessness onto the next, marking the shift from one concept of meaning to another. We could therefore say that Fluxus complements Dada's use of senselessness as an artistic strategy of shock with its inverse: shock as a means to reach a changed understanding of the senseless.

In Fluxus, the experience of shock functions as a step of transition between two concepts of meaning and aims at what was described as an "aestheticization" of our daily perception. Thus, Fluxus conforms to the dominating use of shock within art of seeking to communicate and initiate an important change. Using this terminology, Fluxus attempts to communicate a different take on the world by using shock and boredom as means to irritate spectators' or listeners' receptive attitude and to defamiliarize their perceptive activity. Shock functions here as a means to estrange recipients from their very expectations. It seeks to initiate a different approach toward sensibility both on a perceptive and cognitive level. In this, it ultimately intends to change the recipient's perception and understanding of the world.

Turning our attention back to Dada, it becomes clear that it shares neither the use of shock as a means of defamiliarization nor the related aspiration to achieve an aestheticization of experience. Dada does not seek to aestheticize the recipient's perception by modifying conventionalized forms of reception; instead, as we saw, it sought to promote precisely a nonartistic receptive attitude. Fostering the recipient's distraction, it deliberately thwarted the basic preconditions for an aesthetic experience based on contemplation. Whereas Fluxus sought to transfer an aesthetic attitude to the reception of life, Dada performed the inverse movement by pursuing a "radical *anaesthetícization of aesthetics*."[18] By exposing the recipient to an excess of incongruous, contradictory impulses, Dada ushered him into a receptive situation that rather required "a mode of technical problem-solving and not [of] aesthetic enjoyment," as Frederic Schwartz phrased it.[19] It deprived the audience of the means of controlling its perception. Coming from this angle, Dada's use of shock can be seen as encapsulating the movement's attempt to destroy art by destroying the possibility of an aesthetic experience. If one wished to describe Dada's approach in aesthetic terms, one would have to redefine those terms so profoundly as to end the conception of art as existing in a realm of its own.

> *Aisthitikos* is the ancient Greek word for that which is "perceptive by feeling." *Aisthisis* is the sensory experience of perception. The original field of aesthetics is not art but reality—corporeal, material nature. . . . This physical-cognitive apparatus . . . is "out front" of the mind, encountering the world prelinguistically, hence prior not only to logic but to meaning as well.[20]

With these reflections in mind, any answer to the question of whether Dada uses shock as a means of communication will appear contrived. In attempting to provide one, however, it is worth revisiting an excerpt from Francis Picabia's *DADA Manifesto* quoted earlier, in which he describes Dada's intention as "doing something so that the public can say: 'We understand nothing, nothing, nothing.' "[21] The aspect that is of interest to us here is the notion of reaction expressed in this quote. Picabia grounds the motivation for the Dadaists' strategies in their desire to make the audience respond, and he specifies this as a reaction to the experience of understanding nothing. The audience responds to an expression by the performer but this response is not based on any moment of understanding and consent. Dada's approach to shock thus presents a contrived use of its communicative capacities. On the one hand, it complies with the interactive aspect of communication, requesting an interchange of action and reaction.[22] On the other hand, however, Dada does not comply with the general assumption that "the act of communication on the part of the communicator requires a corresponding act of understanding on the part of the recipient."[23] Whereas Dada communicates insofar as it involves a "conscious and intentional acting," it does not pursue "the aim of reaching an act of understanding."[24] The Dadaists *intend* the audience *not* to understand, as Picabia put it perfectly. They pursue an intentional communication of the senseless, or, to choose a different wording, they seek to deliver the experience of being confronted with an absence of sense. In giving expression to their incomprehension, the audience complies precisely with the performers' intentions, which were not so much about making the public say they disapprove, as Picabia puts it euphemistically, but rather about making them shout, scream, and throw eggs, apples, and chairs, thus giving expression to their irritation and provocation at being confronted by something utterly void of meaning.

Christopher Bigsby perceives Dada's paradoxical use of communication as a dilemma, believing that artistic production as such implies "the possibility and desirability of communication."[25] Based on the preceding argument, we can reply to Bigsby as follows: Dada did not engage with artistic production—and with shock—*despite* its implying the possibility and desirability of communication, but precisely *because* of these capacities, (mis-)using them to produce an "empty statement." "Art objects were not important in themselves for most of the Dadaists but were used as a means of communication"[26]—or, as we can now say, as a means to subvert communication as part of the intended subversion of the concept of art. Thus, the blow to communication demanded by Adorno is delivered by undermining its basic principles. When Hausmann states that "Dada had ripped everything away from man and pushed him into the void deprived even of the fig-leaf he had in paradise,"[27] he indicates that what Dada seeks to deliver is the experience of this void—the shock of the void—and not its repletion or replacement with something else. We could therefore say with some justification that Dada is quite literally a shock for shock's sake.

It is here that we find the basis for the prevailing characterization (and condemnation) of Dada as profoundly nihilistic and interested in destruction for the sake of it. Renato Poggioli even came to state "that the nihilistic tendency functioned as the primary, even solitary, psychic condition" for Dada, taking "the form of an intransigent puerility, an extreme infantilism."[28] Tristan Tzara consequently asked whether "this movement, only the destructive side of which had been seen by most critics, [was] really necessary?" answering: "It is certain that the *tabula rasa* which we made into the guiding principle of our activity, was of value only in so far as *something else* would succeed in. A state of affairs considered noxious and infamous demanded to be changed."[29] Huelsenbeck indicates a similar counterbalance by outlining that "Dada had both destructive and constructive sides," with the latter being "not so easily discernible" and requiring to "be elucidated in some detail if it is to be understood."[30] He corresponds with Marcel Janco, observing that "each time the Dada flame flared again . . . it began with the same purifying and scandalous fire to consume the past and open up a new creative route."[31] However, by leaving this new route inchoate, neither Tzara, Huelsenbeck, nor Janco explicate this supposed positive value and constructive aspect, and thus—more specifically—indicate to what end, if not for its own sake, the experience of shock was triggered.

How can we recognize any positive aspect within a use of shock for shock's sake, and how can we consider the lack of any added meaning as constructive in itself? "So long as it fails to understand what the shock of the unintelligible [*Schock des Unverständlichen*] can communicate, the whole dispute resembles shadow-boxing,"[32] wrote Adorno, and he continued by offering an answer as to how these shocks might be understood: "The shocks of incomprehension, emitted by artistic technique in the age of its meaninglessness, undergo a sudden change. They illuminate the meaningless world."[33] Referring to contemporaneous composers, he becomes more specific:

> The terror [*Schrecken*] which Schönberg and Webern spread, today as in the past, comes not from their incomprehensibility but from the fact that they are all too correctly understood. Their music gives form to that anxiety, that terror, that insight into the catastrophic situation which others merely evade by regressing.[34]

Here, Adorno recognizes the shock of the senseless—understood as the shock of the unintelligible—as a metaphor for the state of the world. This seems to be an approach valuable still today, as a press review of the recent exhibition *Bad Art for Bad People* by the Chapman brothers suggests: "We should be appalled—not because the brothers have created these things, but because we have created a world in which they make sense."[35] On the part of the recipient, such metaphoric understanding of an experience of shock presupposes that this experience becomes the subject of a contemplative activity and thus comes to be understood as delivering or confirming some insight or truth about the world.

However, I would argue that the constructive or positive aspect inherent in Dada's shock of the senseless cannot be straightforwardly understood in that manner, at least as far as the artists' own intentions are concerned. As I see it, the Dadaists did not conceive of shock as functioning on the level of reflection but on that of immediate experience. They wanted the shock of the senseless to be *experienced* rather than *understood*, to enact a repetition of the world's absurdity rather than create an intelligible representation of it. Different from Fluxus's later use, Dada's employment of shock does not seek to deliver any shift in perception or any insight other than that generated by the present reality. Striving for an artistic production that "fits the moment," and seeking to achieve a commensurate and faithful portrayal of reality, this attempt required Dada to move the artistic tradition of representation from the level of visual appearance onto that of sensorial impulses, from the creation of a coherent, sensible entity into a shattered heap of incoherent, disjunctive fragments, and finally from the level of reflection to that of immediate experience. The recipient's experience of shock completes Dada's endeavor to deliver a representation of reality as experienced by the artists, in which the senseless presents itself as the essence of shock. The artists' mimesis of the sensorial landscape of their time and context is completed once the recipient's experience of the work of art mimics his experience of daily life.

Although my research thus confirms that the shock of the senseless was an artistic concept specific to the historical avant-garde and, more precisely, to Dada, we are able to revise Peter Bürger's explanation summarized at the very beginning of this book. He considered the fading value of the use of shock within art to be a consequence of the neo-avant-garde's repeating an outdated and obsolete avant-garde strategy. Contrary to this, my examination of Fluxus characterizes its use of shock not so much as a *repetition* but a *revision* of avant-garde strategies, formulating a response to its own artistic and, more important, its sociocultural context. In these changed circumstances, the experience of shock was no longer dominant but had given way to a prevailing receptive passivity. Fluxus's use of shock was a reaction to this state, but did not take the form of a mimetic approach. Instead, Fluxus aimed to trigger a moment of transformation. In this Fluxus differs crucially from Dada and the conceptual immediacy of its use of shock, which embedded shock for shock's sake within a larger artistic endeavor.

At the end of her exploration of shock in Dada and Surrealist poetry, Elizabeth Allen Chabert comes to the following conclusion:

> The rhetoric of surprise, shock, and violence in dada and surrealist poetry does not necessarily correspond to a quest for pure novelty or sensation. . . . To deny that the dada and surrealist movements were not in the least concerned to "épater le bourgeois" would be senseless. But I hope to have shown a more serious side.[36]

Chabert finds this more serious side in "their attempts to shock the public into some sort of awakening."[37] My own conclusion with regard to Dada is thus not—or not only—a contradiction but also a refinement of Chabert's suggestion, having taken a different route. While she distinguishes between an "*épater le bourgeois*"—or what I called "shock for shock's sake"—and a more serious use of shock that aims at a moment of awakening or transformation, I set out to show that these two sides are in fact inseparable one from another. This makes Dada's notion of shock conceptually distinct and exceptional.

Bertolt Brecht once described art as being "not a mirror held up to reality, but a hammer with which to shape it."[38] As I have argued, the artists' interest in shock was fostered by the hope that it might function as such a hammer. However, comparing our conclusions about Fluxus and Dada with this statement, the latter's deviation from this request becomes apparent. Dada makes no distinction between mirroring and changing society—or, more precisely, it takes mirroring as the first step toward change. This approach not only informs the whole concept of Dada but also explains its distinctive pursuit of shock in particular. Responding to a sociocultural context in which shock had been made an issue of intellectual history, Dada embedded it within an artistic concept where shock is needed for the experience it is, without seeking to integrate it into an aesthetic tradition, contemplative process, or cathartic transgression.

Our comparison of Dada and Fluxus and their place within the larger framework of an artistic interest in shock has shown that Dada's unique relationship with shock is not a matter of using it earliest or most intensely. Even if Dada was the first artistic movement to exploit shock to a substantial degree, its use of shock, as we have learned by comparing it with Fluxus, is distinct from other approaches not by virtue of presenting the climax of an ongoing concept of shock but of manifesting a conceptual singularity.

Acknowledgments

I would like to express my profound gratitude to a range of individuals and institutions who have supported the research for this book in various ways and at different stages. Substantial financial supported has been granted by the Arts and Humanities Research Council (AHRC) as well as by the Terra Foundation for American Art. To both institutions I express my sincere thanks for having facilitated the pursuit and completion of this work.

I thank Prof. Ursula Frohne from the University of Cologne and Philip Dodd from the London Consortium, for their munificent investment of attention, advice, and time as supervisors of the Ph.D. thesis that constituted the basis for this book. In this context, my sincere thanks also go to the two examiners, Dr. Astrit Schmidt-Burkhardt from the Freie Universität Berlin and Dr. Frederic J. Schwartz from University College London. Other experts in the field have supported my work in different phases of its completion, notably Prof. Steven Connor, Prof. Colin MacCabe, and the late Prof. Paul Hirst from the London Consortium, Dr. Veerle Thielemans from the Terra Foundation of American Art in Giverny and Prof. Winfried Fluck from the Freie Universität in Berlin. I thank Dr. Ken Friedman and Dr. Bertrand Clavez for sharing their knowledge on Fluxus. I owe my thanks to Thomas Mansell and Dr. Catherine Nichols for a careful reading and copyediting of the manuscript, Harald Niessner for his support in visual aspects, and Dr. Benjamin Meyer-Krahmer for having been a highly appreciated continual reader and critic of my research.

I would like to thank all the individuals and institutions who have generously given their permission to reproduce images in this book, notably all the artists and their representatives. My grateful appreciation goes to the photographers Dorine van der Klei, Manfred Leve, Manfred

Montwé, as well as Ken Hakuta of the Paik Estate, Anneliese Jährling, Barbara Wien, Wilma Lukatsch and the tomas schmit archiv, Jon Hendricks from the Gilbert and Lila Silverman Fluxus Collection, Tess Carota from the Robert Mapplethorpe Foundation, Marijke Mosheuvel-Lie from ESTeeLIE, Kathryn Hillier and Karen Polack from Yvon Lambert, Karin Seinsoth from Hauser & Wirth, Ila Furman from the Corcoran Gallery of Art, Gretchen Wagner from MoMA, Uwe Lewitzky from Sammlung Falckenberg, Lisa Franzen from Galerie Gisela Capitain as representative of the Estate Martin Kippenberger, Kate Murphy from the Maya Stendhal Gallery as representative of the George Maciunas Foundation, Ilona Lütken from the Archiv Sohm/Staatsgalerie Stuttgart, Brigitte Jacobs van Renswou from ZADIK, Norbert Ludwig from bpk, Tanja Witsch from VG-Bild Kunst, and Dr. Susanne Neuburger and Alexandra Pinter from MUMOK.

I am extremely happy that this book can be part of the Dartmouth College Press series "Interfaces: Studies in Visual Culture" and express my gratitude to the publisher and especially Richard Pult for having made this possible.

Notes

1. Introduction

1. Peter Bürger, *Theory of the Avant-Garde*, trans. Michael Shaw (Minneapolis: University of Minnesota Press, 1984), p. 22. Using an almost identical phrase, Hubert van den Berg describes Dada as "the most radical formation of the historical avant-garde"—see "On the Historiographic Distinction between Historical and Neo-Avant-Garde," in *Avant-Garde/Neo-Avant-Garde*, vol. 17 of *Avant-Garde Critical Studies*, ed. Dietrich Scheunemann (Amsterdam: Rodopi, 2005), p. 69, see also p. 68.

2. Harry Ruhé, *Fluxus: The Most Radical and Experimental Art Movement of the Sixties* (Amsterdam: Gallery 'A,' 1979), n.p.

3. Kai Hoffmann, "Wagnis Kunst?" available at: www.propellerkick.de/introduktion/Kunst01/kai_lesen/wagnis_kunst/wagnis_kunst.html.

4. Unidentified French publication, March 5, 1920, Fond Doucet; reprinted in Harriett Watts, *Dada and the Press*, vol. 9 of *Crisis and the Arts*, ed. Stephen C. Foster (New Haven, CT: Thomson/Gale, 2004), p. 104, reprint not translated.

5. Unknown author (B.B.), "Kunst-Terroristen," in *Deutsche Zeitung*; reprinted in *Happenings: Fluxus, Pop Art, Nouveau Réalism*, ed. Jürgen Becker and Wolf Vostell (Reinbeck/Hamburg: Rowohlt, 1965), p. 274.

6. For Dada see: Richard Huelsenbeck, "Erklärung" (probably presented during the first Dada soirée at the Cabaret Voltaire in spring 1916); reprinted in Huelsenbeck, *Dada: Eine literarische Dokumentation* (Reinbeck/Hamburg: Rowohlt, 1964), p. 30; see for Fluxus: Emmett Williams, *My Life in Fluxus—and Vice Versa* (London: Thames and Hudson, 1992), p. 164.

7. Georges Ribemont-Dessaignes, "History of Dada," in *The Dada Painters and Poets*, ed. Robert Motherwell, 2nd ed. (New York: Wittenborn, Schultz, Inc., 1967), p. 101. Throughout the book, I quote from this second edition, as it includes as appendices two texts by Tzara and Huelsenbeck that were excluded from the first edition, published in 1951. For all other texts in this anthology, the page numbers of the first and second editions are identical.

8. Robert Watts, as quoted by Robert Silberman, "Minneapolis: In the Spirit of Fluxus," *Burlington Magazine*, vol. 135, no. 1083 (June 1993), p. 432.

9. *Mit dem Kopf durch die Wand . . . und etwas Neues finden: Fluxus aus der Sammlung René Block*, an exhibition of the Kunst- und Museumsverein, Wuppertal in 1996.

10. Richard Huelsenbeck, "Erinnerungen," in *Urlaute dadaistischer Poesie: Der Berliner Dada-Abend am 12. April 1918*, ed. Jeanpaul Goergen (Hannover: Postskriptum Verlag, 1994), p. 106.

11. Ribemont-Dessaignes, "History of Dada," p. 113.

12. Bürger, *Theory of the Avant-Garde*, p. 80.

13. Ibid.

14. Raoul Hausmann, "Massenpsychologie Dadas," in *Am Anfang war Dada*, ed. Karl Riha and Günter Kämpf (Steinbach/Giessen: Anabas-Verlag: Günter Kämpf, 1972), p. 144.

15. Tristan Tzara, "An Introduction to Dada," in Motherwell, *Dada Painters and Poets*, p. 395. This text was not included in the first edition; see also p. 7 n. 9.

16. Klaus von Beyme, *Das Zeitalter der Avantgarden. Kunst und Gesellschaft 1905–1955* (Munich: Verlag C.H.Beck, 2005), pp. 16–17.

17. See Peter Bürger, *Der französische Surrealismus: Studien zum Problem der avantgardistischen Literatur* (Frankfurt: Athenäum Verlag, 1971); Hubert van den Berg, "Tristan Tzara's 'Manifeste Dada 1918,'" *Neophilologus*, vol. 79, no. 3 (1995), pp. 353–76; Alfons Backes-Haase, "Wir wollen triezen, stänkern, bluffen . . ." in *"Die ganze Welt ist eine Manifestation": Die europäische Avantgarde und ihre Manifeste*, ed. Wolfgang Asholt and Werner Fähnders (Darmstadt: Wissenschaftliche Buchgesellschaft, 1997), pp. 259–64; and Hanno Ehrlicher, *Kunst der Zerstörung* (Berlin: Akademie Verlag, 2001), p. 197.

18. See Albrecht Riethmüller, "Hermetik, Schock, Fasslichkeit: Zum Verhältnis von Musikwerk und Publikum in der ersten Hälfte des 20. Jahrhunderts," *Archiv für Musikwissenschaft*, vol. 73, no. 1 (1980), p. 43 and n. 47.

19. Leah Dickerman, ed., *Dada: Zurich, Berlin, Hannover, Cologne, New York, Paris*, exhibition catalog, National Gallery of Art, Washington et al. (New York: Distributed Art Publishers, Inc., 2005).

20. Brigid Doherty, "'See: We Are All Neurasthenics!' or, The Trauma of Dada Montage," *Critical Inquiry*, vol. 24 (Autumn 1997), p. 88.

21. Elizabeth Allen Chabert, *Transforming Impact: The Shock Experience in Dada and Surrealist Poetry*, Ph.D. thesis, Columbia University, New York, microfiche, 1995.

22. Greil Marcus, *Lipstick Traces: A Secret History of the Twentieth Century* (London: Faber and Faber, 1989).

23. Anthony Julius, *Transgressions: The Offences of Art* (London: Thames & Hudson, 2002).

24. Paul Ardenne, *Extrême: Esthétique de la limite dépassée* (Paris: Flammarion, 2006).

25. Kieran Cashell, *Aftershock: The Ethics of Contemporary Transgressive Art* (London: I. B. Tauris, 2009).

26. Ian Dunlop, *The Shock of the New: Seven Historic Exhibitions of Modern Art* (New York: American Heritage Press, 1972).

27. Robert Hughes, *The Shock of the New* (New York: Alfred A. Knopf, 1980). In

the summer of 2004, the BBC broadcast a new documentary by Hughes entitled *The New Shock of the New.*

28. Susan Buck-Morss, "Aesthetics and Anaesthetics: Walter Benjamin's Artwork Essay Reconsidered" (1992), in *October: The Second Decade, 1986–1996*, ed. Rosalind Krauss et al. (Cambridge, MA: MIT Press, 1997), pp. 375–413.

29. Riethmüller, "Hermetik, Schock, Fasslichkeit," pp. 32–60.

30. Francesca Alfano Miglietti, *Extreme Bodies: The Use and Abuse of the Body in Art* (Milan: Skira, 2003).

31. Linda S. Kauffman, *Bad Girls and Sick Boys* (Berkeley: University of California Press, 1998), p. 1.

32. Monika Wagner, *Das Material der Kunst: Eine andere Geschichte der Moderne* (Munich: Beck, 2001).

33. William Ian Miller, *Anatomy of Disgust* (Cambridge, MA: Harvard University Press, 1997); Winfried Menninghaus, *Ekel: Theorie und Geschichte einer starken Empfindung* (Frankfurt/Main: Suhrkamp, 1999); English: *Disgust: The Theory and History of a Strong Sensation*, trans. Howard Eiland and Joel Golb (Albany: State University of New York Press, 2000; Robert Rawdon Wilson, *The Hydra's Tale: Imagining Disgust* (Edmonton: University of Alberta Press, 2002); Chris Turner, *The Disgusting: The Unrepresentable from Kant to Kristeva*, unpublished Ph.D. thesis, University of London, 2000. Turner uses the terms *shock* and *disgust* interchangeably, which I consider problematic.

34. Despite his having lived in the United Kingdom as foreign correspondent for the *Frankfurter Allgemeine Zeitung* from 1975 to 1982, only one of Bohrer's many books has been translated into English: *Suddenness: On the Movement of Aesthetic Appearance*, trans. Ruth Crowley (New York: Columbia University Press, 1994).

35. See, for example, Karl Heinz Bohrer, "Ästhetik und Gewalt als Bedingungsverhältnis: Jenseits anthropologischer Begründungen," in Bohrer, *Die Grenzen des Ästhetischen* (Munich: Hanser, 1998), pp. 140–41; see also Bohrer, "Die permanente Theodizee: Über das verfehlte Böse im deutschen Bewusstsein," *Merkur*, no. 458 (April 1987), pp. 267–386; reprinted in Bohrer, *Nach der Natur: Über Politik und Ästhetik* (Munich and Vienna: Carl Hanser Verlag, 1988), p. 133; see also Bohrer, "Das Böse—Eine ästhetische Kategorie?" *Merkur*, no. 436 (June 1985), pp. 459–73.

36. Bohrer, *Suddenness*, p. vii.

37. See Laura Wixley Brooks, "Damien Hirst and the Sensibility of Shock," in *The Contemporary Sublime—Sensibilities of Transcendence and Shock*, Art & Design, profile no. 40, ed. Paul Crowther (London: London Academy Editions, 1995), pp. 55–67.

38. Both were shown at the Salon des Indépendants, the former in the year of its creation and the latter in 1865.

39. The original title reads *Was ist der Unterschied zwischen Casanova und Jesus: Der Gesichtsausdruck beim Nageln* and thus contains a pun by using "nailing" as a vulgar expression for sexual penetration.

40. Xiao Yu in an e-mail to the author via ESTeeLIE gallery, Dec. 2, 2009.

41. Julius, *Transgressions*, p. 17.

42. Dunlop, *Shock of the New*, p. 7. It becomes readily apparent that these categories are neither exhaustive nor clearly separated. Quite evidently, works such as

Stelarc's biotechnologically grown version of his ear or Orlan's sarcastic commentary on the perversions of cosmetic surgery not only violate principles of ethical rules of behavior, but are also questioned regarding their claim to pass as works of art, which here, however, might not be the principal reason for a reaction of shock.

43. Ibid.

44. Ibid. For my purposes it is relevant to note that Dunlop does not differentiate between modernist and avant-garde art and interrogates exhibitions representing art from either field.

45. Ibid. The assumption of an inherent and causal connection between the confrontation with something new (i.e., something never experienced before) and a consequent reaction of shock or distress can still be found today. A recent example was given by David McNeill, spokesman for Arts Council England, in November 2004, when stating that anything, which is truly "new and . . . groundbreaking . . . must, by definition, do something to upset people," pointing toward contemporary cultural production (as quoted by Mathew Sweet, "Trouble at Mall," *Evening Standard*, November 19, 2004, p. 30). However, one would need to examine to what extent this correlation represents the revival of a distinctly avant-garde correlation.

46. See ibid., p. 254.

47. Bohrer, *Suddenness*, p. 72.

48. Ibid., p. 83.

49. Cashell, *Aftershock*, p. 1.

50. Immanuel Kant, *The Critique of Judgement*, trans. James Creed Meredith (Oxford: Clarendon Press, 1964 [1790]), pp. 85–86.

51. Ibid., p. 8.

52. Ibid., p. 12 (italics in original).

53. As quoted by Dunlop, *Shock of the New*, p. 8.

54. Bürger, *Theory of the Avant-Garde*, pp. 80–81.

55. Ibid., p. 81. As Wulf Herzogenrath states correspondingly, "shocks are effective just once—but tremendously." See Wulf Herzogenrath, "Nam June Paik: Die subversiven Spiele der Doppelbödigkeit," in *Künstler: Kritisches Lexikon der Gegenwartskunst*, ed. Lothar Romain and Detlef Bluemler (Munich: Zeitverlag), p. 3.

56. Dunlop, *Shock of the New*, p. 7.

57. Andreas Huyssen, *After the Great Divide* (Indianapolis: Indiana University Press, 1986), p. 163; see also, for example, Bürger, *Theory of the Avant-Garde*, pp. 47–54.

58. Van den Berg, "On the Historiographic Distinction between Historical and Neo-Avant-Garde," p. 65.

59. Ralf Burmeister, "Dada 1958: Der Versuch, eine explodierte Bombe zu kitten," in *Grotesk! 130 Jahre Kunst der Frechheit*, ed. Pamela Kort, exhibition catalog (Munich: Prestel, 2003), p. 151.

60. See Bürger, *Theory of the Avant-Garde*, p. 4.

61. Ibid., p. 53.

62. Hal Foster, "What's Neo about the Neo-Avant-Garde?" *October*, vol. 70 (Autumn 1994), p. 13.

63. Foster, "What's Neo about the Neo-Avant-Garde?" p. 30.

64. See Bürger, *Theory of the Avant-Garde*, p. 58.

65. Anonymous, "Shock-Art with a Purpose," *Times Literary Supplement*, February 4, 1965, p. 80.

66. Bohrer, *Suddenness*, pp. 77–78.

67. Bürger's influential analysis of the avant-garde has triggered a wide range of critical responses, for example W. M. Lüdke, ed., *"Theorie der Avant-garde": Antworten auf Peter Bürgers Bestimmung von Kunst und bürgerlicher Gesellschaft* (Frankfurt: Suhrkamp Verlag, 1976); Benjamin Buchloh, "Theorizing the Avant-Garde," *Art in America*, vol. 72, no. 10 (November 1984), pp. 19–21.

68. Foster, "What's Neo about the Neo-Avant-Garde?" p. 8; see also n. 64.

69. Ibid., p. 16; see also p. 20.

70. Ibid., p. 8.

2. The Notion of Shock

1. Chris Turner, "Shock Treatment," *Tate: The Art Magazine* 22 (Summer 2000), p. 45.

2. Jeffrey Thompson Schnapp, "Crash (Speed as Engine of Individuation)," *Modernism/modernity*, vol. 6, no. 1 (1999), p. 7.

3. Patricia De Montfort, "White Muslin: Joanna Hiffernan and the 1860s," in *Whistler, Women, and Fashion*, ed. Margaret F. MacDonald et al. (New York: Frick Collection and Yale University Press, 2003), p. 80.

4. Nicholas Daly, "The Woman in White: Whistler, Hiffernan, Courbet, Du Maurier," *Modernism/modernity*, vol. 12, no. 1 (2005), p. 8.

5. Henry L. Mansel, "Sensation Novels," *Quarterly Review* 113 (1863), p. 482.

6. Walter Benjamin, "On Some Motifs in Baudelaire," in *Walter Benjamin: Selected Writings*, vol. 4: *1938–1940*, ed. Michael W. Jennings with Howard Eiland, trans. Edmund Jephcott, Rodney Livingstone et al. (Cambridge, MA: Belknap Press of Harvard University Press, 2003), pp. 313–55; Karl Heinz Bohrer, *Die Ästhetik des Schreckens: Die pessimistische Romantik und Ernst Jüngers Frühwerk* (Munich: Hanser, 1978).

7. Stephan Burgdorff and Klaus Wiegrefe, eds., *Der Erste Weltkrieg: Die Urkatastrophe des 20. Jahrhunderts* (Munich: Deutsche Verlags-Anstalt, 2004); see also Wolfgang J. Mommsen, *Die Urkatastrophe Deutschlands: Der Erste Weltkrieg 1914–1918*, vol. 17 of *Gebhardt: Handbuch der deutschen Geschichte*, ed. Jürgen Kocka (Stuttgart: Klett-Cotta, 2002).

8. See Leah Dickerman, "Introduction," in *Dada: Zurich, Berlin, Hannover, Cologne, New York, Paris*, ed. Dickerman, exhibition catalog, National Gallery of Art, Washington et al. (New York: Distributed Art Publishers, Inc., 2005), p. 3.

9. Gerd Krumeich, "Kriegsgeschichte im Wandel," in *"Keiner fühlt sich hier mehr als Mensch . . .": Erlebnis und Wirkung des Ersten Weltkriegs*, ed. Gerhard Hirschfeld and Gerd Krumeich (Essen: Klartext, 1993), p. 11, 14.

10. Klaus Vondung, "Propaganda oder Sinndeutung?" in *Kriegserlebnis: Der Erste Weltkrieg in der literarischen Gestaltung und symbolischen Deutung der Nationen*, ed. Klaus Vondung (Göttingen: Vandenhoeck & Ruprecht, 1980), p. 11.

11. Dickerman, "Introduction," in Dickerman, *Dada*, p. 3.

12. F. W. Mott, "Special Discussion on Shell Shock without Visible Signs of Injury," *Proceedings of the Royal Society of Medicine*, vol. 9 (1916), pp. i–xxiv; see also Dickerman, "Zurich," in Dickerman, *Dada*, p. 42 n. 42. One of the most recent publications is Peter Leese's *Shell Shock: Traumatic Neurosis and the British Soldiers of the First World War* (Basingstoke: Palgrave Macmillan, 2002). The author examines the phenomenon of shell shock, focusing on the technological and strategic specificities of World War I; there is no noteworthy consideration of psychoanalysis.

13. Fernand Leger, "Contemporary Achievement in Painting," as quoted by Elizabeth Allen Chabert, *Transforming Impact: The Shock Experience in Dada and Surrealist Poetry*, Ph.D. diss., Columbia University, New York, microfiche, 1995, p. 48.

14. The text's German title is more commonly translated as "The Work of Art in the Age of Its Mechanical Reproduction." I adopt the revised and more accurate translation "The Work of Art in the Age of Its Technological Reproducibility," as found in the recent edition of *Walter Benjamin: Selected Writings*, vol. 4: *1938–1940*, ed. Michael W. Jennings with Howard Eiland, trans. Edmund Jephcott, Rodney Livingstone et al. (Cambridge, MA: Belknap Press of Harvard University Press, 2003), pp. 251–83.

15. José Ortega y Gasset, *The Revolt of the Masses* (London: Allen and Unwin, 1932), 54, 119; see also John Carrey, *The Intellectuals and the Masses: Pride and Prejudice among the Literary Intelligentsia, 1880–1939* (London: Faber and Faber, 1992), p. 3.

16. Ortega y Gasset, *Revolt of the Masses*, p. 54.

17. Sidney V. Pearson, *The Growth and Distribution of Population* (New York: Wiley, 1935), p. 211.

18. Friedrich Lütge, *Deutsche Sozial- und Wirtschaftsgeschichte* (Berlin: Springer-Verlag, 1952), p. 506.

19. See Volker Berghahn, *Das Kaiserreich 1871–1914*, vol. 16 of *Gebhardt: Handbuch der deutschen Geschichte*, ed. Jürgen Kocka (Stuttgart: Klett-Cotta, 2003), pp. 91–92.

20. Louis Wirth, "Urbanism as a Way of Life," *American Journal of Sociology*, vol. 44, no. 1 (July 1938), p. 2.

21. Ibid., p. 5.

22. Wilhelm Graff, *Wie muss der Neurastheniker leben und wie wird er gesund?* (Berlin: Hugo Steinitz Verlag, 1907), p. 11.

23. George Miller Beard, "Neurasthenia, or Nervous Exhaustion," *Boston Medical and Surgical Journal*, vol. 80 (1869), pp. 217–21.

24. Graff, *Wie muss der Neurastheniker leben und wie wird er gesund?* p. 3.

25. Carl Ludwig Schleich, *Vom Schaltwerk der Gedanken* (Berlin: S. Fischer, 1916), p. 254, as quoted by Lothar Müller, "Modernität, Nervosität und Sachlichkeit: Das Berlin der Jahrhundertwende als Hauptstadt der 'neuen Zeit,'" in *Mythos Berlin: Zur Wahrnehmungsgeschichte einer industriellen Metropole*, ed. Ulrich Baehr, exhibition catalog, Berlin (Berlin: Verlag für Ästhetik und Kommunikation, 1987), p. 90.

26. For a historical analysis of the preoccupation with the phenomena of nervousness and neurasthenia, see Müller, "Modernität, Nervosität und Sachlichkeit."

27. John Bornemann, *After the Wall: East Meets West in the New Berlin* (New York: Basic Books, 1991), p. 6.

28. See Gottfried Korff, "Mentalität und Kommunikation in der Grossstadt: Berliner Notizen zur 'inneren' Urbanisierung," in *Grossstadt. Aspekte empirischer Kulturforschung*, ed. Theodor Kohlmann, exhibition catalog (Berlin: Museum für Deutsche Volkskunde Berlin, 1985), pp. 363–64.

29. See Georg Holmsten, *Die Berlin-Chronik* (Düsseldorf: Droste Verlag, 1990), p. 297.

30. See Werner Hegemann, *Das steinerne Berlin: Geschichte der grössten Mietskasernenstadt der Welt* (Berlin: Ullstein, 1963), p. 333; see also Hermann Schwabe, *Berliner Südwestbahn und Centralbahn: Beleuchtet vom Standpunkt der Wohnungsfrage und der industriellen Gesellschaft* (Berlin: Guttentag, 1873); and Korff, "Mentalität und Kommunikation in der Grossstadt," pp. 343, 345, 349.

31. See Holmsten, *Die Berlin-Chronik*, p. 297.

32. Gottfried Korff and Reinhard Rürup, eds., *Berlin, Berlin: Die Ausstellung zur Geschichte der Stadt*, exhibition catalog, Berliner Festspiele GmbH (Berlin: Nicolaische Verlagsbuchhandlung, 1987), p. 40; see also Bodo Harenberg, ed., *Die Chronik Berlins* (Dortmund: Chronik Verlag, 1991), p. 303.

33. Heinrich Grunholzer, "Erfahrungen eines jungen Schweizers im Vogtland," in Bettina von Arnim, *Dies Buch gehört dem König* (Berlin: E. H. Schrüder, 1843), pp. 534–98.

34. See Ignaz Wrobel, "Die Kinderhölle in Berlin," *Freie Welt*, Nov. 28, 1920, pp. 2–3.

35. See, for example, Harenberg, *Die Chronik Berlins*, p. 322; see also Korff and Rürup, *Berlin, Berlin*, pp. 38–9. The most recent publication on this subject is Andreas Killen, *Berlin Electropolis: Shock, Nerves, and German modernity* (Berkeley: University of California Press, 2006).

36. See Wolfgang Ribbe, ed., *Geschichte Berlins*, vol. 2: *Von der Märzrevolution bis zur Gegenwart* (Berlin: Berliner Wissenschafts-Verlag, 2002), pp. 736–37.

37. See Ingo Materna, Wolfgang Ribbe, et al., *Berlin: Geschichte in Daten* (Munich: Koehler and Amelang, 1997), p. 155; see also Harenberg, *Die Chronik Berlins*, pp. 255, 275, 308.

38. See Ribbe, *Von der Märzrevolution bis zur Gegenwart*, p. 737.

39. See Materna, Ribbe, et al., *Berlin: Geschichte in Daten*, pp. 137, 160.

40. Egon Friedell, *Ecce poeta* (Berlin: S. Fischer, 1912), p. 259, as quoted by Müller, "Modernität, Nervosität und Sachlichkeit," p. 92.

41. For a comprehensive account on the development of the railway and railway traveling in nineteenth-century Europe and its impact on people, see Wolfgang Schivelbusch, *The Railway Journey: The Industrialisation of Time and Space in the 19th Century* (Berkeley: University of California Press, 1992).

42. See Holmsten, *Die Berlin-Chronik*, p. 277; see also Materna, Ribbe, et al., *Berlin: Geschichte in Daten*, p. 145.

43. See Holmsten, *Die Berlin-Chronik*, p. 304; see also Ribbe, *Von der Märzrevolution bis zur Gegenwart*, p. 738.

44. John E. Erichsen, *On Railway and Other Injuries of the Nervous System* (London: Walton & Maberly, 1866).

45. See Müller, "Modernität, Nervosität und Sachlichkeit," p. 87.

46. See Inka Mülder-Bach, "Einleitung," in *Modernität und Trauma*, ed. Mülder-Bach (Vienna: WUV, 2000), p. 8.

47. Description of post-traumatic stress disorder (PTSD), as given in Brigid Doherty, "'See: We Are All Neurasthenics!'" or, The Trauma of Dada Montage," *Critical Inquiry* 24 (Autumn 1997), p. 84.

48. See Mülder-Bach, "Einleitung," in Mülder-Bach, *Modernität und Trauma*, p. 8.

49. See Walter Benjamin, "A Berlin Chronicle," in *Walter Benjamin: Selected Writings*, vol. 2: *1927–1934*, ed. Michael W. Jennings with Howard Eiland and Gary Smith, trans. Edmund Jephcott and Rodney Livingstone et al. (Cambridge, MA: Belknap Press of Harvard University Press, 1999), pp. 599–600.

50. See Korff and Rürup, *Berlin, Berlin*, 39; see also Harenberg, *Die Chronik Berlins*, p. 292.

51. Walter Benjamin, "The Paris of the Second Empire in Baudelaire," in *Selected Writings*, vol. 4, ed. Jennings, p. 29.

52. See Benjamin, "A Berlin Chronicle," p. 595 and following.

53. See Karl Scheffler, *Berlin: Ein Stadtschicksal* (Berlin: Reiss, 1910), pp. 51 and following, 181; see also Müller, "Modernität, Nervosität und Sachlichkeit," pp. 79–80.

54. Mark Twain, "The German Chicago," in *The Complete Essays of Mark Twain*, ed. Charles Neider (Garden City, NY: Doubleday & Co. 1963), pp. 87, 88.

55. Benjamin, "A Berlin Chronicle," p. 596.

56. See Gustav Janouch, *Gespräch mit Kafka* (Frankfurt/Main: Fischer, 1961), p. 93.

57. Richard Hamann, *Der Impressionismus in Leben und Kunst* (Cologne: DuMont-Schauberg, 1907), 204; see also Müller, "Modernität, Nervosität und Sachlichkeit," p. 89.

58. Benjamin, "On Some Motives in Baudelaire," p. 328.

59. See Benjamin, "A Berlin Chronicle," pp. 597–98.

60. See ibid., p. 619; see also Walter Benjamin, "Berlin Childhood around 1900" (final version), in *Walter Benjamin: Selected Writings*, vol. 3: *1935–1938*, ed. Michael W. Jennings with Howard Eiland, trans. Edmund Jephcott and Rodney Livingstone et al. (Cambridge, MA: Belknap Press of Harvard University Press, 2002), pp. 349–50.

61. Benjamin, "A Berlin Chronicle," p. 600.

62. Ibid., p. 601.

63. See Benjamin, "Ein Jakobiner von Heute: Zu Werner Hegemanns *Das steinerne Berlin*," in *Walter Benjamin: Gesammelte Schriften*, vol. 3, ed. Rolf Tiedemann and Hermann Schweppenhäuser (Frankfurt: Suhrkamp, 1972), p. 265.

64. Walter Benjamin to Gershom Scholem, April 17, 1931; reprinted in English in *The Correspondence of Walter Benjamin 1910–1940*, ed. Gershom Scholem and Theodor W. Adorno, trans. Manfred R. Jacobson and Evelyn M. Jacobson (Chicago: University of Chicago Press, 1994), p. 377.

65. Benjamin, "The Work of Art in the Age of Its Technological Reproducibility," p. 255.

66. Clemens Zimmermann and Jürgen Reulecke, "Einleitung," in *Die Stadt als Moloch? Das Land als Kraftquell?* ed. Clemens Zimmermann and Jürgen Reulecke (Basel: Birkhäuser Verlag, 1999), p. 10.

67. Georg Simmel, "Metropolis and Mental Life," in *Simmel on Culture: Selected Writings*, ed. David Frisby and Mike Featherstone (London: Sage Publications, 1997), p. 175.

68. Georg Simmel, as quoted in Michael Landman, "Arthur Steins Erinnerungen an Georg Simmel," in *Ästhetik und Soziologie um die Jahrhundertwende: Georg Simmel*, ed. Hannes Böhringer and Karl Gründer (Frankfurt/Main: Vittorio Klostermann, 1976), p. 274.

69. Simmel, "Metropolis and Mental Life," p. 178.

70. See the curriculum vitae that Benjamin submitted to Frankfurt University in 1926 along with his "Habilitationsschrift," in *Walter Benjamin: Gesammelte Schriften*, vol. 6, ed. Tiedemann and Schweppenhäuser, pp. 215–16.

71. David Frisby compares Benjamin's figure of the flâneur and Simmel's essayistic type of sociological research and writing; see David Frisby, *Sociological Impressionism: A reassessment of Georg Simmel's Social Theory* (London: Heinemann, 1981), pp. 68–102.

72. See Benjamin's letter to Adorno of February 23, 1939, in *Walter Benjamin: Selected Writings*, vol. 4, p. 209.

73. Benjamin, quoted in Lothar Müller, "'Die Grossstadt als Ort der Moderne," in *Die Unwirklichkeit der Städte: Grossstadtdarstellungen zwischen Moderne und Postmodern*, ed. Klaus R. Scherpe (Rheinbeck bei Hamburg: Rowohlt, 1988), p. 30.

74. See *Walter Benjamin: Selected Writings*, vol. 1: *1892–1926*, ed. Michael W. Jennings with Marcus Bullock, trans. Edmund Jephcott and Rodney Livingstone et al. (Cambridge, MA: Belknap Press of Harvard University Press, 1996), p. 494.

75. See Adorno's letter to Benjamin of November 10, 1938, in *Walter Benjamin: Selected Writings*, vol. 4, p. 101; see also Werner Fuld, *Walter Benjamin: Zwischen den Stühlen* (Munich: Carl Hanser Verlag, 1979), p. 153; and also p. 257 for Benjamin's and Adorno's differing evaluations of Simmel.

76. Simmel, "Metropolis and Mental Life," p. 175.

77. Willy Hellpach, *Mensch und Volk der Grossstadt* (Stuttgart: Ferdinand Enke Verlag, 1939), p. 69 and following.

78. See Hans Simmel, "Auszüge aus den Lebenserinnerungen," in *Ästhetik und Soziologie um die Jahrhundertwende: Georg Simmel*, ed. Böhringer and Gründer, p. 247; see ibid., pp. 248, 249, 251.

79. See ibid., p. 265.

80. Benjamin, "The Paris of the Second Empire in Baudelaire," p. 27.

81. Ralph Hoppe, *Die Friedrichstrasse: Pflaster der Extreme* (Berlin: be.bra-Verlag, 1999).

82. Ibid., p. 50.

83. See ibid., p. 42; and Dietmar Jazbinsek, "'The Metropolis and the Mental Life

of Georg Simmel: On the History of Antipathy," *Journal of Urban History*, vol. 30, no. 1 (November 2003), p. 103.

84. Hildegard von Spitzemberg, *Das Tagebuch der Baronin Spitzemberg, geb. Freiin v. Varnbühler: Aufzeichnungen aus der Hofgesellschaft des Hohenzollernreiches*, ed. Rudolf Vierhaus (Göttingen: Vandenhoeck & Ruprecht, 1960), p. 377. See also Müller, "Modernität, Nervosität und Sachlichkeit," p. 88.

85. See Jazbinsek, "The Metropolis and the Mental Life of Georg Simmel," p. 103.

86. See ibid.; see Theodor Lessing, *Philosophie als Tat*, vol. 2 (Göttingen: Otto Hapke Verlag, 1914), p. 302.

87. W. Hartenau (alias Walter Rathenau), "Die schönste Stadt der Welt," *Zukunft*, vol. 7, no. 15 (1899), as quoted in Müller, "Modernität, Nervosität und Sachlichkeit,"p. 79.

88. Jazbinsek, "The Metropolis and the Mental Life of Georg Simmel," p. 484.

89. See Hans Simmel, "Auszüge aus den Lebenserinnerungen," p. 248.

90. Karl Joël, "Eine Zeitphilosophie," *Neue Deutsche Rundschau* (Freie Bühne), no. 12 (1901), 813; as quoted in Müller, "Die Grossstadt als Ort der Moderne," p. 22.

91. Simmel as quoted in Hans Simmel, "Auszüge aus den Lebenserinnerungen," p. 265 (English trans. as given in Jazbinsek, "The Metropolis and the Mental Life of Georg Simmel," p. 104).

92. Simmel as quoted in Hans Simmel, "Auszüge aus Lebenserinnerungen," p. 265.

93. See Ilja Scrubar, "Zur Formierung des soziologischen Blicks," in *Die Grossstadt als "Text,"* ed. Manfred Smuda, 37–52 (Munich: Wilhelm Fink Verlag, 1992), p. 37.

94. Ibid., p. 38.

95. Simmel, "Sociology of the Senses," p. 110.

96. Ibid., p. 117.

97. Ibid., p. 178.

98. Ibid., p. 119.

99. Ibid.

100. Ibid.

101. Ibid., p. 118.

102. Ibid.

103. See, for example, Jazbinsek, "The Metropolis and the Mental Life of Georg Simmel," pp. 107–8.

104. Buck-Morss, "Aesthetics and Anaesthetics," p. 388.

105. Simmel, "Metropolis and Mental Life," p. 178.

106. Ibid.

107. Ibid., p. 173.

108. Ibid., pp. 173–74.

109. Ibid., p. 174.

110. Ibid., p. 178.

111. Ibid., p. 179.

112. For contemporaneous discussions of distraction as a specifically modern mode of perception see, for example, Jonathan Crary, *Suspension of Perception: Attention, Spectacle, and Modern Culture* (Cambridge, MA: MIT Press, 1999), pp. 48, 49 n. 111.

113. See, for example, Ralf Thies, *Wiener Grossstadt-Dokumente: Erkundungen in der Metropole der k.u.k Monarchie* (The Vienna Grossstadt-Documents: Explorations of the Imperial Metropolis), 2001, Schriftenreihe der Forschungsgruppe "Metropolenforschung" am Wissenschaftszentrum Berlin für Sozialforschung (WZB), Berlin, text available at: http://bibliothek.wz-berlin.de/pdf/2001/ii01–503.pdf.

114. Ibid, p. 4.

115. Freud to Karl Abraham of August 25, 1914, in *The Complete Correspondence of Sigmund Freud and Karl Abraham, 1907–1925*, ed. Ernst Falzeder (London: Karnac, 2002), p. 272.

116. See Hubert Danler, *Sigmund Freud in seiner Epoche (1856–1939)* (Norderstedt: Books on Demand, 2001), pp. 97–98.

117. Freud to Ferenczi, October 17, 1915, in *The Correspondence of Sigmund Freud and Sándor Ferenczi,* vol. 2: *1914–1919*, ed. Eva Brabant and Ernst Falzeder, trans. Peter T. Hoffer (Cambridge, MA: Belknap Press of Harvard University Press, 1996), p. 82.

118. See Freud to Ferenczi, February 4, 1916, in *Correspondence of Sigmund Freud and Sándor Ferenczi,* vol. 2, p. 111.

119. Freud, as quoted in Ronald W. Clark, *Freud: The Man and the Cause* (London: Jonathan Cape, Weidenfeld & Nicolson, 1980), p. 377.

120. Freud to Ferenczi, February 4, 1916, in *Correspondence of Sigmund Freud and Sándor Ferenczi,* vol. 2, p. 111.

121. Freud to Karl Abraham, December 10, 1917, in *Complete Correspondence of Sigmund Freud and Karl Abraham*, ed. Falzeder, p. 364.

122. Freud to Lou Andreas-Salomé, November 25, 1914, as quoted in Danler, *Sigmund Freud in seiner Epoche*, p. 76.

123. Freud to Ernest Jones, December 25, 1914, in *The Complete Correspondence of Sigmund Freud and Ernest Jones, 1908–1939*, ed. R. Andrew Paskauskas (Cambridge, MA: Belknap Press of Harvard University Press, 1993), p. 309.

124. See Clark, *Freud: The Man and the Cause*, p. 378.

125. See ibid., p. 365.

126. See Heinrich Wietfeldt, *Kriegsneurosen als psychisch-soziale Mangelkrankheit* (Leipzig: Georg Thieme Verlag, 1936), p. 15.

127. Ernest Jones, "War Shock and Freud's Theory of the Neuroses," *Proceedings of the Royal Society of Medicine*, vol. 11, 1918 (Sect Psych), p. 24.

128. See Bernd Ulrich, "'... als wenn nichts geschehen wäre': Anmerkungen zur Behandlung der Kriegsopfer während des Ersten Weltkrieges," in Hirschfeld and Krumeich, *"Keiner fühlt sich hier mehr als Mensch ...,"* p. 117.

129. Sándor Ferenczi in his paper given to the Fifth Psycho-Analytical Congress, Budapest, 1918, in *Psycho-Analysis and the War Neurosis*, ed. Sándor Ferenczi et al. (London: International Psycho-Analytical Press, 1921), p. 6.

130. See, for example, Louis Puussep, *Traumatische Kriegsneurose* (Tartu: Typographie J. Mällo, 1925), p. 1.

131. See, for example, Martha N. Evans, *Fits and Starts: A Genealogy of Hysteria in Modern France* (Ithaca, NY: Cornell University Press, 1991), p. 78 and following.

132. Sigmund Freud, "Memorandum on the Electrical Treatment of War Neurot-

ics," in Kurt R. Eissler, *Freud as an Expert Witness: The Discussion of War Neuroses between Freud an Wagner-Jauregg* (Madison, CT: International Universities Press, 1986), p. 24; see also Sigmund Freud, "Beyond the Pleasure Principle," in *The Standard Edition of the Complete Psychological Works of Sigmund Freud*, vol. 18: *Group Psychology and the Analysis of the Ego*, ed. and trans. James Strachey (London: Hogarth Press and Institute of Psycho-Analysis, 1955), p. 12.

133. Ewald Stier, "Wie kann der Entstehung von Kriegsneurosen bei der Feldarmee vorgebeugt werden?" *Deutsche Militärärztliche Zeitschrift* 47 (1918), p. 62; an English translation of this quotation can be found in Paul Lerner, "An Economy of Memory: Psychiatrists, Veterans and Traumatic Narratives in Weimar Germany," in Mülder-Bach, *Modernität und Trauma*, p. 86.

134. Hans-Ulrich Wehler, *Deutsche Gesellschaftsgeschichte*, vol. 4: *Vom Beginn des Ersten Weltkriegs bis zur Gründung der Beiden Deutschen Staaten 1914–1949* (Munich: C. H. Beck, 2003), p. 103.

135. Ernst Falzeder, Einleitung, in *Sigmund Freud—Sandor Ferenczi: Briefwechsel*, vol. 2: *1917–1919*, ed. Brabant and Falzeder (Vienna: Böhlau Verlag, 1996), p. 12 (my italics). See also Sigmund Freud in his introduction to the Fifth International Psycho-Analytical Congress, Budapest, 1918, in *Psycho-Analysis and the War Neurosis*, ed. Ferenczi et al., p. 1.

136. See, for example, Lerner, "An Economy of Memory," p. 79.

137. See Ben Shephard, *A War of Nerves* (Cambridge, MA: Harvard University Press, 2001), pp. 82–83.

138. See Doherty, "'See: We Are All Neurasthenics!'" p. 102; and Ernst Simmel, *Kriegs-Neurosen und "Psychisches Trauma"* (Munich: Nemnich, 1918).

139. See Shephard, *A War of Nerves*, p. 57.

140. See, for example, Karl Heinz Roth, "Die Modernisierung der Folter in den beiden Weltkriegen: Der Konflikt der Psychotherapeuten und Schulpsychiater um die deutschen 'Kriegsneurotiker' 1915–1941," *1999: Zeitschrift für Sozialgeschichte des 20. und 21. Jahrhunderts* 3 (July 1987): pp. 15–16. See also Freud, "Memorandum on the Electrical Treatment of War Neurotics," pp. 24–26.

141. Freud to Ferenczi, November 17, 1918, in *Correspondence of Sigmund Freud and Sándor Ferenczi*, vol. 2, p. 311.

142. See Ferenczi, in *Psycho-Analysis of the War Neuroses*, ed. Ferenczi et al., p. 194.

143. See Freud, "Beyond the Pleasure Principle," pp. 12, 33.

144. Ibid., p. 70 (my italics).

145. Heinrich Wietfeldt uses a similar analogue between physical and psychological harm when comparing the polar explorer's danger of freezing with the soldier's exposure to a "coldness of the soul" (*Seelenkälte*); see Wietfeldt, *Kriegsneurosen als psychisch-soziale Mangelkrankheit*, p. 13. In his autobiographical short story "The Blackbird," recalling an experience as soldier in World War I, Robert Musil draws an interesting analogy between a physical and psychological wounding, leading to an experience of shock. See Robert Musil, *The Blackbird*, trans. Thomas Frick and Wilhelm Wiegandt (Cambridge, MA: Simba Editions, 1981).

146. Freud, "Beyond the Pleasure Principle," p. 29.

147. Ibid., p. 31.

148. See, for example, Ernst Simmel, *Kriegs-Neurosen und "Psychisches Trauma,"* p. 6; and Puussep, *Traumatische Kriegsneurose*, p. 2. Puusep notably refers to Carl Moeli, "Über psychische Störungen nach Eisenbahnunfällen," *Berliner Klinische Wochenschrift: Organ für practische Aerzte*, vol. 18, no. 6 (1881), pp. 73–75; and to Jean-Martin Charcot, "Deux nouveaux cas de paralysie hysterotraumatique chez l'homme," in J.-M. Charcot, *Oeuvres complètes de J.-M. Charcot*, vol. 4 (Paris: Bureaux du Progrès Médical, 1887).

149. Charles Dickens to Thomas Mitton, June 13, 1865, as quoted in Mülder-Bach, "Einleitung," in Mülder-Bach, *Modernität und Trauma*, p. 7.

150. Ibid.

151. Freud, "Beyond the Pleasure Principle," p. 31.

152. See ibid., p. 85.

153. Wietfeldt, *Kriegsneurosen als psychisch-soziale Mangelkrankheit*, pp. 12, 34.

154. Sigmund Freud, "Two Artificial Groups: The Church and the Army," in *Group Psychology and the Analysis of the Ego*, p. 95.

155. See Ernst Simmel, *Kriegs-Neurosen und "Psychisches Trauma,"* p. 5.

156. Hirschfeld and Krumeich, *"Keiner fühlt sich hier mehr als Mensch . . . ,"* book title and p. 4.

157. Hugo Ball, *Flight Out of Time: A Dada Diary*, ed. John Elderfield, trans. Ann Raimes (New York: Viking Press, 1974), entry of June 26, 1915, p. 22.

158. Ibid., entry of March 5, 1916, p. 55.

159. Ibid., entry of March 3, 1916, p. 56.

160. See Dickerman, "Introduction," in Dickerman, *Dada*, p. 6; and Doherty, "'See: We Are All Neurasthenics!'" pp. 93, 95, 102. Huelsenbeck refers to an encounter with Karl Bonhoeffer in 1923–25, who was treating war neuroses at the Charité in Berlin—see Doherty, "'See: We Are All Neurasthenics!'" p. 91.

161. Wieland Herzfelde, "The Curious Merchant from Holland," *Harper's*, Nov. 1943, p. 569.

162. See Doherty, "'See: We Are All Neurasthenics!'" pp. 102, 105–6, 115.

163. Wietfeldt, *Kriegsneurosen als psychisch-soziale Mangelkrankheit*, p. 13.

164. Johannes Volmert, *Ernst Jünger "In Stahlgewittern"* (Munich: Wilhelm Fink Verlag, 1985), p. 53.

165. See Mülder-Bach, "Einleitung," in Mülder-Bach, *Modernität und Trauma*, p. 9; see also Helmut Lethen, "'Knall an sich': Das Ohr als Einbruchstelle des Traumas," in ibid., p. 207.

166. Sigmund Freud, "The Disillusionment of the War," in *Standard Edition of the Complete Psychological Works of Sigmund Freud*, vol. 14: *Thoughts for the Times on War and Death*, p. 275.

167. Ernst Jünger, *The Storm of Steel: From the Diary of a German Storm-Troop Officer on the Western Front*, trans. Basil Creighton (New York: Howard Fertig, 1975), p. 3.

168. Jünger, *Storm of Steel*, p. 2.

169. Robert Graves, *Goodbye to All That* (Harmondsworth, UK: Penguin, 1960), p. 205.

170. Ball, *Flight Out of Time*, entry of November 25, 1914, p. 10.

171. Ibid., p. 11.

172. Ulrich Linse, "Das wahre Zeugnis: Eine psychohistorische Deutung des Ersten Weltkriegs," in *Der Erste Weltkrieg in der literarischen Gestaltung und symbolischen Deutung der Nationen*, ed. Klaus Vondung (Göttingen: Vandenhoeck & Ruprecht, 1980), p. 98.

173. Linse, "Das wahre Zeugnis," p. 103.

174. Freud, "Beyond the Pleasure Principle," p. 31.

175. Ibid., p. 28.

176. Ibid., p. 27.

177. See, for example, Sigmund Freud, "A Note upon the 'Mystic Writing-Pad,'" in *The Standard Edition of the Complete Psychological Works of Sigmund Freud*, vol. 19, p. 228.

178. Freud, "Beyond the Pleasure Principle," p. 12 and following.

179. Sigmund Freud, *Vorlesungen zur Einführung in die Psychoanalyse*, Studienausgabe, vol. 1, 6th ed. (Frankfurt/Main: Suhrkamp, 1975), p. 382.

180. Freud, "Beyond the Pleasure Principle," p. 12.

181. Ibid.

182. Ortega y Gasset, *Revolt of the Masses*, p. 11.

183. Ibid., pp. 11, 13, 15.

184. Sigmund Freud, "New Introductory Lectures on Psychoanalysis," in *Standard Edition of the Complete Psychological Works of Sigmund Freud*, vol. 22, p. 72.

185. Benjamin, "The Work of Art in the Age of Its Technological Reproducibility," p. 268.

186. See Crary, *Suspension of Perception*, p. 302 and following.

187. Walter Benjamin, "Moscow," in *Walter Benjamin: Selected Writings*, vol. 2, p. 32.

188. Ibid., p. 23.

189. Benjamin to Siegfried Kracauer, February 23, 1927, as quoted in *Walter Benjamin: Gesammelte Schriften*, vol. 6, p. 781.

190. Benjamin to Martin Buber, as quoted in *The Correspondence of Walter Benjamin* (Chicago: University of Chicago Press, 1994), p. 313; see also *Walter Benjamin: Selected Writings*, vol. 2, p. 824.

191. See for example Adorno to Benjamin, November 10, 1938, in *Walter Benjamin: Selected Writings*, vol. 4, pp. 100, 102.

192. Buck-Morss, "Aesthetics and Anaesthetics," p. 388.

193. Benjamin to Hugo von Hofmannsthal, June 5, 1927; reprinted in English in *The Correspondence of Walter Benjamin 1910–1940*, ed. Gershom Scholem and Theodor W. Adorno, trans. Manfred R. Jacobson and Evelyn M. Jacobson (Chicago: University of Chicago Press, 1994), p. 314.

194. Robert Musil, *The Man without Qualities*, vol. 1 (London: Picador, 1995), p. 4. (The first volume was written in the late 1920s and published in 1930.)

195. Benjamin, "Moscow," p. 32.

196. Benjamin, "The Work of Art in the Age of Its Technological Reproducibility," p. 268.

197. "The Flâneur" is the second chapter of "The Paris of the Second Empire in Baudelaire," pp. 18–39.

198. Benjamin, "The Work of Art in the Age of Its Technological Reproducibility," p. 268.

199. Ibid.

200. See Crary, *Suspension of Perception*, p. 248.

201. Frederic J. Schwartz, *Blind Spots: Critical Theory and the History of Art in Twentieth-Century Germany* (New Haven, CT: Yale University Press, 2005), p. 62.

202. Richard Shusterman, *Performing Live: Aesthetic Alternatives for the Ends of Art* (New York: Cornell University Press: 2000), p. 18; the relevant chapter on "The End of Aesthetic Experience" (pp. 15–34) was first published in *Journal of Aesthetics and Art Criticism* 55 (1999), pp. 29–41.

203. See Hamann, *Der Impressionismus in Leben und Kunst*, p. 204.

204. Filippo Tommaso Marinetti, "Tactilism" (1924), in *Manifesto: A Century of Isms*, ed. Mary Ann Caws (Lincoln: University of Nebraska Press, 2001), p. 198.

205. Walter Benjamin, "Theory of Distraction," in *Walter Benjamin: Selected Writings*, vol. 3, p. 141.

206. See Crary, *Suspension of Perception*, p. 248.

207. Benjamin, "Theory of Distraction," p. 141.

208. See Benjamin, "On Some Motifs in Baudelaire," p. 319.

209. Buck-Morss, "Aesthetics and Anaesthetics," p. 388.

210. Freud, "Beyond the Pleasure Principle," p. 25 (my italics; in the original, the entire phrase is in italics). See also Freud, "A Note upon the 'Mystic Writing-Pad,'" p. 228.

211. Freud, "Beyond the Pleasure Principle," p. 25.

212. Ibid., p. 27.

213. Benjamin, "A Berlin Chronicle," pp. 632–33.

214. Benjamin, "On Some Motifs in Baudelaire," p. 319.

215. Ibid.

216. Max Horkheimer, "The End of Reason," in *The Essential Frankfurt School Reader*, ed. Andrew Arato and Eike Gebhardt (New York: Urizen Books, 1978), p. 38.

217. Hal Foster, "Amour Fou," *October*, vol. 56 (Spring 1991): p. 73, with reference to Freud's "Beyond the Pleasure Principle," pp. 6–7, 23–27.

218. Freud, "Beyond the Pleasure Principle," p. 18.

219. Walter Benjamin, "Das Kunstwerk im Zeitalter seiner technischen Reproduzierbarkeit" (first version), in *Walter Benjamin: Gesammelte Schriften*, vol. 1, 2, ed. Tiedemann and Schweppenhäuser, p. 464. This quoted phrase is not contained in the final version of the text.

220. Benjamin, "The Work of Art in the Age of Its Technological Reproducibility," p. 267.

221. Ibid., p. 269, see also Benjamin, "Theory of Distraction," p. 141.

222. See Benjamin, "Theory of Distraction," p. 141.

223. Buck-Morss, "Aesthetics and Anaesthetics," p. 390.

3. Shock and the Senseless in Dada

1. Hanne Bergius, *"Dada Triumphs!" Dada Berlin, 1917–1923, Artistry of Polarities: Montages, Metamechanics, Manifestations*, trans. Brigitte Pichon, vol. 5 of *Crisis and the Arts: The History of Dada*, ed. Stephen C. Foster (New Haven, CT: Thomson/Gale), 2003, p. 26. The text was first published in German under the title *Montage und Metamechanik. Dada Berlin: Artistik von Polaritäten* (Berlin: Gebr. Mann Verlag, 2000); the second chapter on "Club Dada Berlin" has been added to the English edition.

2. Peter Bürger, *Theory of the Avant-Garde* (Minneapolis: University of Minnesota Press, 1984), p. 18.

3. See Matei Calinescu, *Five Faces of Modernity* (Durham, NC: Duke University Press, 1987), p. 124.

4. Tristan Tzara, "Erinnerungen an Dada," in *Der Querschnitt: Das Magazin der aktuellen Ewigkeitswerte, 1924–1933*, ed. Christian Ferber (Berlin: Ullstein Verlag: 1981), p. 129.

5. Peter Bürger, *Der französische Surrealismus* (Frankfurt: Athenäum Verlag, 1971), p. 38.

6. P. H., "Da-Da. Literatur-Narrenheiten in der Sezession," in *Urlaute dadaistischer Poesie: Der Berliner Dada-Abend am 12. April 1918*, ed. Jeanpaul Goergen (Hannover: Postskriptum Verlag, 1994), p. 73.

7. See ibid., p. 77.

8. Tristan Tzara, "An Introduction to Dada," in *Dada Painters and Poets*, ed. Robert Motherwell, 2nd ed. (New York: Wittenborn, Schultz, Inc., 1967), p. 395.

9. Raoul Hausmann, "Aussichten oder Ende des Neodadaismus" (1962), in Adelheid Koch, *Ich bin immerhin der grösste Experimentator Österreichs: Raoul Hausmann—Dada und Neodada* (Innsbruck: Haymon-Verlag, 1994), n.p.

10. Walter Mehring, *Berlin Dada* (Zurich: Die Arche, 1959), p. 51.

11. Ibid.

12. George Grosz, *A Little Yes and a Big No: The Autobiography of George Grosz*, trans. Lola Sachs Dorin (New York: Dial Press, 1946), p. 182.

13. Tristan Tzara, "Erinnerungen an Dada, " p. 128.

14. Richard Huelsenbeck, "Dada siegt!" in *Dada siegt!: Bilanz und Erinnerung*, ed. Richard Huelsenbeck and Tristan Tzara (Hamburg: Nautilus/Nemo Press et al., 1985), p. 27.

15. Tzara, "Erinnerungen an Dada," p. 129.

16. See Jürgen Hotz, ed., *Der Brockhaus: Moderne Kunst—vom Impressionismus bis zur Gegenwart* (Leipzig: Brockhaus, 2003), p. 71.

17. Raoul Hausmann, "Dada empört sich, regt sich und stirbt in Berlin," in Raoul Hausmann, *Am Anfang war Dada*, ed. Karl Riha and Günter Kämpf (Steinbach/Giessen: Anabas-Verlag: Günter Kämpf, 1972), p. 15.

18. Raoul Hausmann, commenting on the Berlin Dada Soirée, April 12, 1918, in Hausmann, *Am Anfang war Dada*, p. 27.

19. See Hausmann, "Aussichten oder Ende des Neodadaismus," n.p.

20. Kurt Schwitters, "Katalog" (1927), in Kurt Schwitters, *Das literarische Werk*, vol. 5, ed. Friedhelm Lach (Cologne: DuMont Schauberg, 1973–1981).

21. Marcel Duchamp in an interview with George Heard Hamilton (1959), in *Marcel Duchamp: Interviews and Statements*, ed. Susanne Gauss, trans. Serge Stauffer (Ostfildern: Cantz, 1991), p. 78.

22. Hausmann, "Aussichten oder Ende des Neodadaismus," n.p.

23. Hans Richter, *Dada: Art and Anti-Art* (London: Thames and Hudson, 1965), p. 65.

24. Richard Huelsenbeck, "Collective Dada Manifesto" (1918), in Motherwell, *Dada Painters and Poets*, p. 244.

25. Dada's own references to Nietzsche are mostly of implicit nature. However, Hugo Ball wrote a text on "Nietzsche in Basel" in 1909–10, and started a Ph.D. dissertation on Nietzsche, which remained unfinished, about the affinities between Nietzsche and Dada; see also Bergius, *"Dada Triumphs!"* pp. 11–20.

26. Raoul Hausmann, "Dada ist mehr als Dada," in Hausmann, *Am Anfang war Dada*, p. 89 (my italics).

27. Raoul Hausmann, "Bilanz der Feierlichkeit," *Die Erde: Politische und kulturpolitische Halbmonatsschrift*, vol. 8, no. 1 (1919), p. 519. English translation as quoted by Bergius, *"Dada Triumphs!"* p. 9.

28. Marcel Janco, "Die Kunst will und muss wieder zum Leben zurückkehren . . ." (1919), reprinted in *Manifeste und Proklamationen der europäischen Avantgarde (1909–1938)*, ed. Wolfgang Asholt and Walter Fähnders (Stuttgart: Verlag J. B. Metzler, 1995), p. 162.

29. Ibid.

30. Ball, *Flight out of Time: A Dada Diary*, ed. John Elderfield, trans. Ann Raimes (New York: Viking Press, 1974), entry of April 5, 1916, p. 58.

31. Huelsenbeck, "Collective Dada Manifesto," pp. 242–46. The translation of the title in Motherwell is inexact insofar as the original German title reads "Dadaistisches Manifest" (Dada Manifesto). Motherwell gives the date of 1920; however, it was written early in 1918 and presented at the first Berlin Dada soirée on April 12 that year—see, for example, Goergen, *Urlaute dadaistischer Poesie*, p. 112; see also Georges Hugnet, *Dictionnaire du Dadaïsme 1916–1922* (Paris: Jean-Claude Simoën, 1976), p. 223. It was first published in Huelsenbeck's collection of writings, *Dada Almanach*, in 1920.

32. See Karl Riha, Nachwort, in *Dada Zürich: Texte, Manifeste, Dokumente*, ed. Karl Riha (Stuttgart: Reclam, 1992), p. 174.

33. Huelsenbeck, "Collective Dada Manifesto," p. 242. Huelsenbeck repeats these sentences in his text "Die dadaistische Bewegung: Eine Selbstbiographie" (1920), *Die neue Rundschau* 31, Jahrgang der freien Bühne, Bd. 2, 1920; reprinted in Goergen, *Urlaute dadaistischer Poesie*, p. 103.

34. Francis Picabia, "Art," in *Dadas on Art*, ed. Lucy Lippard (Englewood Cliffs, NJ: Prentice Hall, 1971), p. 167.

35. Hausmann, "Dada empört sich, regt sich und stirbt in Berlin," p. 16.

36. Owen F. Smith, "Pre-Fluxus Conceptual Developments and Generative Influences," available at: www.thing.net/~grist/ld/smith-fl.htm, n.p. Reprinted as chapter 1 of Owen Smith, *Fluxus: The History of an Attitude* (San Diego, CA: San Diego State University Press, 1998).

37. Huelsenbeck, "Die dadaistische Bewegung," p. 101.

38. Leah Dickerman, "Introduction" in *Dada: Zurich, Berlin, Hannover, Cologne, New York, Paris*, ed. Dickerman, exhibition catalog, National Gallery of Art, Washington, D.C., and other museums (New York: Distributed Art Publishers, Inc., 2005), p. 9.

39. Huelsenbeck, "Die dadaistische Bewegung," p. 102.

40. Hausmann, "Aussichten oder Ende des Neodadaismus, " n.p.

41. Raoul Hausmann in a speech given at the opening of an exhibition of photomontage at the Kunstgewerbemuseum in Berlin, curated by Cesar Domela-Nieuwenhhuis, in Hausmann, "Aussichten oder Ende des Neodadaismus," n.p.

42. Hausmann, "Aussichten oder Ende des Neodadaismus," n.p.

43. See Walter Benjamin, "The Work of Art in the Age of Its Technological Reproducibility," in *Walter Benjamin: Selected Writings*, vol. 4: *1938–1940*, ed. Michael W. Jennings with Howard Eiland, trans. Edmund Jephcott, Rodney Livingstone, et al., (Cambridge, MA: Belknap Press of Harvard University Press, 2003), pp. 266–67.

44. See Adolf Hitler, "Der Führer eröffnet die 'Grosse Kunstausstellung 1937,'" *Die Kunst im Dritten Reich*, vol. 1, nos. 7–8 (1937), pp. 47–61.

45. See *Zwischen Revolutionskunst und sozialistischem Realismus*, ed. Hubertus Gassner and Eckhart Gillen (Cologne: DuMont, 1991), p. 323; see also: John Heartfield, *John Heartfield* (Cologne: DuMont, 1991), p. 14.

46. See Andrei B. Nakov, "Dada Gives Me an Intolerable 'Malaise' . . ." in *Dada—Constructivism: The Janus Face of the Twenties*, ed. Annely Juda (London: Annely Juda Fine Art, 1984), p. 21.

47. Man Ray in an interview with Arturo Schwarz, in Arturo Schwarz, *New York Dada: Duchamp, Man Ray, Picabia* (Munich: Prestel, 1973), p. 99.

48. Huelsenbeck, "Dada Lives!" in Motherwell, *Dada Painters and Poets*, pp. 280–81.

49. Fernand Léger, *Contemporary Achievements in Painting*, trans. Alexander Anderson (New York: Viking Press, 1973), p. 1.

50. Wassily Kandinsky, "Über das Geistige in der Kunst," as quoted in *Blast: Review of the Great English Vortex*, no. 2 (July 1915), p. 119.

51. Wyndham Lewis et al., "Manifesto," *Blast: Review of the Great English Vortex*, no. 1 (June 20, 1914), ed. Wyndham Lewis, p. 34.

52. Hausmann, "Post-Dada," in Hausmann, *Am Anfang war Dada*, p. 149.

53. See for example Hans-Georg Kemper, *Vom Expressionismus zum Dadaismus* (Kronberg/Taunus: Scriptor Verlag, 1974), see also Dickerman, "Zurich," in Dickerman, *Dada*, pp. 20, 24.

54. Ludwig Meidner, "Anleitung zum Malen von Grossstadtbildern," *Kunst und Künstler*, vol. 12, no. 6 (1914), p. 312; extracts translated by Nicholas Walker, in *Art*

in Theory 1900–2000: An Anthology of Changing Ideas, ed. Charles Harrison and Paul Wood (London: Blackwell: 2003), p. 168.

55. Hausmann, "Aussichten oder Ende des Neodadaismus," n.p.

56. Huelsenbeck, "Collective Dada Manifesto," p. 243.

57. Huelsenbeck, "En Avant Dada" (1920), in Motherwell, *Dada Painters and Poets*, p. 40.

58. Hausmann, as quoted by Elizabeth Allen Chabert, *Transforming Impact: The Shock Experience in Dada and Surrealist Poetry*, Ph.D. thesis, Columbia University, New York, microfiche, 1995, p. 149.

59. Huelsenbeck, "Collective Dada Manifesto," p. 244.

60. See, for example, Smith, "Pre-Fluxus Conceptual Developments and Generative Influences," n.p.

61. Hubert van den Berg distinguishes four different strands of political attitude within Dada. Hubert van den Berg, *Avantgarde und Anarchismus: Dada in Zürich und Berlin* (Heidelberg: Winter, 1999), p. 169.

62. See Hubert van den Berg, "Dada Subjectivity and the Politics of Indifference: On Some Contrasts and Correspondences between Dada in Zürich and Berlin," in *Subjectivity*, vol. 12 of *Avant-Garde Critical Studies*, ed. Willem van Reijen and Willem G. Weststeiin (Amsterdam: Rodopi, 1999), p. 29. Tristan Tzara joined communist activities, but only after the end of Dada. See Klaus von Beyme, *Das Zeitalter der Avantgarden: Kunst und Gesellschaft, 1905–1955* (Munich: Verlag C.H.Beck, 2005), p. 546.

63. Robert Motherwell, "Introduction," in Motherwell, *Dada Painters and Poets*, p. xxv.

64. See Rudolf E. Kuenzli, "Dada gegen den ersten Weltkrieg: Die Dadaisten in Zürich," in *Sinn aus Unsinn: Dada International 12, Amherster Kolloquium zur deutschen Literatur* (Bern: Franke, 1982), p. 92.

65. Translation taken from Klaus Vondung, *The Apokalypse in Germany* (Columbia: University of Missouri Press, 2000, p. 326).

66. Jefim Golyscheff, Raoul Hausmann, and Richard Hülsenbeck, "What Is Dadaism and What Does It Want in Germany?" in Motherwell, *Dada Poets and Painters*, p. 41.

67. The exhibition also contained a poster that positioned Dada "on the side of the revolutionary Proletariat"; see Berlinische Galerie, ed., *Hannah Höch: Eine Lebenscollage*, vol. 1: *1889–1930* (Berlin: Argon, 1989), p. 679; English translation of the slogan in *Theories of Modern Art: A Source Book by Artists and Critics*, ed. Hershel B. Chipp (Berkeley: University of California Press, 1968), p. 376. The poster can be seen in a documentary photography of the fair; reprinted in: Brigid Doherty, "'See: We Are All Neurasthenics!' or, The Trauma of Dada Montage," *Critical Inquiry* 24 (Autumn 1997), p. 87 (fig. 2).

68. See Hausmann, "Aussichten oder Ende des Neo-Dadaismus," n.p.

69. Walter Serner, "Qu'est-ce que le Dadaïsme?" *Le Mondain*, no. 3 (January 14, 1920); reprinted in French in Walter Serner, *Das Gesamte Werk*, vol. 2: *Das Hirngeschwür* (Munich: Renner, 1981), p. 108.

70. Theodor Adorno, *Aesthetic Theory*, ed. Gretel Adorno and Rolf Tiedemann,

trans. Robert Hullot-Kentor (London: Athlone Press, 1997), p. 230; here as quoted in *The Adorno Reader*, ed. Brian O'Connor (Oxford: Blackwell Publishers Ltd., 2000), p. 246, as O'Connor offers the better translation in this case.

71. Adorno, *Aesthetic Theory*, p. 229.

72. Adorno, "Commitment" (1962), in *Aesthetics and Politics*, ed. Ernst Bloch et al., trans. Ronald Taylor et al. (London: Verso, 1980), p. 178.

73. Adorno, *Aesthetic Theory*, p. 227.

74. Ball, *Flight Out of Time*, p. 4.

75. Dickerman, "Zurich," p. 20.

76. See Marguerite Bonnet, ed., *L'Affaire Barrès* (Paris: Corti, 1987), pp. 19–20; see also Hanno Ehrlicher, *Die Kunst der Zerstörung* (Berlin: Akademie-Verlag, 2001), p. 206.

77. Dickerman, "Introduction," in Dickerman, *Dada*, p. 2.

78. Richard Huelsenbeck, "Erinnerungen" in *Urlaute dadaistischer Poesie: Der Berliner Dada-Abend am 12. April 1918*, ed. Jeanpaul Goergen (Hannover: Postskriptum Verlag, 1994), p. 105; see also Tuck-Chee Phung, *Dada and the First World War: Origins of an Art Movement in Political Conflict*, Ph.D. diss., University of Aberdeen, Aberdeen,1983.

79. See Dickerman, "Introduction," in Dickerman, *Dada*, p. 6; see also Dickerman "Zurich," in ibid., pp. 20–21, 23; also, on Ernst, see Hal Foster, "Amour Fou, " *October* 56 (Spring 1991), p. 69.

80. See Foster, "Amour Fou," p. 69.

81. See Kuenzli, "Dada gegen den ersten Weltkrieg," pp. 87–100.

82. Filippo Tommaso Marinetti, "The Founding and Manifesto of Futurism" (1909), in *A Century of Isms*, ed. Mary Ann Caws (Lincoln: University of Nebraska Press, 2001), pp. 185–89.

83. Max Ernst, *Beyond Painting* (New York: Wittenborn and Schultz, 1948), p. 14.

84. Grosz, *A Little Yes and a Big No*, p. 181.

85. Klaus Vondung, "Propaganda oder Sinndeutung?" in *Kriegserlebnis: Der Erste Weltkrieg in der literarischen Gestaltung und symbolischen Deutung der Nationen*, ed. Klaus Vondung (Göttingen: Vandenhoeck & Ruprecht, 1980), p. 31.

86. Richter, *Dada: Art and Anti-Art*, p. 58.

87. Max Ernst in an interview with Patrick Waldberg, "La Partie de Boules: Die Boule-Partie," in *Max Ernst in Selbstzeugnissen und Bilddokumenten*, ed. Lothar Fischer (Reinbek/Hamburg: Rowohlt 1969), p. 35; extracts translated into English in *Max Ernst: A Retrospective*, ed. Diane Waldman (New York: Solomon R. Guggenheim Museum, 1975), p. 21.

88. Hans Arp, "Dada Was No Childish Romp," in Rex W. Last, *Hans Arp, the Poet of Dadaism* (London: Oswald Wolff, 1969), p. 78.

89. Ibid.

90. Bergius, "*Dada Triumphs!*" p. 1.

91. Ernst, in *Max Ernst: A Retrospective*, ed. Waldman, p. 21.

92. Tzara, "An Introduction to Dada," p. 394.

93. Georges Ribemont-Dessaignes, "History of Dada," in Motherwell, *Dada Painters and Poets*, p. 102.

94. Ball, *Flight out of Time*, entry of June 12, 1916, p. 66.

95. Tristan Tzara, "Dada Manifesto 1918," in Motherwell, *Dada Painters and Poets*, p. 79.

96. Willy Verkauf, *Dada. Monograph of a Movement* (London: Alec Tiranti, 1957), p. 8.

97. See Hugo Ball, "Dada Manifesto," in Ball, *Flight out of Time*, pp. 219–21; see also Ball, *Flight Out of Time*, entry of April 18, 1916, p. 63; regarding the reference to a soap, Ball alludes to the Dresden-based drug company, Bergmann & Co., which had opened a branch in Zurich in 1891 and had launched a range of products for personal hygiene under the name of "Dada," a name for which they took out a patent in 1906. Among the products were a soap and cream containing essences of lilies. See Raimund Meyer, "Dada ist gross, Dada ist schön: Zur Geschichte von Dada Zürich," in *Dada in Zürich*, ed. Hans Bollinger, Guido Magnaguagno, and Raimund Meyer (Zurich: Arche Verlag, 1985), pp. 9–79, pp. 25–7.

98. Raoul Hausmann, "Was ist dada?" (text collage), *Der Dada*, no. 2, ed. Hausmann (Berlin 1919); reprinted in Hausmann, *Am Anfang war Dada*, p. 8.

99. Hausmann, "Dada ist mehr als Dada," *De Stijl*, vol. 4, no. 3 (May 1921); reprinted in Hausmann, *Am Anfang war Dada*, p. 85.

100. See Hausmann, "Aussichten oder Ende des Neodadaismus," n.p.

101. Francis Picabia, "DADA Manifesto" (1920), trans. Margaret I. Lippard, in *Dadas on Art*, ed. Lucy Lippard (Englewood Cliffs, NJ: Prentice Hall, 1971), p. 166.

102. Richard Huelsenbeck, "Erklärung," presented at the Cabaret Voltaire in spring 1916; reprinted in Huelsenbeck, *Dada: Eine literarische Dokumentation* (Reinbek/Hamburg: Rowohlt, 1964), p. 30.

103. Tristan Tzara, "Zurich Chronicle," in Motherwell, *Dada Painters and Poets*, p. 236.

104. Theo van Doesburg, "Characteristics of Dadaism," in Lippard, *Dadas on Art*, p. 112.

105. Bergius, "*Dada Triumphs!*" p. 21.

106. Tzara, "Dada Manifesto 1918," p. 76.

107. Tzara, "An Introduction to Dada," p. 396.

108. Ehrlicher, *Kunst der Zerstörung*, p. 197.

109. Richter, *Dada. Art and Anti-Art*, p. 60.

110. Tzara, "Dada Manifesto 1918," p. 76.

111. Tristan Tzara, "Unpretentious Proclamation," in Tzara, *Seven Dada Manifestos and Lampisteries* pp. 15–17 (London: John Calder Ltd., 1977), p. 16.

112. Huelsenbeck, "Collective Dada Manifesto," p. 246.

113. Tzara, "Erinnerungen an Dada," p. 129.

114. See Harriett Watts, "Dada and the Press: An Introduction," in *Dada and the Press*, ed. Watts, vol. 9 of *Crisis and the Arts*, ed. Stephen C. Foster (New Haven, CT: Thomson/Gale, 2004), p. 4, see also pp. 1–9.

115. Tzara, "An Introduction to Dada," p. 396.

116. Kuenzli, "Dada gegen den ersten Weltkrieg," p. 94.

117. Ibid.

118. Henning Grunwald, "Dadatropismus oder Die alexandrinische Paralyse," in "Dada–Neodada–Kryptodada–?" ed. Walter Höllerer and Norbert Miller, special issue, *Sprache im technischen Zeitalter* 55 (1975), pp. 192–93.

119. Ball, *Flight out of Time*, entry of July 9, 1915, p. 25.

120. Ibid., entry of June 18, 1916, p. 68 (my italics).

121. Ball, "Dada Manifesto," p. 221.

122. Ball, *Flight out of Time*, entry of June 18, 1916, p. 67.

123. Ibid., p. 68.

124. Christopher W. E. Bigsby, *Dada and Surrealism* (London: Methuen, 1972), p. 27.

125. Ball, "Dada Manifesto," p. 221. Slightly inappropriately, the German word *Unfug* (nonsense) has here been translated as stuff; the German text is reprinted in Riha, *Dada Zürich. Texte, Manifeste, Dokumente*, p. 30.

126. See Raoul Hausmann, "Zur Geschichte des Lautgedichts," in Hausmann, *Am Anfang war Dada*, pp. 34–43: p. 35; see also Walter Mehring, *Dada Berlin* (Zurich: Die Arche, 1967), pp. 75–76.

127. Hans Richter, "Zur Geschichte des Lautgedichts," in Hausmann, *Am Anfang war Dada*, p. 35.

128. Ball, *Flight out of Time*, entry of June 18, 1916, p. 68.

129. Hans Arp, as quoted by Richter, *Dada. Art and Anti-Art*, p. 34; see also Hans Arp, "dear monsieur brzekowski," as quoted by Dawn Ades, "Dada—Constructivism," in Juda, *Dada—Constructivism*, p. 33.

130. Theodor Lessing, *Geschichte als Sinngebung des Sinnlosen* (Hamburg: Rütten and Loening Verlag, 1962), p. 28. Unless otherwise stated, italics within quotations are as in the original publication.

131. Ibid., p. 304.

132. See van den Berg, "Tristan Tzara's 'Manifeste Dada 1918': Anti-Manifest oder manifestierte Indifferenz?" *Neophilologus*, vol. 79, no. 3 (1995), pp. 353–76.

133. Hausmann, as quoted by Koch, *Ich bin immerhin der grösste Experimentator Österreichs*, p. 82.

134. Duchamp in William Seitz, "What's Happened to Art?" *Vogue*, Feb. 15, 1963, p. 113; as quoted by Schwarz, *New York Dada*, p. 10.

135. See Renato Poggioli, *The Theory of the Avant-Garde* (Cambridge, MA: Belknap Press of Harvard University Press, 1968), p. 62. An interesting dispute about Dada's nihilism emerged between Peter Bürger's analysis of Dada as total repudiation, including the negation of itself, based on an analysis of Tzara's "Dada Manifesto 1918" and Hubert van den Berg's counteranalysis of the same manifesto. See Bürger, *Der französische Surrealismus*, and van den Berg, "Tristan Tzara's 'Manifeste Dada 1918'"; see also Ehrlicher, *Kunst der Zerstörung*, p. 197.

136. Anonymous, "Dada-Abend," *Neue Zürcher Zeitung*, second evening edition, July 18, 1916; reprinted in Brigitte Pichon and Karl Riha, eds., *Dada Zürich: A Clown's Game from Nothing*, vol. 2 of *Crisis and the Arts*, ed. Stephen C. Foster

(New Haven, CT: Thomson/Gale, 1996), pp. 203–4: p. 203 (reprinted press releases not translated).

137. Ball, "Dada Manifesto," p. 220.

138. Anonymous, untitled article in *Zürcher Morgen-Zeitung*, July 29, 1918; reprinted in Pichon and Riha, *Dada Zürich*, p. 220 (reprinted press releases not translated).

139. Franz Schulz, "Prager Tagblatt," June 17, 1919; reprinted in Watts, *Dada and the Press*, p. 97.

140. Hausmann, "Aussichten oder Ende des Neodadaismus," n.p. (capitalization as in original).

141. See Ian Dunlop, *The Shock of the New: Seven Historic Exhibitions of Modern Art* (New York: American Heritage Press, 1972), p. 251.

142. Ibid., p. 255.

143. Werner Leibbrand, "Da-Da, Betrachtung eines Arztes," *Generalanzeiger*, July 21, 1920 (first in *Tägliche Rundschau*, Berlin); see also: Doherty, "'See: We Are All Neurasthenics!'" p. 90.

144. Press review on Zurich Dada; as quoted by Richter, *Dada: Art and Anti-Art.*

145. Anonymous, "Die Simulanten des Irrsinns auf dem Vortragspult," *Neue Berliner 12. Uhr Zeitung*, May 20, 1919. Reprinted in Pichon and Riha, *Dada Zürich*, pp. 221–22.

146. Dickerman, "Zurich," in Dickerman, *Dada*, p. 26.

147. Doherty, "'See: We Are All Neurasthenics!'" pp. 129–30.

148. Ibid., p. 90.

149. Ibid., p. 128.

150. See Chabert, *Transforming Impact*, p. 125.

151. George Grosz, "Kaffeehaus," *Neue Blätter für Kunst und Dichtung*, vol. 1 (November 1918), p. 155; English translation taken from Doherty, "'See: We Are All Neurasthenics!'" pp. 94–95.

152. Doherty, "'See: We Are All Neurasthenics!'" p. 95.

153. Bergius, *"Dada Triumphs!"* p. 12.

154. Huelsenbeck, "Die dadaistische Bewegung," p. 103.

155. Huelsenbeck, "Collective Dada Manifesto," p. 242.

156. Ibid., p. 244.

157. Hausmann, "Synthetisches Cino der Malerei" (1918), in Hausmann, *Am Anfang war Dada*, p. 27. The text had been presented by Hausmann at the first Berlin Dada soirée on April 12, 1918, entitled "Das neue Material in der Malerei," but was only published in 1972, with the typescript, dated April 1918, carrying the same title; see Goergen, *Urlaute dadaistischer Poesie*, pp. 9, 54–56, 65, 117, 121; see also: van den Berg, "Tristan Tzara's 'Manifeste Dada 1918,'" p. 357.

158. Huelsenbeck, "Collective Dada Manifesto," p. 244. Although using a terminology strikingly close to Marinetti's "The Founding and Manifesto of Futurism" (in Caws, *A Century of Isms*, pp. 185–89), the reasons for their mutual requests to acknowledge the changed paradigms of the present society are different.

159. See, for example, Huelsenbeck, "En Avant Dada," p. 40.

160. Reprinted in Riha, *Dada Zürich: Texte, Manifeste, Dokumente*, pp.130–31.

161. Huelsenbeck, "Die dadaistische Bewegung," p. 111.

162. Huelsenbeck, "En Avant Dada," p. 12.

163. George Grosz to Otto Schmalhausen, December 6, 1917, and June 30, 1917; as quoted by Hans Hess, *George Grosz* (New Haven: Yale University Press, 1974), p. 44.

164. Georges Hugnet, *Dictionnaire du Dadaïsme 1916–1922* (Paris: Simoën, 1976), pp. 277–78.

165. Hugnet, *Dictionnaire du Dadaïsme*, p. 278.

166. Unknown author as quoted in Richard Huelsenbeck, *Dada Almanac*, trans. Malcolm Green et al. (London: Atlas Press, 1993), p. 51.

167. Hausmann, "Synthetisches Cino der Malerei," p. 28.

168. Hausmann, "Aussichten oder Ende des Neodadaismus," n.p.

169. Hausmann, "Presentismus: Gegen den Puffkeismus der teutschen Seele" (1921), in Hausmann, *Am Anfang war Dada*, p. 132; excerpts translated in English in Caws, *Manifesto: A Century of Isms*, p. 164, quoted paragraph not included.

170. See Fedele Azari, "Vita simultanea futurista," *Scrivo*, no. 68, 1968.

171. Ehrlicher, *Kunst der Zerstörung*, p. 189.

172. Huelsenbeck, "Die dadaistische Bewegung," p. 104. The translation of the German term *Rentier* as "coupon clipper" is not quite correct, as it describes someone living from interests on capital and rent. Rentier Schulze was, in fact, board member of the landholder association of parts of the Berlin district Prenzlauer Berg during the first decades of the twentieth century. Thus, the manifesto refers to a stereotypical bourgeois figure. "Herr Schulze" reappears, for example, in Ball's "Dada Manifesto": "Mr. Schulz's words are only two and a half centimeters long" (Ball, "Dada Manifesto," p. 221).

173. Huelsenbeck, "Das Bruitistische Gedicht" (introduction to his performance given at the "Autoren-Abend," first Dada soirée, held in Zurich at the Zunfthaus Waag, on July 14, 1916), in Raoul Schrott, *Dada 15/25: Dokumentation und Chronologischer Überblick zu Tzara and Co.* (Cologne: Dumont, 2004), p. 57.

174. Hausmann, "Synthetisches Cino der Malerei," p. 29.

175. Huelsenbeck, "En Avant Dada," p. 7.

176. Huelsenbeck, as quoted by Verkauf, *Dada: Monograph of a Movement*, p. 92.

177. Verkauf, *Dada: Monograph of a Movement*, p. 92.

178. Isaac Goldberg, "Dada Putting the Jazz into Modern Verse: The Strange Cult Which Riots in Paradox and Negation, and Is the Dancing Spirit Over the Morals of the Earth, the Point of Indifference Between Contact and Form," *Boston Evening Transcript*, January 12, 1921; see also Watts, *Dada and the Press*, p. 2.

179. Huelsenbeck, "Die dadaistische Bewegung," pp. 101–2.

180. Ball, *Flight out of Time*, entry of March 3, 1916, p. 56.

181. Hausmann, "Presentismus," p. 132.

182. Hausmann, "Synthetisches Cino der Malerei," p. 28.

183. Huelsenbeck, "Die dadaistische Bewegung, p. 104.

184. Adorno, *Aesthetic Theory*, p. 321.

185. Ibid., p. 145. The latter part of the quotation is my own translation, as Robert

Hullot-Kentor translated the German phrase "Betrieb der Kommunikation" as "culture industry."

186. Ibid., pp. 29–30.

187. Ibid., p. 20.

188. Ibid., p. 22.

189. Ibid., p. 20.

190. Henri Bergson, *Creative Evolution* (London: Macmillan, 1913), pp. 172–74; as quoted by Bigsby, *Dada and Surrealism*, p. 30.

191. Lenin, as quoted in Hausmann, "Aussichten oder Ende des Neodadaismus," n.p.

192. Huelsenbeck, "Erinnerungen," p. 106.

193. Huelsenbeck, "First Dada Lecture in Germany," in *Dada Almanac*, ed. Huelsenbeck, p. 113.

194. Alexander Partens, "Dada Art," in *Dada Almanac*, ed. Huelsenbeck, p. 95.

195. Hausmann, "Presentismus," p. 133.

196. Patrick Waldenberg, *Dada. La fonction de refus* (Paris: Editions de la Différence, 1999), pp. 18–19.

197. Ribemont-Dessaignes, as quoted in Nakov, "Dada Gives Me an Intolerable 'Malaise' . . . ," pp. 16–17.

198. Tzara, "Manifesto of Mr. Antipyrine," in Motherwell, *Dada Painters and Poets*, p. 75.

199. See Nakov, "Dada Gives Me an Intolerable 'Malaise' . . . ," p. 16.

200. Ernesto de Fiori, in *Neue Zürcher Zeitung*, October 10, 1918, first morning edition; reprinted in German in Pinchon and Riha, *Dada Zürich: A Clown's Game from Nothing*, p. 223.

201. Boris Groys, *Über das Neue. Versuch einer Kulturökonomie* (Munich: Hanser, 1992); English excerpt available at: www.artnodes.com/eng/art/groys1002/groys1002.html (pdf), p. 4.

202. Bürger, *Theory of the Avant-Garde*, p. 59.

203. Adorno, *Aesthetic Theory*, p. 21.

204. Karl Heinz Bohrer, *Suddenness: On the Movement of Aesthetic Appearance*, trans. Ruth Crowley (New York: Columbia University Press, 1994), p. 79.

205. On the distinction and definition of *modernism* and *avant-garde* see, for example, Poggioli, *Theory of the Avant-Garde*; Peter Bürger, *Theory of the Avant-Garde*, pp. 18, 53, and 56; and Andreas Huyssen, *After the Great Divide: Modernism, Mass Culture, Postmodernism* (Bloomington: Indiana University Press, 1986).

206. Calinescu, *Five Faces of Modernity*, p. 124, see also p. 140.

207. Ball, *Flight Out of Time*, entry of March 22, 1917, p. 101.

208. Ezra Pound, as quoted in Astradur Eysteinsson, *The Concept of Modernism* (Ithaca, NY: Cornell University Press, 1990), p. 144.

209. Eysteinsson, *Concept of Modernism*, p. 144.

210. Rosalind E. Krauss, *The Originality of the Avant-Garde and Other Modernist Myths* (Cambridge, MA: MIT Press, 1985), p. 157. See also Harold Rosenberg, *The Tradition of the New* (New York: McGraw-Hill, 1965).

211. Adorno, *Aesthetic Theory*, p. 23.

212. See ibid., p. 321.

213. Adorno refers to Victor Hugo's description of Rimbaud's poetry as a "frisson nouveau."

214. Adorno, *Aesthetic Theory*, p. 20.

215. Theodor Adorno, "Über Jazz," in Adorno, *Musikalische Schriften IV*, vol. 17 of *Gesammelte Schriften*, ed. Rolf Tiedemann (Frankfurt: Suhrkamp, 1982), p. 80. In his text "Engagement" ("Commitment," 1962), Adorno modifies this phrase slightly, speaking of the "Schock des Unverständlichen"; see Adorno, "Engagement," in Adorno, *Noten zur Literatur*, vol. 11 of *Gesammelte Schriften*, ed. Rolf Tiedemann (Frankfurt: Suhrkamp, 1974), p. 412.

216. Bürger, *Theory of the Avant-Garde*, p. 80.

217. Bohrer, *Suddenness*, p. 71.

218. Ibid., p. 78.

219. Raoul Hausmann, "Massenpsychologie Dadas," in Hausmann, *Am Anfang war Dada*, p. 144.

220. See Tristan Tzara, "Erinnerungen an Dada," p. 129; see also Hausmann, "Aussichten oder Ende des Neodadaismus," n.p.

221. Grosz, *A Little Yes and a Big No*, p. 185.

222. Elias Canetti, *The Torch in My Ear*, trans. Joachim Neugroschel (New York: Farrar Straus Giroux, 1982), p. 253.

223. Ernst Bloch, "The Unbearable Moment," in Bloch, *Literary Essays*, vol. 6, trans. Andrew Joron (Stanford, CA: Stanford University Press, 1998), p. 190.

224. Nicholas Daly, "The Woman in White: Whistler, Hiffernan, Courbet, Du Maurier," *Modernism/modernity*, vol. 12, no. 1 (2005), p. 9.

225. Benjamin to Adorno, June 30, 1936, in *Walter Benjamin: Gesammelte Schriften*, vol. 1, 3, p. 190.

226. Adorno, "Über Jazz," pp. 80, 97.

227. See Albrecht Riethmüller, "Hermetik, Schock, Fasslichkeit: Zum Verhältnis von Musikwerk und Publikum in der ersten Hälfte des 20. Jahrhunderts," *Archiv für Musikwissenschaft* 73, no. 1 (1980), p. 47 n. 73.

228. Adorno, "Über Jazz, Appendix: Oxforder Nachträge" (1937), in Adorno, *Musikalische Schriften IV*, p. 102.

229. See, for example, Eberhart Thiel, *Sachwörterbuch der Musik* (Stuttgart: Alfred Kröner Verlag, 1977), as quoted in Frank Hellberg, *Walter Mehring: Schriftsteller zwischen Kabarett und Avantgarde* (Bonn: Bouvier Verlag Herbert Grundmann, 1983), p. 84; see also Klaus Birkenhauer, *Die eigenrhythmische Lyrik Bertolt Brechts* (Tübingen: Max Niemeyer Verlag, 1971), p. 21.

230. See Ewin Rotermund, *Die Parodie in der modernen deutschen Lyrik* (Munich: Eidos Verlag, 1963), p. 124.

231. Bertolt Brecht, "On Unryhmed Lyrics in Irregular Rhythms," trans. Beatrice Gottlieb, *Tulane Drama Review*, vol. 2, no. 1 (November 1957), p. 37.

232. Brecht, "On Unryhmed Lyrics," p. 34.

233. See Goergen *Urlaute dadaistischer Poesie*, p. 126.

234. See, for example, Grosz, "Aus den Gesängen" (1917), and "Gesang an die Welt" (1918), both in Goergen, *Urlaute dadaistischer Poesie*, p. 49 and pp. 50–52.

235. Hellberg, *Walter Mehring*, p. 133 n. 5.

236. Hausmann, "Synthetisches Cino der Malerei," pp. 27–28.

237. See Verkauf, *Dada: Monograph of a Movement*, p. 91.

238. Benjamin, "The Work of Art in the Age of Its Technological Reproducibility," p. 267.

239. Huelsenbeck, "Erklärung," p. 29. Regarding the difficulties of dating this text, as well as doubts about its authenticity, see Ehrlicher, *Kunst der Zerstörung*, pp. 193–94 n. 74.

240. Hausmann, "Presentismus," p. 131.

4. Shock and the Senseless in Fluxus

1. Estera Milman, "Fluxus History and Trans-History: Competing Strategies for Empowerment," in *The Fluxus Reader*, ed. Ken Friedman (London: Academy Editions, 1998), p. 163.

2. Edith Decker, *Paik: Video* (Cologne: DuMont Buchverlag, 1988), p. 182.

3. John Corr, in the *Philadelphia Inquirer*, as quoted in *CHARLOTTE MOORMAN * NAM JUNE PAIK QUOTES (AMERICAN)*, photocopied typescript, 1 page, undated, Sohm-Archiv, Staatsgalerie Stuttgart (folder: "Nam June Paik—Charlotte Moorman: Bibliografie und Dokumentation"; in box: *Nam June Paik: Dokumentation allgemein: Bio-Bibliografie, Beiträge, Publikationen, Drucksachen, Private Misc., Charlotte Moorman*).

4. Tomas Schmit, Ben Patterson, and Wolf Vostell, among others, participated in the evening.

5. Günter Schab, "Zuviel Klamauk mit Neo-Dada," *Neue Ruhrzeitung*, June 1962, quoted in Jürgen Becker and Wolf Vostell, eds., *Happenings: Fluxus, Pop Art, Nouveau Réalism* (Reinbek/Hamburg: Rowohlt, 1965), p. 269.

6. Willi Wolfradt, "Der Dadaismus," *Der Friede*, vol. 1, no. 16 (May 24, 1918), pp. 434–35, reprinted in Harriet Watts, *Dada and the Press* (New Haven, CT: Thomson/Gale, 2004), p. 95; see also Tonio Finta, "Kaka, Sch und geplatzte Torte," *Der Mittag*, February 6, 1963; reprinted in Becker and Vostell, *Happenings*, p. 271.

7. Wolf-Eberhard von Lewinsky, "Stumpfsinn—stundenlang! Festspiele neuester Musik," *Die Welt*, September 24, 1963; reprinted in Becker and Vostell, *Happenings*, p. 272.

8. Maciunas in a letter to La Monte Young, 1963, in *Fluxus: Selections from the Gilbert and Lila Silverman Collection*, ed. Clive Phillpot and Jon Hendricks (New York: Museum of Modern Art, 1988), p. 35.

9. Emmett Williams in an interview with Hans-Ulrich Obrist, October 11, 2004, available at: www.udno.net/Features, n.p.

10. Ibid.

11. Emmett Williams, "St. George and the Fluxus Dragons," in *Upheavals. Manifestos, Manifestations: Conceptions in the Arts at the Beginning of the Sixties*, ed. Klaus Schrenk, exhibition catalog, Städtische Kunsthalle, Düsseldorf (Cologne: DuMont, 1984), p. 27 (German and English).

12. See Robert Filliou, *Jinji Japsu Sosunika No. 3 for George Maciunas*, 1963–1964; excerpt reprinted in *Mr Fluxus: A Collective Portrait of George Maciunas 1931–1978*, ed. Ann Noël and Emmett Williams (London: Thames and Hudson, 1997), p. 76.

13. See Hal Foster, "What's Neo about the Neo-Avant-Garde?" *October* 70, (Autumn 1994), pp. 22–23.

14. Anonymous, "Trend to the 'Anti-Art,'" *Newsweek*, March 31, 1958, p. 94.

15. Richard Hamilton, "For the Finest Art, Try Pop," *Gazette*, vol. 1 (1961).

16. See Nauman's 1967 interview with Joe Raffaele, and with Willoughby Sharp in 1979; both reprinted in *Bruce Nauman, Interviews 1967–1988*, ed. and trans. Christine Hoffmann (Amsterdam: Verlag der Kunst, 1996), pp. 9 and 34–35.

17. Maria Müller, *Aspekte der Dada-Rezeption 1950–1960* (Essen: Verlag Die Blaue Eule, 1987), p. 49.

18. William S. Rubin, "Reflexions on Marcel Duchamp," *Art International*, vol. 4, no. 9 (December 1960), pp. 49–53.

19. See Kieran Cashell, *Aftershock: The Ethics of Contemporary Transgressive Art* (London: I.B. Tauris, 2009), p. 197ff; see also Isabelle Anscombe, *Punk* (New York: Urizen, 1978).

20. Tzara in a letter to Hausmann, October 6, 1962; cit. after Adelheid Koch, *Ich bin immerhin der grösste Experimentator Österreichs: Raoul Hausmann—Dada und Neodada* (Innsbruck: Haymon-Verlag, 1994), p. 228.

21. See Raoul Hausmann, "Aussichten oder Ende des Neodadaismus," in Koch, *Ich bin immerhin der grösste Experimentator Österreichs*, n.p.

22. Complete exhibition title: *Mouvement Dada 1916–1966: Berlin, Genêve, Madrid, New York, Zurich: Yesterday, Today, Tomorrow: Arman, Raysse, Spoerri, Dufrêne, Rotella, Villeglé.*

23. Hilton Kramer, paper delivered to *A Symposium on Pop Art*, MoMA, New York, December 13, 1962; reprinted in *Arts Magazine* (April 1963), p. 38.

24. *Fantastic Art, Dada, Surrealism*, MoMA, New York, 1936. The show was curated by Alfred H. Barr.

25. Wolf Vostell, "Dada und die mentale Energie: Interview von Doña Mercedes Guardado Olivenza de V. mit Vostell, Juli 1975 in Malpartida/Spanien," in "Dada–Neodada–Kryptodada–?" ed. Walter Höllerer and Norbert Miller, special issue, *Sprache im technischen Zeitalter* 55 (1975), p. 214.

26. Vostell, "Dada und die mentale Energie," p. 214.

27. Ibid.

28. Williams in an interview with Obrist, *www.udno.net/Features*, n.p.

29. See Ian Dunlop, *The Shock of the New: Seven Historic Exhibitions of Modern Art* (New York: American Heritage Press, 1972), p. 248.

30. Rühm, as quoted by Koch, *Ich bin immerhin der grösste Experimentator Österreichs*, p. 216.

31. Robert Motherwell, ed., *The Dada Painters and Poets*, 2nd ed. (New York: Wittenborn, Schultz, Inc., 1967).

32. Other publications soon followed, such as George Hugnet's *L'Aventure Dada: 1916–1922* (Paris: Galerie de l'Institut, 1957); the exhibition catalog by Karl-Heinz

Hering and Ewald Rathke, *Dada: Dokumente einer Bewegung* (Düsseldorf: Kunstverein für die Rheinlande und Westfalen, 1958); and Willi Verkauf, *Dada: Monograph of a Movement* (London: Alec Tiranti, 1961). With his collection of essays *L'Esprit Dada dans la Peinture*, published in the *Cahiers* between 1932 and 1934, Georges Hugnet had delivered the earliest historical account of the group—see Hugnet, "L'Esprit de Dada dans la Peinture," *Cahiers d'Art*, vol. 7, nos. 1–2, 6–7, 8–10 (1932); vol. 9, nos. 1–4 (1934); see also Müller, *Aspekte der Dada-Rezeption 1950–1960*, p. 14.

33. Walter Serner, *Letzte Lockerung* (Hannover: Paul Steegemann Verlag, 1920); English translation in *Blago Bung Blago Bung Bosso Fataka! First Texts of German Dada by Hugo Ball, Richard Huelsenbeck, Walter Serner*, trans. Malcolm Green (London: Atlas, 1995); *Dada Almanach*, ed. Richard Huelsenbeck (Berlin: Reiss, 1920); English edition: *Dada Almanac*, trans. Malcolm Green et al. (London: Atlas, 1993); and Richard Huelsenbeck, *En-avant Dada* (Hamburg: Nautilus, 1920); no published English edition.

34. Peter Schifferli, *Die Geburt des Dada . . . Dichtung und Chronik der Gründer* (Zurich: Verlag der Arche, 1957) (no English edition); Richard Huelsenbeck, *Mit Witz, Licht und Grütze: Auf den Spuren des Dadaismus* (Wiesbaden: Limes, 1957), see p. 28 and following.

35. Walter Mehring, *Berlin Dada: Eine Chronik mit Photos und Dokumenten* (Zurich: Arche Verlag, 1959); Richard Huelsenbeck, ed., *Dada: Eine literarische Dokumentation* (Reinbek/Hamburg: Rowohlt, 1964); Hans Richter, *Kunst und Anti-Kunst: Der Beitrag Dadas zur Kunst des 20. Jahrhunderts* (Cologne: DuMont Schauberg, 1964).

36. A German translation of the text was read by Arthur Caspari. In the following, I will quote from George Maciunas, "Neo-Dada in Music, Theater, Poetry Art," in *In the Spirit of Fluxus*, ed. Elizabeth Armstrong and Joan Rothfuss, exhibition catalog (New York: Walker Art Center, 1993), pp. 156–57.

37. See Jon Hendricks, "Fluxus," in *Stationen der Moderne*, ed. Michael Bollée, exhibition catalog (Berlin: Berlinische Galerie, 1988), p. 494.

38. Maciunas, "Neo-Dada in Music, Theater, Poetry Art," p. 156.

39. Hendricks, "Fluxus," p. 494.

40. Dick Higgins, "In einem Minensuchboot um die Welt" ("In a Minesweeper around the World"), in *1962 Wiesbaden Fluxus 1982: Eine kleine Geschichte von Fluxus in drei Teilen*, ed. René Block (Wiesbaden: Harlekin Art, 1983), p. 127 (German and English).

41. Huelsenbeck, as quoted in Michael Oven, "Fluxus-Kästen und Dada-Konstruktionen," in *Sinn aus Unsinn: Dada International 12, Amherster Kolloquium zur deutschen Literatur* (Bern: Franke, 1982), p. 277.

42. Hausmann in a letter to Tzara, September 30, 1962; reprinted in Koch, *Ich bin immerhin der grösste Experimentator Österreichs*, p. 228.

43. Hausmann, "Aussichten oder Ende des Neodadaismus," n.p.

44. Ibid.

45. Hausmann in a letter to Dick Higgins, November 12, 1963, as quoted in Koch, *Ich bin immerhin der grösste Experimentator Österreichs*, p. 82.

46. Hausmann, "Aussichten oder Ende des Neodadaismus," n.p.

47. See Huelsenbeck, *Mit Witz, Licht und Grütze*, p. 25 and following.

48. Ben Vautier, "What is Fluxus?" *Flash Art* 84–85 (1978), p. 52.

49. Kate Millett, "Fluxus Is" (1981), in *What's Fluxus? What's Not! Why*, ed. Jon Hendricks, exhibition catalog (Rio de Janeiro: Centro Cultural Banco Do Brasil, 2002), p. 122.

50. Vostell, "Dada und die mentale Energie," p. 214.

51. See, for example, Maciunas, *Fluxus (Its Historical Development and Relationship to Avant-garde Movements*, chart, c. 1966; Maciunas, *Diagram of Historical Development of Fluxus and other 4 Dimensional, Aural, Optic, Olfactory, Epithelial and Tactile Art Forms* (incomplete), 1973. For these two works and an analysis and reprint of Maciunas's charts, see Astrit Schmidt-Burkhardt, *Maciunas' Learning Machines: From Art History to a Chronology of Fluxus* (Berlin: Vice Versa, 2003). See also Astrit Schmidt-Burkhardt, *Stammbäume der Kunst: Zur Genealogie der Avantgarde* (Berlin: Akademie Verlag, 2005), pp. 357–90.

52. Ken Friedman, "Fluxus and Company," in Friedman, *Fluxus Reader*, p. 245.

53. Dick Higgins, "Theory and Reception," in Friedman, *Fluxus Reader*, p. 218.

54. See Higgins, "In einem Minensuchboot um die Welt," p. 127.

55. Higgins, however, published Huelsenbeck's *Dada Almanac* in his Something Else Press in 1966.

56. Maciunas in a letter to Schmit, January 1964, in Hendricks, *What's Fluxus? What's Not! Why*, p. 163 (typeface and punctuation according to Maciunas).

57. Maciunas in a letter to Vostell, November 3, 1964; a German translation by Tomas Schmit is in Becker and Vostell, *Happenings*, p. 202.

58. See Hausmann, "Nachhall," in Hausmann, *Am Anfang war Dada*, ed. Karl Riha and Günter Kämpf (Steinbach/Giessen: Anabas-Verlag: Günter Kämpf, 1972), p. 152.

59. Andreas Huyssen, "Postmoderne—Eine amerikanische Internationale?" in *Postmoderne. Zeichen eines kulturellen Wandels*, ed. Andreas Huyssen and Klaus R. Scherpe (Reinbek/Hamburg, 1986), p. 13.

60. Maciunas, *Fluxus (Its Historical Development and Relationship to Avant-garde Movements)*, chart, c. 1966.

61. Harrison and Wood, *Art in Theory 1900–2000*, vol. 1, p. 549.

62. David Doris, "Zen Vaudeville: A Medi(t)ation in the Margins of Fluxus," available at: www.thing.net/~grist/ld/koppany/doris-e.htm, n.p.

63. Friedman, "Fluxus and Company," p. 242.

64. Jon Hendricks, foreword to *Fluxus Codex*, ed. Hendricks (Detroit: Gilbert and Silverman Fluxus Collection and Harry N. Abrams, Inc, 1988), p. 21.

65. See Doris, "Zen Vaudeville," n.p.

66. See Nam June Paik, *John Cage: Studie III*, typed manuscript, n.d., 15 pages (incomplete), p. 5, Sohm-Archiv, Staatsgalerie Stuttgart (folder: "Nam June Paik, Original, Notizen zu John Cage: Studie 1, Studie III"; in box: *Nam June Paik: Originaltexte und -manuskripte (7 Mappen) "MY LIFE" (1964), Symphonie No. 5*).

67. Higgins, "In einem Minensuchboot um die Welt," p. 135.

68. See Harry Ruhé, *Fluxus: The Most Radical and Experimental Art Movement of*

the Sixties (Amsterdam: "A," 1979), ring folder, n.p. (3. Hir); see also Gabriele Knapstein, "Fluxus International," in *Berlin–Tokyo: Die Kunst zweier Städte*, ed. Angela Schneider, exhibition catalog, Neue Nationalgalerie Berlin (Ostfildern: Hatje Cantz, 2006), pp. 232–33. A parallel connection between Dada and Japan was an adaptation of Dada in Japan—see Omuka Toshiharu, "Dadaismus in Japan," in Schneider, *Berlin–Tokyo,* pp. 120–21.

69. Geoffrey Hendricks, in "Flux Generation: A Conversation between Janet A. Kaplan and Bracken Hendricks, Geoffrey Hendricks, Alison Knowles, Hannah Higgins," held on November 6, 1999, ed. Kaplan, *Art Journal* 59, no. 2 (Summer 2000), p. 12.

70. See preparatory material, Sohm-Archiv, Staatsgalerie Stuttgart (folder: Nachlass George Maciunas Inv. Nr. 28: "Circumnavigation of the World with 145 Ft Converted Mine Sweeper, 1976–1984"—Originaltyposkripte und Kartenentwürfe, 20 pp.; in box: *Nachlass George Maciunas: Originale für Fluxus u. Allg.* [*Zeichnungen, Partituren, Manuskripte, z.T. von Kollegen*]).

71. Hannah Higgins, in Kaplan, "Flux Generation," p. 12.

72. For comprehensive biographical information on individual Fluxus artists see James Lewes, "Biography Fluxus," in *Fluxus Virus: 1962–1992*, exhibition catalog, ed. Ken Friedman (Cologne: Galerie Schüppenhauer, 1992), pp. 260–316.

73. Higgins, "In einem Minensuchboot um die Welt," p. 126.

74. See Paik, *A Music History*, photocopy of a typescript, 5 pages, p. 5, Sohm-Archiv, Staatsgalerie Stuttgart (folder: "Nam June Paik: Beiträge für Zeitschriften"; in box: *Nam June Paik: Dokumentation allgemein: Bio-Bibliografie, Beiträge, Publikationen, Drucksachen, Private Misc., Charlotte Moorman*); see also Tomas Schmit, "If I Remember Correctly," *Art and Artists: Free Fluxus Now*, vol. 7, no. 7, issue 79 (October 1972), London, p. 39. The majority of the primary Fluxus artists were students of Cage at some point, for example, George Brecht, Jackson Mac Low, Dick Higgins, Al Hansen, Toshi Ichiyanagi at the New School of Social Research in New York, and La Monte Young and Nam June Paik at the International Summer Course for New Music in Darmstadt in 1958.

75. On Mary Bauermeister's studio and pre-Fluxus activities, see Robert von Zahn, "'Refusierte Gesänge': Musik im Atelier Bauermeister," in *Intermedial, Kontrovers, Experimentell: Das Atelier Mary Bauermeister in Köln, 1960–1962* (Cologne: Emons Verlag, 1993); see also Wilfried Dörsel, Rainer Steinberg, and Robert von Zahn, "The Bauermeister Studio: Proto-Fluxus in Cologne, 1960–1962," in Friedman, *Fluxus Virus*, p. 56.

76. See, for example, Huyssen, "Postmoderne—Eine amerikanische Internationale?" p. 13.

77. Nam June Paik in a photocopied collage, Sohm-Archiv, Staatsgalerie Stuttgart (folder: "Nam June Paik: Dokumentation 1967"; in box: *Nam June Paik: Dokumentation 1959–1973*).

78. Finta, "Kaka, Sch und geplatzte Torte," p. 271. Finta refers here to Jean-Pierre Wilhelm's introduction to Fluxus held at the *festum fluxorum fluxus*.

79. Peter Frank, "New York Fluxus," in *New York-Downtown Manhattan: Soho: Ausstellungen, Theater, Musik, Performance, Video, Film*, ed. René Block, exhibition catalog (Berlin: Akademie der Künste, 1976), p. 150.

80. Hubert van den Berg, "On the Historiographic Distinction between Historical and Neo-Avant-Garde," in Scheunemann, *Avant-Garde/Neo-Avant-Garde*, p. 64.

81. Ralph Burmeister, "Fluxus besucht Heiligensee," in *Hanna Höch: Eine Lebens-collage*, vol. 3: *1946–1978* (Berlin: Berlinische Galerie, 2001), p. 145.

82. Paul Dickson, *Sputnik: The Shock of the Century* (New York: Walker & Co, 2001).

83. See, for example, C. Wright Mills, *White Collar: The American Middle Classes* (New York: Oxford University Press, 1951), p. 326 and following.

84. Ibid., p. 328.

85. Arthur M. Schlesinger Jr., "The New Mood in Politics," in Schlesinger, *The Politics of Hope* (Boston, MA: Riverside Press, 1963), p. 85.

86. Lisa Phillips, *The American Century: Art and Culture 1950–1960*, exhibition catalog, Whitney Museum of American Art (New York: W. W. Norton & Company, 1999), p. 27. Dwight D. Eisenhower was U.S. president between 1953 and 1961.

87. See Samuel R. Delany, *The Motion of Light on Water: Sex and Science Fiction Writing in the East Village, 1957–1965* (New York: Arbor House/W. Morrow, 1988), p. 183.

88. Ronald Berman, *America in the Sixties. An Intellectual History* (New York: Free Press, 1968), p. 4.

89. David Riesman, *The Lonely Crowd: A Study of the Changing American Character* (New Haven, CT: Yale University Press, 1950), p. 190.

90. Klaus von Beyme, *Zeitalter der Avantgarden: Kunst und Gesellschaft, 1905–1955* (Munich: Verlag C. H. Beck, 2005), p. 836. Regarding this influence see also Serge Gilbaut, *How New York Stole the Idea of Modern Art* (Chicago: University of Chicago Press, 1983).

91. Von Beyme, *Zeitalter der Avantgarden*, p. 836.

92. Gilbaut, *How New York Stole*, p. 190.

93. See, for example, Lee Krasner, in Robert C. Hobbs, *Lee Krasner* (New York: Abbeville Press, 1993), p. 18; Robert Motherwell, *The Collected Writings of Robert Motherwell* (Berkley: University of California Press, 1999), pp. 47 and 79; Clyfford Still's letters and diary entries, in *Clyfford Still 1904–1980*, ed. Thomas Kellein (Munich: Prestel, 1992), pp. 141–64; and von Beyme, *Zeitalter der Avantgarden*, p. 827.

94. Samuel M. Kootz, *The Intrasubjectives*, exhibition catalog (New York: Samuel M. Kootz Gallery, 1949), reprinted in Ellen G. Landau, ed., *Reading Abstract Expressionism* (New Haven, CT: Yale University Press, 2005), pp. 154–55.

95. Christine Lindey, *Art in the Cold War: From Vladivostok to Kalamazoo, 1945–1962* (London: Herbert Press, 1990), p. 83. Compare also von Beyme, *Zeitalter der Avantgarden*, p. 826 and following.

96. Barnett Newman, "The Sublime Is Now," in Newman, *Selected Writings and Interviews*, ed. John P. O'Neill (New York: Alfred A. Knopf, 1990), p. 173.

97. Hendricks, foreword to *Fluxus Codex*, p. 21.

98. Gilbaut, *How New York Stole*, pp. 165–94. Counter-arguments can be found, for example, in von Beyme, *Zeitalter der Avantgarden*, p. 833.

99. See Thomas Crow, *The Rise of the Sixties: American and European Art in the Era of Dissent 1955–69* (London: Weidenfeld & Nicolson, 1996), p. 48.

100. See ibid.

101. Ibid.

102. Schlesinger, "The New Mood in Politics," p. 84.

103. Ibid., p. 83.

104. Ibid., p. 91.

105. Tom Lavazzi offers an interesting reading of the hippie movement as a continuation of Fluxus principles; see Lavazzi, "Punching the Line: Fluxus, Yippie, and the 1968 DNC," *Rhizomes*, vol. 9 (Fall 2004), n.p., available at: www.rhizomes.net/issue9/lavazzi.htm.

106. Hendricks, "Foreword," in Hendricks, *Fluxus Codex*, p. 21.

107. Berman, *America in the Sixties*, p. 2; see also Howard Zinn, *Postwar America 1945–1971* (Boston, MA: South End Press: 1973), p. 89; see also Schlesinger, "The New Mood in Politics," p. 83.

108. See Barbara Ward, as quoted by Schlesinger, "The New Mood in Politics," p. 88.

109. See Sidra Stich, ed., *Made in the USA: An Americanization in Modern Art, the '50s and '60s*, exhibition catalog, University Art Museum, Berkeley (Berkeley: University of California Press, 1987), pp.110, 237, 245.

110. See Phillips, *The American Century*, p. 27.

111. Ibid., p. 28.

112. Bertrand Clavez in a presentation at the Terra Museum of American Art, Giverny, France, July 3, 2006.

113. Ibid.

114. Maciunas to Williams, June 1963, The Jean and Leonard Brown Collection, Getty Center; reprinted with annotations in Emmett Williams, *My Life in Fluxus—and Vice Versa* (London: Thames and Hudson, 1992), p. 168.

115. Ibid.

116. Henry Flynt and George Maciunas, "Communists Must Give Revolutionary Leadership in Culture," in Block, *1962 Wiesbaden Fluxus 1982*, p. 195.

117. Maciunas in the typescripted draft of a letter, undated, Sohm-Archiv, Staatsgalerie Stuttgart (folder: Nachlass George Maciunas Inv. Nr. 87: George Maciunas. Maschinenschriftliche Typoskripte [z.T. Fotokopie]; in box: *Nachlass George Maciunas: Originale für Fluxus u. Allg.[Zeichnungen, Partituren, Manuskripte* (*z.T. von Kollegen*)]).

118. Maciunas in a (September?) 1963 letter to La Monte Young, in Phillpot and Hendricks, *Fluxus: Selections*, p. 37. See also the excerpt reprinted in Noël and Williams, *Mr Fluxus*, p. 92.

119. See Jackson Mac Low, "Wie George Maciunas die New Yorker Avantgarde kennenlernte" (December 1980), in Block, *1962 Wiesbaden Fluxus 1982*, p. 122 (German and English).

120. Eric Andersen in a letter to Emmett Williams, September 12, 1993, in Noël and Williams, *Mr Fluxus*, p. 110.

121. George Maciunas, *For press release. Statement from Fluxus committee regarding so called Fluxus concerts recently presented at Warshaw* [*sic*], *Prague, Budapest, Kiew* [*sic*], *Moscow and Leningrad by 4 Fluxus Renegades and impostors*, photocopy of typescripted or printed document, Sohm-Archiv, Staatsgalerie Stuttgart (folder: Nachlass George Maciunas, Inv. Nr. 87: George Maciunas. Maschinenschriftliche Typoskripte [z.T. Fotokopie]; in box: *Nachlass George Maciunas: Originale für Fluxus u. Allg.* [*Zeichnungen, Partituren, Manuskripte* (*z.T. von Kollegen*)]).

122. George Maciunas in a letter to Emmett Williams, October 1964, in Noël and Williams, *Mr Fluxus*, p. 112.

123. Gerd Wilbert, *Entstehung und Entwicklung des Programms der "linken" Kunst und der "Linken Front der Künste" (LEF) 1917–1925*, vol. 13 of Marburger Abhandlungen zur Geschichte und Kultur Osteuropas (Giessen: Schmitz, 1976), p. 183; see also p. 179.

124. Cit. after ibid.

125. See ibid., p. 188.

126. See ibid., pp. 174–75.

127. On the dispute between Maciunas and other Fluxus artists concerning their relationship with the USSR and its political system, see the interesting material compiled in Noël and Williams, *Mr Fluxus*, pp. 91–115.

128. Flynt, as quoted in Ruhé, *Fluxus: The Most Radical*, n.p. (3. Fly).

129. Mac Low, "Wie George Maciunas die New Yorker Avantgarde kennenlernte," in Block, *1962 Wiesbaden Fluxus 1982*, p. 123; Maciunas made this proposal in the *Fluxus News-Policy Letter*, no. 6, April 6, 1963; facsimile in *Fluxus etc. Addendum I*, ed. Jon Hendricks (Detroit: Gilbert and Lila Silverman Fluxus Collection, 1981–1983), p. 156.

130. See *Fluxus News Letter No. 7*, May 1, 1963; facsimile in Hendricks, *Fluxus etc.*, p. 157, see also Noël and Williams, *Mr Fluxus*, p. 95.

131. See Maciunas in a letter to Williams, June 1963, as quoted by Williams in *My Life in Flux*, pp. 168–69.

132. See George Brecht, *White for Governor Wallace*, event score at the Foundation for Contemporary Performance Art, Music Manuscript Collection, Music Library, Northwestern University, Chicago.

133. See Maciunas's manifesto from 1965; see also Maciunas in a letter to Vostell, November 3, 1964, a German translation by Tomas Schmit is in Becker and Vostell, *Happenings*, p. 202.

134. Vautier, as quoted in Hendricks, *Fluxus etc*, p. 54.

135. Reprinted in Hendricks, *What's Fluxus? What's Not! Why*, pp. 161–65; see also Hendricks, in Kaplan, "Flux Generation," p. 7.

136. Paik as quoted by Calvin Tomkins, "Profiles: Video Visionary," *New Yorker*, May 5, 1975, p. 48.

137. Maciunas, "Neo-Dada in Music, Theater, Poetry, Art," p. 157.

138. Vautier as quoted in Friedman, *Fluxus Virus*, p. 388.

139. Maciunas, "Neo-Dada in Music, Theater, Poetry, Art," p. 157.

140. Victor Musgrave, "The Unknown Art Movement," *Art and Artists*, vol. 7, no. 7, p. 14.

141. Musgrave, "The Unknown Art Movement," p. 14; see also Mike Sell, *Avant-Garde Performance and the Limits of Criticism* (Ann Arbor: University of Michigan Press, 2005), p. 174.

142. Paik, handwritten note addressed to George Maciunas and labeled as "IMPORTANT," blue pen on transparent paper (torn), Sohm-Archiv, Staatsgalerie Stuttgart (folder: "Nam June Paik: Verschiedene Manuskripte und Stücke"; in box: *Nam June Paik: Originaltexte und -manuskripte (7 Mappen) "MY LIFE" (1964), Symphonie No. 5*).

143. Quoted after Paik, *Afterlude to the EXPOSITION OF EXPERIMENTAL TELEVISION, march 1963, Galerie Parnass (Text für Fluxus Newspaper VTRE No. 5, June 1964)*, copy of typed manuscript, 9 pages, p. 8 (typesetting according to Paik), Sohm-Archiv, Staatsgalerie Stuttgart (folder: "Nam June Paik: Div. maschinenschrftl. Typoskripte"; in box: *Nam June Paik: Originaltexte und -manuskripte [7 Mappen] "MY LIFE" [1964], Symphonie No. 5*). Here, Paik transforms Akutagawa's sentences into a slightly differing variation: "the perpetual Unsatisfaction is the perpetual evolution."—see ibid.

144. Nam June Paik, "Experimentelles Fernsehen," typed manuscript, n.d., 5 pages, p. 4, Sohm-Archiv, Staatsgalerie Stuttgart (folder: "Nam June Paik: Div. maschinenschrftl. Typoskripte"; in box: *Nam June Paik: Originaltexte und -manuskripte [7 Mappen] "MY LIFE" [1964], Symphonie No. 5*).

145. Nam June Paik, *John Cage: Studie III*, p. 2; see also ibid., p. 7.

146. Joseph Beuys in an interview with the magazine *Kunst*; reprinted in Becker and Vostell, *Happenings*, p. 327.

147. Hausmann, as quoted by Koch, *Ich bin immerhin der grösste Experimentator Österreichs*, p. 82.

148. Hans Arp, "dear monsieur brzekowski," as quoted by Dawn Ades, "Dada—Constructivism," in *Dada—Constructivism: The Janus Face of the Twenties*, ed. Annely Juda (London: Annely Juda Fine Art, 1984), p. 33. Elsewhere Arp states, "Dada stands for art without sense. This does not mean nonsense." Arp as quoted by Richter, *Art and Anti-Art*, p. 34.

149. Owen F. Smith, "Playing with Difference: Fluxus as a World View," in Friedman, *Fluxus Virus*, p. 118.

150. Ibid., pp. 116–17.

151. Tristan Tzara, "Dada Manifesto 1918," in Motherwell, *Dada Painters and Poets*, p. 79.

152. See also David Doris, "Fluxus and Zen? Shut My Mouth, Quick!" in Friedman, *Fluxus Virus*, pp. 133–40. For statements about Zen by Fluxus artists, see Geoffrey Hendricks, in Kaplan, *Flux Generation*, p. 7; Robert Filliou in a letter to the editor of the *Berlinske Tidende*, December 21, 1963, reprinted in *Happening & Fluxus: Materialien*, ed. Hans Sohm and Harald Szeemann (Cologne: Kölnischer Kunstverein, 1970), n.p.; see also Paik's paralleling of cybernetics with the idea of Karma in Buddhism—see Paik, typed manuscript, untitled, undated, signed with: Nam June Paik (1789–1848), Sohm-Archiv, Staatsgalerie Stuttgart (folder "Nam June Paik: Div. maschinenschrftl. Typoskripte"; in box: *Nam June Paik: Originaltexte und -manuskripte [7 Mappen] "MY LIFE" [1964], Symphonie No. 5*). There are also explicit references to Zen in

Fluxus works: for example Mac Low's *Warum kam Bodhidharma von Westen? Um auf die andere Seite zu gelangen* and Paik's performances *Zen for Hand*, *Zen for Face*, *Zen for Walking*, *Zen for Wind*, *Old Zen*, which formed part of his *Exhibition of Music*, Wuppertal, 1963.

153. See Williams, *My Life in Flux*, p. 163 and following.

154. See, for example, Steve Odin, *The Social Self in Zen and American Pragmatism* (Albany: State University of New York Press, 1996), p. 258; and Jeff Kelley, *Childsplay: The Art of Allan Kaprow* (Berkeley: University of California Press, 2004), pp. 199–207.

155. Schlesinger, "New Mood in Politics," p. 89; see also Thomas W. Tweed, *The American Encounter with Buddhism, 1844–1912* (Bloomington: Indiana University Press, 1992), p. 158.

156. On Cage, see David Revill, *The Roaring Silence: John Cage—A Life* (New York: Arcade, 1992), pp. 107–25; see also: John Cage, *Musicage: John Cage in Conversation with Joan Retallack*, ed. Joan Retallack (Middletown, CT: Wesleyan University Press, 1996), p. 52 n. 8. On Mac Low, see Mac Low, *Representative Works: 1938–1985* (New York: Roof, 1986), p. xvi. On Paik, see Paik, *John Cage: Studie 1*, typed manuscript, n.d., 13 pages, p. 11, Sohm-Archiv, Staatsgalerie Stuttgart (folder: "Nam June Paik, Original, Notizen zu John Cage: Studio 1, Studio III"; in box: *Nam June Paik: Originaltexte und -manuskripte [7 Mappen] "MY LIFE" [1964], Symphonie No. 5*). On Brecht, see his interview with Irmeline Lebeer, in Henry Martin, *An Introduction to George Brecht's Book of the Tumbler on Fire* (Milan: Multhipla Edizioni, 1978), p. 83.

157. See Williams, *My Life in Flux-and Vice Versa*, p. 163.

158. Vautier, "What Is Fluxus?" in *Flash Art*, nos. 84–85 (1978), p. 52. See also Hannah Higgins, in Kaplan, *Flux Generation*, p. 9.

159. Introduction to "Magnum-Interview: Die Fluxus-Leute" (interview with Jean-Pierre Wilhelm, Nam June Paik, Wolf Vostell, Arthus C. Caspari), *Magnum: Die Zeitschrift für das moderne Leben*, 47 (1963), p. 32.

160. Maciunas in a videotaped interview with Larry Miller, March 24, 1978; transcript in Hendricks, *Fluxus etc. Addenda I*, p. 26.

161. See Suzuki, "The Meaning of Satori: A Talk to the Buddhist Society" (September 1963), in Suzuki, *The Field of Zen*, p. 21. Alternatively, *prajna* is also translated as "wisdom."

162. Suzuki, "The Essence of Buddhism," in Suzuki, *Essentials of Zen Buddhism*, p. 387.

163. Ibid.

164. Doris, "Fluxus and Zen?" p. 133.

165. Musgrave, "The Unknown Art Movement," p. 12.

166. Allan Kaprow, "Nam June Paik," in *Nam June Paik: Electronic Art II*, exhibition catalog (New York: Galeria Bonino, Ltd., 1968), p. 1.

167. See *CHARLOTTE MOORMAN NAM JUNE PAIK BIOGRAPHICAL MATERIAL*, photocopied print, 2 pages, p. 2, Sohm-Archiv, Staatsgalerie Stuttgart (folder: "Nam June Paik—Charlotte Moorman: Bibliografie und Dokumentation"; in

box: *Nam June Paik: Dokumentation allgemein: Bio-Bibliografie, Beiträge, Publikationen, Drucksachen, Private Misc., Charlotte Moorman*). The Sohm-Archive holds at least four copies of this text, varying in layout, format, and content.

168. See Maciunas's proposed program for a Fluxfest in Prague, 1966, copy of typescript, Sohm-Archiv, Staatsgalerie Stuttgart (folder: "Nachlass George Maciunas Inv. Nr. 143: George Maciunas: Typoskripte zu geplanten und angekündigten Fluxus-Veranstaltungen"; in box: *Nachlass George Maciunas: Originale für Fluxus u. Allg. [Zeichnungen, Partituren, Manuskripte, z.T. von Kollegen]*).

169. Nam June Paik, "Postmusic: The Monthly Review of the University for Avant-garde Hinduism, edited by N. J. PAIK. FLUXUS a publication—an essay for the new ontology of music," typescript, 1 page, Sohm-Archiv, Staatsgalerie Stuttgart (folder: "Nam June Paik: 'Monthly Review of University for Avantgarde Hinduism.' Mail Art"; in box: *Nam June Paik: Originaltexte und -manuskripte [7 Mappen] "MY LIFE" [1964], Symphonie No. 5*).

170. Paik as quoted in John A. Twaites, "Der Philosoph und die Katze: Nam June Paik in der Galerie Parnass in Wuppertal," *Deutsche Zeitung*, April 9, 1963, p. 10. The article is included in a photocopied collage of various newspaper cutouts with articles on Paik taken from international newspapers, photocopied document (1 page, Din-A3), Sohm-Archiv, Staatsgalerie Stuttgart (folder: "Nam June Paik: Bio—Bibliografie"; in box: *Nam June Paik: Dokumentation allgemein: Bio-Bibliografie, Beiträge, Publikationen, Drucksachen, Private Misc., Charlotte Moorman*).

171. Karlheinz Stockhausen, as quoted by Decker, *Paik: Video*, p. 28.

172. Kaprow, "Nam June Paik," p. 1.

173. John Cage, as quoted in *CHARLOTTE MOORMAN * NAM JUNE PAIK QUOTES (AMERICAN)*, Sohm-Archiv, Staatsgalerie Stuttgart.

174. Paik in "Magnum-Interview: Die Fluxus-Leute," p. 64.

175. John Dwyer, as quoted in *CHARLOTTE MOORMAN * NAM JUNE PAIK QUOTES (AMERICAN)*, Sohm-Archiv, Staatsgalerie Stuttgart.

176. Higgins, "In einem Minensuchboot um die Welt," p. 129.

177. See Phillpot and Jon Hendricks, *Fluxus: Selections*, p. 35.

178. Twaites, "Der Philosoph und die Katze," p. 10.

179. Nam June Paik, as quoted by Justin Hoffmann, *Destruktionskunst: Der Mythos der Zerstörung in der Kunst der frühen sechziger Jahre* (Munich: Verlag Silke Schreiber, 1995), p. 86. In *My Life* (1964), a modified issue of the magazine *Life*, no. 1142 (September 15, 1904), pp. 264–65, Paik circles the word *shocking* in the caption of an illustration; Sohm-Archiv, Staatsgalerie Stuttgart (folder: "Nam June Paik: My Life 1964"; in box: *Nam June Paik: Originaltexte und -manuskripte [7 Mappen] "MY LIFE" [1964], Symphonie No. 5*).

180. See Ken Friedman, Owen Smith, and Lauren Sawchyn, eds., *Fluxus Performance Workbook*, Performance Research e-publication, 2002, available at: www.performance-research.net/documents/fluxus_workbook_print.pdf, p. 88. Similar elements appear in Paik's description of *Moving Theater No. 2*: "DECORATE A TRUCK . . . with . . . mothers or motors and Films and naked or bleeding Dolls and real HUMAN BODIES"—see copy of manuscript (reworked), Sohm-Archiv, Staatsgalerie Stuttgart

(folder: "Eigene Drucksachen"; in box: *Nam June Paik: Originaltexte und -manuskripte [7 Mappen] "MY LIFE" [1964], Symphonie No. 5*), typeface as in original document.

181. Benjamin, "Theses on the Philosophy of History," in *Illuminations*, ed. Hannah Arendt, trans. Harry Zohn (New York: Schocken, 1969), p. 262.

182. Bloch, "The Unbearable Moment," pp. 189–90.

183. Nam June Paik, as quoted in Toni Stooss and Thomas Kellein, eds., *Nam June Paik Video Time—Video Space* (New York: Harry N. Abrams, 1993), p. 12.

184. Paik in a leaflet accompanying the exhibition *TV as a Creative Medium* at the Howard Wise Gallery, New York, 1969.

185. Nam June Paik, as quoted in Heinz Peter Schwerfel, *Kunst-Skandale: Über Tabu und Skandal, Verdammung und Verehrung zeitgenössischer Kunst* (Cologne: DuMont, 2000), p. 147.

186. See, for example, Joachim Diederichs, *Allan Kaprow*, Ph.D. diss., Ruhr-Universität Bochum, Bochum, 1975, pp. 61, 146.

187. Kaprow, "Nam June Paik," p. 1.

188. Ben Vautier, "Text on the Fluxus," in *Fluxus Subjektiv*, exhibition catalog (Vienna: Galerie Krinzinger, 1997), pp. IV/2–3, also available at: www.artnotart.com/fluxus/bvautier-textonthefluxus.html.

189. Mieko Shiomi, in Hendricks, *Fluxus etc.*, p. 51.

190. Ben Patterson, "Bekenntnis," November 14, 1964, in Becker and Vostell, *Happenings*, p. 241.

191. Paik, *John Cage: Studie 1*, p. 11, Sohm-Archiv, Staatsgalerie Stuttgart.

192. Bracken Hendricks, in Kaplan, *Flux Generation*, p. 14.

193. Hausmann, "Aussichten oder Ende des Neo-Dadaismus," n.p.

194. Wolf Vostell, as quoted in Ulrike Rüdiger, *Vostell: Leben = Kunst = Leben*, exhibition catalog, Kunstgalerie Gera (Leipzig: Seemann, 1993), p. 151; see also Burmeister, "Fluxus besucht Heiligensee," p. 148.

195. John Cage, *4'33"* (New York: Henmar Press/Edition Peters, 1960).

196. Mac Low, "The Poetics of Chance and the Politics of Simultaneous Spontaneity, or the Sacred Heart of Jesus," in *Talking Poetics from Naropa Insitute*, vol. 1, ed. Anne Waldman and Marilyn Webb (Boulder, CO: Shambhala, 1978), as quoted by Mac Low, *Representative Works: 1938–1985* (New York: Roof, 1986), p. viii.

197. Tomas Schmit, "Sensatorium Minimaximum" (1964), in Becker and Vostell, *Happenings*, p. 246, typeface and punctuation as in original.

198. Mac Low, as quoted in Noël and Williams, *Mr Fluxus*, p. 91.

199. Marcel Duchamp on the role of Mr Mutt, as quoted by Ian Chilvers, ed., *A Dictionary of Twentieth-Century Art* (Oxford: Oxford University Press, 1998), p. 508.

200. Jackson Mac Low, La Monte Young, et al., eds., *An Anthology of Chance Operations: Concept Art Anti-Art Indeterminacy Improvisation Meaningless Work Natural Disasters Plans of Action Stories Diagrams Music Poetry Essays Dance Constructions Mathematics Compositions* (New York: J. Mac Low and L. Young, 1963).

201. Walter De Maria, "Meaningless Work" (1960), in *An Anthology of Chance Operations*, ed. Mac Low and Young et al., n.p.

202. Ibid.

203. John Cage in an interview with Joan Retallack on October 22, 1991, in Cage, *Musicage*, p. 103.

204. Maciunas, "Neo-Dada in Music, Theater, Poetry, Art," p. 157.

205. Tzara, as quoted in Susan Hapgood and Jennifer Rittner, "Neo-Dada: Redefining Art, 1958–1962," *Performing Arts Journal*, vol. 17, no. 1 (January 1995), p. 69.

206. Maciunas in a letter to Schmit, November 8, 1963, in Hendricks, *What's Fluxus? What's Not! Why*, p. 160. In the original, this phrase is underlined.

207. Ibid.

208. *Absolument n'importe quoi est art*, October 26–November 8, 1962, Galerie A and Centre d'Art Total "Fluxus," Nice.

209. Philip Corner in a letter to Harry Ruhé, March 1, 1977, as quoted in Ruhé, *Fluxus: The Most Radical*, n.p. (3. Cor).

210. La Monte Young, "Lecture 1960," in *Ubi Fluxus ibi Motus 1990–1962*, ed. Achille Bonito Oliva, Gabriella De Mila, and Claudio Cerritelli (Milano: Mazzotta, 1990), p. 203.

211. George Brecht, "The Origin of Events," in Sohm and Szeeman, *Happening & Fluxus*, n.p.

212. Nam June Paik, "Manuskript about Exposition . . ." (probably 1963), facsimile in Hendricks, *Fluxus etc, Addendum II*, p. 292 (italics as in original).

213. Nam June Paik, as quoted in *CHARLOTTE MOORMAN NAM JUNE PAIK BIOGRAPHICAL MATERIAL*, p. 2 (my italics), Sohm-Archiv, Staatsgalerie Stuttgart.

214. Ralf Burmeister, "Dada 1958: Der Versuch, eine explodierte Bombe zu kitten," in *Grotesk! 130 Jahre Kunst der Frechheit*, ed. Pamela Kort, exhibition catalog (Munich: Prestel, 2003), p. 154.

215. Musgrave, "The Unknown Art Movement," p. 12.

216. Ken Friedman, "Rethinking Fluxus," in *Fluxus!* ed. Nicholas Tsoutas and Nicholas Zurbrugg, exhibition catalog (Brisbane: Institute of Modern Art, Brisbane, 1990), p. 19.

217. Maciunas, as quoted by Thomas Kellein, *Fluxus* (London: Thames & Hudson, 1995), p. 19.

218. Unknown author (B.B.), "Kunst-Terroristen," *Deutsche Zeitung*; reprinted in Becker and Vostell, *Happenings*, p. 274.

219. Nam June Paik, "Essay: To the Symphony for 20 Rooms," in Mac Low and Young et al., eds., *An Anthology of Chance Operations*, n.p.

220. See invitation card sent to "Herrn H. Sohm, 7145 Markgröningen, Postfach 7"), Sohm-Archiv, Staatsgalerie Stuttgart (folder: "Nam June Paik: Dokumentation 1966"; in box: *Nam June Paik: Dokumentation 1959–1973*).

221. Karl Heinz Bohrer, "Surrealismus und Terror oder die Aporien des Juste-Milieu," in *Surrealismus*, ed. Peter Bürger (Darmstadt: Wissenschaftliche Buchgesellschaft, 1982), p. 53.

222. Riethmüller, "Hermetik, Schock, Fasslichkeit," p. 43.

223. Nam June Paik, *John Cage: Studie III*, p. 5.

224. See Paik in a typed manuscript, Sohm-Archiv, Staatsgalerie Stuttgart (folder: "Nam June Paik: Div. maschinenschrftl. Typoskripte"; in box: *Nam June Paik: Originaltexte und -manuskripte [7 Mappen] "MY LIFE" [1964], Symphonie No. 5*).

225. Sianne Ngai, "Stuplimity: Boredom and Shock in Twentieth-Century Aesthetics," *Postmodern Culture*, vol. 10, no. 2 (January 2000), n.p., sec.10.

226. Ibid.

227. Jon Hendricks, "Fluxus," in *Stationen der Moderne*, ed. Michael Bollée, exhibition catalog (Berlin: Berlinische Galerie, 1988), p. 495.

228. Dick Higgins, *Postface* (New York: Something Else Press, 1964), p. 69.

229. Von Lewinsky, "Stumpfsinn—stundenlang!" p. 272.

230. Jackson Mac Low, *Representative Works: 1938–1985* (New York: Roof, 1986), p. 132.

231. Cage in an interview with Joan Retallack, October 22, 1991, in Cage, *Musicage*, p. 134.

232. Ibid.

233. Henry Geldzahler, as quoted by Branden W. Joseph, "The Play of Repetition: Andy Warhol's Sleep," *Gray Room*, vol. 19 (2005), p. 26.

234. See, for example, Eric Andersen, in "On New York's Avant-Garde," *Paletten* 1 (1967), p. 11; or Mac Low, *Representative Works*, p. 132. The magazine's title varied with each issue but always included the letters *VTRE*, for example, "cc Valise eTRanglE." It had been started by George Brecht under the title *V TRE* in 1963.

235. John Cage, in Richard Kostelanetz, *Conversing with Cage* (New York: Limelight, 1994), p. 222.

236. See Joseph: "The Play of Repetition," pp. 23–4.

237. Cage, as quoted by Richard Kostelanetz, *Metamorphosis in the Arts: A Critical History of the 1960s* (1967, reprinted New York: Assembling Press, 1980), p. 161.

238. Dick Higgins, "Boredom and Danger," in *A Dialectic of Centuries: Notes Towards a Theory of the New Arts*, ed. Dick Higgins (New York: Printed Editions, 1978), p. 45.

239. Ibid., pp. 43–44; see also Sell, *Avant-Garde Performance*, p. 87 and following.

240. Nam June Paik, *Utopian Laser TV Station*, draft of "TV Programs to Be Telecast March 1, 1996 A.D." (1966), typed manuscript, 2 pages, Sohm-Archiv, Staatsgalerie Stuttgart (folder: "Nam June Paik: Div. maschinenschrftl. Typoskripte"; in box: *Nam June Paik: Originaltexte und -manuskripte (7 Mappen) "MY LIFE" (1964), Symphonie No. 5*).

241. Wulf Herzogenrath, "Boredom—Notes on an Increasingly Relevant Theme," in *Langeweile / Boredom, BE Magazine # 3*, October 1996, Berlin: Künstlerhaus Bethanien, p. 10.

242. Nam June Paik, "Towards More *Sensible* Boredom," program of a performance evening at the Film-Maker's Cinematheque, New York, April 21, 1966; 1 page (photocopy, damaged), Sohm-Archiv, Staatsgalerie Stuttgart (folder: "Nam June Paik:

Notizzettel, Notizhefte u. misc.—Originale"; in box: *Nam June Paik: Originaltexte und -manuskripte [7 Mappen] "MY LIFE" [1964], Symphonie No. 5)*. A second copy of this page is equally available at the Sohm-Archiv (folder: "Nam June Paik: Dokumentation 1966"; in box: *Nam June Paik: Dokumentation, 1959–1973*).

243. Cage, as quoted in Joseph, "The Play of Repetition," p. 25.

244. Jackson Mac Low, "Wie George Maciunas die New Yorker Avantgarde kennenlernte," in Block, *1962 Wiesbaden Fluxus 1982*, pp. 123–24.

245. See Mac Low, "Wie George Maciunas die New Yorker Avantgarde kennenlernte," pp. 124–25.

246. Kathryn Chiong, "Naumans Beckett Gang," in *Samuel Beckett, Bruce Nauman*, ed. Michael Glasmeier, exhibition catalog (Vienna: Kunsthalle Wien, 2000), pp. 88–107.

247. Byrd, in Mac Low and Young et al., eds., *An Anthology of Chance Operations*, n.p.

248. Christian Kellerer, *Objet trouvé und Surrealismus: Zur Psychologie der modernen Kunst* (Reinbek/Hamburg: Rowohlt, 1968), p. 81.

249. Dick Higgins, "A Something Else Manifesto," in Higgins, *A Dialectic of Centuries*, p. 102.

250. D. T. Suzuki, *Zen Buddhism: Selected Writings of D. T. Suzuki*, ed. William Barrett (Garden City, NY: Doubleday & Co., 1956), p. 130.

251. Suzuki, "Zen in the Modern World" (1958), in Suzuki, *The Essentials of Zen Buddhism*, p. 378.

252. Suzuki, "The Break-Through to Reality: A Talk to the Buddhist Society" (July 1954), in Suzuki, *The Field of Zen*, p. 54.

253. Kellerer, *Objet trouvé und Surrealismus*, p. 80.

254. See Ngai, "Stuplimity: Boredom and Shock," sec. 21; see also: Jacques Lacan, *The Seminar of Jacques Lacan*, book 7: *The Ethics of Psychoanalysis* (New York: W. W. Norton, 1992), pp. 113–14.

255. John Ruskin, *The Elements of Drawing* (New York: J. Wiley, 1863), p. 22.

256. Daisetz T. Suzuki, "The Break-Through to Reality," p. 54.

257. See Friedman, Smith, and Sawchyn, *Fluxus Performance Workbook*, p. 115.

258. Higgins, "Boredom and Danger," pp. 43, 46.

259. Ina Blom, "Boredom and Oblivion," in Friedman, *Fluxus Reader*, p. 66.

260. Ibid., p. 64.

261. See Decker, *Paik: Video*, p. 24.

262. Jürging, *Tradition des Traditionsbruchs*, p. 86.

263. John Cage, "Juilliard Lecture" (1952), in John Cage, *A Year from Monday: New Lectures and Writings* (Middletown, CT: Wesleyan University Press, 1967), p. 105.

264. Suzuki, "The Meaning of Satori," p. 22; see also Doris, "Fluxus and Zen?" p. 135.

265. Hannah Higgins, *The Fluxus Experience* (Berkeley: University of California Press, 2002), p. 85.

266. Viktor Shklovsky, "Art as Technique," in *Contemporary Literary Criticism*, ed. Robert Con Davies and Ronald Schleifer (New York: Longman, 1989), p. 58.

267. Shklovsky, "Art as Technique," p. 58.

268. Viktor Shklovsky, "The Resurrection of the Word," in *Russian Formalism*, ed. Stephen Bann and John E. Bowlt (New York: Barnes & Noble, 1973), p. 46.

269. Shklovsky, "Art as Technique," p. 58.

270. See Wolfgang Iser, "Image und Montage," in *Immanente Ästhetik, ästhetische Reflexion: Lyrik als Paradigma der Moderne*, ed. Wolfgang Iser, vol. 2 of *Poetik und Hermeneutik* (Munich: Fink, 1966), pp. 368, 369. English excerpts as quoted by Winfried Fluck, "In Search for Distance: Negation and Negativity in Wolfgang Iser's Literary Theory," *New Literary History*, vol. 31 (2000), p. 183.

271. See Iser, "Image und Montage," p. 368.

5. Conclusion

1. Andrei B. Nakov, "Dada Gives Me an Intolerable 'Malaise,'" in *Dada—Constructivism: The Janus Face of the Twenties*, ed. Annely Juda (London: Annely Juda Fine Art, 1984), p. 7.

2. John Dewey, *Psychology* (New York: Harper, 1887), p. 127.

3. Roland Barthes, "Shock-Photos," in Barthes, *The Eiffel Tower and Other Mythologies* (Berkeley: University of California Press, 1997), p. 72.

4. Mark Quinn in Robert Preece, "Just a Load of Shock? An Interview with Marc Quinn," *Sculpture*, vol. 19, no. 8 (October 2000), p. 16.

5. Wolfgang Flatz, "Ich bin schon eher eine Ratte: Ein Gespräch zwischen Justin Hoffmann und Flatz," in *Out of Control*, exhibition catalog (Linz: Ars Electronica, 1991); also available at: http://90.146.8.18/de/archives/festival_archive/festival_catalogs/festival_catalog.asp.

6. Ibid.

7. See Daniel Süss et al., *Kommunikationsstrategien in der Gesundheitsförderung*, conducted by K.E.A.P. (Kompetenzzentrum für Evaluationsforschung in Angewandter Psychologie) in 2002 (Kurzbericht); available at: www.psychologie.zhaw.ch/de/psychologie/forschung-und-entwicklung/medienpsychologie/forschungsprojekte-archiv/gesundheitsfoerderung.html.

8. Richard Shiff, "Handling Shocks: On the Representation of Experience in Walter Benjamin's Analogies," *The Oxford Art Journal*, vol. 15, no. 2 (1992), p. 90.

9. Sean Kernan, "Camera Art: An interview with John Paul Caponigro," *Camera Arts*, December 1999–January 2000, p. 14.

10. Howard Brenton, as quoted by Vanessa Thorpe, "Welcome to the New Brutalism," *Observer*, August 20, 2000.

11. James G. Ballard, ibid.

12. Joachim Diederichs, *Allan Kaprow*, Ph.D. diss., Ruhr-Universität Bochum, 1975, p. 146.

13. See Anthony Julius, *Transgressions: The Offences of Art* (London: Thames & Hudson, 2002), p. 33.

14. Ibid., p. 26.

15. Ibid., p. 27.

16. Norman Rosenthal as quoted in Jonathan Jones, "Shock treatment," *The Guardian*, September 7, 2000.

17. Unspecified source as quoted in Julius, *Transgressions*, p. 32.

18. Richard Shusterman, "The End of Aesthetic Experience," in Shusterman, *Performing Live: Aesthetic Alternatives for the Ends of Art* (New York: Cornell University Press: 2000), p. 31. The text was first published in *Journal of Aesthetics and Art Criticism* 55 (1999), pp. 29–41.

19. Frederic Schwartz, *Blind Spots: Critical Theory and the History of Art in Twentieth-Century Germany* (New Haven, CT: Yale University Press, 2005), p. 62.

20. Susan Buck-Morss, "Aesthetics and Anaesthetics: Walter Benjamin's Artwork Essay Reconsidered" (1992), in *October: The Second Decade, 1986–1996*, ed. Rosalind Krauss et al. (Cambridge, MA: MIT Press, 1997), p. 413.

21. Francis Picabia, "DADA Manifesto," in *Dadas on Art*, ed. Lucy Lippard (Englewood Cliffs, NJ: Prentice Hall, 1971), p. 166.

22. See Roland Burkart, "Kommunikationstheorien," in *Öffentliche Kommunikation. Handbuch Kommunikations- und Medienwissenschaft*, ed. Günter Bentele et al. (Wiesbaden: Westdeutscher Verlag, 2003), p. 170.

23. Ibid.

24. Ibid.

25. Christopher W. E. Bigsby, *Dada and Surrealism* (London: Methuen, 1972), p. 29.

26. Owen F. Smith, "Pre-Fluxus Conceptual Developments and Generative Influences," available at: www.thing.net/~grist/ld/smith-fl.htm, n.p.

27. Raoul Hausmann, "Aussichten oder Ende des Neodadaismus," (1962), in Adelheid Koch, *Ich bin immerhin der grösste Experimentator Österreichs: Raoul Hausmann—Dada und Neodada* (Innsbruck: Haymon-Verlag, 1994), n.p.

28. Renato Poggioli, *Theory of the Avant-Garde* (Cambridge, MA: Belknap Press of Harvard University Press, 1968), p. 62.

29. Tristan Tzara, "An Introduction to Dada," in *The Dada Painters and Poets*, ed. Robert Motherwell, 2nd ed. (New York: Wittenborn, Schultz, Inc., 1967), p. 397.

30. Richard Huelsenbeck, "Dada Manifesto, 1949," in Motherwell, *Dada Painters and Poets*, p. 391.

31. Marcel Janco, "Dada at Two Speeds," in Lippard, *Dadas on Art*, p. 37.

32. Theodor W. Adorno, "Commitment" (1962), in *Aesthetics and Politics*, ed. Ernst Bloch et al., trans. Ronald Taylor et al. (London: Verso, 1980), p. 180.

33. Theodor W. Adorno, *Philosophy of Modern Music*, trans. Anne G. Mitchell and Wesley V. Blomster (New York: Seabury Press, 1973), p. 133.

34. Theodor W. Adorno, "On the Fetish-Character in Music and the Regression of Listening" (1938), in *The Essential Frankfurt School Reader*, ed. Andrew Arato and Eike Gebhardt (Oxford: Basil Blackwell, 1978), p. 298.

35. Rachel Campbell-Johnson, "Bad Art for Bad People," *Times*, Dec. 14, 2006. *Bad Art for Bad People* was on display at Tate Liverpool from December 15, 2006 to March 4, 2007.

36. Elizabeth Allen Chabert, *Transforming Impact: The Shock Experience in Dada and Surrealist Poetry*, Ph.D. diss., Columbia University, New York, microfiche, 1995, p. 444.

37. Ibid.

38. Bertolt Brecht, as quoted by Martin Esslin, *Brecht: The Man and His Work* (Garden City, NY: Anchor Books, 1969), p. 143. In their manifesto "Towards a Free Revolutionary Art" (1938), André Breton, Diego Rivera, and Leon Trotsky came to formulate the same request: "True art, which is not content to play variations on ready-made models but rather insists on expressing the inner needs of man and of mankind in its time—true art is unable not to be revolutionary, not to aspire to a complete and radical reconstruction of society." See André Breton, Diego Rivera, and Leon Trotsky, "Towards a Free Revolutionary Art," trans. Dwight MacDonald, *Partisan Review*, vol. 4, no. 1 (Fall 1938), p. 50.

Bibliography

Ades, Dawn. "Dada—Constructivism." In *Dada—Constructivism: The Janus Face of the Twenties*. Edited by Annely Juda. London: Annely Juda Fine Art, 1984, pp. 33–34.

Adorno, Theodor W. *Philosophy of Modern Music*. Translated by Anne G. Mitchell and Wesley V. Blomster. New York: Seabury Press, 1973. First: *Philosophie der neuen Musik*. Tübingen: J. C. B. Mohr, 1949.

———. *The Adorno Reader*. Edited by Brian O'Connor. Oxford: Blackwell Publishers, 2000.

———. "On the Fetish-Character in Music and the Regression of Listening." In *The Essential Frankfurt School Reader*. Edited by Andrew Arato and Eike Gebhardt. Oxford: Basil Blackwell, 1978, pp. 270–99. First: "Über den Fetischcharakter in der Musik und die Regression des Hörens," *Zeitschrift für Sozialforschung*, vol. 2 (1938).

———. "Commitment." In *Aesthetics and Politics*. Edited by Ernst Bloch et al. Translated by Ronald Taylor et al. London: Verso, 1980, pp. 177–95. First: "Engagement" (1962). In *Noten zur Literatur*. Vol. 11 of *Gesammelte Schriften*. Edited by Rolf Tiedemann. Frankfurt: Suhrkamp, 1974, pp. 409–30.

———. "Über Jazz." In *Musikalische Schriften IV*. Vol. 17 of *Gesammelte Schriften*. Edited by Rolf Tiedemann. Frankfurt: Suhrkamp, 1982, pp. 74–100. First: Hektor Rottweiler (pseudonym). "Über Jazz." *Zeitschrift für Sozialforschung*, vol. 1 (1936).

———. "Über Jazz, Appendix: Oxforder Nachträge" (1937). In *Musikalische Schriften IV*. Vol. 17 of *Gesammelte Schriften*. Edited by Rolf Tiedemann. Frankfurt: Suhrkamp, 1982, pp. 100–108.

———. *Aesthetic Theory*. Edited by Gretel Adorno and Rolf Tiedemann. Translated by Robert Hullot-Kentor. London: Athlone Press, 1997. First: *Ästhetische Theorie*. Vol. 7 of *Gesammelte Schriften*. Edited by Rolf Tiedemann. Frankfurt: Suhrkamp, 1970.

Allen, Richard W. "The Aesthetic Experience of Modernity: Benjamin, Adorno, and Contemporary Film Theory." *New German Critique*, no. 40, Winter 1987, pp. 225–40.

Andersen, Eric. "On New York's Avant-Garde." *Paletten*, no. 1, 1967, p. 11.

Anonymous. "Dada Abend am 14. Juli 1916 im Zunfthaus zur Waag." *Neue Zürcher Zeitung*, second evening edition (July 18, 1916). Reprinted in Pichon and Riha, *Dada Zürich: A Clown's Game from Nothing*, 203–4.

———. "Die Simulanten des Irrsinns auf dem Vortragspult." *Neue Berliner 12 Uhr Zeitung* (May 20, 1919). Reprinted in Pichon and Riha, *Dada Zürich: A Clown's Game from Nothing*, pp. 221–22.

———. "Shock-Art with a Purpose." *Times Literary Supplement*, February 4, 1965, p. 80.

———. "Trend to the 'Anti-Art.'" *Newsweek*, March 31, 1958, pp. 94–96.

———. Untitled article in *Zürcher Morgen-Zeitung* (July 29, 1918). Reprinted in Pichon and Riha, *Dada Zürich: A Clown's Game from Nothing*, pp. 219–20.

Ardenne, Paul. *Extrême: Esthétique de la Limite Dépassée*. Paris: Flammarion, 2006.

Arp, Hans. "Dada Was No Childish Romp." In Rex William Last, *Hans Arp, the Poet of Dadaism*. London: Oswald Wolff, 1969, pp. 77–80. First: "Dada war kein Rüpelspiel." In *Unsern täglichen Traum . . . Erinnerungen, Dichtungen und Betrachtungen aus den Jahren 1914–1954*. Edited by Peter Schifferli. Zurich: Arche, 1955, pp. 20–28.

Azari, Fedele. "Vita simultanea futurista" (1928). *Scrivo*, no. 68, 1968.

B., B. (unknown author). "Kunst-Terroristen." *Deutsche Zeitung*. In Becker and Vostell, *Happenings*, p. 274.

Backes-Haase, Alfons. "Wir wollen triezen, stänkern, bluffen . . . ." In *"Die ganze Welt ist eine Manifestation": Die europäische Avantgarde und ihre Manifeste*. Edited by Wolfgang Asholt and Werner Fähnders. Darmstadt: Wissenschaftliche Buchgesellschaft, 1997, pp. 259–64.

Baehr, Ulrich (ed.). *Zur Wahrnehmungsgeschichte einer industriellen Metropole*, exhibition catalog, 2nd ed. Berlin: Verlag für Ästhetik und Kommunikation, 1987 (1984).

Bagdikian, Ben H. "Endings, Beginnings, and Endings: Media in the 1950s." In Stich, *Made in the USA*, pp. 228–33.

Ball, Hugo. "Dada Manifesto" (Opening manifesto of the first Dada evening in Zurich, July 14, 1916). In *Flight Out of Time*, pp. 219–21. First: "Eröffnungs-Manifest." In *Flucht aus der Zeit*. Munich: Duncker and Humblot, 1927.

———. *Flight Out of Time: A Dada Diary*. Edited by John Elderfield. Translated by Ann Raimes. New York: Viking Press, 1974. First: *Flucht aus der Zeit*. Munich: Duncker and Humblot, 1927.

Barr, Alfred H. *What Is Modern Painting?* New York: Museum of Modern Art, 1946.

Barthes, Roland. "Shock-Photos." In *The Eiffel Tower and Other Mythologies*. Berkeley: University of California Press, 1997, pp. 71–75.

Beard, George Miller. *American Nervousness: Its Causes and Consequences*. New York: G. P. Putnam's Sons, 1881.

———. "Neurasthenia, or Nervous Exhaustion." *Boston Medical and Surgical Journal*, vol. 80 (1869), pp. 217–21.

———. *Practical Treatise on Nervous Exhaustion (Neurasthenia): Its Symptoms, Nature, Sequences, and Treatment*. New York: Wood, 1880.

Becker, Jürgen, and Wolf Vostell. *Happenings: Fluxus, Pop Art, Nouveau Réalism.* Reinbek/Hamburg: Rowohlt, 1965.

Bell, Daniel. *The End of Ideology: On the Exhaustion of Political Ideas in the Fifties.* Cambridge, MA: Harvard University Press, 1988. First: Glencoe, Ill.: Free Press, 1960.

Benjamin. Walter. "Berlin Childhood around 1900" (final version). In *Walter Benjamin: Selected Writings,* vol. 3: *1935–1938.* Edited by Michael W. Jennings, and Howard Eiland. Cambridge, MA: Belknap Press of Harvard University Press, 2002, pp. 344–433. First: *Berliner Kindheit um Neunzehnhundert.* Frankfurt: Suhrkamp, 1987.

———. "A Berlin Chronicle." In *Walter Benjamin: Selected Writings,* vol. 2: *1927–1934.* Edited by Michael W. Jennings, Howard Eiland, and Gary Smith. Cambridge, MA: Belknap Press of Harvard University Press, 1999, pp. 595–637. First: *Berliner Chronik.* Edited by Gershom Scholem. Frankfurt: Suhrkamp, 1970.

———. "Das Kunstwerk im Zeitalter seiner technischen Reproduzierbarkeit" (first version), in *Walter Benjamin: Gesammelte Schriften.* Vol. 1, 2. Edited by Rolf Tiedemann and Hermann Schweppenhäuser. Frankfurt: Suhrkamp: 1974, pp. 431–69. First: *L'Oeuvre d'art à l'époque de sa reproduction mécanisée.* Translated by Pierre Klossowski. *Zeitschrift für Sozialforschung,* vol. 5, no. 1 (1936).

———. *The Correspondence of Walter Benjamin 1910–1940.* Edited by Theodor Adorno and Gershom Scholem. Translated by Manfred R. Jacobson and Evelyn M. Jacobson. Chicago: University of Chicago Press, 1994.

———. "Ein Jakobiner von Heute: Zu Werner Hegemanns 'Das steinerne Berlin.'" In *Walter Benjamin: Gesammelte Schriften.* Vol. 3. Edited by Rolf Tiedemann and Hermann Schweppenhäuser. Frankfurt: Suhrkamp: 1972, pp. 260–65. First: *Frankfurter Zeitung,* Sept. 14, 1930.

———. "Moscow." In *Walter Benjamin: Selected Writings,* vol. 2: *1927–1934.* Edited by Michael W. Jennings, Howard Eiland, and Gary Smith. Cambridge, MA: Belknap Press of Harvard University Press, 1999, pp. 22–46. First: "Moskau." *Die Kreatur,* vol. 2 (1927).

———. "On Some Motifs in Baudelaire." In *Walter Benjamin: Selected Writings,* vol. 4: *1938–1940.* Edited by Michael W. Jennings and Howard Eiland. Cambridge, MA: Belknap Press of Harvard University Press, 2003, pp. 313–55. First: "Über einige Motive bei Baudelaire." *Zeitschrift für Sozialforschung,* vol. 8, nos. 1–2 (1939).

———. "The Paris of the Second Empire in Baudelaire." In *Walter Benjamin: Selected Writings,* vol. 4: *1938–1940.* Edited by Michael W. Jennings and Howard Eiland. Cambridge, MA: Belknap Press of Harvard University Press, 2003, pp. 3–92. First: *Das Paris des Second Empire bei Baudelaire.* Edited by Rosemarie Heise. Berlin and Weimar: Aufbau-Verlag, 1971.

———. "Theory of Distraction." Translated by Howard Eiland. In *Walter Benjamin: Selected Writings,* vol. 3: *1935–1938.* Edited by Michael W. Jennings and Howard Eiland. Cambridge, MA: Belknap Press of Harvard University Press, 2002, pp. 141–42. First: "Theorie der Zerstreuung. In *Gesammelte Schriften.* Vol. 7. Edited

by Rolf Tiedemann and Hermann Schweppenhäuser. Frankfurt: Suhrkamp, 1989, pp. 678–79.
———. "Theses on the Philosophy of History" (1940). In *Illuminations*. Edited by Hannah Arendt. Translated by Harry Zohn. New York: Schocken 1969, pp. 253–64.
———. "The Work of Art in the Age of Its Technological Reproducibility" (final version). In *Walter Benjamin: Selected Writings*, vol. 4: *1938–1940*. Edited by Michael W. Jennings and Howard Eiland. Cambridge, MA: Belknap Press of Harvard University Press, 2003, pp. 251–83. First: *Das Kunstwerk im Zeitalter seiner technischen Reproduzierbarkeit*. Frankfurt: Suhrkamp, 1963.
Berend, Alice. *Spreemann and Co.* Berlin: Fischer, 1916.
Berg, Hubert van den. *Avantgarde und Anarchismus: Dada in Zürich und Berlin*. Heidelberg: Winter, 1999.
———."Dadaist Subjectivity and the Politics of Indifference: On Some Contrasts and Correspondences between Dada in Zürich and Berlin." In *Subjectivity*. Edited by Wilhelm van Reijen and Willem G. Weststeijn. Vol. 12 of *Avant-Garde Critical Studies*. Amsterdam: Rodopi, 1999, pp. 29–57.
———. "On the Historiographic Distinction between Historical and Neo-Avant-Garde." In *Avant-Garde/Neo-Avant-Garde*. Edited by Dietrich Scheunemann. Vol. 17 of *Avant-Garde Critical Studies*. Amsterdam: Rodopi, 2005, pp. 63–74.
———. "Tristan Tzara's 'Manifeste Dada 1918.'" *Neophilologus*, vol. 79, no. 3 (1995), pp. 353–76.
Berghahn, Volker. *Das Kaiserreich 1871–1914*. Vol. 16 of *Gebhardt Handbuch der deutschen Geschichte*. Edited by Jürgen Kocka. Stuttgart: Klett-Cotta, 2003.
Bergius, Hanne. "*Dada Triumphs!*" *Dada Berlin, 1917–1923, Artistry of Polarities: Montages, Metamechanics, Manifestations*. Translated by Brigitte Pichon. Vol. 5 of *Crisis and the Arts: The History of Dada*, ed. Stephen C. Foster. New Haven, CT: Thomson/Gale, 2003. First: *Montage und Metamechanik: Dada Berlin; Artistik von Polaritäten*. Berlin: Gebr. Mann Verlag, 2000. (The second chapter of the English edition ("Club Dada Berlin") is not contained in the German publication.)
———. "Zur Wahrnehmung und Wahrnehmungsästhetik im Berliner Dadaismus." In Höllerer and Miller, "Dada–Neodada–Kryptodada–?" pp. 234–55.
Bergson, Henri. *Creative Evolution*. London: Macmillan, 1913.
Berman, Ronald. *America in the Sixties: An Intellectual History*. New York: Free Press, 1968.
Beyme, Klaus von. *Das Zeitalter der Avantgarden: Kunst und Gesellschaft 1905–1955*. Munich: Verlag C. H. Beck, 2005.
Bigsby, Christopher W. E. *Dada and Surrealism*. London: Methuen, 1972.
Binswanger, Ludwig. *Die Pathologie und Therapie der Neurasthenie*. Jena: Fischer, 1896.
Birkenhauer, Klaus. *Die eigenrhythmische Lyrik Bertolt Brechts*. Tübingen: Max Niemeyer Verlag, 1971.
Bloch, Ernst. "The Unbearable Moment." In *Literary Essays*. Vol. 6. Translated by Andrew Joron. Stanford, CA: Stanford University Press, 1998, pp. 189–90. First

"Der unerträgliche Augenblick." In *Gesamtausgabe*. Vol. 9. Frankfurt: Suhrkamp, 1965, pp. 219–20.

Block, René (ed.). *Eine lange Geschichte mit vielen Knoten: Fluxus in Deutschland 1962–1994*, exhibition catalog. Stuttgart: IfA Galerie, 1995.

——— (ed.). *1962 Wiesbaden Fluxus 1982: Eine kleine Geschichte von Fluxus in drei Teilen*, exhibition catalog. Wiesbaden: Harlekin Art, 1983 (German and English).

Blom, Ina. "Boredom and Oblivion." In Friedman, *Fluxus Reader*, pp. 64-90.

Bluemler, Detlef, and Lothar Romain (eds.) *Künstler: Kritisches Lexikon der Gegenwartskunst*. Munich: Zeitverlag, ongoing.

Bohrer, Karl Heinz. "Ästhetik und Gewalt als Bedingungsverhältnis: Jenseits Anthropologischer Begründungen." In *Die Grenzen des Ästhetischen*. Munich: Hanser, 1998, pp. 138–59.

———. "Das Böse—Eine Ästhetische Kategorie?" *Merkur*, no. 436 (June 1985), pp. 459–73.

———. *Die Ästhetik des Schreckens: Die pessimistische Romantik und Ernst Jüngers Frühwerk*. Munich: Hanser, 1978.

———. "Die permanente Theodizee: Über das verfehlte Böse im deutschen Bewusstsein." *Merkur*, no. 458 (April 1987), pp. 267–386

———. *Nach der Natur: Über Politik und Ästhetik*. Munich and Vienna: Carl Hanser Verlag, 1988.

———. *Suddenness: On the Moment of Aesthetic Appearance*. Translated by Ruth Crowley. New York: Columbia University Press, 1994. First: *Plötzlichkeit: Zum Augenblick des ästhetischen Scheins*. Frankfurt/Main: Suhrkamp, 1981.

———."Surrealismus und Terror oder die Aporien des Juste-Milieu" (1969). In *Surrealismus*. Edited by Peter Bürger. Darmstadt: Wissenschaftliche Buchgesellschaft, 1982, pp. 51–66. First: Bohrer. *Die gefährdete Phantasie, oder Surrealismus und Terror*. Munich: Hanser, 1970, pp. 32–61.

Böhringer, Hannes, and Karl Gründer (eds.). *Ästhetik und Soziologie um die Jahrhundertwende: Georg Simmel*. Frankfurt/Main: Vittorio Klostermann, 1976.

Bollé, Michael (ed.). *Stationen der Moderne*, exhibition catalog. Berlin: Berlinische Galerie, 1988.

Bonhoeffer, Karl (ed.). *Geistes- und Nervenkrankheiten*. Vol. 4 of *Handbuch der Ärztlichen Erfahrungen im Weltkriege 1914/1918*, ed. Otto Schjerning. Leipzig: Verlag von Johann Ambrosius Barth, 1922.

Bonnet, Marguerite (ed.). *L'Affaire Barrès*. Paris: Corti, 1987.

Bornemann, John. *After the Wall: East Meets West in the New Berlin*. Boston: Basic Books, 1991.

Brecht, Bertolt. "On Unrhymed Lyrics in Irregular Rhythms." Translated by Beatrice Gottlieb. *The Tulane Drama Review*, vol. 2, no. 1 (Nov. 1957), pp. 33–38, First: "Über reimlose Lyrik mit unregelmässigen Rhythmen." In *Versuche*. Edited by Bertolt Brecht and Elisabeth Hauptmann, issue 12, 27/32. Berlin: Aufbau-Verlag, 1957.

Brecht, George. "The Origin of Events." In Sohm and Szeemann, *Happening and Fluxus*, n.p.

Breton, André, Diego Rivera, and Leon Trotsky. "Manifesto: Towards a Free Revolutionary Art" (1938). Translated by Dwight MacDonald. *Partisan Review*, vol. 4, no. 1 (Fall 1938), pp. 49–53.

Buchloh, Benjamin H. D. "The Primary Colors for the Second Time: A Paradigm Repetition of the Neo-Avant-Garde." *October*, vol. 37 (Summer 1986), pp. 41–52.

———. "Theorizing the Avant-Garde." *Art in America*, vol. 72, no. 10 (Nov. 1984), pp. 19–21.

———. "The Twilight of the Idol: Preliminary Notes for a Critique." *Artforum*, vol. 18, no. 5 (January 1989), pp. 35–43.

Buck-Morss, Susan. "Aesthetics and Anaesthetics: Walter Benjamin's Artwork Essay Reconsidered." *October*, no. 62 (Fall 1992), pp. 3–41. Reprinted in: *October: The Second Decade, 1986–1996*. Edited by Rosalind Krauss et al. Cambridge, MA: MIT Press, 1997, pp. 375–413.

Burgdorff, Stephan, and Klaus Wiegrefe (eds.). *Der Erste Weltkrieg: Die Urkatastrophe des 20. Jahrhunderts*. Munich: Deutsche Verlags-Anstalt, 2004.

Bürger, Peter. *Der französische Surrealismus: Studien zum Problem der avantgardistischen Literatur*. Frankfurt: Athenäum Verlag, 1971.

———. *Theory of the Avant-Garde*. Minneapolis: University of Minnesota Press, 1984. First: *Theorie der Avantgarde*, Frankfurt: Suhrkamp, 1974.

Burkart, Roland. "Kommunikationstheorien." In *Öffentliche Kommunikation: Handbuch Kommunikations- und Medienwissenschaft*. Edited by Günter Bentele, Hans-Bernd Brosius and Otfried Jarren. Wiesbaden: Westdeutscher Verlag, 2003, pp. 169–92.

Burke, Edmund. *A Philosophical Enquiry into the Origin of Our Ideas of the Sublime and Beautiful*. Oxford: Oxford University Press, 1990. First: London: Scott, Webster and Geary (printed for R. and J. Dodsley), 1757.

Burmeister, Ralf. "Dada 1958: Der Versuch, eine explodierte Bombe zu kitten." In *Grotesk! 130 Jahre Kunst der Frechheit*, exhibition catalog. Edited by Pamela Kort. Munich: Prestel, 2003, pp. 148–54.

———. "Fluxus besucht Heiligensee." In *Hanna Höch: Eine Lebenscollage*, vol. 3: *1946–1978*. Berlin: Berlinische Galerie, 2001, pp. 122–53.

Cage, John. *4'33"*. New York: Henmar Press/Edition Peters, 1960.

———. "Juilliard Lecture" (1952). In *A Year from Monday: New Lectures and Writings*. Middletown, CT: Wesleyan University Press, 1967, pp. 95–111.

———. *Musicage: John Cage in Conversation with Joan Retallack*. Edited by Joan Retallack. Hanover, NH: Wesleyan University Press, 1996.

Calinescu, Matei. *Five Faces of Modernity*. Durham, NC: Duke University Press, 1987.

Campbell-Johnson, Rachel. "Bad Art for Bad People," *Times*, December 14, 2006.

Canetti, Elias. *The Torch in My Ear*. Translated by Joachim Neugroschel. New York: Farrar Straus Giroux, 1982. First: *Die Fackel im Ohr*. Munich and Vienna: Hanser, 1980.

Carrey, John. *The Intellectuals and the Masses: Pride and Prejudice among the Literary Intelligentsia, 1880–1939*. London: Faber and Faber, 1992.

Cashell, Kieran. *Afershock: The Ethics of Contemporary Transgressive Art*. London: I. B.Tauris, 2009.

Caws, Mary-Ann (ed.). *Manifesto: Century of Isms*. Lincoln: University of Nebraska Press, 2000.

Chabert, Elizabeth Allen. *Transforming Impact: The Shock Experience in Dada and Surrealist Poetry*. Ph.D. dissertation, Columbia University, New York, 1995, microfiche.

Chilvers, Ian (ed.). *A Dictionary of Twentieth-Century Art*. Oxford: Oxford University Press, 1998.

Chiong, Kathryn. "Naumans Beckett Gang." In *Samuel Beckett, Bruce Nauman*, exhibition catalog. Edited by Michael Glasmeier. Vienna: Kunsthalle Wien, 2000, pp. 88–107.

Chipp, Hershel B. (ed.). *Theories of Modern Art: A Source Book by Artists and Critics*. Berkeley: University of California Press, 1968.

Clark, Ronald W. *Freud: The Man and the Cause*. London: Jonathan Cape, Weidenfeld and Nicolson, 1980.

Crary, Jonathan. *Suspension of Perception: Attention, Spectacle, and Modern Culture*. Cambridge, MA: MIT Press, 1999.

Crow, Thomas. *The Rise of the Sixties: American and European Art in the Era of Dissent 1955–69*. London: Weidenfeld and Nicolson, 1996.

Crowther, Paul. *Critical Aesthetics and Postmodernism*. Oxford: Clarendon Press, 1993.

Daly, Nicholas. "The Woman in White: Whistler, Hiffernan, Courbet, Du Maurier." *Modernism/modernity*, vol. 12, no. 1 (2005), pp. 1–25.

Damus, Martin. *Kunst in der BRD 1945–1990: Funktionen der Kunst in einer demokratisch verfassten Gesellschaft*. Reinbek/Hamburg: Rowohlt, 1995.

Danler, Hubert. *Sigmund Freud in seiner Epoche (1856–1939)*. Norderstedt: Books on Demand, 2001.

Decker, Edith. *Paik. Video*. Cologne: DuMont Buchverlag, 1988.

Delany, Samuel R. *The Motion of Light on Water: Sex and Science Fiction Writing in the East Village, 1957–1965*. New York: Arbor House/W. Morrow, 1988.

Dewey, John. *Psychology*. New York: Harper, 1887.

Dickerman, Leah, ed. *Dada: Zurich, Berlin, Hannover, Cologne, New York, Paris*, exhibition catalog. National Gallery of Art, Washington, D.C., and other museums. New York: Distributed Art Publishers, 2005.

Dickson, Paul. *Sputnik: The Shock of the Century*. New York: Walker and Co., 2001.

Diederichs, Joachim. *Allan Kaprow*, Ph.D. dissertation, Ruhr-Universität Bochum, Bochum, 1975.

Doesburg, Theo van. "Characteristics of Dadaism" (1923). In Lippard, *Dadas on Art*, p. 112.

Doherty, Brigid. "'See: We Are All Neurasthenics!' or, The Trauma of Dada Montage." *Critical Inquiry*, vol. 24 (Autumn 1997), pp. 82–132.

Doris, David. "Fluxus und Zen? Halt meinen Mund, schnell!" ("Fluxus and Zen? Shut My Mouth, Quick!") In Friedman, *Fluxus Virus*, pp. 124–32, 133–40 (German and English).

———. "Zen Vaudeville: A Medi(t)ation in the Margins of Fluxus." Available at: www.thing.net/~grist/ld/koppany/doris–e.htm.

Dörsel, Wilfried, Rainer Steinberg, and Robert von Zahn. "Das Atelier Bauermeister: Proto-Fluxus in Köln 1960–62" ("The Bauermeister Studio: Proto-Fluxus in Cologne, 1960–1962"). In Friedman, *Fluxus Virus*, pp. 48–55, 56–62 (German and English).

Duhamel, Georges. *Scènes de la vie future*. Paris: Mercure de France, 1930.

Dunlop, Ian. *The Shock of the New: Seven Historic Exhibitions of Modern Art*. New York: American Heritage Press, 1972.

Ehrlicher, Hanno. *Die Kunst der Zerstörung*. Berlin: Akademie-Verlag, 2001.

Eiland, Howard. "Reception in Distraction." *Boundary* 2, vol. 30, no. 1 (Spring 2003), pp. 51–66.

Engels, Friedrich. "The Impression Produced by London." In *The Condition of the Working Class in England in 1844*. Translated by Florence Kelly Wischnewetsky. New York: J. W. Lovell Compagny, 1887. First: *Die Lage der arbeitenden Klasse in England*, Leipzig: Wigand, 1885.

Erb, Wilhelm Heinrich. *Über die wachsende Nervosität unserer Zeit*. Heidelberg: Koester, 1894.

Erichsen, John Eric. *On Railway and Other Injuries of the Nervous System*. London: Walton and Maberly, 1866.

Ernst, Max. *Beyond Painting and Other Writings by the Artist and His Friends*. New York: Wittenborn and Schultz, 1948.

Esslin, Martin. *Brecht: The Man and His Work*. Garden City, NY: Anchor Books, 1969.

Evans, Martha Noel. *Fits and Starts. A Genealogy of Hysteria in Modern France*. Ithaca, NY: Cornell University Press, 1991.

Eysteinsson, Astradur. *The Concept of Modernism*. Ithaca, NY: Cornell University Press, 1990.

Falzeder, Ernst. Einleitung. In *Sigmund Freud—Sandor Ferenczi: Briefwechsel*, vol 2: *1917–1919*. Edited by Eva Brabant and Ernst Falzeder. Vienna: Böhlau Verlag, 1996, pp. 7–18.

Ferber, Christian (ed.). *Der Querschnitt. Das Magazin der aktuellen Ewigkeitswerte, 1924 –1933*. Berlin: Ullstein Verlag: 1981.

Ferenczi, Sándor. Untitled (paper held at the 5th International Psycho-analytical Congress in Budapest, 1915). In Ferenczi et al., *Psycho-Analysis and the War Neurosis*, pp. 5–22.

Ferenczi, Sándor, et al. (eds.). *Psycho-Analysis and the War Neuroses*. London: International Psycho-analytical Press, 1921.

Finta, Tonio. "Kaka, Sch und geplatzte Torte." *Der Mittag*, February 6, 1963. Reprinted in: Becker and Vostell, *Happenings*, pp. 270–71.

Fiori, Ernesto de. Untitled article. *Neue Zürcher Zeitung*, October 10, 1918, 1st morning edition.

Fischer, Lothar (ed.). *Max Ernst in Selbstzeugnissen und Bilddokumenten*. Reinbek/Hamburg: Rowohlt, 1969.

Flatz, Wolfgang. "Ich bin schon eine Ratte: Ein Gespräch zwischen Justin Hoffmann und Flatz." In *Out of Control*, exhibition catalog. Linz: Ars Electronica, 1981. Available at: http://www.aec.at/20Jahre/archiv/1991/1991_129.rtf. Also available at http://90.146.8.18/de/archives/festival_archive/festival_catalogs/festival_catalog.asp.

Fluck, Winfried. "In Search for Distance: Negation and Negativity in Wolfgang Iser's Literary Theory," *New Literary History*, vol. 31 (2000), pp. 175–210.

Foster, Hal. "Amour Fou." *October*, vol. 56 (Spring 1991), pp. 65–97.

———. "What's Neo about the Neo-Avant-Garde?" *October*, vol. 70 (Autumn 1994): The Duchamp Effect, pp. 5–32.

Frank, Peter. "New York Fluxus." In *New York-Downtown Manhattan: Soho: Ausstellungen, Theater, Musik, Performance, Video, Film*, exhibition catalogue. Edited by René Block. Berlin: Akademie der Künste, 1976, pp. 150–79.

Freud, Sigmund. "Beyond the Pleasure Principle." In *Group Psychology and the Analysis of the Ego*." Vol. 18 of *Standard Edition of the Complete Psychological Works of Sigmund Freud*, ed. Strachey, 1955, pp. 7–66.

———. "Die 'kulturelle' Sexmoral und die moderne Nervosität" (1908). In *Werke aus den Jahren 1906–1909*. Vol. 7 of *Gesammelte Werke*. London: Imago Publ., 1955, pp. 143–67.

———. "The Disillusionment of the War." In *Thoughts for the Times on War and Death*. Vol. 14 of *Standard Edition of the Complete Psychological Works of Sigmund Freud*, ed. Strachey, 1950, pp. 275–88.

———. "Memorandum on the Electrical Treatment of War Neurotics." In Kurt R. Eissler, *Freud as an Expert Witness: The Discussion of War Neuroses between Freud an Wagner-Jauregg*. Translated by Christine Trollope. Madison, CT: International Universities Press, 1986, pp. 24–26. First: "Gutachten über die elektrische Behandlung der Kriegsneurotiker." In Kurt R. Eissler, *Freud und Wagner-Jauregg vor der Kommission zur Erhebung militärischer Pflichtverletzungen*. Vienna: Löcker, 1979, pp. 31–4.

———. *New Introductory Lectures on Psychoanalysis* (1933). Vol. 22 of *Standard Edition of the Complete Psychological Works of Sigmund Freud*, ed. James Strachey, 1964, pp. 5–182.

———. "A Note upon the 'Mystic Writing-Pad.'" In *The Ego and the Id*. Vol. 19 of *Standard Edition of the Complete Psychological Works of Sigmund Freud*, ed. Strachey, 1971, pp. 227–334. First: "Notiz über den 'Wunderblock.'" *Internationale Zeitschrift für Psychoanalyse*, vol. 11 (1925), pp. 1–5.

———. *The Standard Edition of the Complete Psychological Works of Sigmund Freud*. Edited by James Strachey. 24 vols. London: Hogarth Press, 1953–74.

———. "Two Artificial Groups: The Church and the Army." In *Group Psychology and the Analysis of the Ego*." Vol. 18 of *Standard Edition of the Complete Psychological Works of Sigmund Freud*, ed. Strachey, 1955, pp. 93–99.

———. Untitled (introduction held at the 5th International Psycho-analytical Congress in Budapest, 1915). In Ferenczi et al., *Psycho-Analysis and the War Neurosis*, pp. 1–4.

———. *Vorlesungen zur Einführung in die Psychoanalyse*. Studienausgabe, vol. 1. (6th ed.). Frankfurt/Main: Suhrkamp, 1975. First: Leipzig: Heller, 1917.

Freud, Sigmund, and Karl Abraham. *The Complete Correspondence of Sigmund Freud and Karl Abraham, 1907–1925*. Edited by Ernst Falzeder. London: Karnac, 2002.

Freud, Sigmund, and Sándor Ferenczi. *The Correspondence of Sigmund Freud and Sándor Ferenczi,* vol. 2: *1914–1919*. Edited by Eva Brabant and Ernst Falzeder. Translated by Peter T. Hoffer. Transcription by Ingeborg Meyer-Palmedo. Cambridge, MA: Belknap Press of Harvard University Press, 1996.

Freud, Sigmund, and Ernest Jones. *The Complete Correspondence of Sigmund Freud and Ernest Jones, 1908–1939*. Edited by Andrew R. Paskauskas. Cambridge, MA: Belknap Press of Harvard University Press, 1993.

Friedell, Egon. *Ecce poeta*. Berlin: S. Fischer, 1912.

Friedman, Ken (ed.). *The Fluxus Reader*. London: Academy Editions, 1998.

——— (ed.). *Fluxus Virus 1962–1992*. Cologne: Galerie Schüppenhauer, 1992.

———. "Rethinking Fluxus." In *Fluxus!* exhibition catalogue. Edited by Nicholas Tsoutas and Nicholas Zurbrugg. Brisbane: Institute of Modern Art, Brisbane, 1990, pp. 10–27.

Friedman, Ken, Lauren Sawchyn, and Owen Smith (eds.). *Fluxus Performance Workbook*. Edited by Performance Research e-publication, 2002. Available at: www.performance-research.net/documents/fluxus_workbook_print.pdf.

Frisby, David. *Sociological Impressionism: A Reassessment of Georg Simmel's Social Theory*. London: Heinemann, 1981.

Fuld, Werner. *Walter Benjamin. Zwischen den Stühlen*. Munich: Carl Hanser Verlag, 1979.

Gassner, Hubertus, and Eckhart Gillen (eds.). *Zwischen Revolutionskunst und Sozialistischem Realismus*. Cologne: DuMont, 1991.

Gauss, Susanne (ed.). *Marcel Duchamp: Interviews and Statements*. Translated by Serge Stauffer. Ostfildern: Cantz, 1991.

Gilbaut, Serge. *How New York Stole the Idea of Modern Art*. Chicago: University of Chicago Press, 1983.

Goergen, Jeanpaul (ed.). *Urlaute dadaistischer Poesie: Der Berliner Dada-Abend am 12. April 1918*. Hannover: Postskriptum Verlag, 1994.

Goldberg, Isaac. "Dada Putting the Jazz into Modern Verse: The Strange Cult Which Riots in Paradox and Negation, and Is the Dancing Spirit over the Morals of the Earth, the Point of Indifference Between Contact and Form." *Boston Evening Transcript*, Jan. 12, 1921.

Golyscheff, Jefim, Raoul Hausmann, and Richard Huelsenbeck. "What Is Dadaism and What Does It Want in Germany?" (1919). In Motherwell, *Dada Poets and Painters*, pp. 41–47. First: "Was ist der Dadaismus und was will er in Deutschland?" In Raoul Hausmann, *Bilanz der Feierlichkeiten: Texte bis 1933*. Vol 1. Edited by Michael Erlhoff. Munich: Richard Boorberg Verlag, 1982, pp. 60–61.

Graff, Wilhelm. *Wie muss der Neurastheniker leben und wie wird er gesund?* Berlin: Hugo Steinitz Verlag, 1907.

Graves, Robert. *Goodbye to All That*. London: Penguin Books, 1960. First: London: Jonathan Cape, 1929.

Grimm, Jacob, and Wilhelm, *Deutsches Wörterbuch von Jacob und Wilhelm Grimm*. Leipzig: Verlag von S. Hirzel, 1899.

Grosz, George. *Ach Knallige Welt, Du Lunapark*. Edited by Klaus Peter Dencker. Munich: Carl Hanser Verlag, 1986.

———. "Kaffeehaus" (poem). *Neue Blätter für Kunst und Dichtung*, vol. 1 (Nov. 1918), p. 155.

———. *A Little Yes and a Big No: The Autobiography of George Grosz*. Translated by Lola Sachs Dorin. New York: Dial Press, 1946. First: *Ein kleines Ja und ein grosses Nein: Sein Leben von ihm selbst erzählt*. Reinbek/Hamburg: Rowohlt, 1955.

Groys, Boris. *Über das Neue: Versuch einer Kulturökonomie*. Munich: Hanser, 1992. English excerpt available at: www.uoc.edu/artnodes/eng/art/groys1002/groys1002.html.

Grunholzer, Heinrich. "Erfahrungen eines jungen Schweizers im Vogtland." In Bettina von Arnim, *Dies Buch gehört dem König*. Berlin: E. H. Schröder, 1843, pp. 534–98.

Grunwald, Henning. "Dadatropismus oder Die Alexandrinische Paralyse." In Höllerer and Miller, "Dada–Neodada–Kryptodada–?" pp. 190–201.

Hamann, Richard. *Der Impressionismus in Leben und Kunst*. Cologne: DuMont-Schauberg, 1907.

Hamilton, Richard. "For the Finest Art, Try Pop." *Gazette*, vol. 1 (1961).

Hanhardt, John. "De-Collage and Television: Wolf Vostell in New York, 1963–1964." *Visible Language*, vol. 26, nos. 1–2 (Winter/Spring 1992), pp. 109–25.

Hapgood, Susan, and Jennifer Rittner. "Neo-Dada: Redefining Art, 1958–1962." *Performing Arts Journal*, vol. 17, no. 1 (January 1995), pp. 63–70.

Harenberg, Bodo (ed.). *Die Chronik Berlins*. Dortmund: Chronik Verlag, 1991.

Harrison, Charles, and Paul Wood (eds.). *Art in Theory 1900–2000. An Anthology of Changing Ideas*. Oxford: Blackwell, 2003. First published as: *Art in Theory 1900–1990*, Oxford: Blackwell, 1992.

Hartenau W. (alias Walter Rathenau). "Die schönste Stadt der Welt." *Zukunft*, vol. 7, no. 15 (1899).

Hausmann, Raoul. *Am Anfang war Dada*. Edited by Karl Riha and Günter Kämpf. Steinbach/Giessen: Anabas-Verlag: Günter Kämpf, 1972.

———. "Aussichten oder Ende des Neodadaismus" (1962). In Koch, *Ich bin immerhin der grösste Experimentator Österreichs*, n.p.

———."Bilanz der Feierlichkeit." *Die Erde: Politische und kulturpolitische Halbmonatsschrift*, vol. 8, no. 1 (1919).

———. "Dada empört sich, regt sich und stirbt in Berlin." In Hausmann, *Am Anfang war Dada*, 1972, pp. 15–21.

———. "Dada ist mehr als Dada." *De Stijl*, vol. 4, no. 3 (May 1921). Reprinted in Hausmann, *Am Anfang war Dada*, 1972, pp. 83–89.

———. "Massenpsychologie Dadas." In Hausmann, *Am Anfang war Dada*, 1972, pp. 144–48.

———. "Nachhall." In Hausmann, *Am Anfang war Dada*, 1972, pp. 151–53.

———. "Post-Dada." In Hausmann, *Am Anfang war Dada*, 1972, pp. 149–50.

———. “Presentismus: Gegen den Puffkeismus der teutschen Seele” (1921). In Hausmann, *Am Anfang war Dada*, 1972, pp. 129–34.

———. “Synthetisches Cino der Malerei” (1918). In Hausmann, *Am Anfang war Dada*, 1972, pp. 27–29.

Hegemann, Werner. *Das steinerne Berlin: Geschichte der grössten Mietskasernenstadt der Welt.* Berlin: Kiepenheuer, 1930.

Hellberg, Frank. *Walter Mehring: Schriftsteller zwischen Kabarett und Avantgarde.* Bonn: Bouvier, 1983.

Hellpach, Willy. *Mensch und Volk der Grossstadt.* Stuttgart: Ferdinand Enke Verlag, 1939.

———. *Nervosität und Kultur.* Berlin: Räde, 1902.

Hendricks, Jon“Fluxus.” In Bollé, *Stationen der Moderne*, pp. 493–99.

———. (ed.). *Fluxus etc, Addendum I, Addendum II*, 3 vols. Detroit: Gilbert and Lila Silverman Fluxus Collection, 1981–1983.

———. Foreword. In *Fluxus Codex.* Edited by Hendricks. Detroit: Gilbert and Silverman Fluxus Collection. In association with Harry N. Abrams, New York, 1988, pp. 21–29.

——— (ed.). *What's Fluxus? What's Not! Why*, exhibition catalogue. Rio de Janeiro: Centro Cultural Banco Do Brasil, 2002.

Hermann, Helmut G., and Wolfgang Paulsen (eds.). *Sinn aus Unsinn: Dada International, 12: Amherster Kolloquium zur deutschen Literatur.* Bern: Franke, 1982.

Hering, Karl Heinz, and Ewald Rathke (eds.). *Dada: Dokumente einer Bewegung*, exhibition catalogue. Düsseldorf: Kunstverein für die Rheinlande und Westfalen, 1958.

Herzfelde, Wieland. “The Curious Merchant from Holland.” *Harper's*, Nov. 1943, pp. 569–76. First German publication: “Ein Kaufmann aus Holland.” In Herzfelde, *Immergrün: Merkwürdige Erlebnisse und Erfahrungen eines fröhlichen Waisenknaben.* Berlin: Aufbau-Verlag, 1949.

Herzogenrath, Wulf. “Die Geburt der Kunstmetropole Köln aus dem Geist der Musik-Aktion um 1960.” In *Die 60er Jahre. Kölns Weg zur Kunstmetropole: Vom Happening zum Kunstmarkt*, exhibition catalog. Edited by Wulf Herzogenrath and Gabriele Lueg. Cologne: Henke, 1986, pp. 12–25.

Hess, Hans. *George Grosz.* London: Studio Vista, 1974.

Higgins, Dick. “Boredom and Danger.” In Higgins, *A Dialectic of Centuries*, pp. 42–50.

——— (ed.). *A Dialectic of Centuries: Notes Towards a Theory of the New Arts.* New York: Printed Editions, 1978.

———. “In einem Minensuchboot um die Welt” (“In a Minesweeper around the World”). In Block, *1962 Wiesbaden Fluxus 1982*, pp. 126–35 (German and English).

———. *Postface.* New York: Something Else Press, 1964.

———. “A Something Else Manifesto.” In Higgins, *A Dialectic of Centuries*, pp. 102–3.

———. “Theory and Reception.” In Friedman, *Fluxus Reader*, pp. 217–36.

Higgins, Hannah. *The Fluxus Experience*. Berkeley: University of California Press, 2002.

Hirschfeld, Gerhard. "Erster Weltrieg—Zweiter Weltkrieg: Kriegserfahrung in Deutschland." Zeitgeschichte Online: Fronterlebnis und Nachkriegsordnung. Wirkung und Wahrnehmung des Ersten Weltkriegs, May 2004. Available at: www.zeitgeschichte–online.de.

Hirschfeld, Gerhard, and Gerd Krumeich (eds.). *Keiner fühlt sich hier mehr als Mensch . . . Erlebnis und Wirkung des Ersten Weltkriegs*. Essen: Klartext, 1993.

Hitler, Adolf. "Der Führer eröffnet die 'Grosse Kunstausstellung 1937,'" *Die Kunst im Dritten Reich*, vol. 1, nos. 7–8 (1937), pp. 47–61.

Hobbs, Robert C. *Lee Krasner*. New York: Abbeville Press, 1993.

Höch, Hannah. *Hannah Höch: Eine Lebenscollage*, 3 vols. Edited by Cornelia Thater-Schulz and Berlinische Galerie. Berlin: Argon, 1989.

Höllerer, Walter, and Norbert Miller (eds.). "Dada–Neodada–Kryptodada–?" Special issue. *Sprache im technischen Zeitalter*, no. 55, 1975.

Hoffmann, Christine (ed.). *Bruce Nauman: Interviews 1967–1988*. Amsterdam: Verlag der Kunst, 1996.

Hoffmann, Justin. *Destruktionskunst: Der Mythos der Zerstörung in der Kunst der frühen sechziger Jahre*. Munich: Verlag Silke Schreiber, 1995.

Honnef, Klaus, and Peter Pachnicke. *John Heartfield*, exhibition catalog. Berlin: Akademie der Künste. Cologne: DuMont, 1991.

Holmsten, Georg. *Die Berlin-Chronik*. Düsseldorf: Droste Verlag, 1990.

Hoppe, Ralph. *Die Friedrichstrasse: Pflaster der Extreme*. Berlin: Be.Bra-Verlag, 1999.

Horkheimer, Max. "The End of Reason." In *The Essential Frankfurt School Reader*. Edited by Andrew Arato and Eike Gebhardt. New York: Urizen Books, 1978, pp. 26–48.

Hotz, Jürgen (ed.) *Der Brockhaus: Moderne Kunst—Vom Impressionismus bis zur Gegenwart*. Leipzig: Brockhaus, 2003.

Huelsenbeck, Richard. "Collective Dada Manifesto" (1918). In Motherwell, *Dada Painters and Poets*, pp. 242–46. First: "Dadaistisches Manifest." *Der Zweemann*, no. 3, 1920.

———. *Dada Almanac*. Translated by Malcolm Green et al. London: Atlas Press, 1993. First: *Dada Almanach*. Berlin: Reiss, 1920.

——— (ed.). *Dada: Eine literarische Dokumentation*. Reinbek/Hamburg: Rowohlt, 1964.

———. "Dada Lives!" In Motherwell, *Dada Painters and Poets*, pp. 279–81.

———. "Dada siegt!" In Huelsenbeck and Tzara, *Dada siegt! Bilanz und Erinnerung*, 1985, pp. 7–53.

———. "Die Dadaistische Bewegung: Eine Selbstbiographie." *Die neue Rundschau*, vol. 2, no. 8 (August 1920), pp. 972–79.

———. *En Avant Dada*. In Motherwell, *Dada Painters and Poets*, pp. 23–41 First: Hamburg: Nautilus, 1920.

———. "Erinnerungen" (1930). In Goergen, *Urlaute dadaistischer Poesie*, pp. 101–12.

———. “Erklärung” (probably 1916). In Huelsenbeck, *Dada: Eine literarische Dokumentation*, pp. 29–30.

Huelsenbeck, Richard, and Tristan Tzara. *Dada siegt! Bilanz und Erinnerung.* Hamburg: Nautilus/Nemo Press et al., 1985.

Hugnet, Georges. *Dictionnaire du Dadaïsme 1916–1922.* Paris: Jean-Claude Simoën, 1976.

———. *L'Aventure Dada: 1916–1922.* Paris: Galerie de l'Institut, 1957.

———. *L'Esprit Dada dans la Peinture* (collection of essays). *Cahier d'Art*, vol. 7, nos. 1–2, 6–7, 8–10 (1932); vol. 9, nos. 1–4 (1934).

Humphreys, Christmas. “Obituary for Dr. D. T. Suzuki.” In Suzuki, *The Field of Zen*, 1966, pp. xiii–xvii.

Huyssen, Andreas. *After the Great Divide: Modernism, Mass Culture, Postmodernism.* Bloomington: Indiana University Press, 1986.

———. “Postmoderne—Eine amerikanische Internationale?” In *Postmoderne: Zeichen eines kulturellen Wandels.* Edited by Andreas Huyssen and Klaus R. Scherpe. Reinbek/Hamburg: Rowohlt, 1986, pp. 13–44.

Iser, Wolfgang. “Image und Montage: Zur Bildkonzeption in der imagistischen Lyrik und in T. S. Eliot's ‘Waste Land.’ ” In *Immanente Ästhetik, ästhetische Reflexion: Lyrik als Paradigma der Moderne.* Munich: Fink, 1966, pp. 361–93.

Janco, Marcel. “Dada at Two Speed.” In Lippard, *Dadas on Art*, pp. 36–38.

———. “Die Kunst will und muss wieder zum Leben zurückkehren . . .” (1919). In *Manifeste und Proklamationen der europäischen Avantgarde (1909–1938).* Edited by Wolfgang Asholt and Walter Fähnders. Stuttgart and Weimar: Verlag J. B. Metzler, 1995, p. 162.

Janouch, Gustav. *Gespräch mit Kafka.* Frankfurt/Main and Hamburg: Fischer, 1961.

Jazbinsek, Dietmar. “The Metropolis and the Mental Life of Georg Simmel: On the History of Antipathy.” *Journal of Urban History*, vol. 30, no.1 (Nov. 2003), pp. 102–26. First: “Die Grossstädte und das Geistesleben. Zur Geschichte einer Antipathie,” Publication Series “Metropolenforschung,” Social Science Research Center Berlin (WZB). Available at: http://skylla.wz-berlin.de/pdf/2001/ii01–504.pdf.

Joël, Karl. “Eine Zeitphilosophie.” *Neue Deutsche Rundschau*, no. 12, 1901, pp. 812–26.

Jones, Ernest. “War Shock and Freud's Theory of the Neuroses.” *Proceedings of the Royal Society of Medicine*, vol. 11 (1918) (Sect Psych), pp. 21–36.

Jones, Jonathan. “Shock Treatment.” *Guardian*, September 7, 2000.

Joseph, Branden W. “The Play of Repetition: Andy Warhol's Sleep.” *Gray Room*, vol. 19 (2005), pp. 23–53.

Julius, Anthony. *Transgressions: The Offences of Art.* London: Thames and Hudson, 2002.

Jünger, Ernst. *The Storm of Steel: From the Diary of a German Storm-Troop Officer on the Western Front.* Translated by Basil Creighton. New York: Howard Fertig, 1975. First: *In Stahlgewittern. Aus dem Tagebuch eines Stosstruppführers.* Leisnig: Robert Meier, 1920.

Jürging, Stefan. *Die Tradition des Traditionsbruchs: John Cages amerikanische Ästhetik*. Frankfurt: Peter Lang, 2002.

Kant, Immanuel. *The Critique of Judgement* (1790). Translated by James Creed Meredith. Oxford: Clarendon Press, 1964.

Kaplan, Janet A. (ed.). "Flux Generation: A Conversation between Janet A. Kaplan and Bracken Hendricks, Geoffrey Hendricks, Alison Knowles, Hannah Higgins" (Nov. 6, 1999). *Art Journal*, vol. 59, no. 2 (Summer 2000), pp. 6–17.

Kaprow, Allan. "Nam June Paik." In *Nam June Paik: Electronic Art II*, exhibition catalog. New York: Galeria Bonino, 1968, pp. 1–2.

Kauffman, Linda S. *Bad Girls and Sick Boys*. Berkeley: University of California Press, 1998.

Kernan, Sean. "Camera Art: An interview with John Paul Caponigro." *Camera Arts* (December 1999–January 2000), pp. 13–16.

Kellein, Thomas (ed.). *Clyfford Still 1904–1980*. Munich: Prestel, 1992.

———. *Fluxus*. London: Thames and Hudson, 1995.

Kellein, Thomas, and Toni Stooss (eds.). *Nam June Paik Video Time—Video Space*. New York: Harry N. Abrams, 1993. First: Stuttgart: Edition Cantz, 1991.

Kellerer, Christian. *Objet Trouvé und Surrealismus: Zur Psychologie der modernen Kunst*. Reinbek/Hamburg: Rowohlt, 1968.

Kelley, Jeff. *Childsplay. The Art of Allan Kaprow*. Berkeley: University of California Press, 2004.

Kemper, Hans-Georg. *Vom Expressionismus zum Dadaismus*. Kronberg/Taunus: Scriptor Verlag, 1974.

Killen, Andreas. *Berlin Electropolis: Shock, Nerves, and German Modernity*. Berkeley: University of California Press, 2006.

Kirker, Anne. "Engaging Discontent: Fluxus Printed Matter" (2005). Available at: www.artspacemackay.com.au/artists_books/second_australian_artists_books_forum_2005/anne_kirker_paper.

Knapstein, Gabriele. "Fluxus International." In Schneider, *Berlin–Tokyo: Die Kunst zweier Städte*, pp. 232–33.

Koch, Adelheid. *Ich bin immerhin der grösste Experimentator Österreichs. Raoul Hausmann—Dada und Neodada*. Innsbruck: Haymon-Verlag, 1994.

König, Gottfried M., and John A. Thwaites. "Magnum-Interview: Die Fluxus Leute" (Interview with Jean-Pierre Wilhelm, Nam June Paik, Wolf Vostell, and Arthus C. Caspari). *Magnum*, no. 47 (1963), pp. 32–35, 62–68.

Kootz, Samuel M. *The Intrasubjectives*, exhibition catalogue. New York: Samuel M. Kootz Gallery, 1949.

Korff, Gottfried. "Mentalität und Kommunikation in der Grossstadt: Berliner Notizen zur 'inneren' Urbanisierung." In *Grossstadt: Aspekte empirischer Kulturforschung*, exhibition catalog. Edited by Theodor Kohlmann. Berlin: Staatliche Museen Preussischer Kulturbesitz, 1985, pp. 343–62.

Korff, Gottfried, and Reinhard Rürup (eds.). *Berlin, Berlin: Die Ausstellung zur Geschichte der Stadt*, exhibition catalog. Berliner Festspiele GmbH. Berlin: Nicolaische Verlagsbuchhandlung, 1987.

Kostelanetz, Richard. *Conversing with Cage*. New York: Limelight, 1994.

———. *Metamorphosis in the Arts: A Critical History of the 1960s*. New York: Assembling Press: 1980.
Kramer, Hilton. Untitled (paper given at the *Symposium on Pop Art*, MoMA, Dec. 13, 1962). *Arts Magazine*, April 1963, pp. 36–44.
Krauss, Rosalind E. "The Originality of the Avant-Garde." In *The Originality of the Avant-Garde and Other Modernist Myths*. Cambridge, MA: MIT Press, 1985, pp. 151–70.
Krumeich, Gerd. "Kriegsgeschichte im Wandel." In Hirschfeld and Krumeich, *Keiner fühlt sich hier mehr als Mensch . . .*, pp. 11–24.
Kuenzli, Rudolf E. "Dada gegen den ersten Weltkrieg: Die Dadaisten in Zürich." In Hermann and Paulsen, *Sinn aus Unsinn: Dada International*, pp. 87–100.
Kuspit, Donald. "Joseph Beuys: Between Showman and Shaman." In *Joseph Beuys: Diverging Critiques*. Edited by David Thistlewood, Tate Gallery Liverpool Critical Forum Series, vol. 2. Liverpool: Liverpool University Press: 1995, pp. 27–49.
Lacan, Jacques. *The Seminar of Jacques Lacan*. Book 7: *The Ethics of Psychoanalysis*. Translated by Dennis Porter. New York: W.W. Norton, 1992.
Landau, Ellen G. (ed.). *Reading Abstract Expressionism*. New Haven, CT: Yale University Press, 2005.
Landman, Michael. "Arthur Steins Erinnerungen an Georg Simmel." In Böhringer and Gründer, *Ästhetik und Soziologie um die Jahrhundertwende: Georg Simmel*, pp. 272–76.
Lavazzi, Tom. "Punching the Line: Fluxus, Yippie, and the 1968 DNC." *Rhizomes*, vol. 9 (Fall 2004), n.p. Available at: www.rhizomes.net/issue9/lavazzi.htm.
Lebeer, Irmeline. "Interview with George Brecht." In Henry Martin, *An Introduction to George Brecht's Book of the Tumbler on Fire*. Milan: Multhipla Edizioni, 1978, pp. 83–84.
Leese, Peter. *Shell Shock: Traumatic Neurosis and the British Soldiers of the First World War*. Basingstoke: Palgrave Macmillan, 2002.
Léger, Fernand. *The Function of Painting*. Translated by Alexander Anderson. New York: Viking Press, 1973, pp. 11–17. First: *Fonctions de la Peinture*. Paris: Gonthier, 1965.
Lerner, Paul. "An Economy of Memory: Psychiatrists, Veterans and Traumatic Narratives in Weimar Germany." In Mülder-Bach, *Modernität und Trauma*, pp. 79–103.
Lessing, Theodor. *Geschichte als Sinngebung des Sinnlosen*. Hamburg: Rütten and Loening Verlag, 1962. First: Munich: Beck, 1919.
———. *Philosophie als Tat*. Göttingen: Otto Hapke Verlag, 1914.
Lethen, Helmut. "'Knall an sich': Das Ohr als Einbruchstelle des Traumas." In Mülder-Bach, *Modernität und Trauma*, pp. 192–210.
Lewes, James. "Biography Fluxus," in Friedman, *Fluxus Virus*, pp. 260–316.
Lewinsky, Wolf-Eberhard von. "Stumpfsinn—stundenlang! Festspiele Neuester Musik." *Die Welt*, Sept. 24, 1962.
Lewis, Wyndham (ed.). *Blast: Review of the Great English Vortex*, no. 1 (June 20, 1914).

Lindey, Christine. *Art in the Cold War: From Vladivostok to Kalamazoo, 1945–1962*. London: Herbert Press, 1990.
Linse, Ulrich. "Das wahre Zeugnis. Eine psychohistorische Deutung des Ersten Weltkriegs." In Vondung, *Kriegserlebnis*, pp. 90–114.
Lippard, Lucy R. (ed.). *Dadas on Art*. Englewood Cliffs, NJ: Prentice Hall, 1971.
Locher, David. "Unacknowledged Roots and Blatant Imitation: Postmodernism and the Dada Movement." *Electronic Journal of Sociology*, 1999. Available at: www.sociology.org/content/vol004.001/locher.html.
Lüdke Werner M. (ed.). *"Theorie der Avant-garde." Antworten auf Peter Bürgers Bestimmung von Kunst und bürgerlicher Gesellschaft*. Frankfurt: Suhrkamp Verlag, 1976.
Lütge, Friedrich. *Deutsche Sozial- und Wirtschaftsgeschichte*. Berlin: Springer-Verlag, 1952.
Mac Low, Jackson. "The Poetics of Chance and the Politics of Simultaneous Spontaneity, or the Sacred Heart of Jesus." In *Talking Poetics from Naropa Insitute*, vol. 1. Edited by Anne Waldman and Marilyn Webb. Boulder, CO: Shambhala, 1978.
———. *Representative Works: 1938–1985*. New York: Roof, 1986.
———. "Wie George Maciunas die New Yorker Avantgarde kennenlernte" ("How Maciunas Met the New York Avant Garde) (1980). In Block, *1962 Wiesbaden Fluxus 1982*, pp. 110–25 (German and English).
Mac Low, Jackson, and La Monte Young. *An Anthology of Chance Operations*. New York: Mac Low and Young, 1963.
Maciunas, George. *Fluxus News Letter No. 7*, May 1, 1963. Facsimile in Hendricks, *Fluxus etc. Addendum I*, p. 157.
———. *Fluxus News-Policy Letter No. 6*, April 6, 1963. Facsimile in Hendricks, *Fluxus etc. Addendum I*, p. 156.
———. "Neo-Dada in Music, Theater, Poetry, Art" (1962). In *In the Spirit of Fluxus*, exhibition catalog. Edited by Elizabeth Armstrong and Joan Rothfuss. New York: Walker Art Center, 1993, pp. 156–57.
Mansel, Henry L. "Sensation Novels." *Quarterly Review*, no. 113, 1863, pp. 481–514.
Maria, Walter de. "Meaningless Work" (1960). In Mac Low and Young et al., *An Anthology of Chance Operations*, n.p.
Marcus, Greil. *Lipstick Traces: A Secret History of the Twentieth Century*. London: Faber and Faber Ltd., 1989.
Marinetti, Filippo Tommaso. "Fondazione e Manifesto del Futurismo." *Le Figaro*, February 20, 1909, Paris, p. 1.
———. "Tactilism" (1924). In Caws, *Manifesto: A Century of Isms*, pp. 197–200.
Materna, Ingo, Wolfgang Ribbe, et al. *Berlin: Geschichte in Daten*. Munich: Koehler and Amelang, 1997.
Mehring, Walter. *Berlin Dada: Eine Chronik mit Photos und Dokumenten*, Zurich: Arche Verlag, 1959.
———. *Dada Berlin*. Zurich: Die Arche, 1967.
Meidner, Ludwig. "Anleitung zum Malen von Grossstadtbildern." *Kunst und Künstler*, vol. 12, no. 6 (1914), pp. 32–314.

Menninghaus, Winfried. *Disgust: The Theory and History of a Strong Sensation*. Translated by Howard Eiland and Joel Golb. Albany: State University of New York Press, 2000. First: *Ekel: Theorie und Geschichte einer starken Empfindung*. Frankfurt/Main: Suhrkamp, 1999.

Meyer, Raimund. "Dada ist gross, Dada ist schön: Zur Geschichte von Dada Zürich." In *Dada in Zürich*. Edited by Hans Bollinger, Guido Magnaguagno, and Raimund Mexer. Zurich: Arche Verlag, 1985, pp. 9–79.

Michaelidis, Lee. "Interview with Ken Friedman." Available at: http://king.dom.de/fluxus/archive1/1195.html.

Miglietti, Francesca Alfano. *Extreme Bodies: The Use and Abuse of the Body in Art*. Milan: Skira, 2003.

Miller, Larry. "Interview with Maciunas" (March 24, 1978). Transcript of videotaped interview in Hendricks, *Fluxus etc. Addenda I*, pp. 11–28.

Miller, William Ian. *Anatomy of Disgust*. Cambridge, MA: Harvard University Press, 1997.

Millett, Kate. "Fluxus Is (1981)." In Hendricks, *What's Fluxus? What's Not! Why*, p. 122.

Mills, C. Wright. *White Collar: The American Middle Classes*. New York: Oxford University Press, 1951.

Milman, Estera. "Fluxus History and Trans-History: Competing Strategies for Empowerment." In Friedman, *Fluxus Reader*, pp. 155–65.

Mommsen, Wolgang J. *Die Urkatastrophe Deutschlands: Der Erste Weltkrieg 1914–1918*. Vol. 17 of *Gebhardt Handbuch der deutschen Geschichte*. Edited by Jürgen Kocka. Stuttgart: Klett-Cotta, 2002.

Montfort, Patricia de. "White Muslin: Joanna Hiffernan and the 1860s." In *Whistler, Women, and Fashion*. Edited by Margaret F. MacDonald et al. New York: Frick Collection and Yale University Press, 2003.

Moritz, Peter. "Der Schock des Unverständlichen: Medienethik und Medienkultur im Kreuzfeuer medial arrangierter Provokation." *Medien Impulse*, December 1997, pp. 49–60.

Motherwell, Robert. *The Collected Writings of Robert Motherwell*. Berkeley: University of California Press, 1999.

——— (ed.). *The Dada Painters and Poets*. 2nd ed. New York: Wittenborn, 1967 (1951).

Mott, F. W. "Special Discussion on Shell Shock without Visible Signs of Injury." *Proceedings of the Royal Society of Medicine*, vol. 9 (1916), pp. i–xxiv.

Mülder-Bach, Inka (ed.). *Modernität und Trauma: Beiträge zum Zeitenbruch des Ersten Weltkrieges*. Vienna: WUV, 2000.

Müller, Lothar. "Die Grossstadt als Ort der Moderne." In *Die Unwirklichkeit der Städte. Grossstadtdarstellungen zwischen Moderne und Postmoderne*. Edited by Klaus R. Scherpe. Rheinbeck/Hamburg: Rowohlt, 1988, pp. 14–36.

———. "Modernität, Nervosität und Sachlichkeit: Das Berlin der Jahrhundertwende als Hauptstadt der 'neuen Zeit.'" In *Mythos Berlin: Zur Wahrnehmungsgeschichte einer industriellen Metropole*. Edited by Baehr, 1987, pp. 79–92.

Müller, Maria. *Aspekte der Dada-Rezeption 1950–1960*. Essen: Verlag Die Blaue Eule, 1987.

Musgrave, Victor. "The Unknown Art Movement." In "Free Fluxus Now," special issue. *Art and Artists*, vol. 7, no. 7, pp.12–14.

Musil, Robert. *The Blackbird* (1916). Translated by Thomas Frick and Wilhelm Wiegandt. Cambridge, MA: Simba Editions, 1981. First: "Die Amsel." In: Musil, Nachlass zu Lebzeiten. Zurich: Humanitas Verlag, 1936.

———. *The Man without Qualities*. London and Basingstoke: Picador, 1995. First: *Der Mann ohne Eigenschaften*. Berlin: Rowohlt, 1930.

Nakov, Andrei B. "Dada Gives Me an Intolerable 'Malaise' . . ." In Juda, *Dada—Constructivism*, pp. 7–32.

Newman, Barnett. *The Sublime Is Now* (1949). In Newman, *Selected Writings and Interviews*. Edited by John P. O'Neill. New York: Alfred A. Knopf, 1990, pp. 170–73.

Ngai, Sianne. "Stuplimity: Boredom and Shock in Twentieth-Century Aesthetics." *Postmodern Culture*, vol. 10, no. 2 (Jan. 2000), n.p.

Noël, Ann, and Emmett Williams (eds.). *Mr Fluxus: A Collective Portrait of George Maciunas, 1931–1978*. London: Thames and Hudson, 1997.

Obrist, Hans-Ulrich. "Interview with Emmett Williams," October 11, 2004. Available at: http://www.udno.net/Features/.

Odin, Steve. *The Social Self in Zen and American Pragmatism*. Albany: State University of New York Press, 1996.

Ortega y Gasset, José. *The Revolt of the Masses*. London: Allen and Unwin, 1932. First: *La Rebelión de las Masas*. Madrid: Espasa-Calpe, 1930.

Oven, Michael. "Fluxus-Kästen und Dada-Konstruktionen." In Hermann and Paulsen, *Sinn aus Unsinn: Dada International*, pp. 277–93.

P., H. (unknown author). "Da-Da. Literatur-Narrenheiten in der Sezession." *Berliner Börsen-Courier*, April 1918. Reprinted in Goergen, *Urlaute dadaistischer Poesie*, pp. 73–74.

Paik, Nam June. "Essay: To the Symphony for 20 Rooms." In Mac Low and Young, *An Anthology of Chance Operations*, n.p.

———. "Manuskript about Exposition . . ." (probl. 1963). Facsimile in Hendricks, *Fluxus etc, Addendum II*, pp. 289–300.

Partens, Alexander. "Dada Art." In Huelsenbeck, *Dada Almanac*, pp. 91–97.

Patterson, Ben. "Bekenntnis" (1964). In Becker and Vostell, *Happenings: Fluxus, Pop Art, Nouveau Réalism*, p. 241.

Pearson, Sidney V. *The Growth and Distribution of Population*, New York: Wiley, 1935.

Phillips, Bernard. Introduction. In *The Essentials of Zen Buddhism: Selected from the Writings of Daisetz T. Suzuki*. Edited by Phillips. New York: Dutton, 1962, pp. xiii–xl.

Phillips, Lisa. *The American Century: Art and Culture 1950–1960*, exhibition catalog. Whitney Museum of American Art. New York: W. W. Norton, 1999.

Phillpot, Clive, and Jon Hendricks (eds.). *Fluxus: Selections from the Gilbert and Lila Silverman Collection*. New York: Museum of Modern Art, 1988.

Phung, Tuck-Chee. *Dada and the First World War: Origins of an Art Movement in Political Conflict*. Ph.D. dissertation, Aberdeen University, 1983, unpublished.

Picabia, Francis. "Art." In Lippard, *Dadas on Art*, p. 167.

———. "DADA Manifesto," trans. Claire Nicholas White. In Lippard, *Dadas on Art*, p. 166.

Pichon, Brigitte, and Karl Riha (eds.). *Dada Zürich: A Clown's Game from Nothing*. Vol. 2 of *Crisis and the Arts*, ed. Stephen Foster. New Haven, CT: Thomson/Gale, 1996.

Poggioli, Renato. *The Theory of the Avant-Garde*. Cambridge, MA: Belknap Press of Harvard University Press, 1968.

Preece, Robert. "Just a Load of Shock? An Interview with Marc Quinn." *Sculpture*, vol. 19, no. 8 (Oct. 2000), pp. 14–19.

Puusepp, Louis. *Traumatische Kriegsneurose*. Tartu: Typographie J. Mällo, 1925.

Rawdon Wilson, Robert. *The Hydra's Tale: Imagining Disgust*. Edmonton: University of Alberta Press, 2002.

Revill, David. *The Roaring Silence: John Cage—A Life*. New York: Arcade, 1992. p. 107–25.

Ribbe, Wolfgang (ed.). *Von der Märzrevolution bis zur* Gegenwart. Vol. 2 of *Geschichte Berlins*. Berlin: Berliner Wissenschafts-Verlag, 2002.

Ribemont-Dessaignes, Georges. "History of Dada." In Motherwell, *Dada Painters and Poets*, pp. 99–120.

Richter, Hans. *Dada: Art and Anti-Art*. London: Thames and Hudson, 1965.

———. *Kunst und Anti-Kunst: Der Beitrag Dadas zur Kunst des 20. Jahrhunderts*. Cologne: DuMont Schauberg, 1964.

———. "Zur Geschichte des Lautgedichts." In Hausmann, *Am Anfang war Dada*, pp. 35–43.

Riesman, David. *The Lonely Crowd. A Study of the Changing American Character*. New Haven, CT: Yale University Press, 1950.

Riethmüller, Albrecht. "Hermetik, Schock, Fasslichkeit: Zum Verhältnis von Musikwerk und Publikum in der ersten Hälfte des 20. Jahrhunderts." *Archiv für Musikwissenschaft*, vol. 73, no. 1 (1980), pp. 32–60.

Riha, Karl (ed.). *Dada: 113 Gedichte*. Berlin: Wagenbach, 2003 (1982).

——— (ed.). *Dada Zürich: Texte, Manifeste, Dokumente*. Stuttgart: Reclam, 1992.

———. Nachwort. In Riha, *Dada Zürich: Texte, Manifeste, Dokumente*, pp. 167–76.

Ronte, Dieter. "Dada/Fluxus." In Friedman, *Fluxus Virus*, pp. 144–47, 148–51 (German and English).

Rosenberg, Harold. *The Tradition of the New*. New York: McGraw-Hill, 1965.

Rotermund, Erwin. *Die Parodie in der modernen deutschen Lyrik*. Munich: Eidos Verlag, 1963.

Roth, Karl Heinz. "Die Modernisierung der Folter in den beiden Weltkriegen: Der Konflikt der Psychotherapeuten und Schulpsychiater um die deutschen 'Kriegsneurotiker' 1915–1941." *1999: Zeitschrift für Sozialgeschichte des 20. und 21. Jahrhunderts*, issue 3 (July 1987), pp. 8–75.

Rubin, William S. "Reflexions on Marcel Duchamp." *Art International*, vol. 4, no. 9 (Dec. 1960), pp. 49–53.

Rüdiger, Ulrike. *Vostell: Leben = Kunst = Leben*, exhibition catalog. Kunstgalerie Gera: Leipzig: Seemann, 1993.

Ruhé, Harry. *Fluxus: The Most Radical and Experimental Art Movement of the Sixties*. Amsterdam: "A", 1979, ring folder, n.p.

Ruskin, John. *The Elements of Drawing: In Three Letters to Beginners*. New York: J. Wiley, 1863 (1857).

Schab, Günter. "Zuviel Klamauk mit Neo-Dada." *Neue Ruhrzeitung*, June 1962. Reprinted in Becker and Vostell, *Happenings*, p. 269.

Scheffler, Karl. *Berlin. Ein Stadtschicksal*. Berlin: Reiss, 1910.

Schifferli, Peter (ed.). *Die Geburt des Dada . . . Dichtung und Chronik der Gründer*. Zurich: Verlag der Arche, 1957.

Schivelbusch, Wolfgang. *The Railway Journey: The Industrialisation of Time and Space in the 19th Century*. Berkeley: University of California Press, 1992. First: *Geschichte der Eisenbahnreise: Zur Industrialisierung von Raum und Zeit im 19. Jahrhundert*. Munich: Hanser, 1977.

Schleich, Carl Ludwig. *Vom Schaltwerk der Gedanken*. Berlin: S. Fischer, 1916.

Schlesinger, Arthur M., Jr. "The New Mood in Politics." In Schlesinger, *The Politics of Hope*. Boston, MA: Riverside Press, 1963, pp. 81–93. First: *Esquire*, January 1960.

Schmidt-Burkhardt, Astrit. *Maciunas' Learning Machines: From Art History to a Chronology of Fluxus*. Berlin: Vice Versa, 2003.

———. *Stammbäume der Kunst. Zur Genealogie der Avantgarde*. Berlin: Akademie Verlag, 2005.

Schmit, Tomas. "If I Remember Correctly." In "Free Fluxus Now," special issue. *Art and Artists*, vol. 7, no. 7 (Oct. 1972), pp. 34–39.

———."Sensatorium Minimaximum." In Becker and Vostell, *Happenings*, pp. 246–50.

Schnapp, Jeffrey Thompson. "Crash (Speed as Engine of Individuation)." *Modernism/modernity*, vol. 6, no. 1 (1999), pp. 1–49.

Schneider, Angela (ed.). *Berlin–Tokyo: Die Kunst zweier Städte*, exhibition catalog. Neue Nationalgalerie Berlin. Ostfildern: Hatje Cantz, 2006.

Schrott, Raoul. *Dada 15/25: Dokumentation und chronologischer Überblick zu Tzara und Co*. Cologne: Dumont: 2004.

Schwabe, Hermann. *Berliner Südwestbahn und Centralbahn. Beleuchtet vom Standpunkt der Wohnungsfrage und der industriellen Gesellschaft*. Berlin: Guttentag, 1873.

Schwarz, Arturo. *New York Dada: Duchamp, Man Ray, Picabia*. Munich: Prestel, 1973.

Schwartz, Frederic J. *Blind Spots: Critical Theory and the History of Art in Twentieth-Century Germany*. New Haven, CT: Yale University Press, 2005.

Schwerfel, Heinz Peter. *Kunst-Skandale: Über Tabu und Skandal, Verdammung und Verehrung zeitgenössischer Kunst*. Cologne: DuMont, 2000.

Schwitters, Kurt. "Katalog" (1927). In Schwitters, *Das literarische Werk*. Vol. 5. Edited by Friedhelm Lach. Cologne: DuMont Schauberg, 1973–1981.

Scrubar, Ilja. "Zur Formierung des soziologischen Blicks." In *Die Grossstadt als*

"*Text.*" Edited by Manfred Smuda. Munich: Wilhelm Fink Verlag, 1992, pp. 37–52.

Seitz, William C. *The Art of Assemblage*, exhibition catalog. New York: Museum of Modern Art, 1961.

———. "What's Happened to Art? An Interview with Duchamp." *Vogue*, Feb. 15, 1963, p. 113.

Sell, Mike. *Avant-Garde Performance and the Limits of Criticism*. Ann Arbor: University of Michigan Press, 2005.

Serner, Walter. Last Loosening Manifesto. In *Blago Bung Blago Bung Bosso Fataka! First Texts of German Dada by Hugo Ball, Richard Huelsenbeck, Walter Serner*. Translated by Malcolm Green. London: Atlas, 1995. First: Serner. *Letzte Lockerung*. Hannover: Paul Steegemann Verlag, 1920.

———. "Qu'est-ce que le Dadaïsme?" *Le Mondain*, no. 3 (January 14, 1920). Reprinted in Walter Serner, *Das Hirngeschwür*. Vol. 2 of *Walter Serner: Das Gesamte Werk*. Munich: Renner, 1981, pp. 107–9.

Seuphor, Michel. "L'Internationale Dada." *L'Oeil* (December 1956), pp. 64–75.

Shephard, Ben. *A War of Nerves*. Cambridge, MA: Harvard University Press, 2001.

Sheppard, Richard. "Dada und Futurismus." In Hermann and Paulsen, *Sinn aus Unsinn: Dada International*, pp. 29–70.

Shiff, Richard. "Handling Shocks: On the Representation of Experience in Walter Benjamin's Analogies." *Oxford Art Journal*, vol. 15, no. 2 (1992), pp. 88–103.

Shklovsky, Viktor. "Art as Technique" (1917). In *Contemporary Literary Criticism*. Edited by Robert Con Davies and Ronald Schleifer. New York: Longman, 1989, pp. 54–66.

———. "The Resurrection of the Word" (1914). In *Russian Formalism*. Edited by Stephen Bann and John E. Bowlt. New York: Barnes & Noble, 1973, p. 46.

Shusterman, Richard. "The End of Aesthetic Experience." In Shusterman, *Performing Live: Aesthetic Alternatives for the Ends of Art*. Ithaca, NY: Cornell University Press: 2000, pp. 15–34. First: *Journal of Aesthetics and Art Criticism*, vol. 55, no. 1 (Winter 1997), pp. 29–41.

Smith, Owen F. "Pre-Fluxus Conceptual Developments and Generative Influences." Available at: http://www.thing.net/~grist/ld/smith-fl.htm. Reprinted chapter 1 of Smith, *Fluxus: The History of an Attitude*. San Diego, CA: San Diego State University Press, 1998.

———. "Spielen mit Unterschied: Fluxus als Weltanschauung" ("Playing with Difference: Fluxus as a World View"). In Friedman, *Fluxus Virus*, pp. 110–15, 116–20 (German and English).

Silberman, Robert. "Minneapolis: In the Spirit of Fluxus" (exhibition review). *Burlington Magazine*, vol. 135, no. 1083 (June 1993), pp. 432–33.

Simmel, Ernst. *Kriegs-Neurosen und "Psychisches Trauma."* Munich: Nemnich, 1918.

Simmel, Georg. "The Metropolis and Mental Life." In Simmel, *Simmel on Culture*, pp. 174–86. First: "Die Grossstädte und das Geistesleben." In *Die Grossstadt: Vorträge und Aufsätze zur Städteausstellung; Jahrbuch der Gehe-Stiftung Dresden*. Edited by Theodor Petermann. Vol. 9, 1903, pp. 185–206.

———. *The Philosophy of Money*. London: Routledge, 1990. First: *Philosophie des Geldes*. Leipzig: Duncker and Humblot, 1900.

———. *Simmel on Culture: Selected Writings*. Edited by Mike Featherstone and David Frisby. London: Sage Publications, 1997.

———. "Sociology of the Senses." In Simmel, *Simmel on Culture*, pp. 109–19. First: "Soziologie der Sinne." *Die Neue Rundschau*, vol. 9 (September 1907), pp. 1025–36.

Simmel, Hans. "Auszüge aus den Lebenserinnerungen." In Böhringer and Gründer, *Ästhetik und Soziologie um die Jahrhundertwende: Georg Simmel*, pp. 247–68.

Sohm, Hanns, and Harald Szeemann (ed.). *Happening and Fluxus: Materialien*. Cologne: Kölnischer Kunstverein, 1970.

Spitzemberg, Hildegard von. *Das Tagebuch der Baronin Spitzemberg, geb. Freiin v. Varnbühler. Aufzeichnungen aus der Hofgesellschaft des Hohenzollernreiches* (1865–1914). Edited by Rudolf Vierhaus. Göttingen: Vandenhoeck and Ruprecht, 1960.

Sterneck, Wolfgang. *Der Kampf um die Träume—Musik und Gesellschaft*. Hanau: Komista-Verlag, 1998.

Stich, Sidra (ed.). *Made in USA: An Americanization in Modern Art, the '50s and '60s*, exhibition catalog. University Art Museum, Berkeley. Berkeley: University of California Press, 1987.

Stier, Ewald. "Wie kann der Entstehung von Kriegsneurosen bei der Feldarmee vorgebeugt werden?" *Deutsche Militärärztliche Zeitschrift*, no. 47, 1918, p. 62.

Stolnitz, Jerome. *Aesthetics and the Philosophy of Criticism*. Cambridge, MA: Riverside Press, 1960.

Süss, Daniel, et al. *Kommunikationsstrategien in der Gesundheitsförderung: Eine Studie zur optimalen Gestaltung von Botschaften in Gesundheitsförderungsprogrammen*, 2002; conducted by K.E.A.P. (Kompetenzzentrum für Evaluationsforschung in Angewandter Psychologie). Available at: http://www.hapzh.ch/download/Kurzbericht_KKStrategien.pdf.

Suzuki, Daisetz Teitaro. "The Break-Through to Reality: A Talk to the Buddhist Society" (July 1954). In Suzuki, *Field of Zen*, pp. 53–54.

———. "The Essence of Buddhism" (1948). In Suzuki, *Essentials of Zen Buddhism*, pp. 383–414.

———. *The Essentials of Zen Buddhism: Selected from the Writings of Daisetz T. Suzuki*. Edited by Bernard Philips. New York: Dutton, 1962.

———. *The Field of Zen: Contributions to The Middle Way*. Edited by Christmas Humphreys. London: Buddhist Society, 1966.

———. "The Meaning of Satori: A Talk to the Buddhist Society" (September 1963). In Suzuki, *Field of Zen*, pp. 21–27.

———. *Zen Buddhism: Selected Writings of D.T. Suzuki*. Edited by William Barrett. Garden City, NY: Doubleday and Co., 1956.

———. "Zen in the Modern World" (1958). In Suzuki, *Essentials of Zen Buddhism*, pp. 371–82.

Sweet, Matthew. "Trouble at Mall." *Evening Standard Magazine* (November 19, 2004), pp. 28–30.

Thiel, Eberhard (ed.). *Sachwörterbuch der Musik*, 3rd ed. Stuttgart: Alfred Kröner Verlag, 1977.

Thies, Ralf. *Wiener Grossstadt-Dokumente: Erkundungen in der Metropole der k.u.k Monarchie*, 2001, Publication Series "Metropolenforschung," Social Science Research Center Berlin (WZB). Available at: http://skylla.wz-berlin.de/pdf/2001/ii01-503.pdf.

Thorpe, Vanessa. "Welcome to the New Brutalism." *Observer*, August 20, 2000. Available at: www.observer.guardian.co.uk/review/story/0,6903,356245,00.html.

Thwaites, John A. "Der Philosoph und die Katze: Nam June Paik in der Galerie Parnass in Wuppertal." *Deutsche Zeitung*, April 9, 1963, p. 10.

Tomkins, Calvin. "Profiles: Video Visionary." *New Yorker*, May 5, 1975, pp. 44–49; shortened version reprinted in: *Nam June Paik: Eine Database*. Edited by Klaus Bussmann and Florian Matzner. Ostfildern: Edition Cantz, 1993, pp. 34–36.

Toshiharu, Omuka. "Dadaismus in Japan." In Schneider, *Berlin–Tokyo. Die Kunst zweier Städte*, pp. 120–21.

Turner, Chris. *The Disgusting: The Unrepresentable from Kant to Kristeva*. Ph.D. dissertation, University of London, 2000, unpublished.

———. "Shock Treatment." *Tate: The Art Magazine*, no. 22 (Summer 2000), pp. 44–51.

Twain, Mark. "The German Chicago." In *The Complete Essays of Mark Twain*. Edited by Charles Neider. Garden City, NY: Doubleday and Co. 1963, pp. 87–98.

Tweed, Thomas W. *The American Encounter with Buddhism 1844–1912*. Bloomington: Indiana University Press, 1992.

Tzara, Tristan. "Dada Manifesto 1918." In Motherwell, *Dada Painters and Poets*, pp. 76–82. First: "Manifeste Dada 1918," *Dada*, no. 3, December 1918.

———. "Erinnerungen an Dada" (1927). In *Der Querschnitt: Das Magazin der aktuellen Ewigkeitswerte, 1924–1933*. Edited by Christian Ferber (Berlin: Ullstein Verlag: 1981), pp. 127–30. First: *Der Querschnitt: Das Magazin der aktuellen Ewigkeitswerte*, no. 2 (February 1927).

———. "An Introduction to Dada" (1948). In Motherwell, *Dada Painters and Poets*, pp. 394–98.

———. "Manifeste de Monsieur Antipyrine" (1916). In Motherwell, *Dada Painters and Poets*, pp. 75–76.

———. "Unpretentious Proclamation" (1919). In Tzara, *Seven Dada Manifestos and Lampisteries*. London: John Calder Ltd., 1977, pp. 15–17.

———. "Zurich Chronicle" (1916). In Motherwell, *Dada Painters and Poets*, pp. 235–42. First: "Zürich Chronik." In Huelsenbeck, *Dada Almanach*.

Ulrich, Bernd. "'. . . als wenn nichts geschehen wäre'": Anmerkungen zur Behandlung der Kriegsopfer während des Ersten Weltkrieges." In Hirschfeld and Krumeich, *Keiner fühlt sich hier mehr als Mensch . . .*, pp. 115–30.

Vautier, Ben. "Text über den Fluxus" ("Text on the Fluxus"). In *Fluxus Subjektiv*, exhibition catalog. Ed. Ursula Krinzinger. Vienna: Galerie Krinzinger, 1997, pp. 2–3. Available also at: www.artnotart.com/fluxus/bvautier-textonthefluxus.html.

———. "What Is Fluxus?" *Flash Art*, nos. 84–85, 1978, p. 52.

Verkauf, Willi. *Dada: Monograph of a Movement*. London: Alec Tiranti, 1957. First: *Dada: Monograph of a Movement—Monographie einer Bewegung—monographie d'un movement*. Teuffen: Niggli, 1957 (English, German, French).

Volmert, Johannes. *Ernst Jünger: "In Stahlgewittern."* Munich: Wilhelm Fink Verlag, 1985.

Vondung, Klaus (ed.). *Kriegserlebnis: Der Erste Weltkrieg in der literarischen Gestaltung und symbolischen Deutung der Nationen*. Göttingen: Vandenhoeck and Ruprecht, 1980.

———. "Propaganda oder Sinndeutung?" In *Kriegserlebnis*, pp. 11–37.

Vostell, Wolf. "Dada und die mentale Energie: Interview mit Doña Mercedes Guardado Olivenza" (July 1975). In Höllerer and Miller, "Dada–Neodada–Kryptodada–?" pp. 214–16.

Wagner, Monika. *Das Material der Kunst: Eine andere Geschichte der Moderne*. Munich: Beck, 2001.

Waldenberg, Patrick. *Dada: La fonction de refus*. Paris: Editions de la Différence, 1999.

Waldman, Diane (ed.). *Max Ernst: A Retrospective*. New York: Solomon R. Guggenheim Museum, 1975.

Watts, Harriett (ed.). *Dada and the Press*. Vol. 9 of *Crisis and the Arts*, ed. Foster. New Haven, CT: Thomson/Gale, 2004.

Wehler, Hans-Ulrich. *Vom Beginn des Ersten Weltkriegs bis zur Gründung der beiden deutschen Staaten 1914–1949*. Vol. 4 of *Deutsche Gesellschaftsgeschichte*. Munich: C. H. Beck, 2003.

Wietfeldt, Heinrich. *Kriegsneurosen als psychisch-soziale Mangelkrankheit*. Leipzig: Georg Thieme Verlag, 1936.

Wilbert, Gerd. *Entstehung und Entwicklung des Programms der "linken" Kunst und der "Linken Front der Künste" (LEF) 1917–1925*. Vol. 13 of the Marburger Abhandlungen zur Geschichte und Kultur Osteuropas. Giessen: Schmitz, 1976.

Williams, Emmett. *My Life in Flux—and Vice Versa*. New York: Thames and Hudson, 1992.

———. "St. George and the Fluxus Dragons." In *Upheavals. Manifestos, Manifestations: Conceptions in the Arts at the Beginning of the Sixties*, exhibition catalog. Edited by Klaus Schrenk. Städtische Kunsthalle, Düsseldorf et al. Cologne: DuMont, 1984, pp. 19–38 (German and English).

Wirth, Louis. "Urbanism as a Way of Life." *American Journal of Sociology*, vol. 44, no. 1 (July 1938), pp. 1–24.

Wixley Brooks, Laura. "Damien Hirst and the Sensibility of Shock." In *The Contemporary Sublime: Sensibilities of Transcendence and Shock*. Edited by Paul Crowther. Art and Design Profile No. 40. London: London Academy Editions, 1995, pp. 55–67.

Wolfradt, Willi. "Der Dadaismus." *Der Friede*, vol. 1, no. 16 (May 24, 1918), pp. 434–35.

Wrobel Ignaz (alias Kurt Tucholsky). "Die Kinderhölle in Berlin." *Freie Welt*, Nov. 28, 1920, pp. 2–3.

Young, La Monte. "Lecture 1960." In *Ubi Fluxus ibi Motus 1990–1962*. Edited by Achille Bonito Oliva and Claudio Cerritelli and Gabriella de Mila (ed.). Milano: Mazzotta, 1990.

Youngblood, Gene. *Expanded Cinema*. London: Studio Vista, 1970.

Zahn, Robert von. "'Refusierte Gesänge': Musik im Atelier Bauermeister." In *Intermedial, Kontrovers, Experimentell: Das Atelier Mary Bauermeister in Köln 1960–1962*. Edited by Historisches Archiv der Stadt Köln. Cologne: Emons H J, 1993.

Zinn, Howard. *Postwar America 1945–1971*. Boston: South End Press, 1973.

Illustration Credits

Figures 1 and 2. © Paul McCarthy. Videography by Mike Cram; photos by Spandau Parks/Karen McCarthy. Courtesy the artist and Hauser & Wirth.

Figure 3. © The Robert Mapplethorpe Foundation.

Figure 4. © Estate Martin Kippenberger, Galerie Gisela Capitain, Cologne. Courtesy Sammlung Falckenberg, Hamburg, and Galeria Gisela Capitain, Cologne.

Figure 5. © Marc Quinn. Photo by Stephen White. Courtesy White Cube.

Figures 6–7. © Xiao Yu. Courtesy ESTeeLIE.

Figure 8. © Paul McCarthy. Photo by Spandau Parks. Courtesy the artist and Hauser & Wirth.

Figure 9. © bpk.

Figure 10. © VG Bild-Kunst, Bonn 2010/bpk/Staatsbibliothek zu Berlin/Ruth Schacht.

Figures 11–12. © VG Bild-Kunst, Bonn 2010/bpk/Staatsbibliothek zu Berlin/Ruth Schacht.

Figure 13. © VG Bild-Kunst, Bonn 2010/bpk/CNAC-MNAM/Philippe Migeat.

Figure 14. © The Heartfield Community of Heirs/VG Bild-Kunst, Bonn 2010. Photo by Markus Hawlik. Courtesy Akademie der Künste, Berlin.

Figure 15. © VG Bild-Kunst, Bonn 2010/bpk/CNAC-MNAM.

Figure 16. © bpk/Scala.

Figure 19. All rights reserved. Courtesy of The George Maciunas Foundation, Inc., New York.

Figure 20. All rights reserved. Courtesy of The George Maciunas Foundation, Inc., New York.

Figure 21. All rights reserved. Courtesy of The George Maciunas Foundation, Inc., New York.

Figure 24. All rights reserved. Courtesy of The George Maciunas Foundation, Inc., New York.

Figures 25–27. © tomas schmit archiv, Berlin/Manfred Leve. Photo by Manfred Leve. Courtesy Barbara Wien Wilma Lukatsch, Berlin.

Figure 28. © The Nam June Paik Estate/Manfred Montwé. Photo by Manfred Montwé. Courtesy MUMOK, Vienna.

Figure 29. © The Nam June Paik Estate/Manfred Montwé. Photo by Manfred Montwé. Courtesy MUMOK, Vienna.

Figure 30. © The Nam June Paik Estate/Manfred Montwé. Photo by Manfred Montwé. Courtesy MUMOK, Vienna.

Figure 31. © The Nam June Paik Estate/Anneliese Jährling, Cologne/Zentralarchiv des internationalen Kunsthandels (ZADIK), Cologne/The Museum of Modern Art, New York. Photo by Rolf Jährling. Courtesy MUMOK, Vienna.

Figure 32. © The Nam June Paik Estate/bpk/Nationalgalerie im Hamburger Bahnhof, Staatliche Museen zu Berlin/Jens Ziehe. Photo by Jens Ziehe.

Figures 33–35. © tomas schmit archiv, Berlin/Dorine van der Klei. Photo by Dorine van der Klei. Courtesy Barbara Wien Wilma Lukatsch, Berlin.

Figure 36. © Andres Serrano. Courtesy of the artist, Corcoran Gallery of Art, Washington, D.C., and Yvon Lambert Paris, New York.

Index